FROM OLD QUEBEC TO LA BELLE PROVINCE

ÉTUDES D'HISTOIRE DU QUÉBEC / STUDIES ON THE HISTORY OF QUEBEC

Magda Fahrni et/and Jarrett Rudy
DIRECTEURS DE LA COLLECTION / SERIES EDITORS

FROM **OLD QUEBEC** TO **LA BELLE PROVINCE**

TOURISM PROMOTION,
TRAVEL WRITING,
and NATIONAL IDENTITIES,
1920–1967

NICOLE NEATBY

McGILL-QUEEN'S UNIVERSITY PRESS
MONTREAL & KINGSTON | LONDON | CHICAGO

© McGill-Queen's University Press 2018

ISBN 978-0-7735-5495-5 (cloth)
ISBN 978-0-7735-5496-2 (paper)
ISBN 978-0-7735-5573-0 (ePDF)
ISBN 978-0-7735-5574-7 (ePUB)

Legal deposit third quarter 2018
Bibliothèque nationale du Québec

Printed in Canada on acid-free paper

This book has been published with the help
of a grant from the Canadian Federation for
the Humanities and Social Sciences, through
the Awards to Scholarly Publications Program,
using funds provided by the Social Sciences
and Humanities Research Council of Canada.
Funding has also been received from the
Faculty of Graduate Studies and Research,
Saint Mary's University.

Funded by the   Financé par le
Government   gouvernement | Canadä
of Canada   du Canada

 Canada Council   Conseil des arts
for the Arts   du Canada

We acknowledge the support of the Canada
Council for the Arts, which last year invested
$153 million to bring the arts to Canadians
throughout the country.

Nous remercions le Conseil des arts du Canada
de son soutien. L'an dernier, le Conseil a
investi 153 millions de dollars pour mettre
de l'art dans la vie des Canadiennes et des
Canadiens de tout le pays.

LIBRARY AND ARCHIVES CANADA
CATALOGUING IN PUBLICATION

Neatby, Nicole, 1962–, author
From Old Quebec to La Belle Province :
tourism promotion, travel writing, and national
identities, 1920–1967 / Nicole Neatby.

(Studies on the history of Quebec ; 34)
Includes bibliographical references and index.
Issued in print and electronic formats.
ISBN 978-0-7735-5495-5 (cloth). –
ISBN 978-0-7735-5496-2 (paper). –
ISBN 978-0-7735-5573-0 (ePDF). –
ISBN 978-0-7735-5574-7 (ePUB)

1. Tourism – Québec (Province) –
Marketing – History – 20th century.
2. Tourism – Government policy – Québec
(Province) – History – 20th century. 3. Travel
writing – Québec (Province) – History –
20th century. 4. National characteristics,
French-Canadian – History – 20th century.
5. National characteristics, French-Canadian,
in literature. 6. Québec (Province) – In
literature. 7. Québec (Province) – Description
and travel. I. Title. II. Series: Studies on the
history of Quebec ; 34

G155.C2N43 2018
306.4'819097140904
C2018-903575-7

C2018-903576-5

Set in 10.5/13.5 Goudy Oldstyle with
League Spartan and Gotham
Book design & typesetting
by Garet Markvoort, zijn digital

IN LOVING MEMORY OF MY FATHER

CONTENTS

ILLUSTRATIONS

ACKNOWLEDGMENTS

Not many can imagine the joy and relief I feel arriving at the stage when I can thank many of those who over the years, the many years, provided support both through wise scholarly advice and enduring friendship. The idea for this project came out of conversations with the much regretted and ever insightful Pierre Savard, but I was further motivated by my exchanges with Alain Roy, Karen Dubinsky, and Serge Jaumain who may not realize that I followed through with many of their suggestions. One of the most telling indications of this project's long maturation period is the fact that I owe much to the outstanding and thorough research conducted in the archives by Matthew Hayday in the long gone days when he was a graduate student.

Friends, many of them fellow tourists with whom I have travelled extensively over the years, including through Quebec, also accompanied me throughout the life of this study. I am so very grateful to Ann Collins, Julie Dompierre, Andrée Dumulon, Robert Kadas Marcel Lauzière, Stuart McGee, Sylvie Paquette for their friendship and the encouragement I needed to reach the finish line. A special thanks to Natalie Neville and Bronwen Woods who also read several drafts and offered insightful comments. I also had the good fortune to work with Brian Hotson whose meticulous copyediting (and deleting) made the lives of those who read the manuscript later easier. I also owe a great debt to Sandra Barry who produced the index. My parents will not have the chance to read the bound version of this book, but they read many loose-leaf drafts. As with all my projects, big and small over the years, they made me feel that what I was doing was worthwhile, never tiring to ask me what I had discovered and to listen to my long answers. Having been trained as an historian in an earlier time, my father, to whom I dedicate this book, might have been surprised that tourism would one day become a subject of historical inquiry. But as with all new and unexpected developments, he wanted to make sense of them. Through his probing inquiries and love of debating, he helped me make sense of puzzling findings I encountered along the way.

I also had the good luck to benefit from amazing support and guidance working with the professionals at McGill-Queen's University Press. First among them, Jonathan Crago who went beyond the call of duty with his wise and expert advice right through the last miles and on to completion. Finn Purcell patiently walked me through the process of locating and preparing the numerous images the press generously agreed to include in the book. Shelagh Plunkett's keen eye and Garet Markvoort's meticulous overview ensured that what I meant was truly conveyed on the page, and Ryan Van Huijstee was only an email away to provide me with clear instructions. Much of the research during the early stages of this study was made possible by a Social Sciences and Humanities Research Council Standard Research Grant. I also thank the Federation for the Humanities and Social Sciences for its generous support through its Awards to Scholarly Publication Program as well as the contribution of Saint Mary's University's Faculty of Graduate Studies and Research for the additional funds it provided to make this publication possible.

FROM **OLD QUEBEC** TO LA **BELLE PROVINCE**

INTRODUCTION

In the summer of 1935, Kathrine Gordon Sanger (pen name, Gordon Brinley), an American author and travel writer, and her husband, illustrator Putman Brinley, left their home in Hartford, Connecticut, for a three-month summer trip to the Gaspé.[1] In the opening pages of their travel book, *Away to the Gaspé* (1935), they recount that they had agreed upon this destination after some negotiation. She apparently told her husband that she had collected information about the region because "I knew *you* wanted to go to France and I knew *I* wanted to go to the Gaspé Peninsula. So, it seemed wise to be prepared, in case we compromised on French Canada." The Gaspé, she felt, would better meet her interests as "[it's] not the old France of today ... but the new France of yesterday that's occupying my mind." Puzzled, he inquired, "What do you mean?" She specified, "Canada, colonial Canada, in particular the Gaspé Peninsula."[2] While her husband came around to agree, he, in turn, was apparently able to convince his wife to make the journey into a camping trip: "[t]hink of all the things that might happen in a tent that would bring you into relation with the 'habitant.'"[3] Having finally agreed on a destination, they set off in their car, pens and drawing boards in hand. The resulting travel book constitutes a lively and witty account of their adventures in the "new France of yesteryear" – the one she was looking forward to visiting.

As this exchange suggests, the couple was not venturing into unknown territory. Gordon Brinley had gathered information about their destination beforehand. Some of it came from Quebec government publicity, which would have certainly reinforced her expectations that they were destined for an "Old World" in the Gaspé where "Yesterday meets Today."[4] Quebec, more generally, was labelled "Old Quebec," a place "where they would meet the *habitants* who still followed 'old French customs.'"[5] She also referred specifically to "Mr. Boutwell's article in the *National Geographic*."

At face value, the gist of the Brinleys' exchange that summer neatly en-capsulates the expectations and reactions of American as well as English Canadian travel writers who visited Quebec well into the 1950s. Their ac-count did, as so many would in the following decades, tell of the pleasures they experienced, walking back in time in a New France of yesteryear, where the sense of embarking on an adventure afforded them the unique opportun-ity to encounter people living as did their seventeenth-century ancestors. And Quebec's tourism publicity material during that time also confirms that government promoters represented the province as the one place in North America where visitors could indeed step into an Old World. This being said, it remains that the Brinleys' experience does not fully capture the broad range and notable diversity of travel writers' assumptions about and reactions to Quebec. By examining American and English Canadian travel accounts pub-lished between the early 1920s and late 1960s, this book reveals the extent to which their distinct national identities shaped in significantly different ways their preconceptions about the province before they set off on their trip and their reactions to the people and sites they encountered once they got there. Paying attention as well to the reactions of French Quebec travel writ-ers, I illustrate how they also read the Quebec landscape and their compatri-ots, informed by their own distinct national allegiances.[6] Furthermore, by taking into account these travel writers' reactions to Montreal, it is possible to confirm that Quebec modernity long held appeal among a wide range of visitors. In parallel, this study tracks the provincial government tourist pro-moters' evolving objectives and initiatives, drawing particular attention to the intentions of the principal officials involved through a detailed reading of their marketing strategies and tourism publicity. In their case as well, it will become clear that their thoughts about what made Quebec a distinct travel destination and how they chose to promote the province during the same period was directly shaped by their own sense of national identity.

My study also brings to light the ways in which travel writing can be used as "a barometer for changing views on other ... cultures."[7] As will become apparent, these travel writers' impressions gradually changed in tandem with changes taking place in the province. Notably, by the 1960s, American and English Canadian travel writers were compelled to reassess long-standing pre-conceptions about French Quebeckers. Thus, focusing on the decades which span the interwar period to the years leading up to Expo 67 as Quebec went through the transformative period of the Quiet Revolution, offers an ideal time frame from which to tease out how Americans and English Canadians, negotiated French Quebec's rapidly changing sense of national identity and how French Quebeckers "re-viewed" their homeland. By then, travel writers' expectations, like those of the Brinleys, of finding a New France of yesteryear, were long gone. As for government tourist promoters, by this time they had stopped inviting tourists to an "Old Quebec," encouraging them instead to visit "La Belle Province."

My interest lies in those who engaged in cultural or ethnic tourism. I have therefore focused on information that speaks to travel writers' "ethnocultural" curiosity, revealing the reactions of those who "seek exotic peoples and different cultures."[8] Of course, many visitors to Quebec were hunting and fishing enthusiasts attracted by Quebec's reputed northern wilderness or in search of opportunities to practise winter sports. However, I have chosen to turn my attention to what travel writers had to say specifically about the province's French-speaking society, its inhabitants, and their way of life and culture. And while anthropologist Pierre van den Berghe reminds us that "tourism is always in some sense a form of ethnic relations, for it puts into contact people who are strangers to one another, and who invariably belong to different cultures or subcultures," it remains that there are travellers who are more inclined to leave home to "actively sear[ch] for the ethnically exotic, in as untouched, pristine, authentic a form as [they] can find it."[9]

Furthermore, a few women wrote travel accounts either on their own or occasionally in collaboration with their husbands. While I flagged when possible the evidence I came across which reveals how traditional gendered assumptions coloured the way travel writers recounted their experiences, I did not find a sufficient number of accounts to produce a fully fleshed-out gendered analysis of their experiences and reactions "on the road." More to the point, in the context of this study, there was not enough evidence to distinguish between a female and male sense of national identity.

It should be noted that Quebec offered opportunities to encounter Indigenous peoples as well.[10] Indeed, early on travellers from abroad and the rest of Canada expressed an interest in visiting the more easily accessible reserves, most notably the Mohawk Kahnawake reserve (commonly known as Caughnawaga) across from Montreal. It was originally a Jesuit Mission at the time of New France. The Huron – Wendat (Wendake) reserve of Lorette near Quebec City also attracted visitors. Tourists were propelled by a desire to see firsthand, and before it was too late, those who belonged to a "race" presumed vanishing through its gradual assimilation into the "civilized" world of white Christian colonizers. Private companies offered excursion packages that included side trips to such reserves, and Natives developed ways to profit from the curiosity of white tourists, mostly by selling an array of souvenirs which those visitors could take home as tangible evidence of encounters with a people supposedly quickly disappearing. It would seem that interest in this particular type of "ethnic tourism" was losing its luster by the interwar period, to say nothing of the fact that such cultural tourism was not promoted by government officials.[11] Instead, the state held up French Quebecers as the authentic "natives" of the province – those worthy of interest – and travellers in search of exotic cultural encounters apparently concurred. Well into the 1950s, their travel accounts suggest that, to their minds, those who counted as exotic and worthy of the trip were the *habitants* – the French Quebeckers of yesteryear.[12]

I begin my study in the 1920s, which mark the emergence of mass tourism as automobile ownership made long-distance travel an affordable option for a larger number of North Americans. These were also the years when the Quebec government became fully involved in the tourism industry. It is apparent that the way it represented the province to the outside world, even in these early days, could not simply be captured by focusing on the long-standing "Old Quebec" publicity slogan. The government's marketing strategies were directly linked to its economic priorities and changing views regarding Quebec's defining traits and attributes. Indeed, it represented the province as both old and new as promoters also sought to attract capital investors. This changed in the 1930s when the "Old Quebec" brand took pride of place as traditional nationalists gained increasing influence on government tourism promotion policies. By the 1960s, the objectives of those at the helm changed in significant ways, and in a relatively short period of time, also in tune with the major transformations in the way French-speaking Quebeckers defined their national identity. These were encapsulated by the "La Belle Province" slogan and fully acted out during Expo 67.

During this period, Montreal also underwent significant changes in the way it was promoted. This had much to do with the fact that before the Quiet Revolution tourism promotion was mostly left in the hands of the English Montreal business elite who chose to brand the city as the "Paris of the New World" and featured Montreal's French population as a backdrop simply to remind visitors of the city's past. In the early 1960s, things changed markedly as the city's French-dominated municipal government took over tourism promotion and chose to market it instead as the "New Montreal" in tune with the times.

Overall, accounting for these remarkable rebranding developments can enrich a wider and long-standing debate among those who track the origins and meaning of the Quiet Revolution and Quebec modernity. More specifically, while it will become apparent that the showcasing of Quebec's modernity was recognized as worthwhile, however modestly, in the early part of the century, this study will add more evidence that the 1960s were indeed a turning point in the way French Quebeckers defined themselves and were perceived by English-speaking North Americans.[13]

This book situates itself in a wider historiography directly pertaining to the history of Quebec tourism. The field of Quebec tourism history is a relatively recent one. Scholars developed an interest in tourism in Canada in the 1980s, and their findings have mostly appeared in articles, tangentially in a few book-length studies, or in unpublished theses.[14] Initially, historians who turned their attention to visitors' impressions and experiences primarily focused on those of the late nineteenth and early twentieth centuries. They were also primarily interested in ascertaining the attitudes and experiences of European travellers. Doug Owram, for one, studied the attitudes of British travellers who visited Quebec between 1880 and 1914. He concluded that, to their minds, the "real" Quebec was represented by the rural French Canadians, the *habitants,* who stood as the "charming relic of a backward society."[15] French literature scholar Sylvain Simard analyzed the reactions of the French elite who came to Quebec between 1850 and 1914. He, too, revealed the extent to which their reactions were shaped by homegrown prejudices and ideological allegiances.[16] While not explicitly informed by post-colonial criticism and theory, these authors established that the views and reactions of European visitors were very much shaped by a British-imperialist outlook in the first case and a French one in the second.

By the 1990s, a few historians turned their sights on English-speaking North American travellers who also visited the province in the late nineteenth and first half of the twentieth century, mostly those who came from the US. They essentially offered broad generalizations to the effect that American tourists were drawn to rural Quebec because they viewed it as a traditional society, if not a primitive one, and were primarily curious about its rural *habitant* population steeped in a distinctive French culture and steadfastly faithful to the Catholic religion.[17] Over time, historians drew connections between these impressions and a wider, North American antimodernist cultural context.[18] Their conclusions were partly inspired by the work of cultural historians, many of whom illustrate how this outlook oriented travellers' preferred destinations in certain regions of the continent.[19] They established that Quebec was of interest to these antimodernist visitors because, to their minds, here lived a people who remained faithful to their ancestors' simple and traditional way of life and offered a much needed escape from the hectic and less meaningful urban industrial age – a representation which was, in certain ways, in line with the one described by earlier visitors from the "old" countries, although for very different reasons.

Following in their footsteps, historians have sought to illuminate the changing reactions of nineteenth- and early twentieth-century British and English-speaking North American travellers. They offer a nuanced analysis, pointing to the ways in which evolving impressions of the British Empire can be accounted for through shifting views on what constituted attractive landscapes along with differing perspectives on Quebec, the former British colony.[20] More recently, emerging scholars have turned their attention to yet wider factors that influenced the Quebec tourist experience, including the environment and gender. This has involved a more detailed study of how car travel shaped the reactions of visitors, men and women, to sights and people they met along the way, and how the provincial government catered to their needs by adapting the Quebec landscape to their expectations.[21] By focusing on the expectations and reactions of twentieth-century English-speaking North American travel writers, my study adds to this body of knowledge by revealing that, just as with their nineteenth-century counterparts, theirs varied considerably and evolved over time in equally different ways.

Those who visited Montreal have attracted less attention from twentieth-century tourism scholars.[22] Yet, their reactions are instructive. Indeed, contrasting American and English Canadians' preconceptions and impressions of Canada's largest urban and industrial metropolis with those they held towards the province's rural areas belies the view that Quebec was unvaryingly appreciated for being "old." At a time when most travel writers viewed parts of Quebec through an antimodernist lens, I demonstrate that many were also eager to experience its modern centre, praising Montreal for attributes that were at polar opposites to those they admired in rural areas.

As noted earlier, my study also illustrates the fact that Quebec government tourism promoters were themselves directly influenced by nationalism. Scholars have already brought to light some aspects of the connection between the government's marketing initiatives and national identity. Geographers (who have to date shown the most sustained interest in the way Quebec was promoted by the state) have brought forward the influence of specific members of Quebec's traditionalist elite in the promotion of this brand of tourism. More specifically, they point to the role played by members of the province's traditional nationalist intelligentsia during the 1920s and 1930s in marketing the province as "Old Quebec." Not surprisingly, their attention has been mostly drawn to the initiatives and policies of the provincial government that contributed to a transformation of the Quebec landscape.[23] More specifically, they reveal that the Quebec state's gradual intervention in the field of tourism, starting in the 1920s, was geared towards "highlighting the rural identity of the countryside" along with the accompanying traditional lifestyle of the *habitants* "for the benefit of the tourists."[24] They also note that the countryside's traditional cultural landscape, built up over the years for tourist consumption, came to be identified as an authentic repository of French Canadian national heritage. Underpinning some of their research is a question articulated by Lucie Morriset who wonders: "which one of the two, Quebec's national identity or its cultural landscape has first shaped the other"?[25] While this desire to establish the extent to which tourist representations contribute to the shaping of contemporary national identities is of interest to a wide range of tourism scholars, answers backed by solid evidence are hard to come by.[26] What has been more easily confirmed is that the elite of this period believed that tourism would revitalize past traditions and culture and so help rejuvenate and secure what they perceived to be French Canadians' authentic national identity.[27]

In line with this type of inquiry a few other tourism scholars have turned their attention to the ways in which outsiders – from ethnographers and anthropologists to private sector entrepreneurs – have identified certain provincial regions as places where old-world traditions survived. They argue that their initiatives and findings, in effect, gave credibility to the notion that certain regions of the province were home to a people who lived much as did their ancestors. Here, upper- and middle-class city dwellers influenced by an antimodernist outlook would find the *habitant* folk they were so keen to encounter.[28] This being said, few researchers have explicitly set out to measure in any detail the extent to which visitors' vision of the province as "Old Quebec" reflected reality on the ground. Geographer Lynda Villeneuve stands out as an exception, as she reveals contrasts between the Charlevoix region as it was and as represented during the nineteenth century.[29]

What comes out of this overview is that, when analyzing how nationalism influenced the marketing strategies of government tourist promoters, both historians and geographers tend to focus on the impact of *traditional* Quebec nationalism during the early decades of the twentieth century. This means they have paid less attention to promoters' attempts at highlighting some of Quebec's modern-day developments. Most notably, they have shown less interest in analyzing how the evolution of French Quebec nationalist thought, up to the 1960s, played out and was reflected in Quebec tourism promotion. In fact, a few contend that the "Old Quebec" marketing brand survived well up to the end of the 1960s.[30] My findings suggest otherwise: while some ves-tiges of the "Old Quebec" branding remained, Quebec was by then "La Belle Province," showcased with full fanfare during Expo 67.

Available sources to document these developments are both abundant and diverse. They include government documents and an extensive collection of tourism publicity, including ads and other forms of material that reveal multi-faceted and evolving marketing strategies as well as the goals that informed them. I have also made extensive use of the Paul Gouin and Robert Prévost fonds – two of the most prominent government officials responsible for tour-ism promotion during the period – as well as the rich collection of documents and press clippings at the City of Montreal archives. These fonds and other sources contain correspondence, speeches, government reports – all offering an insider's look at evolving government and municipal promoters' inten-tions as well as their ongoing concerns.

My decision to exclusively study the records of travel writers reflects my conviction that they are of interest in and of themselves, but they also con-stitute a source that reveals the thoughts and experiences of rank-and-file tourists. It should be added that they are also more accessible than private documents – unpublished diaries, private letters, or other visual sources such as postcards – written by those with no thought of recounting their trip other than to friends and family. In contrast, travel writers, by virtue of their profes-sional responsibilities, leave behind readily available and imposing numbers of detailed records of their visits. Some of their accounts are published in book format, but a greater number appear in numerous serial publications, which makes it possible to document change and continuity over time more thoroughly and systematically. And, precisely because of their wide distribu-tion, steady reoccurrence, and similar formats, one can produce more detailed and consistent comparisons between travellers of different nationalities.

In addition to these quantitative advantages, travel accounts offer histor-ians the opportunity to gain a closer understanding of what may have gone through the minds of the more silent majority of tourists. For one, having been, in all likelihood, exposed to the same information about the province (e.g. in novels, visual art, textbooks, or tourism publicity), they would have built up similar preconceptions about Quebec as those of English-speaking North Americans in general. Moreover, by definition, travel writers' responsibilities are to put themselves in the shoes of would-be tourists, anticipating readers' expectations, making assumptions about what they might find interesting. Thus, these accounts provide insight into what they believed the average tourist would likely look for and how they would react to what they encoun-tered.[31] Certainly those who have compared published and unpublished travel accounts have uncovered both differences and similarities. Literary historian Eva-Marie Kröller, in her analysis of Canadian travellers in Europe during the second half of the nineteenth century, explains that, contrary to letters and diaries, "rarely is there a sense in the published travel-books of spontaneous and potentially controversial responses."[32] Cecilia Morgan, on the other hand, in her study of the letters and diaries as well as the published travel accounts of middle-class English Canadian tourists visiting Europe in the late nineteenth century, warns against separating the two "into overly rigid categories." While she observed "important distinctions" as both types of writers "did not always concur on the significance and meaning of what they had seen and experienced," she nonetheless argues that, in many ways, "travel writers were as much tourists as were the travelers who did not publish accounts." She discovered, for instance, that "both groups agreed on the general lineaments and structures of their journeys. They visited mostly the same places and the recommended sites." And, similar to tourists' private recollections, "travel writers also filled their pages with reflections on their emotional reactions."[33]

This being said, such sources have clear limitations and cannot simply be considered as a convenient "substitute" documenting the thoughts and experiences of ordinary tourists. Indeed, one has to consider the possibility that, as Michael Cronin puts it, the "rhetorical strategies of travel writing actually shape the way a destination is perceived by travelers."[34] Furthermore, it may safely be assumed that travel writers were more likely to share positive experiences or impressions in order to pique the interest of prospective tourists to encourage them to travel to these locations. This did not stop writers from occasionally warning their readers of inconveniences or disappointments they may experience along the way, but, above all, readers were meant to understand that less rewarding experiences should not discourage them from leaving home. In short, this type of source is more likely to reveal what travel writers *liked* or found interesting about Quebec and less about what they found unappealing.

In examining these travel-writing texts in more detail, a sense that these accounts cannot simply be taken at face value is revealed from a closer look at the conditions under which the Brinleys left for Quebec. Their decision to go to the Gaspé was not only the result of spousal give-and-take. They stood to financially benefit from this trip, taken, in fact, as a result of an offer made by their friend, Frank Dodd (of Dodd, Mead, and Co. publishers). Dodd had asked them to write a travel book on the Gaspé because he believed the book would fill a niche given that travel accounts of the region were not then available.[35] Moreover, several travel writers explicitly referred to their association with government promoters by acknowledging their support, which made them, to a certain degree, promoters themselves. Further muddying the waters, following a well-established marketing practice, government promoters produced "anonymous" travel accounts, which they distributed to various publications targeting unsuspecting would-be tourists. In fact, there is evidence to suggest that the *National Geographic* travel account flagged by Gordon Brinley may have been one such account. In other words, here was travel writing pretending to be something it was not. For an historian, of course, such discoveries raise key questions. To begin with, can the Brinleys' account – and all others in this genre for that matter – be treated as a genuine, unfiltered, first-hand impression, or, to the contrary, are their reactions simply informed by self-interested motives? If nothing else, such insights confirm that making hard and fast pronouncements about what can be gleaned from travel accounts to illuminate tourist reactions is far from a straightforward endeavour.

Further, there are challenges for scholars in defining the genre itself. Not surprisingly, the topic is of particular interest to literary scholars, specifically when applying a cultural studies approach.[36] What stands out immediately is that all, regardless of their area of study, concur that "the genre itself is notoriously refractory to definition."[37] This is, in part, due to the fact that travel writing "is a loose generic label, and has always embraced a bewilderingly diverse range of material."[38] It is a hybrid and androgynous being, as it is part diary, part guidebook, part fiction.[39] And "travel books are difficult to define … because of their complex association with other forms, including the essay, the pastoral, the picaresque, and the quest romance."[40]

A few of those interested in tourism history have made other distinctions more in tune with the context in which these publications emerge, situating them on a time continuum. Historian Alan Gordon notes that "[f]rom the late eighteenth century through the nineteenth century, two main forms of travel literature captured the attention of literate Europeans and Americans: travelogues and guidebooks."[41] The first "typically recorded the experiences of a leisured traveler in narrative form" whereas guidebooks were "ephemeral publication[s] produced for commercial gain" and more "prescriptive."[42] Notably, after the Second World War, travel writing became "mainstream" as more newspapers included travel sections and specialized travel magazines emerged at a time when travelling itself became a more mainstream leisure activity and prospective tourists became increasingly interested in learning about various travel options from which to choose.[43] But as this study makes clear, further distinctions can be made between travel genres with the appearance of government-issued travel guidebooks during the interwar period.

These were state-sanctioned publications intended to further develop the tourism industry, and, for the scholar, they open a window onto the changing ways governments represented the nation.

This book alternates between chapters that chart the provincial government's marketing objectives and strategies, and the views of travel writers. Chapter 1 follows the provincial government's growing involvement in the tourism industry during the late 1910s and 1920s. Officials worked to modernize the province's infrastructure, marketing it as a place where visitors would have access to a modern road grid and benefit from the most up-to-date hospitality services. I note that while their publicity material confirms they believed that tourists were looking for an old Quebec, there are clear indications that government officials also wanted to project an image of the province as economically progressive. Chapter 2 continues the investigation into the promotional initiatives of the provincial government starting in the 1930s. That decade marked a clear break from past practices, as government promoters were by then directly influenced by the priorities of traditional nationalists. This is when "Old Quebec" becomes the slogan of choice. Furthermore, a close reading of government publicity in the 1940s and 1950s brings to light a few changes in the way the province was represented, announcing greater changes to come. Having established how the government wished to represent the province to the outside world, chapter 3 focuses on American, English Canadian and French Quebec travel writers' preconceived views about Quebec and French Quebeckers more specifically – notably the *habitants*. Analyzing the novels, visual art, and textbooks they may have come across before setting out on their trip reveals how these travellers had, in effect, seen the province before leaving home. These sources of information set the criteria by which travel writers determined what was worth seeing and, more significantly, what constituted for them the authentic French Quebec. Chapter 4 establishes whether American, English Canadian, and French Quebec travel writers up to the 1950s saw their preconceived ideas about the province borne out once they arrived in its rural areas. What stands out is the extent to which national origins shaped the ways those writers processed the information they might have previously come across and how they read the places and people they encountered. Chapter 5 is devoted to Montreal and brings out the multiple ways in which the city's promotion and travel writers' reactions to it differed from what was happening elsewhere. Mostly promoted by the private sector, the marketing of Montreal was dominated by English Quebeckers intent on highlighting its racy Parisian modernity, and travel writers, both American and English Canadian, in turn lauded it for this very same modernity confirming that they were not simply propelled by antimodernist yearnings. Chapter 6 charts the process by which "Old Quebec" came to be marketed as "La Belle Province" by provincial promoters in the early 1960s in lockstep with the other transformations coming to fruition during the Quiet Revolution. It details the ways in which Quebec tourism was divested of the role many traditional nationalists had ascribed to it to revitalize a traditional French Canada and began to reflect a progressive and forward-looking Quebec. The last chapter analyzes how this wider context of change played out in Montreal. Vigorous debates involving commentators of all stripes – journalists, English Quebec members of the private sector, and French Montreal municipal authorities – questioned the way the city was promoted, clashing over how to best represent it in a context of heightened nationalist debate. The focus here is more specifically on the roles played by Mayor Jean Drapeau and Lucien Bergeron (director of Montreal's Municipal Bureau of Tourism), intent as they were on revamping the city's image to reflect the face of modern Quebec leading up to Expo 67. Travel writers' accounts, for their part, confirm the extent of their awareness of and enthusiasm for these changes. The epilogue brings to light how Expo 67, meant to showcase contemporary human accomplishments in all fields of activity, stands as an *aboutissement* of tourist promoters' efforts to market the province and Montreal as modern, an image both visitors and French Quebeckers could view as authentic.

1

BECOMING "MODERN" WHILE STAYING "OLD": THE STATE STEPS IN

During the late 1910s and at an accelerated pace in the 1920s, the Quebec government became an active participant in marketing the province as a tourist destination. Up to that time, the private sector, mostly large transportation companies, e.g., Canadian Pacific Railway (CPR), the Canadian Steamship Lines (CSL), and the Canadian National Railways (CNR), along with several hotel establishments were the driving forces behind the tourist industry's development and the province's main tourist promoters. From the outset, they imaged the province as "Old Quebec." Prospective visitors were promised they could travel back in time, making "a trip to yesterday,"[1] with "beautiful religious festivals ... sturdy reverent peasantry ... ox-drawn ploughs and dog-drawn cars."[2] Although the past was presented as timeless, it was also circumscribed – visitors, for instance, could expect to discover "sixteenth century France"[3] or enjoy the "Twentieth Century in a Seventeenth Century Setting."[4] Occasionally it was further narrowed down to Normandy. Thus, the CPR ads for their Château Frontenac describe "Jaunts Through Normandy in Historic Quebec"[5] or "Explore! ... North America's Normandy."[6] It should be noted that private companies in no way overlooked the bustling metropolitan centre of Montreal. The publicity about Montreal would further highlight the extent to which the outlying areas offered an enticing contrast to what tourists would encounter in that most modern metropolis: a place that was generically old and, as such, indisputably foreign.

Government tourist promoters, then, found a well-established and widely publicized promotion and branding of Quebec as a destination. This was not a development exclusive to Quebec. Notably, the private sector in British Columbia, Nova Scotia, and Prince Edward Island also predate provincial government involvement in the tourism promotion business.[7] In the following decades, they would fully commit to this imaging, continuing to market the province as old. Yet, their early forays into the tourism industry should not be understood simply as the government falling into line with the private sector's existing marketing strategies. It was also a time when the priority of government officials in charge of tourism promotion was to modernize and expand the province's tourism infrastructure, just as Quebec entered an extraordinary period of industrial and manufacturing expansion – developments government officials were proud of and also hoped to publicize. An analysis of government tourism promoters' early objectives, initiatives, and promotional material reflect the way in which they attempted to conciliate efforts to brand the Quebec destination as old while showcasing it as a place of modern economic development.

Early government incursions into the tourist industry went hand-in-hand with state road infrastructure development and modernization. This pairing is not unique to Quebec. In the first two decades of the twentieth century, provincial governments across Canada and state governments in America embarked on massive road projects.[8] Recalling those early days, the minister of the Roads Department, J.L. Perron, summed up the situation with an overstatement intended to highlight his department's accomplishments – claiming that in 1912 "for all intents and purposes there were no roads."[9] Certainly many existing roads were better suited for horse-drawn carriages than cars, with a clear need for improvement. (See figure 1.1.) Initially though, the Roads Department's mandate was to modernize the road grid for the benefit of its own citizens, notably to improve trading conditions and increase commercial activity and prosperity in farming communities. Increased competitive advantage was linked to commercial trade capacity, getting goods and services to markets, clients, or middlemen as expediently as possible. Motorized vehicles offered possibilities obviously unmatched by horse transportation or even by train and boat. Paving old roads and building new ones became a priority, connecting small, rural communities, which, in turn, linked Quebec to Ontario, as well as to the US. As such, in 1911, the Quebec government passed the "Good Roads Policy." Numbers attest to the government's resolve: between 1912 and 1918, a provincial road network covering a total of 350 miles was created. By the end of 1922, this network included forty-four large arteries covering 3,100 miles. By 1928, 4,972 miles of so-called first-class roads were laid. (See figure 1.2.) And finally, by 1934, drivers had access to roads stretching 16,000 miles.[10] Between 1912 and 1934, no less than $150,000,000 was invested for road development by the provincial government, a large sum for the period.[11] (See figure 1.3.)

1.1 | *"The National Route,"* L'Annonciation, c. 1920s.

Such initiatives did not go unnoticed. Well into the 1930s, newspaper articles in both Canada and the US included comments on improving road conditions and safety in Quebec. In 1930, *La Presse* argued that "long ago when the means of transportation were rarer and slower, the issue of going from place to place was important and difficult to solve ... Today this issue of transportation has completely disappeared as it is now so easy to solve."[12] The Roads Department's early annual reports suggest that road development had not yet been officially enlisted as a means to develop a tourist industry. In these documents, no reference is made to motorized vacationers' needs or the potential advantages of having more roads to accommodate them. This absence reflects the limited role the state and, more specifically, the department initially expected to play in tourism development. However, by 1919 expectations had obviously changed. In that same year, its annual report cited a newly emerging "sport" of motorized leisure travel (*automobilisme* or

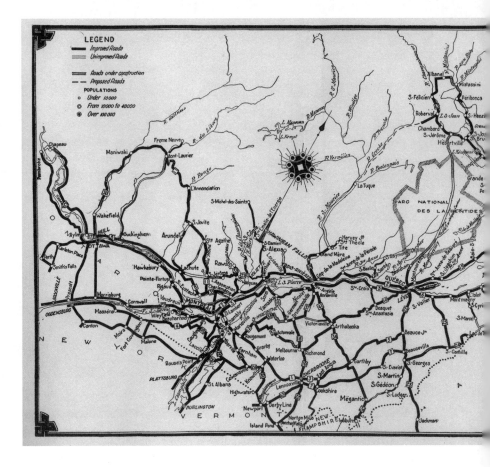

rotarisme). It included Quebeckers who wished to set off on short or more extended excursions not far from home or tourists coming from farther away. It further remarked that this new leisure activity "has all the symptoms of longevity." As if to confirm this prediction, amidst its numerous tables tracking road building, the minister's annual reports began tracking "touring cars" numbers. In 1920, for instance, on the Montreal–Quebec road, there were 231 such cars and by 1923, there were 825.[13] That same year, the department took other initiatives to better serve the needs of motorized visitors, producing a bilingual, bimonthly *Bulletin Officiel du Ministère de la Voierie/ Official Bulletin of the Roads Department* (published between 1923 and 1933) distributed to hotels, automobile associations, tourist bureaus, and the press. This *Bulletin* included detailed road maps and information keeping motorists up-to-date on the latest road conditions, along with safety advice, rules, and regulations. Thus, it becomes clear that the department was, at first, less

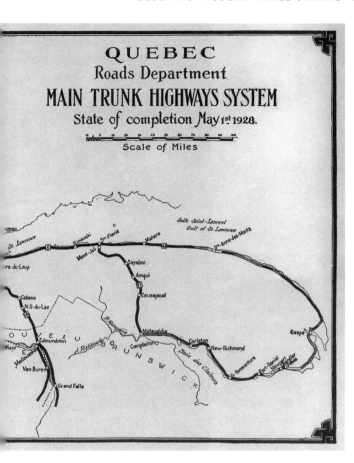

1.2 | Map in 4, 5, and 6 Days in Quebec Canada, 1928.

interested in promoting a distinctive image of the province than in providing motorists with practical information.

Tourism scholars confirm the minister's prediction of the increased popularity of tourism. Indeed, by the 1920s a growing number of North Americans took to motorized travel. In 1935, no less than 85 per cent of leisure travel in North America was done by car.[14] Several factors help account for the increase. For one, cars, which had initially been a luxury, became more affordable. In 1910, "just 500,000 Americans owned cars. By 1920 over eight million cars were registered"[15] and, by "1930, the number had risen to almost 23 million."[16] Canadians followed suit: while 500 could be counted in 1900, the number climbed to 1.2 million in 1930.[17] Directly linked to this development, motorists crossing the US–Quebec border increased from 31,918 in 1920 to 500,000 in 1928.[18] Other factors conducive to this travel increase pertain to changing working conditions: "[b]y the 1920s, most white

1.3 | "Good Roads Everywhere," in *Québec, The French-Canadian Province:*
A Harmony of Beauty, History and Progress, 1927.

collar civil servants in Canada and the United States were entitled to one
or two weeks' paid leave annually."[19] By the 1940s, "vacation with pay" was
made "available to all workers."[20] Richard Popp argues that as a result an
increasing number of people were given the opportunity to carve out free
time from work and, more significantly still, to associate this free time with
leisure understood as leaving home. In fact, this "new mobility" changed the
"the role of vacationing in America ... dramatically between the late 1920s
and 1930s." Furthermore, "cars rendered the feeling of spatial mastery that
came with exploring new places all the more common an experience," if not
"a standard expectation of American life."[21] More recent research also draws
a "connection between tourism and consumerism" and the process by which
tourist destinations can be viewed as a packaged commodity.[22] Indeed, historians point to an emerging consumer society during the 1920s and 1930s to
argue that "the purchasing, accumulating and consuming of goods and services [was] a chief priority for many individuals," including tourists.[23] Thus,
having more time and inclination to do so, an ever-increasing number of
North Americans throughout the period began to travel further from home

by car.[24] However, it is important to keep in mind that tourism remained a middle- and upper-class privilege. Indeed, "the extension of paid vacations to much of the industrial workforce did not mean that lower-middle-class and working-class families suddenly took up tourist travel en masse." Vacations remained "a rare perk for blue-collar employees." It was one thing to have the technology, time to get away, and desire to spend, it was quite another to be in a position to afford the expenses one would incur along the way.[25]

By the mid-1920s, the Quebec government had not only recognized tourism traffic as a growing and permanent phenomenon but also that "the tourist trade is a necessary adjunct" opportunity "to promote our economic life."[26] In other words, this was the decade when it became fully "tourist conscious," recognizing "that tourism is an undisputed source of economic good for all."[27] Reflecting this realization is the fact that officials in the Roads Department started publishing data confirming the ever-increasing revenue these new waves of travelers contributed to the province's economy. Thus, the 1927 annual report points out that in 1915 American motorists spent close to half a million dollars in the province, five years later that amount had climbed up to $5.75 million, ballooning to $45 million in 1925, and, by 1927, revenues totalled $62 million.[28] The following year J.L. Boulanger, deputy minister of Roads, optimistically surmised, "[t]ourism has perhaps become the province's principal industry. It is a gold mine that we must exploit."[29] Not surprisingly, the department then positioned itself as the best suited government organization to increase tourist traffic and to develop the province's tourism industry. For department officials, acquiring this added responsibility stood to reason since the tourism industry was, as they bombastically claimed, "born out of road construction."[30] Whether true or not, the department was officially mandated. To this end, a Provincial Tourist Bureau (PTB) was established in 1926, specifically dedicated to tourism promotion, largely targeting American travellers.[31]

At the same time, government announcements revealed the Quebec "face" they believed should be put forward. For the first time, the department's 1927 annual report included a "Why tourists visit us" subheading. The answer became its leitmotiv for years to come. In addition to pointing to the province's impressive natural beauty and opportunities for sportsmen, it noted that tourists visited the province because it was "characterized by history, traditions, a language and population quite distinct from the rest of America." And promoting these distinct cultural attributes was what "can be the basis of a most flourishing tourist industry." In other words, they recognized that what sold was, in part, old Quebec.[32] In this new age of the automobile, selling this Quebec was made easier as those who travelled by car were able and more than willing to explore. Indeed, contrary to travelling by train or ship, visitors could be less sedentary, more adventurous, and could stop at will several times along the way according to their own schedule. Dona Brown, who studied New England's tourism development, makes a similar point noting that automobilists there "like[d] to 'explore' the back roads and towns off the beaten track, staying only for a night or two at each stopping-place."[33] It also meant that they had a much better chance of coming into contact with Quebec's distinct population. Statistics certainly confirmed that motorized travellers were taking advantage of the ever-expanding road grid leading to the countryside – the closest thing to an old Quebec.[34] This trend further encouraged government expansion of the road network and a modernization of its burgeoning tourist hospitality services in rural areas. More precisely, it extended the available landmass to be promoted as "Old Quebec" so as to "stage the landscape that tourists could frequent"[35] or, viewed from a marketing perspective, was an attempt to commodify the countryside. As noted earlier, geographers refer more generally to such initiatives as "staging the landscape for the benefit of tourists."[36]

Studies by geographers and others go beyond scenery to look at how best to develop a successful industry built on available landmass. This includes "an ensemble of material and social practices and their symbolic representation."[37] It is no coincidence, then, that in 1929, for the first time, the ever-growing waves of tourists were given the opportunity to safely circle the Gaspé Peninsula – a region mostly dependent on fishing and agriculture – with the building of the Perron Boulevard.[38] While this region had been a favoured destination among a wealthy class of tourists as early as the mid-nineteenth century, its roads had been entirely paved with gravel. Once motorists arrived in Matane, they had to park their cars and jump into a horse-drawn carriage. At times, the privileged travellers who undertook the trip could not even make use of these primitive roads and, instead, made their way by *goélettes* (schooners). The situation after 1929 was quite different. The fact that the number of hotels in the Gaspé increased significantly from fifty-six in 1930 to one hundred in 1939 vividly illustrates this change.[39] The Roads Department also took initiatives to make the Île d'Orléans more accessible – yet another region early earmarked as part of old Quebec. In 1927, a highway linking its isolated rural communities was built, and, in 1935, a bridge to the island was constructed that linked to the mainland at Côte Beaupré, making access much easier.

Also during this period, a further highway circling the Lac St-Jean region was built – a destination that long appealed to those who could afford to get there by boat. Following in the footsteps of private companies, govern-

1.4 | Éva Bouchard (Maria Chapdelaine).

ment promoters labelled it the land of "Maria Chapdelaine," inspired by
the Louis Hémon novel of the same name.40 In doing so, they reinforced the
view that this, too, was a place where tourists could find old Quebec. Indeed,
Maria Chapdelaine represented Quebec as a rural province, devoutly faithful
to its traditions and the Catholic Church. In 1938, further cementing the
region's association with the novel, the Société des Amis de Maria Chapdelaine (founded in 1935) established a Louis Hémon museum, and the Bédard
family opened the Foyer de Maria Chapdelaine where travellers could stay
the night and take meals. It was located adjacent to the Bédard family home
with whom Hémon had resided and worked in 1912. (See figures 1.4 and
1.5.) Éva Bouchard, a relative of the Bédard family, would eventually be the
museum curator until her death in 1949. She ended up presenting herself to
tourists has having been the author's model for the novel's central charac-
ter.41 At the museum, tourists could also buy postcards with pictures of Éva
Bouchard, and she would sign these "Éva Bouchard (Maria Chapdelaine),"
which would have, no doubt, incited tourists to associate her with the novel's
heroine. While government tourist promoters never officially endorsed her
claim to fame neither did they contradict this self-appointed muse. One can
only surmise that since this young woman's undocumented contention was
consistent with the "Old Quebec" trademark, officials may have reasoned

1.5 | Louis Hémon Monument. Seated: Éva Bouchard (children unknown).
Péribonka, between 1937 and 1943.

that it did not warrant censorship. No harm was being done – in fact, quite
the contrary. Clearly they were not the only tourism promoters to share such
views. In other parts of Canada, blessed with popular fictional heroines, private sector promoters had long showcased these to lure tourists. In Nova
Scotia, during the later decades of the nineteenth century, "visitors arrived
[...] yearning to see the landscapes they remembered from *Evangeline*" – the
poem written by Henry Longfellow in 1847.[42] In Prince Edward Island, tourists eagerly looked for the places mentioned in Canadian author L.M. Montgomery's famous 1908 novel *Anne of Green Gables*.[43]

Another indication that the government was sensitive to motorists'
countryside interest was the launching of an "Embellishment Campaign." Officials reasoned that it was imperative that the new roads, as well as countryside municipalities, offer opportunities to showcase scenery tourists would
enjoy. The department embarked on an extensive tree planting project such
that, by 1929, the province had planted 210,530 "ornamental trees."[44] Travellers would also have the pleasure of driving by whitewashed telephone and

telegraph poles, and landowners adjoining highways or municipal roads were encouraged, through government publicity, to take responsibility for making a visitor's trip a pleasant one by maintaining their properties. Landowners were told that entranceways should be cleared of unsightly cars or agricultural implements and their fields neatly cultivated. They should also whitewash their barns and fences with lime provided by the government free of charge and plant flowers.[45] Government officials also came up with incentives to motivate proprietors, such as competitions to reward those who had planted the loveliest gardens. They even solicited the support of priests to entreat their parishioners, directly from the pulpit, to do their share in embellishing their surroundings.[46]

Yet, while the government was engaging in obvious "imaging strategies" meant to highlight the province's quaint, rural landscape, it is clear they were trying to do more.[47] Comments made by the Roads Department minister, J.L. Perron, on his return from a visit to Ontario in 1927, are revealing in this respect. For one, he remarked disapprovingly that comparisons between the scenery offered by Ontario and Quebec "are in no way in our favour." In Ontario, he claimed, the "houses are painted or whitewashed, buildings are clean, usually whitewashed and one sees no manure. Cleanliness exists from a physical and moral point of view and this is great progress in the fight against immorality."[48] More significantly, he declared that Quebec should not only try to follow Ontario's example but be in a position to "announce to the whole world that the Province of Quebec is the most advanced not only in terms of roads, administration and education but also in terms of CLEANLINESS, HYGIENE AND ESTHETICS [sic]."[49] Viewed in these terms, the embellishment campaign was meant to inspire the admiration of nonresidents for the province's up-to-date, progressive standards, as well as to increase French Quebeckers' own pride. In short, tourism promotion should be more than a straightforward attempt to highlight the "Old Quebec" brand.

One beautification and modernizing initiative would spawn another. In 1927, the department became involved in a campaign of "Hotel Improvement." This campaign was more explicitly targeted at those working in the tourist industry per se and would involve other branches of government as well. In line with this campaign, it established a Hostelry Service targeted mostly at countryside hotels. While the service was there to ensure that the existing laws and regulations pertaining to hotel services were respected, it was also there to offer advice to hotelkeepers on how best to modernize their establishment.[50] For Roads Department officials there was no doubt that "[n]o good hotels, no tourists, or at least a much reduced influx": tourists should be able to travel in comfort and at affordable prices.[51] Such conditions would entice extended stays and, ideally, return visits. Judging by newspaper editorials, many members of the wider public shared this view. *La Presse*, in particular, was relentless in its criticism of the quality of service found in the province's countryside hotels, deploring that "[t]oo many hotels make use of defective bedding to the disgust of many. Others do not know what it means to offer good service and the dining room, among others, is something awful where not only does one eat poorly but also not enough to eat his fill despite the price that for its part at least has become modern." Put more succinctly, "[t]he truth, the strict truth is that good hotels remain rare along the roads in Quebec."[52] By implication, this meant that the Hotel Improvement campaign would mainly target establishments run by French Quebeckers. Indeed, the majority of these smaller countryside hotels were run by French Quebec families in contrast to their city counterparts, which tended to be larger establishments run by Anglophones and, typically, were well serviced with modern amenities.[53] In all fairness, this state of affairs had much to do with the fact that, until then, countryside hotels' main clientele consisted of mail carriers and travelling salesmen. This meant that hotelkeepers could count on faithful patrons with easily fulfilled needs. They were operating in a non-competitive market, under no pressure to offer up-to-date services. However, with an ever-increasing number of motorized tourists accessing more remote regions, hotelkeepers had to contend with an entirely different set of customers – more demanding ones – and they were simply not up to the task. These establishments required upgrades to their hygiene practices, better quality food, and work to improve the overall comfort level of patrons. Hotelkeepers and their employees were further told to acquire better hospitality etiquette.

The government essentially offered itself as a counselling service, always mindful not to appear as though it was planning to apply a heavily regulatory hand in their affairs. In line with this approach, it distributed a free sixty-page booklet, *L'Hôtellerie moderne*, across the province to advise hotelkeepers how best to upgrade their establishments. Among other things listed were up-to-date and essential services hotelkeepers should provide patrons.

The Roads Department also offered to come directly to hotelkeepers by way of its "lady lecturers" or "teaching housekeepers." Once invited by the hotelkeeper, these women spent some time, if not a few days, at a hotel and gave expert advice on how owners could improve their establishments. No area was overlooked, including decoration, etiquette, and menus, down to staff attire. The credentials of these female officials were not necessarily important. Their expertise as professional consultants clearly rested on the fact that, by being women, they were presumably naturally gifted to impart this type of advice. The department regularly advertised the benefits of inviting their lady lecturers in *L'Hôtellerie* – a monthly publication, which advertised itself as the "[o]fficial French magazine devoted to the interest of Hotels and Tourist Traffic."[54] The magazine's editors did not tire of encouraging readers to make use of their services (while taking great care to reassure them that the lady lecturers were not inspectors), and both the magazine and the department's annual reports occasionally published the names of hotelkeepers who had availed themselves of their services. They were congratulated for demonstrating an admirable "good will by trying to continually improve their hotel."[55] For hoteliers, the message was clear: the road to success was modernization.

From the outset, it appears that countryside hotelkeepers were willing to cooperate with an increasingly proactive state. They recognized that it was in their best interest to do so. The Association des Hôteliers de Campagne (AHC) and *L'Hôtellerie* were active in spreading the state's modernizing word, often by way of the magazine's aptly entitled column "Pour être un bon hôtelier."[56] In fact, by the early 1930s, countryside hotelkeepers were increasingly lobbying the government, asking for various legislative interventions. As the 1929 tourist season was a banner year – following a few years of government hotel improvement campaigns and support – those working in the industry may very well have convinced themselves that the state's involvement could contribute to their success. Then, coming out of the difficult years of the Depression, government involvement may, in fact, have even appeared as a necessity. A case in point, rural hotelkeepers were particularly irked by the increasing competition – disloyal in their opinion – they were experiencing from others in the hospitality business, namely lodging houses and camps. Lodging houses were typically rooms rented by homeowners, providing visitors with access to a living and dining room and running water. Often adjoining the houses was a piece of land that could accommodate those who preferred to camp.[57] Hotelkeepers argued that the province's proud reputation as a hospitable destination was being jeopardized when tourists were being harassed "daily [by] a swarm of boys and men stopping cars and offering them lodging accommodation in hotels or lodging houses."[58] More likely to draw the attention of tourism officials and the general public for that matter, was the hotelkeepers' characterization of these camps as an "insidious menace that has been creeping into our security and corrupting the morals of our youth and young womanhood." Those who stayed in hotels, on the other hand, were "paying for respectability and protection."[59] To protect the unsuspecting tourists and uphold the province's reputation, as well as their own (not to mention their economic interests), hotelkeepers demanded that the Hostelry Service produce an official list of respectable tourist accommodations and disallow those who did not meet an officially sanctioned set of requirements.[60]

Generally speaking, by the end of the decade, many publicly congratulated the department for its efforts in developing the tourist industry. Even the erstwhile critical Quebec press began to publish more laudatory articles. In short, as a *Montreal Gazette* reporter asserted, "[t]he Department has now a fully organized tourist bureau" and it "has done wonders."[61]

This being said, Roads Department officials were well aware that modernization, embellishment, and improvement campaigns alone would not be enough to entice increasing numbers of tourists to visit the newly opened up countryside. They had to convince prospective visitors that it would offer them something different from what they could see at home or in other competing tourist destinations. Reflective of this understanding, the PTB produced a 176-page recipe booklet, *La Bonne cuisine canadienne*. It was meant to encourage hotelkeepers to serve typical *canadienne* recipes, coaching them to showcase the distinct cultural identity of the province's countryside cuisine. The recipes belonged to a repertoire of traditional, French Canadian country cooking including such classics as "*viande de tourtière*" or "*pouding au pain et au sucre d'érable*."[62] In line with the department's modernizing objective, the booklet also offered itself as a "complete treatise of culinary art," a "vade-mecum of the cordon-bleu."[63] Readers were given numerous tips on the best way to cook a wide range of foods. They could also find the meaning of standard culinary terms or, for instance, information on appropriate oven temperatures required for different types of meats, including advice on how to prepare good coffee. Overall, the booklet contained basic instructions to assist hotelkeepers to produce simple yet satisfying and well-served meals. The importance given to good cooking was further reflected in the department's offer, in 1928, to provide free cooking lessons to hotel employees and prospective cooks at the Montreal Provincial Household's Science School. From all accounts, it seems hotelkeepers appreciated this further government initiative, recognizing that serving local cuisine offered their smaller establishments a way to carve out a niche. In the words of the director of the AHC, "Let's not try to imitate the big city hotels, but instead let's offer our visitors the old and delicious *mêts* of the *canadien* cuisine that, be assured, has its own value and is much appreciated by gourmets."[64] This being said, it was not until the 1930s that the government began providing tourism industry workers with advice or direction on how best to promote their services to reflect a distinctive cultural identity.

But to best understand the Roads Department's view of Quebec's distinct cultural personality, an examination of promotional initiatives directed specifically at the travelling public – largely Americans – is required. As noted earlier, government tourist promoters had come to realize that old Quebec was a drawing card. However, their pronouncements and publicity material also make it clear that, during the 1920s, working to promote Quebec as old was not their only objective. Indeed, PTB officials would also make the point that visitors had to be made aware that Quebec was in step with the modern world and not simply a throwback to an old one. The province's impressive economic successes, which "combine[d] a very developed industrial and commercial activity," had to also be showcased. (See figure 1.6.) Among other things, visitors should realize that it was home to "the largest city in Canada, and a large number of less populated centers but no less active."[65] The facts certainly bore this out. This was a time when the province was undergoing a period of massive economic growth on all fronts. For one, "the value of manufacturing doubled between 1901 and 1919."[66] The province was also undergoing extraordinary urbanization. The proportion of city dwellers "increased from 36.1 per cent in 1901 to 63.1 percent in 1931" while the inhabitants of Canada's largest city, Montreal, "quintupled between 1881 and 1931 … which represented 28.4 per cent of the province's population."[67] In fact, in the wider Canadian context, the province could be considered in many areas as an economic powerhouse.[68]

However, the Roads Department officials had to reconcile what they thought outsiders should learn about the province's industrial and financial expansion with what they knew would make Quebec popular among tourists. Such attempts are quite obvious in the PTB's first detailed advertising booklets including a free ninety-page publication tellingly entitled *Québec, The French-Canadian Province: A Harmony of Beauty, History and Progress.*[69] In the booklet's foreword, beauty and history were certainly put on display. The hope expressed is that visitors "enjoy French Canadian hospitality and feel at home in Old Québec." This place "has retained its French character"[70] and "[t]he whole population … lives on [sic] the past." Under the heading "The Historic Province," readers' attention was directed to the countryside where "lives a population which has most faithfully kept the traditions, language, customs and dress of the past." Here the "conservative *habitant* still weaves linen and *étoffe du pays.*"[71] It should be noted that nowhere did this publicity suggest that Indigenous peoples – the original inhabitants of the Quebec territory – were considered part of the province's glorious past. In fact, no mention of them was made. Quebec's history started with the arrival of "Catholic heroes who were its discoverers, its founders, its settlers and its martyrs." Clearly promoters were taking for granted that tourists would only be curious about the descendants of these "first Frenchmen."[72]

Yet, what is intriguing is that, under a section devoted to the "Habitant," readers were in effect told that the traditional rural population, for all intents and purposes, no longer existed. Indeed, as with the voyageurs, "under modern conditions, they have both undergone such a rapid change that they

1.6 | "Old Wind Mill," in *Québec, The French-Canadian Province:
A Harmony of Beauty, History and Progress*, 1927.

1.7 | "An open cast pit in Asbestos Rock," in *Québec, The French-Canadian Province: A Harmony of Beauty, History and Progress*, 1927.

have now almost vanished" – mostly because of the "accessibility to the cities by automobiles." The *habitant* had now "evolved into a practical farmer." In fact, the brochure went out of its way to highlight the Quebec countryside's modernization: "the folk dances and songs are disappearing before phono-graphs, pianos and modern dances, especially in the vicinity of the cities and towns." At most, visitors could find reminders of the old Quebec. (See figure 1.6.) Further, the booklet actually appears to look down upon tourists who were in search of the *habitants* when it warned that "[t]he spinning wheel has been removed to the attic and the *étoffe du pays* is no longer seen except to be sold to unsophisticated tourists."[73] Readers could be forgiven for think-ing that officials were indirectly suggesting that, if they were planning to see an old Quebec, incarnated by the *habitants*, they should think again.

In fact, much of this early advertising publication provides detailed in-formation about the province's progress. The objective was clearly to con-vince readers that, at this time, Quebec as a whole was modern in every way. Indeed, the booklet includes sections on "Forest Resources," "Water Power and Hydraulic Policy," and "The Financial Standing of Quebec," each pep-pered with claims that the province was destined to become an industrial and manufacturing frontrunner in the larger Canadian economic context. Thus, readers were informed that "Quebec stands in the forefront of educational progress and appreciates the value and advantages of education." They also would find out that water power would soon "place Quebec at the head of all the Canadian provinces."[74] Judging solely by this publication, what can be ascertained is that while government publicity claimed that the province's distinctiveness rested on its old Quebec attributes, its officials were not ready to represent it exclusively as such. They clearly wanted prospective visitors coming to Quebec to know they were also coming to a place modern in many impressive ways – "a new-old Province" as they put it in this publication.[75] (See figure 1.7.)

The PTB's sixty-four-page booklet, *4, 5 and 6 Days in Quebec, Canada*, leaves the same impression,[76] as it, too, presented a double image of the province. It provided three itineraries for motorists to choose from, with descriptions of noteworthy cities, small villages, and other sites along the way. As with *Québec, The French-Canadian Province*, some sections of the booklet equated all things reminiscent of the past with French Quebeckers living in the countryside. Thus, motorists travelling between Quebec and La Malbaie learned that they would find "the genuine French Canadian homeland. Here stand sturdy Norman-roofed stone houses ... Where the population is still faithful to the traditions, language, customs and dress of the past; [where] the conservative 'habitant' still weaves linen and 'étoffe du pays.'" As for the Île d'Orléans, "here is the real spirit of French Canada, unaltered, it would seem, by modern progress ... Old houses, windmills, ox-teams and the genuine type of old-time French Canadian will delight the tourist."[77] Yet, in contrast with the government's other booklets, nowhere were readers told that the *habitants*, with their traditional customs and way of life, were a dying race. Searching for the *habitants*, accordingly, would not be a futile endeavour. As far as the modern Quebec was concerned, however, both publications were on the same page. In *4, 5 and 6 Days in Quebec, Canada*, prospective tourists learned that Quebec was a province on the move, developing at an ever-accelerating pace. Detailed information on the economic output of the province's various fields of industrial activity, complete with tables and statistics, were proudly displayed. The description of the four-day itinerary between Montreal and Quebec City, for example, offered a particularly good illustration of how PTB officials represented the province as being both old and new. The trip was characterized as "a historic and scenic promenade, where most up-to-date characteristics in commerce, industry and agriculture blend with a touch of ancient days peculiar to French Canada."[78] In Quebec City, "the tourist at once comes in touch with the past" as "it recalls a medieval city," "rais[ing] monuments to the glories of old France."[79] But it is also described as the "principal industrial and commercial city of the province after Montreal." As for

Montreal, it stands out for its remarkable economic accomplishments being "the largest city in Canada, the fifth largest city of America and is the Canadian commercial, industrial and financial metropolis." The booklet even invited tourists to take time to visit newly emerging cities with newly developing industries: "If sufficient time is available, a side -trip to Shawinigan and Grand'Mère will prove very instructive." Shawinigan, they were told, "owes its birth to water power development. A number of industries are established there," while "Grand'Mère, pop [sic] 8,000 has the same characteristics, and owing to very up-to-date management, is a fast growing town."[80] Even in the PTB's short, twelve-page booklet, *The Old World at Your Door*, specifically promoting what it labelled as "The Historic Quebec," progress was not overlooked. On the one hand, visitors were told that the "population ... has most faithfully kept the traditions, language, customs and dress of the past."[81] They were also invited to associate tradition with French Canadians. On the other hand, the point was, nonetheless, made that "the habitant has in the meantime, evolved into a practical farmer." Indeed, "he reads the city and agricultural papers, wants a rural mail and good roads."[82]

Further, the PTB produced an impressive, 900-page, 1929 publication, *Sur les routes du Québec: Guide du touriste*, translated into English the following year as *Along Quebec Highways, Tourist Guide*. The minister's report of 1929 described it as "the 'vade mecum' of the motorist, and it will, for the whole population of the Province, and American tourist as well, [be] an inexhaustible source of information and instruction."[83] As with its predecessors, it pointed out that the province's "affable and hospitable populace has preserved intact, in the country places at all events [sic], the manners and customs of the French regime." However, such comments were only occasional asides. Compared to the previous publications, less is made of the old Quebec. Even when describing the Île d'Orléans, the guidebook simply pointed to "the unusual character of its inhabitants" and "the number and importance of its historic souvenirs." First and foremost, readers were invited to take stock of the province's rapid modernization and understand that it was "destined to play, in the not far distant future, a preponderant rôle [sic] in the economic life of Canada."[84] All told, then, an overview of the PTB's early promotional material makes clear that it hoped to represent the province as both "old" and "new."

Yet this double imaging, pairing the modern and archaic, essentially contravenes tourism promotion best practices: clear, simple, and direct slogans that allow travellers to identify a destination with a distinctive and easily recognizable personality. Why deviate from this well-established marketing strategy? Was it simply that government promoters were trying to reconcile what they knew would make Quebec popular with tourists while showcasing what they thought these tourists should know about the province's impressive economic development? The Roads Department's double imaging can best be understood if one keeps in mind that the department was also responsible for promoting the economic development of the province. Its double mandate meant that it had to cater to both prospective tourists and potential entrepreneurs, two very distinct types of clientele. This is the reason for including the seemingly contradictory description in the same booklet of the traditional *habitants* as both alive and well and on the verge of disappearing. It also accounts for the fact that some publicity made the point of reassuring readers that the *habitant* "is not a ready listener to the labour agitator or socialistic propagandist. Strong, willing and resourceful, he makes a valuable employee in mills."[85]

While there is no doubt that, from the start, the Roads Department had its sights primarily set on American tourists and investors, it was also intent on attracting another group of visitors: Quebec residents. Quebeckers, after all, travelled as well. Although considerably less plentiful, publicity material intended for this clientele reveals that the government chose to market the province to its own citizens in different ways. In 1926, the PTB published a 154-page bilingual booklet, *Voyez Québec d'abord!/See Quebec First!*, providing itineraries for half-day to six-day tours. As the title made clear, the objective was to "induce motorists to visit their Province first." Quebeckers should understand that "[at] a time when the Province of Quebec is becoming a Mecca for tourists of North America, it would be strange, to say the least, were local motorists to forsake it" and go elsewhere.[86] Department officials viewed this marketing initiative "as quite a novelty in the line of publicity."[87] In point of fact, this initiative was not novel. In the US, for one, "boosters of all kinds including tourism promoters in the first decade of the 20th century," launched a *See America First* campaign "in an effort to encourage domestic tourism."[88] However, it certainly stands out among the booklets aimed at nonresidents. Most significantly Quebeckers would have found much less information to draw from to get a sense of their province's distinctive identity. It was essentially a practical compendium of play-by-play instructions on how to get from place to place, offering only short paragraphs describing "some points of interest on this trip." More significantly, however, is that it included only a few descriptions of the countryside that could have evoked for them an old Quebec. Thus, for instance, on the Île d'Orléans, prospective travellers were told that its "archaic villages" and "peaceful cottages reflect here more than anywhere else the far distant origins." They were also informed that "the old French customs and habits have remained intact in a large number of families on the south shore of the St Lawrence River. The tourist will specially enjoy the gaiety and the gracious hospitality of the French Canadian farmer." But for all this, visitors were not promised that in the countryside they would be plunged into a world of yesteryear, allowing them to travel back in time. At best, they would occasionally encounter vestiges of the past, where "a large number of families" – not whole communities – lived as had their ancestors and where they would discover only "traces of the ancient seigniorial homes."[89] There was, in short, no living old Quebec to be discovered, only reminders of it.

Most noteworthy, in fact, is that in the booklet for Quebeckers there is no specific mention of the *habitants*. Those living and working in the countryside were described simply as farmers – a term divorced of ethnicity and with no association to the past. Clearly, this suggests that the booklet was mainly aimed at city dwellers. From their perspective, those who lived off the land were simply exercising a specific occupation. Furthermore, some of these travellers might actually know or be related to farmers, to say nothing of the fact that to some French Quebeckers the term *habitant* often carried pejorative connotations, used as it was to describe unsophisticated country bumpkins.[90] In short, in *Voyez Québec d'abord!/See Quebec First!* readers would get no sense that French Quebeckers – farmers or otherwise – had distinctive or noteworthy ethnic or cultural traits. This, too, stands to reason. For one, French Quebeckers were less in need of information pertaining to their own way of life or beliefs or that of their compatriots, and they certainly did not recognize them as quaintly foreign. In fact, they would have been much more sensitive to what distinguished them from one another as French Quebeckers.

The type of historical information provided in the booklet was also indicative of the fact that the department counted on readers having a significant amount of knowledge about the province before setting off. Indeed, its short descriptive paragraphs focus on local history and include the kind of detailed information that could only have been of interest to travellers already familiar with the province's wider historical context. For example, prospective travellers could find out who, in the past, had owned specific seigneuries and learn the names of the parishes they would pass by along the way. The names of individual priests and other local figures were provided, as well. Who other than French Quebeckers travelling along the Montréal–Berthier route would be interested to know that "[the] records of the parish of St Pierre de Sorel begin in the year 1675. The first chapel was built in 1672 by Mr de Saurel and Messire L. Petit, third officiating priest"?[91]

As for representations of modern Quebec, differences with other PTB booklets are less obvious. *Voyez Québec d'abord!/See Quebec First!* also offered

Quebec residents a double image of the province. They, too, were invited to take stock of the province's extraordinary economic development. In a description of the Lac St-Jean area, readers were informed that "[t]he industrial development achieved during the past, and the development expected in the future are nothing less than marvellous." Two pages of statistical data confirmed these remarkable economic advances.[92] However, contrary to booklets destined for prospective English-speaking, North American tourists there is no evidence to suggest that this double imaging was a function of department officials wanting to attract both visitors and potential investors. Presenting the modern face of Quebec was first and foremost meant to inspire pride in the residents of the province, not to promote its business opportunities.

The period leading up to the early 1930s is a time during which much was accomplished. Starting in the late 1910s, provincial government officials in the Roads Department increasingly took on a new responsibility – that of increasing tourist traffic in the province. Tourist promotion was no longer the exclusive purview of the private transportation and hotel companies. Government officials' initial efforts would focus on modernizing the province's basic tourist infrastructure, largely in an increasingly popular Quebec countryside, such as extending and upgrading the road grid, embellishing roadsides, and improving service in provincial hotels. By the mid-1920s, more attention was devoted to marketing strategies meant to promote the province as different from other destinations. A PTB was established and issued publicity material, which revealed that officials believed tourists were looking for an old Quebec. Yet, at the same time, these publications contained information that pointed to the province's modernity, showcasing it as an economic powerhouse. This double imaging reflects the fact that, as employees of the Roads Department, they hoped to lure another class of visitor – prospective entrepreneurs who could directly contribute to the province's economic development. At times, would-be tourists could very well have wondered what they would find when they reached the newly accessible countryside. Would they come across an old Quebec or one in which the old was fast disappearing, giving way to a destination just as modern and progressive as anything they could see elsewhere? For their part, French Quebec residents would be invited to yet another Quebec, one that was less old – certainly not one in which they would be plunged in a living past. In the early 1920s then, government tourist promoters were essentially trying to attract different types of visitors compelled to travel for very different reasons and looking for different Quebecs – these were challenging conditions under which an attention grabbing marketing trademark could be developed – one that would confer on the province a unique "personality."

2

"TWO BIRDS WITH ONE STONE": ATTRACTING TOURISTS TO SAVE THE NATION

The government's increasing involvement in the province's tourism industry, starting in the late 1910s, ensured that by the early 1930s it had become a central player in the tourist promotion business. This is not entirely surprising as, more so than the private sector, it had the resources to initiate marketing campaigns and issue publicity material reaching wide audiences, both inside and outside the province. It also had the means to enlist and serve the needs of a wider range of players involved in the industry. In short, the province was best equipped to reach an ever-expanding and diverse tourist clientele. Yet, by the end of the 1920s and the early 1930s, louder and louder voices were heard, persistently criticizing government promotional initiatives. Unlike those who came before, they were less concerned about the province's sub-standard infrastructure and hospitality services. Instead, they argued, it was time for government promoters to devote more energy to showcasing what made the province a truly unique destination. More specifically, they wanted government promoters to fully commit to the "Old Quebec" brand name, and, more significantly still, they should do what was necessary to ensure that it reflected reality.

It is only possible to make sense of these evolving demands by pointing out that a great number of these critics belonged to the French Quebec, traditional nationalist intelligentsia – an elite extremely concerned about the fate of their nation's cultural survival. The sentiments of University of Montreal historian Jean Bruchési are reflective of this deep-rooted apprehension when he claimed that "[we] are noticing all of a sudden ... that this province of Quebec, cradle of our people, the *douce province*, is in the process of rapidly losing the characteristics it has of a French country."[1] Mgr Camille Roy, the rector of Laval University, put it even more pessimistically when he deplored that "there remains nothing of our beautiful ancestral face."[2] This disfigurement was symptomatic of a more alarming condition. It was nothing less than "the caving in of our French soul."[3] Thus, this elite devoted ever-increasing efforts to convince their fellow French Quebeckers to revitalize what it considered their authentic culture – a French-speaking one, imbedded in traditional rural society, upholding the beliefs and values of a strong Catholic Church. These traditional nationalists, though, were in no way advocating a return to preindustrial times, but they were deeply suspicious of those who favoured and praised all things modern, deploring the accelerating pace of urbanization and consolidation of unfettered industrialization. They associated these encroaching and threatening signs of modernization with "Americanization," inspired by their conviction that what took place in the US was, in all probability, a harbinger of things to come north of the border.[4] They "worried above all [that US] moral and cultural domination" would inevitably lead to a decline in moral values among Catholic French Canadians, who would come to prize material goods consumption and fall prey to the lure of an English and Protestant urban mass popular culture.[5]

To counter this creeping Americanization, nationalists turned to politicians. Earlier on they began lobbying the government to use colonization policies to extend rural areas in northwestern Quebec as a means of curbing the exodus to the New England States and Western Canada.[6] Further, they encouraged those living in rural areas to develop a local or regional *petite industrie*, which included the revival of handicraft production that had been gradually eroding since the 1890s. Reintroducing these practices, it was hoped, would make people there more self-sufficient and less reliant on urban markets.

But what stands out is that, by the late 1920s and early 1930s, traditionalists also started to draw direct connections between the survival of the nation and a successful tourism industry. In the words of the prominent economist Édouard Montpetit, "[to] stay ourselves" as French Canadians, we should keep "our traditions: religion, culture, language, *moeurs* and [he argued], tourism [requires] of us this behaviour, incite[s] us to conserve *la ligne d'expression de nos traits*. It deeply defines us and brings to us an economic justification to pursue our resistance to assimilation. It is therefore *bâtisseur*."[7] In short, as historian Alain Roy put it, tourism could serve "as a lever for a part of the elite to strengthen traditional aspects of culture and identity."[8]

Underpinning their position was the claim that when scanning the Quebec landscape through the eyes of American tourists, they could not but be "disillusioned."[9] And this was because these tourists were being assured by the private sector and, in part, by government publicity that, in the province, they would find an old Quebec. Yet, when they got there, traditionalists claimed it was nowhere to be seen. The solution seemed clear: create an old Quebec. Indeed, as Mgr Camille Roy put it: "[since] it is the French character, traditional, of our Quebec that makes it so popular abroad, that attracts to it so many visitors, that directs to our cities and our countryside a flow, ever re-plenished of American tourists: Let us preserve Quebec's French character."[10]

As will become clear in the following chapters, their assumptions were correct: the past made real by traditional ways of life was a drawing card. This was true not only for Quebec. Tourism promoters, as a rule, were quick to understand that, at that time, travellers were not only keen to visit foreign lands but wanted to be transported into foreign times, as well. Indeed, the antimodernist motivations of incoming, city-dwelling tourists during the late nineteenth and early decades of the twentieth century were a recurring explanation to account for the seduction of destinations that offered sharp contrasts to urban and industrial landscapes. And Quebec, along with other destinations on the North American continent, was well positioned to attract those sensitive to the lures of antimodernist scenery, both natural and social.[11]

However, the tourism industry could also serve broader nationalist interests. As Eric G.E. Zuelow argues, "tourism quite naturally prompts discussion about the nature of national identity" as decisions must be made about the nation's "defining characteristics."[12] In the case of Nova Scotia, Ian McKay points to the fact that cultural producers identified the fisher folk as the essential Nova Scotian. This made sense as at the time "what it meant to be a Nova Scotian" was ambiguous. The British connection was losing its centrality, and a Canadian nationalism had not yet proven inclusive to Nova Scotians, thus they were "working out a sense of identity," which, among other things, fed their "neo-nationalism" along with their "diffuse modern sense of anxiety and rootlessness." The fisher folk, with their timeless traditions, "released from the iron cage of modernity"[13] and their simpler life, could very well provide a kind of identity anchor for the wide range of city dwellers who lived both in and out of Nova Scotia, and who came from or were born out of the province. In Quebec, as in Nova Scotia, tourism promotion did not simply feed an antimodernist tourist hunger – all were plunged into a form of national introspection.

Yet, for all these similarities, the Quebec case stands out as distinct: the connections between tourism promotion and questions of national-identity formation were more explicit there. It involved a wider range of players and, more significantly, a unique and more ambitious state-sponsored project of national *survivance*. Moreover, traditional nationalists' recipe for success would require nothing less than a reorienting of Quebec society's contemporary culture and values. This task, it was argued, should not simply be left to a "few traditionalists and a few patriots" making efforts "to safeguard, what is left to us of our ethnic character and our distinct *physionomie!*"[14] For one, government tourist promoters should try, with the means at their disposal, to ensure that the destination they were selling was indeed an old Quebec. While this reorientation would not require a wholesale revamping of the government's marketing strategies, it would involve a refocusing of sorts. The PTB's publicity would have to avoid, as much as possible, double imaging the province as both old and modern to cater to the interests of two distinct sets of visitors – tourists and prospective entrepreneurs. As for French Quebeckers more generally, they could contribute to the success of the tourism industry by resurrecting an old Quebec "on the ground" and, thus, put an end to what tourists surely considered false advertising. More specifically, they must take initiatives to revitalize and preserve the traditions, values, and ways of life of what nationalists viewed as the *authentic* Quebec. Here rested the most challenging and ambitious aspect of traditional nationalists' tourism promotion strategy.

While undoubtedly ambitious, one could argue that by the early 1930s the stars had aligned to strengthen traditional nationalists' powers of persuasion. Indeed, a convergence of wider developments ensured that their understanding of what was best for the tourism industry would fall on receptive ears. For one, the Crash of 1929, which led to the collapse of world markets and unprecedented economic hardship, incited many states in North America and abroad to view tourism as a possible path to recovery. Despite the fact that US and foreign tourist expenditures in Canada plummeted in the early 1930s, the tourism industry fared relatively better than others and appeared to many politicians and economists as a way to kick-start their floundering economies.[15] In line with this way of thinking, the Canadian government set up a Special Senate Committee on Tourist Traffic in 1934 "to consider the immense possibilities of the tourist traffic, to enquire as to the means adopted by the government looking to its encouragement and expansion."[16] The next year, the Canadian Travel Bureau was created, later known as the Canadian Government Tourist Bureau (CGTB), headed by Leo Dolan until 1957.[17] It took on an increasingly important role in developing Canada's tourism industry. In addition to its wide-ranging responsibilities,[18] it took every opportunity to sensitize Canadians to the industry's crucial role in the country's economic development and encourage them to be good hosts. To support provincial tourist promoters, the federal government contributed funds through a shared-cost arrangement with the provinces to help subsidize interprovincial tourism campaigns, but it was understood that provincial officials would remain responsible for their respective tourism promotion. More significantly, the CGTB would have no say on the content of provincial publicity, and while it distributed promotional material in Canada and in the United States to advertise the country as a whole, labelling it a "Vacationland," it mostly promoted the country's natural sites including national parks and outdoor pastimes. In order to avoid appearing as though it was favouring one province over another it also strove to offer equal and "purportedly neutral representation of the country" inhabited by generically friendly, neighbourly people.[19] Focussing on scenery and recreational activities was also a way to avoid having to decide how to represent Canadians in ways that might offend provincial promoters keen on differentiating their inhabitants to their advantage – best to focus on cultural attributes everyone could agree on.[20]

By getting into the tourism business to this extent, the federal government's hope was that, in the future, tourism might offer some level of financial security by stimulating economic growth at relatively low cost. Quebec government officials clearly shared this optimism.[21] Indeed, Roads Department Minister J.E. Perrault invited his compatriots to see in the tourist industry "a reason to hope, a first means to improve our economic situation, one of our most important sources of wealth."[22] Reflective of this conviction, tourism was given greater importance by government tourism policy planners. Thus, the Tourist Act (1933) was passed, establishing a Tourism Council, which brought together representatives from the provincial government and business community to provide advice on how to best develop the province's tourist industry. Although it never amounted to much, meeting as it did only a few times, the council nevertheless brought to light the government's intent to better plan and coordinate tourist promotion initiatives.[23] State officials also created regional initiator syndicates (*syndicats d'initiatives*). These were mandated to group "within a given region or district all the living forces of tourism, that is to say to bring about co-ordination of effort among all individuals and organized bodies working for the promotion of tourism." Each was required, by law, to submit a program for government approval to the minister.[24] Of more enduring significance is the fact that tourism also was relocated in the government bureaucracy providing yet more evidence of how decision-makers viewed this as deserving greater attention. Thus, in 1936, the responsibility of tourism promotion under the Provincial Tourist Bureau was handed over to the Ministry of Municipal Affairs, Industry and Commerce. Its responsibilities were essentially the same as those of its predecessor but moving into a department more directly mandated to promote the province's economy clearly signalled that, more than ever before, tourism was valued as a source of financial prosperity. More telling still, certainly at a symbolic level, the following year, it was relocated once again into the newly formed Department of the Executive Council, which, among other responsibilities, oversaw government publicity as a whole, with its director answering to the premier's chief of staff. In other words, this meant that tourism would officially become the ultimate responsibility of the premier, clearly making it "une affaire d'État."[25] Indeed, during a speech he delivered at the first Canadian National Tourist Congress in Quebec City in 1943, Premier Adélard Godbout explained that "we in Quebec fully realize the importance of tourism and proof of this is to be found in the fact that I have kept tourism in my own Department in order that I may give it particularly careful attention and close supervision."[26] From a nationalist perspective, the fact that up to 1939 and then from 1944 to 1959 the premier would be Maurice Duplessis, leader of the Union nationale party, also boded well for their cause, as Duplessis shared in many ways their traditionalist worldview. Finally, in 1946 the government created a Provincial Publicity Bureau (PPB), directed by Georges Léveillé who remained in that position until his death in 1956.[27] It was charged with managing all government propaganda, divided into three separate branches with the Tourist Branch (TB) as the most important of the three.[28] Notably, it remained under the ultimate responsibility of the premier, suggesting, at least officially, that its administrators would continue to get the attention of the highest authority in the province.[29] All told, these wider economic and political developments provided a propitious context for those offering advice as to how to best develop the tourism industry. Traditional nationalists, with energetic resolve and a clear sense of what needed to be done to increase tourist traffic, were particularly well positioned to draw decision-makers' attention, both in the public and private sector, and did not miss an opportunity to provide them with guidance by way of specific and concrete advice.

For one, they had much to say about the French language. While many nationalists had long voiced criticism of the province's rampant Anglicization and worked to rein it in, by the 1930s they channelled their concerns through a highly publicized *refrancisation* campaign. Initiated in 1932 by the members of the Société des arts et des lettres de Québec, it rapidly obtained the collaboration of prominent members of the nationalist elite and francophone newspapers including *La Presse*, *Le Devoir*, and *Le Soleil*.[30] A host of organizations, regions, and parishes joined in as well and established *refrancisation* committees of their own, urging all – including those working in the tourism industry – to put their French face forward. Typical in this regard were Eudore Couture of Rimouski, editor of the *Progrès du Golfe*, who advised his compatriots to speak French with tourists. Indeed "[let] us not forget that our charm, for them, is to have remained *vieille France,* they like our *parlez doux,* even though they do not fully understand it." He further noted, "they do not appreciate an awkward copy of what they can find at home."[31]

Not surprisingly, French Quebec hotelkeepers became preferred targets. According to nationalists, hotelkeepers were particularly well positioned to contribute to the *refrancisation* of Quebec for the benefit of tourists. They homed in on countryside hotels as French Quebeckers, more often than not, were the managers, and those establishments were also more numerous. Indeed, in 1930, 85 per cent of "hospitality entrepreneurs" were family run and located outside large urban centres. Furthermore, in the opinion of nationalists, French Quebec hotelkeepers had much to reproach themselves for contributing to the province's disfigurement.[32] Indeed, much to their dismay, many hotelkeepers chose to baptize their establishments with English-sounding names such as the "'Hotel Commercial,' 'Hotel Central,' 'Petit Windsor,' 'American House' or 'Hotel Canada.'"[33] A great deal of effort was used to convince them to change their ways. The campaign met with some early success as a few proudly reported small victories to newspapers or campaign promoters. Joseph Ferland, for instance, a member of the Ste-Marie *refrancisation* committee, proudly announced that each parish in the Beauce region had established its own committee and boasted that "[t]he 'New York Coffee' of Ste-Marie has become the *Café Ste-Marie* [and a] garage chose to call itself the '*Garage du Domaine.*'"[34]

A more likely influence at the provincial level, though, were prominent nationalists who took leadership roles, making the most of their sway to change their compatriots' outlook and behaviour, in addition to alerting government tourist promoters of the gravity of the situation. This was the case of Olivar Asselin (1874–1937), whose widespread reputation as a polemicist and a man of action meant that his views attracted attention.[35] Furthermore, as editor-in-chief of *Le Canada,* he had privileged access to an influential journal from which to publicize his opinions. In 1932, he wrote a noted editorial, "Sur une organisation du tourisme."[36] Although short, this text drew much attention as it provided well-thought-out guiding principles, and it was immediately referred to by those who hoped to develop a tourist industry along nationalist lines. Indeed, after alerting his readers to the rampant anglicization of the province and its detrimental impact on the tourism industry, Asselin insisted, among other things, that hotelkeepers and restaurant owners serve their patrons typical, local French Canadian cuisine and not "Mr Kellogg's dry '*bouillies.*'" For the benefit of decision-makers, he suggested that the government use only French terminology to identify landscapes such

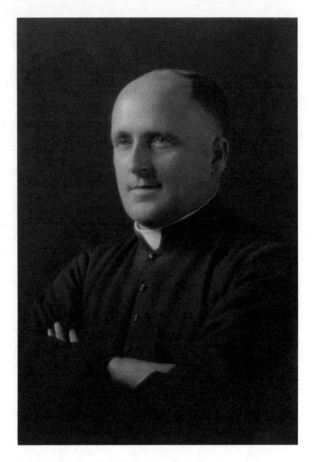

2.1 | Albert Tessier, circa 1938.

as rivers and seaways and that tourist guidebooks include "a French-English glossary."[37] He also argued that, even though all the necessary players involved in tourist promotion were in place, to be truly effective, they should coordinate their efforts and work under the umbrella of a single authority. This idea of having a government body solely dedicated to tourism would be a recurring demand throughout the period.

Asselin had great influence on other nationalists who then played a more active role in developing the tourist industry. Abbé Albert Tessier (1895–1976) is a case in point. (See figure 2.1.) He, too, was a well-known public figure, prolific writer, and pioneer filmmaker promoting the regional history of the St Maurice Valley. More generally, he became an energetic propagandist dedicated to publicizing the traditional French Canadian rural way of life and the beauty of Quebec's landscape.[38] Tessier produced documentary films on the subject, close to seventy films in total between 1932 and 1941, the first, entitled *L'Île d'Orléans, reliquaire d'histoire*, in 1939.[39] He estimated he gave more than 2,200 talks between 1932 and 1960, all meant to increase audiences' knowledge and love of the province.[40] As with other traditional nationalists, he pointed out again and again that French Canadians boastfully proclaim themselves proud citizens of the "Old province of Quebec" and that "this refrain came back like an obsessive leitmotif in all our patriotic speeches and brochures edited to the glory of the 'France of America.'" Yet, for all this, he deplored that this seemingly heartfelt conviction was not reflected in reality.[41] It was incumbent upon French Canadians, therefore, to remedy the disconnect between rhetoric and real life, and, being a nationalist of his time, Tessier invoked tourism to make his case more convincing. In fact, he rapidly acquired the record of someone ready to devote tremendous time and energy to increasing tourist traffic.

Many of Tessier's recommendations directly echoed Asselin, and Tessier would often refer back to his suggestions or quote him directly. He too called upon French Quebeckers to put a stop to the proliferation of English-language signage across the province. To his mind, here was the most visible manifestation of the gradual erasure of Quebec's French face and one that could not but strike tourists when they first arrived. In fact, early on, Tessier collected detailed evidence to prove the gravity of the situation. In 1933, he alerted the members of the Société du parlez français at Laval University that "from the banks of the Outaouais river to the tip of the Gaspésie, one comes across scarcely ten signs that are truly French."[42] Not long after that, Tessier was given the opportunity and resources to document more fully this sorry state of affairs for the direct benefit of government tourism promoters. Indeed, in 1938, the government hired experts, including Jean-Marie Gauvreau, director of the École du meuble in Montreal, to produce an inventory of the province's natural resources, including its arts and crafts.[43] He, in turn, hired Tessier to investigate the state of the tourist industry and to make recommendations about the best way to promote the province. From June to mid-September of that year, Tessier travelled the region from the *comté* of l'Islet to the tip of the Gaspésie. He took copious notes, asked people to fill out questionnaires, conducted home studies, took thousands of photographs, and produced more than 5,000 feet of film with the goal of documenting "our peasant life."[44] This allowed him to provide more detailed and damning evidence. Among others, he calculated that from Trois-Rivières to Quebec City, 77.4 per cent of signs were exclusively in English.[45]

His report also offered a cogent plan of action replete with very specific recommendations – many of them directly inspired by those of Asselin. But, on another level, what makes this document of particular interest is the fact that it provided one of the most detailed articulations of traditionalists' heart-felt conviction that the tourism industry could and should serve a noble, nationalist end.[46] Tessier insisted, "all efforts to intensify our distinct qualities, to give back to our ethnic personality its full vitality, will amplify in direct proportion to our tourist value."[47] More to the point, he asserted, "tourism must be for us a way to strengthen first our ethnic personality."[48] Its value was, in essence, "NATIONAL [sic]."[49] Thus, in what could be read as a veiled criticism of present-day initiatives, he insisted that it was misguided to make tourism "almost exclusively a question of publicity, roads, hotels, chalets, hunting or fishing clubs, ski runs etc."[50] What mattered most was that "meas-ures [be taken] so that visitors attracted by our appeals find *chez nous* what our publicity promises!"[51] Using a term likely to resonate with those primarily preoccupied with the business side of things, he argued that work should be done to promote the province's "capital" assets to tourists. Among others, he identified five points that spoke directly to a traditional understanding of the French Canadian identity. They included, in ranking order, the province's history, spirituality, French atmosphere, human character, and hospitality.[52] What Tessier hoped above all was that promoting these capital assets would encourage French Quebeckers *themselves* to prize and protect them.

While he acknowledged that all these assets were showcased in the prov-ince's advertising, Tessier argued that much more needed to be done to bring them to the fore. Thus, for instance, in order to bring out and make the province's history more accessible and visible to tourists, he proposed the creation of half a dozen *parcs musées* in different regions of the province. After all, Quebec was the only one "on the whole continent that keeps the memory and the imprint of four centuries of French and Catholic life."[53] In fact, in his view, Quebec's spirituality capital also had the potential to draw in tourists. He claimed that it was well known that North American and Euro-pean travellers, including Protestants, were drawn to the outward manifesta-tions of French Canadian Catholicism, be they places of worship, wayside crosses, shrines, or religious processions. Enlisting tourism to serve Catholi-cism would contribute to the *"rayonnement"* of our "best racial qualities" on the continent.[54]

But Tessier's report also identified what he terms "liabilities," regardless of the fact that some of these were extremely popular with tourists. The top liability was the presence of tethered dogs in rural areas – dogs he had actually taken time to count during his field research. (He identified seventeen on the road between Trois-Rivières and Ste-Anne-de-Beaupré.) They were nothing less than "a crime against distinction and good taste that should be subject to

2.2 | Dolled-up dogs for the benefit of tourists.

judicial sanctions." Yet, tourists viewed them as distinctive markers of "Old Quebec."[55] Certainly, some French Quebec promoters and countryside inhabitants had understood the appeal they held with visitors. To Tessier's dismay some even decorated them to amuse tourists. They wore "headdresses, smoke[d] pipes ... and [were] watched over by kids shamelessly begging and soliciting."[56] (See figure 2.2.) Although Tessier did not single them out in his report, French Quebec newspapers often featured these dogs and their carts as tourist attractions. For example, a *La Presse* article on the Laurentians was illustrated by a photo of a young child standing in a cart pulled by a dog with a caption noting that tourists "who will go on the Malbaie route will see how children work while having fun ... they harness their dogs and haul the wood required at home." In fact, these dog carts were occasionally featured in some of the province's own advertising material.[57] (See figure 2.3.) If nothing else, Tessier's reactions to the popular dogcarts bring to light the extent to which using tourism to bolster tradition could be a double-edged sword. On the one hand, it could serve to shore up what nationalists perceived as an authentic French Canadian culture. But, at times, traditional ways of life could also be adapted to serve exclusively market-driven imperatives thus potentially tainting, if not demeaning, Quebec's national capital.

However, while Montpetit, Asselin, Tessier, and others weighed in to give the nationalist point of view on how best to increase tourist traffic, some actually ended up working directly with frontline players in the tourism industry

2.3 | "Dog cart near Quebec," in
4, 5, and 6 Days in Quebec, Canada, 1928.

and as government promoters themselves. Paul Gouin proved to be the most prominent example, working as a promoter until the late 1950s. (See figure 2.4.) He had long since gained respect among a wide swath of both provincial and local elites and high-ranking government officials. Part of his renown can be attributed to the fact that he came from a famous French Canadian family, the son of former Quebec premier Lomer Gouin, and had made his own incursions into Quebec politics. Above all, his highly reputed credentials as an active promoter of French Canadian culture and language are what gave him, more than any of his nationalist counterparts, a unique and privileged opportunity and platform to express his views and promote his understanding of what direction Quebec tourism should take.[58] In the 1930s and beyond, Gouin would be at the forefront of the province's wider *refrancisation* campaigns and other numerous nationalist initiatives, aimed at rejuvenating French Canadian cultural heritage.[59] Not surprisingly, his pronouncements and entreaties to *refranciser* the province were given much public attention

2.4 | Paul Gouin, 1945.

and were well received. Thus, it seemed perfectly fitting that he was invited, in 1948, to join the government as technical consultant to the executive council of the province of Quebec. He was given the mandate to preserve and develop the province's cultural and artistic traditions and shore up the tourism industry – a position he held until 1968.

While Gouin stood out from among his nationalist peers in many ways, he subscribed entirely to their understanding of what ailed his compatriots and how tourism could be put to use as a cure. He too was concerned about the province's Americanization, and, in line with the current traditional nationalist reasoning, he also invoked the economic benefits of resurrecting the province's French character. He never tired of pointing out that tourists "came here to find something new, different from what [they see] every day at home."[60] And hotelkeepers who elected to name their establishments "Tourists' Rest" or "Board and Room" or served "le 'hot dog,' le 'ice-cream cone' and a 'chicken dinner'" were surely not going to convince them that visiting Quebec was worth the trip.[61]

Beginning in the 1930s, he devoted much effort to get hotelkeepers, restaurateurs, and shop owners on side. But rather than simply entreat them to
refranciser, as much as they could, he offered them specific suggestions. He
pointed out, "it is in our customs and our legends, in our history, in our fauna
and our flora that one will find the most flavoursome, the most picturesque
and the most characteristic names."[62] More than that, he strongly encouraged them to seek the counsel of those who, such as himself, were versed in
French Canadian architecture, literature, history, arts, and crafts when looking for advice on how best to *refranciser* their establishments.[63] They clearly
did not hesitate to avail themselves of his cultural consultant services. His
plentiful correspondence throughout the period attests to the fact that many
were indeed eager to seek his advice. Always sensitive to the need to get the
general public involved, he also organized several language competitions in
which contestants were asked to come up with French names and expressions in lieu of the all-too-prevalent English ones. Gouin also felt that more
should be done to preserve typical traditional French Canadian architecture
whether private dwellings, churches, or old farm constructions. This, too, was
part of their distinct, national character and sure to attract tourists.

This barrage of nationalist entreaties and recommendations coming from
such well-respected figures did not go unheard. Countryside hotelkeepers
certainly responded positively to their call for action and, in fact, the AHC
initiated a *refrancisation* campaign of its own in order to, in the words of its
secretary Rodrigue Langlois, "rebaptize the signs of our commercial establishments and our hotels and give them ... a clearly French character."[64] *L'Hôtel-
lerie/The Hostelry* editors reminded readers that, "on several occasions," their
articles "suggested to hotelkeepers and restaurant owners to give their establishments a French name, and French allure as a patriotic and commercial
goal."[65] Their spokespersons concurred that investing resources in promoting
the province was less of an issue than ensuring that the publicity was accurate. Tapping into their members' pecuniary self-interest, officials at the AHC
asked members, "[w]ould it not be more advisable before squandering money
on publicity, advertising a country of French culture, to consider first whether
this culture is visible."[66] To say nothing of the fact that it is "not more ... expensive to advertise your hotel with a sign written up in proper French than
by one with a *baroque* English label or in poor French."[67]

The precarious fortunes of the hotel industry during the first half of the
1930s likely contributed to owners' openness to trying new strategies, including *refrancisation*.[68] In the minds of some, the US Congress's 1933 decision to
repeal the American National Prohibition Act (or Volstead Act) added to
the economic hardships of the Depression.[69] Until 1933, hotelkeepers pointed

out that Quebec had been "the oasis of the dry American continent" and this "brought to us incessantly caravans of tourists, who came to appreciate the moderation of our laws and the warm hospitality of our people." Placing their bets on *refrancisation*, leaders in the industry optimistically contended that by "giv[ing] to our province as quickly as possible that French outside appearance ... we shall soon see the American tourists again."[70]

For traditional nationalists, however, bringing the French language to the fore would not be enough. Throughout the period, they also lobbied persistently to revive local production of handicrafts including "handmade ... objects for utilitarian, decorative and occasionally ritual purposes."[71] As mentioned earlier, nationalists had long called for their compatriots to re-suscitate a rural handicraft industry as a means to encourage farm families to remain on the land. But, by the late 1920s and early 1930s, they would emphasize more forcefully that such a resurrection would also contribute to a more successful tourism industry.[72] For one, it meant that it would be easier to meet the growing tourist demand for souvenirs, as travellers had, from early times, demonstrated an enduring taste for French Canadian handicrafts. They were particularly drawn to homespun textiles, including the famous *catalognes* (hooked rugs), a variety of handmade rustic furniture, and wood-carvings. These typically represented old *habitants* with pipes, often with the telltale toque and *ceinture fléchée*, while women were portrayed at their spinning wheels or in front of outdoor ovens.[73]

Paul Gouin proved to be the most adamant promoter of this handicraft revival, as not only would tourists be less likely to have to settle for inauthentic souvenirs "manufactured in Japan, in Switzerland and in Germany"[74] but, addressing his remarks specifically to countryside hotel owners, he made the point again and again that "the products of our rustic art [such as]: furniture, paintings, materials, carpets, ornaments, etc" would "give to their hotels a French Canadian cachet not only in name but in actual fact." More importantly, from a nationalist perspective, use of such objects would not only serve their business interests but also allow them to perform "a patriotic deed eminently salutary."[75] As he put it "an engraving, a piece of furniture, a carpet, and a book are in some sense the external affirmation of the homeland, its palpable manifestations" and could "constitute a national education opportunity."[76] And, ever the practical consultant, he offered concrete suggestions as to how French Quebeckers could make use of these in their everyday lives. They could, for instance, "decorate the child's room and the home *à la cana-dienne*."[77] Addressing members of the Saint-Jean-Baptiste Society, he even went so far as to suggest that they feel compelled, by way of regulations if necessary, to "buy at least once a year, an article of *fabrication domestique* for their living room or office," and, secondly, "give as a gift at least once a year, an object of the same provenance." Nothing less than a "fine" could be imposed on members who violated these regulations.[78] However, it should be noted that advocates of a handicraft revival, such as Gouin, were not inviting their compatriots to turn back the clock and return to the practices of their forefathers. He believed that while these products should encourage French Canadians to preserve their traditions, they should, at the same time, be adapted to the changing needs and preferences of the host population. Only then could one realistically expect handicrafts to be successfully integrated into their lives.

There was already plenty of evidence to suggest that nationalists' call for increased handicraft production could intersect with the interests of those involved in the tourism industry who had profit seeking foremost in mind. Indeed, French Canadian tourist operators had only to consider the great success of the Canadian Steamship Lines (CSL), under the leadership of William H. Coverdale, president of the company from 1922. He had made selling French Canadian handicrafts an integral part of the company's tourist business. Travellers could purchase these on its cruise ships and in its hotels. The Charlevoix region in particular, with its Manoir Richelieu and Hôtel Tadoussac, were highly prized by tourists as a prime area to purchase CSL souvenirs. But while the company was clearly in the handicrafts business to make a profit, its initiatives were not entirely divorced from the preoccupations of those concerned with French Canadian survival. This was clear when one considers that the CSL had established a working relationship with Marius Barbeau – a reputed anthropologist and folklorist who shared nationalists' alarm at the erasure of French Canada's traditional culture.[79] Beginning in the 1910s, Barbeau had undertaken field trips in the Quebec countryside – most often in the Charlevoix, Île d'Orléans, and Gaspésie regions – recording information on the way of life of the *habitants* in order to ensure the preservation of their traditions, legends, tales, and songs. In the eyes of Barbeau, these *habitants* embodied the folk of Quebec – the province's living repositories of the French Canadian way of life harking back to the days of New France. In fact, the *habitants* and fishermen such as those who lived in the Gaspé were, to his mind, the "true Canadians." Yet, he warned, these bearers of French Canada's authentic culture "represent an age that is quickly passing."[80] By the 1930s, he often seemed overtaken with pessimism, surmising that this age had, in fact, already passed and "one can only speak of a French Canadian culture in retrospect, in other words, in the past."[81] Keeping this in mind, being on the CSL payroll could very well have appeared to him as an opportunity to help preserve French Quebec's authentic culture and forestall its demise. (From the CSL point of view, of course, getting the collaboration of a reputed scholar gave its handicrafts an invaluable stamp of authenticity.) This would have been the case, for instance, when Barbeau offered his expert advice as the company organized fairs meant to showcase traditional songs and *métiers du terroir*.[82] These exhibits would help disseminate a traditional understanding of what constituted an authentic, untainted French Canadian culture to an audience he might otherwise never have reached. At the same time, he could have hoped to incite his compatriots to value this popular traditional heritage among tourists and strive to protect it.[83]

By the 1930s, the PTB government promoters were influenced significantly by this ambient nationalist discourse. While they did not set aside their responsibilities to modernize the industry, by then they were equally engaged in encouraging those involved in the tourist business to preserve and showcase French Canadians' "capital traditions." Reflective of this shift is the increasingly nationalist discourse contained in the Roads Department's Annual Reports. Beginning in 1929, these reports' explicit statements call for the preservation of Quebec's distinct French attributes. In 1929, officials remarked, "another thing that might well be stressed is the necessity of conserving for the Province its French character, one of its greatest attractions to the American visitor." While officials point out that the "Department has brought this to the attention of the public many times," they would now strive to do more to preserve the province's "French character."[84] Echoing the views of nationalists generally, they defined this character as "our sense of hospitality, our enthusiasm, our respect for traditions, our love of the homeland, our love of the arts, nature, music … a special enjoyment of debate and discussion not forgetting our generous sense of humour."[85] In fact, in many respects, the annual reports begin to read as nationalist calls to action. For example, the 1933 report, as though anticipating Tessier's words, declared that the province's French character "must not be considered merely in relation to the tourist industry. It is a function of national survival." In essence, government promoters drew the same connections as nationalists between the conservation of the French Canadian character and the growth of the tourism industry. As they put it, "public opinion has been roused to the urgency of the conservation of that character through the eagerness to develop the tourist trade, and it has therefore become a matter of present day concern." Concretely, officials at the Roads Department started to push for the same changes advocated by nationalists, including *refrancisation*. In fact, they actually claimed that the department had "originated this campaign and ha[d] played a leading role in it."[86] Be that as it may, their official documents certainly started to include regular comments deploring the misguided practice

among those in the tourism business who reverted to English when advertising their establishments. They regretted that there "is still a tendency to
believe that the tourists will be flattered if they are offered accommodation in
hotels and inns with names that are exclusively English or American, and if
they are treated so as to make them feel entirely at home."[87] Roads minister
J.E. Perrault was so intent on modernizing the industry that by the 1930s
he doubled as a strong advocate of *refrancisation*. Addressing an audience in
Trois-Rivières in 1933, he asked "why [we have] these English inscriptions
along our roads."[88] As did nationalists at large, he mostly directed his comments to French Quebeckers working in the countryside with the thought
that the success of the industry depended on a proactive effort on their part.
Sounding a familiar refrain, he argued that "if people of the countryside know
how to dress our province with a distinctive appearance; if they know how to
bring out the features that are its own, hopefully Quebec will appear unique
and foreigners will come back to visit it for its originality."[89] On the ground,
government officials lent their support to various *refrancisation* efforts. Thus,
for instance, in 1937 the Tourist Bureau offered its financial support to the
Syndicat d'initiative de la Mauricie, which organized a French-sign contest
for hotels, restaurants, stores, and products of all kinds.[90]

The department's annual reports also began including a few lines on the
importance of showcasing handicrafts. In 1933, it advised, "[a] tourist organization must give home products a certain importance in its propaganda."
Leading by example, it pointed to its collaboration with the École des arts
domestiques, praising the high quality of the school's training. Of note, this
quality was reflected by its faithful adherence to rural traditions, steering clear
of what they labelled, disapprovingly, as "*art moderne*."[91]

In many ways, by the 1930s traditional nationalists watching the initiatives and statements of PTB officials, whether from afar or as more involved
participants, could very well have felt that the government's priorities had
aligned neatly with their own. The most visible evidence of this may very
well have been the bureau's new advertising initiatives, as this was the period
when the "Old Quebec" brand gained a well-entrenched ascendancy in government publicity, although this development should not simply be seen as
another sign of government promoters' nationalist commitment. Other factors were at play as well. For one, during the years following the Depression
and the repeal of the Volstead Act, the tourist industry became increasingly
competitive. Although Canada fared relatively well in popularity rankings as
a tourist destination – an indirect benefit to Quebec – a worrisome trend was
emerging: the neighbouring province of Ontario and other destinations were

apparently attracting a higher number of visitors.[92] As a result, government tourist promoters were, even more so than before, under pressure to highlight what could be marketed as distinctive or unique about their "product."

This more challenging context would also impel them to extend their marketing reach. Indeed, PTB officials increased their use of magazine and newspaper ads significantly during the 1930s. Previously, the bureau had essentially made use of newspapers as a means to publicize its official bulletin or other more lengthy promotional material. Describing their 1933 publicity campaign as "the largest ever undertaken by the Department," officials inundated the market by sending ads to "all the large dailies in the US and Canada, as well as in the leading magazines."[93] By doing so, they were in effect bringing into line their marketing practices with those that had been emerging in the North American advertising industry. At this time, American "national magazine advertising for commercial products had increased 600 percent in the decade since 1916 and newspaper advertising doubled."[94] If the popular press ensured reaching a significantly large numbers of readers, in many ways, it also shaped advertising content. This medium was best suited for image-based publicity – one that did not lend itself well to multi-faceted representations, such as the one prospective Quebec tourists could find in the PTB's more detailed promotional booklets. In newspaper and magazine ads, Quebec's attractions had to be captured and distilled into an easily consumed, attention-grabbing representation. The "Old Province of Quebec" brand lent itself particularly well to this requirement. Thus it was that the PTB's newspaper and magazine ads featured stock illustrations, easily recognizable as markers of a traditional rural past, including spinning wheels, handlooms, ox drawn ploughs, outdoor ovens, roadside shrines and crosses, and *calèches* set in bucolic rural scenery. As a result, the most easily accessible and widely distributed PTB English publicity ended up being remarkably similar to the one produced by transportation and hotel companies. Tourists were informed that they would come across "the simple, unspoiled, peace-loving French Canadians" abiding by the "old French customs."[95] They were invited to "discover for yourself this ancient corner of New France."[96] This was "Old Historic Quebec," "where the spirit of the Past lives again."[97] (See figure 2.5.) Revealing the same rather elastic notion of historical periodization found in private sector advertisements, tourists were promised that they would be plunged in "the age of the Ancien Regime"[98] or would discover a "Medieval France in America."[99] As for handicrafts, while these were promoted as souvenirs "that may be bought for a song,"[100] they were also to represent French Canadian everyday life. On the Île d'Orléans, for instance, tourists would

2.5 | Provincial Tourist Bureau ad, 1935.

encounter a "still-living folklore" where "grand'mère spins in the sunlight as
grand'mère spun three hundred years ago."[101] All these attractions made the
province so "refreshingly DIFFERENT [*sic*]."[102]

Interestingly, no room was made for iconographic representations of modern industrial and urban Quebec. While this type of advertising did not lend
itself well to double imaging, by the 1930s, this was not seen as a drawback.
On occasion, some mention was made of the present, but such allusions essentially served to better draw attention to a traditional representation of the
province. Thus, when tourists were told that in the Gaspé they would come
across "quaint villages" where "Yesterday meets Today," this "today" was not
depicted in any way.[103]

This being said, the PTB did continue to issue its more detailed advertising material, which revealed both continuity and change. Some years it
reissued a few of its earlier publications, including *Along Quebec Highways*,
The Gaspé Peninsula: History, Legends, Resources, Attractions, *4, 5 and 6 Days
in Quebec, Canada*, and *Tours in Quebec*, which double-imaged the province.
This suggests that the PTB was still keeping in its sights both prospective
tourists and entrepreneurs. As tourism remained ensconced in departments

2.6 | Cover page, *Tours in Quebec*, 1931.

geared to economic development, this is not surprising. These publications also featured tourists – most often couples – in contemporary dress looking at some representation of old Quebec. On such occasions, however, promoters were simply subscribing to what was by then a standard marketing practice, whereby "advertisements [had to] take into account not only the inherent qualities and attributes of the products they [were] trying to sell, but also the way in which they could make those properties *mean something to us*."[104] The idea was that, by seeing people like them reflected in the publicity, prospective tourists could learn to look forward to the pleasures they would derive from visiting Quebec. (See figure 2.6.)

But the PTB also produced new and more targeted tourist brochures aimed to capture the attention of different tourist constituencies – operating a form of market segmentation. More precisely, it homed in on visitors drawn to a specific region of the province or looking to engage in a particular type of activity. New brochures exclusively promoting a distinct region of the province were reflective of this more savvy marketing approach.[105] All these brochures provided mostly practical information for motorized tourists and included short descriptions of what sites tourists would come across along the roads that lead from one city or community to the other.[106] The bureau's *Quebec the Good Roads Province* was meant first and foremost for those who were "Fishing, Bathing, Resorts and Hunting" enthusiasts – a Quebec which was here defined as "The Wonderland of America."[107] While these new publications did refer to the opportunities to come across "reminders of the old régime,"[108] they were mostly intended for those in search of adventure, keen to experience the thrills of roughing it in the bush. They would experience "the same conditions as when travelled by the woodsmen" of that time period. But not much was said about the population they would encounter along the way, save a few short asides referring to the traditional *habitant*. In the Laurentians, for instance, they would find that the *habitant* lived "there today, happy and contented, with the priest not only ministering to his spiritual needs but acting as a guide, philosopher, and friend … All as in bygone days."[109]

It is worthwhile mentioning that the presence of Indigenous peoples was ignored. Even in one of the guidebooks specifically intended for hunters and fishers, readers were only advised to "secure the services of experienced guides"– a generic term that did not inform them that these guides were often Indigenous peoples. Any mention of them was clearly meant to convince that some regions in Quebec would satisfy the wishes of those eager to experience life in the wild. This could be presented as factual information as when readers were told in one guidebook that the route to Lake Mistassini was "well known to the Cree Indians who come annually for their winter supplies." But oblique references to Natives could also be evoked in line with derogatory stereotypes. Thus, the "canoeist" was reassured that he could "tread [the] trails without fear of losing his scalp, but wariness is still called for, as the rapids are as savage as in bygone days."[110] While not enough has been written on Indigenous representations in tourism publicity, we do know that some jurisdictions, such as British Columbia, made a point of highlighting their presence, turning them into attractions to differentiate themselves from their competitors.[111] The fact that traditional nationalists were at the helm of tourism promotion in Quebec meant that Indigenous peoples could simply not have been served up as a drawing card. As we have seen, to nationalists' minds the authentic and unique Quebec was French, Catholic, attached to the land and to continental French traditional ways of life. There was no room in this representation for Indigenous peoples, however exotic and enticingly alien they might have appeared. And if some visitors could be tempted by representations of "vanishing Indians," eager to take advantage of rare and diminishing opportunities to witness a disappearing people, in Quebec, promoters were first and foremost preoccupied with the survival of their own vanishing race. This was the "race" one should turn into the province's central tourist attraction.

Further expanding their reach and diversifying their publicity material, tourist promoters also proved more innovative by occasionally taking advantage of one-off opportunities that came their way. This was the case in 1932, when the PTB proudly reported what it clearly considered a clever initiative. Officials got word that the American caricaturist of "Believe or Not" fame had invited his readers to send him a fact or event the public would likely know nothing about. In its in own words, "the Tourist Bureau saw in this contest an excellent opportunity to advertise the Province of Quebec."[112] Thus, it "anonymously offered a prize which consisted in a tour of the province of Quebec," which meant, "the Province secured during the entire duration of the contest, the attention of millions of readers."[113]

However, the most remarkable strategy to surface at this time was the bureau's use of syndicated feature stories and articles. As the 1932 annual report specified, these were distinct from straight publicity as "the advertiser himself prepares the reading matter as well as the illustrations and sends 'mats' of the complete advertisement to the newspaper. If the reading matter is considered interesting enough, the papers publish them."[114] Year after year the campaign mushroomed. Whereas, in 1931 such articles were published in 600 publications,[115] by 1934 the bureau "distributed fifty-six articles ... of which several were accompanied by photographs" to 1,686 newspapers.[116] These articles highlighted "the 'Old World' charm of the Province, its historic character, its industrial and commercial cities and towns, its natural beauties, its rural life and its domestic arts."[117] During the 1930s, only once did PTB officials identify the author of one of these articles. He was a member of the province's Tourism Council, and the article was published in the *National Geographic* issue on the Gaspé (likely the same one alluded to by travel writer Gordon Brinley in *Away to the Gaspé*).[118]

Judging by the comments made in 1934 by Mr Arthur Bergeron, assistant deputy of Roads, to the members of the Senate Committee on Tourist Traffic, Quebec tourism officials were very proud of this new marketing initiative. While describing all the province's accomplishments on the publicity front, he candidly remarked that, "one of the most interesting branches of our advertising is, I think, the feature story campaign ... Last year we released a certain number of stories. The name of the Provincial Tourist Bureau does not appear and it does not look like advertising. It is simply a story or a news item." The following exchange with committee members revealed that this promotional strategy raised a few eyebrows – at the very least, it was met with some reservations. Indeed, when asked if "those [are] true stories or fiction?" Bergeron unabashedly responded: "Oh, any kind, so long as they present our province well! – celebrations, historical facts, anything that show our province at its best."[119] If only judging by Gordon Brinley's comments in her account, such strategies were clearly well advised.

However, this "feature story" campaign was not directed at French Quebec travellers. As was the case earlier, government promoters engaged with them in significantly different ways. In addressing them, they placed greater emphasis on the preservation and promotion of the province's French character, which also led to more attention paid to French Quebeckers as hosts. In 1935, PTB officials defined their work as "chiefly aimed at educating the public on the importance of the tourist traffic, on the importance of extending a cordial welcome to visitors to the Province."[120] Little evidence suggests that they did more than encourage the host population to be hospitable. Had they been going by what traditional nationalists had to say about how French Quebeckers should behave, one would have expected government officials to entreat the general public, notably those living in the countryside, to play up a lifestyle in tune with the old Quebec marketing brand.[121]

Of course, the PTB did not ignore their fellow citizens as potential tourists, as it began to make a wider use of the French-language popular press.[122] In contrast to ads destined to English-speaking North Americans, however, much less was made of the province's old Quebec attributes. Certainly, some references were made to the past, vaguely defined as "souvenirs historiques."[123] And the "Vieille province de Québec" label occasionally appeared but not always, and when it did, it was not written up in bold or capital letters as it was in the English-language press. More significantly, travellers were not promised they would be stepping into a world of yesteryear, much less coming shoulder-to-shoulder with traditional *habitants*. In the Gaspé, for example, the most they could expect to discover was that "the simple and hospitable ways of the population are in stark contrast to the agitated life … of the big modern cities."[124] Instead, such headlines were mainly meant to attract the attention of French Quebeckers who might not think of their province as a tourist destination. Thus, Quebec was identified as the "Pays du tourisme idéal,"[125] and the Gaspé region was baptized "Le Paradis des inoubliables vacances."[126] And, just in case the message was not clear enough, the possibly sceptical "Québécois [*sic*]" were told that they "should seriously consider the attractions of their province when they outlined their holiday program."[127]

What stands out the most in these French-language ads is the extent to which scenery is given pride of place and advertised as the province's central attraction. Visitors were asked mostly to look forward to admiring "the picturesque beauty of our lakes, our mountains and of our rivers, the munificence of its summers and its unsurpassable sports facilities" as reasons to holiday at home.[128] Interestingly enough, these government ads shared much in common with those issued in the French language press by the private sector. The CSL, for example, gave precedence to descriptions of the stunning or romantic landscapes their passengers would enjoy during their trips along the shores of the St Lawrence. Here, as well, no mention was made of the old world habitants: "The Norwegian fiords have their admirers … the Alaska inland landscape is a great tourist attraction … yet from a picturesque point of view, our majestic Saguenay compares most advantageously to these other marvels of nature!"[129]

Clearly then, government promoters had decided, just as their private-sector counterparts, that, in order to get the attention of French Quebeckers, one had to think of them first and foremost as people in search of relaxation and entertainment. Quebec offered holiday experiences to city dwellers in need of a change of scenery. They might enjoy encounters with compatriots from the countryside, but advertisers had obviously judged that, for them, rural areas were not principally attractive for being old.

These assumptions are further confirmed by the PTB's more detailed publicity. Much of it was, in fact, reissued material. Thus, *Sur les routes du Québec: Guide du touriste* and the detailed brochure on the Gaspé were still available, informing readers of the modern and historic Quebec in the same ways it had at the outset. Quebeckers could also still avail themselves of a new edition of *Voyez Québec d'abord!/See Quebec First!*[130] However, in tune with a more focused marketing strategy and the PTB's attempts at expanding its tourist market, in 1934 it added a new publication to its collection, QUÉBEC: *Ses régions de tourisme*. It was aimed specifically at "French language travellers, whether they live in the province of Quebec, in our sister provinces or in the United States."[131] This brochure did, in some sections, tug more explicitly at French Quebeckers' patriotic heartstrings by invoking the Quebec of the past. Promoters attempted to incite them to "visit more this *canadien* corner of the country that must be dearest to them as it is the cradle of French civilisation in America and that, of all the immense domains formally under the domination of the Kings of France, it has jealously conserved its tradition, the language, and its French character."[132] Yet, for all that, it remains that references to the past were practically absent, save for some vague mention of the province's "historic precious souvenirs"[133] or summary information about churches and old buildings, including historical figures' homes.

In fact, a considerable portion of the guide was devoted, in quite some detail, to describing industrial and economic development throughout the province. This suggests that, in the case of prospective French-speaking travellers, the bureau still considered potential entrepreneurs as a target clientele. In the case of Western Quebec – notably in Abitibi and Temiscamingue – readers would learn that its districts "attract today the attention of numerous tourists, from the businessman, who even while on holidays, wants to find out about the new possibilities for industrial development to the simple wanderer who is attracted to a very picturesque region and little disturbed by the human hand."[134] While readers were informed that this was "a region recently open to colonization," no mention was made of the *habitants* or life on the farm. All told, these new publications sent the message to French Quebeckers that they lived in a province that was unmistakably part and parcel of a modern world and visiting it would allow them to admire how far it had come in terms of economic development even in its more remote regions. More significantly, it also reveals that, however much traditional nationalists would have liked it to be otherwise and however much government officials had convinced themselves that doing their share in preserving tradition was important in order to increase tourist traffic, French Quebec travellers were, in the end, informed that tradition was but one drawing card among several and not the central one at that.

The links made by traditional nationalists between the survival of the province's French character and a healthy tourism industry, essentially remained unchanged through the 1940s and 1950s. During that time, nationalists continued to define Quebec's difference in terms of a distinct culture rooted in the past and encouraged those involved in the tourism industry, along with the population, to do their share to revive this French Canada. In the 1940s, government publicity stressed familiar old Quebec themes, spinning wheels and handmade hooked rugs, and friendly "descendants of some of our settlers."[135] Some differences did emerge, as more emphasis was placed on both old and new Quebec. Notably the point was made that tourists would enjoy traditional and modern amenities and a way of life that included "old world French cuisine and new world air conditioning."[136] They could expect to find "modern hostelries ... against the background of the Old World French Canada."[137] More references to the French language and to the province's special French cuisine also pointed to a veneer of sophistication in Quebec not previously showcased in earlier publicity. Overall, the message was that in Quebec the old world and the new were living side by side.

However, such differences speak less to a changing understanding among government promoters about what made Quebec distinct than to changing conditions brought on by the Second World War. This new context required new strategies. People did not stop travelling during the conflict, but traffic did decrease significantly, as war measures made travelling more challenging.[138] This was particularly true for a wealthier class of Americans who would have otherwise taken their holidays in Europe, with a strong preference for France. As well, the doors of many American hotels, notably in Florida, were closed to ordinary tourists, both American and Canadian, as they were requisitioned for military purposes. While disruptive for some, tourism promoters in Quebec, on the other hand, saw the disaster that befell cross-Atlantic destinations as a unique opportunity. In the words of Premier Adélard Godbout's chief of cabinet, M. Boulanger, "our character as a French Province stands perhaps as the principal gage of our tourism success. It is on this point that we must insist more particularly at a time when the frontiers of Europe are closed to American tourists and that the Province of Quebec is the only corner of French land they can visit without having to cross the seas."[139] But if promoters were to convince Americans that Quebec stood as a worthy surrogate for France, they would have to showcase more than quaint reminders of seventeenth-century New France. They would have to show that Quebec could match the best of what contemporary France had to offer as well. This explains why the invitation to come to an "Old Quebec" was overshadowed by a more neutral and timeless one to enjoy a "French Canadian Vacation." And, to encourage tourists to try something new, slogans such as "Have you ever had a French Canadian vacation" or to "contrast ... atmosphere ... gaiety ... a French Canadian vacation" were used.

But the war brought further challenges. For one, PTB officials quickly became aware that Americans were worried about the type of welcome they would receive in Quebec as a result of their country's neutral stance in the early stages of the war. In 1940, the *Montreal Gazette* published a series of interviews with American tourists that suggested this was a very real issue. For instance, Fred Stater, from Detroit, explained he had been told before coming to Canada that "the Canadians were hostile to Americans because they had not yet entered the war."[140] More than this, word was apparently getting around that, supposedly, people were being held up at the border and subjected to burdensome restrictions. PTB publicity officials thus pulled all the stops to reassure potential tourists that these were nothing but unfounded rumours. No less than a message from the premier was published in one of the bureau's more detailed publicity in which he directly assured his readers: "No people in the whole world are more welcome than you in this friendly Province de Québec. ... Bona fide tourist do not suffer any new restrictions whatsoever as a result of this state of war; their registration with Canadian customs officials is the same simple formality which existed before Canada entered the war and which causes neither delay nor embarrassment."[141] Clearly, however, those involved in tourism promotion were not convinced that these reassuring words would be enough to encourage Americans to make the trip. It is no coincidence that, in 1940, the Quebec government chose to open a new information centre in New York. Some PTB ads revealed that officials also had some apprehensions about damaging preconceptions potential English Canadian tourists might have in these times of heightened French–English tensions over the country's war effort. Some publicity specified, "French Canadian and English Canadian live side by side in neighbourly concord."[142]

It seems the only prospective tourists that government promoters did not worry about were French Quebeckers. True, the content of their French language advertisements were modified in the 1940s, as well but in significantly different ways. The point was to convince Quebec residents that the province was an ideal place to take a holiday during this stressful time, more so than "in times of peace." Prospective travellers were told, a "man needs a yearly time for relaxation and rest." And indeed, men were typical singled out. This is perhaps in anticipation of the reticence some might have holidaying when so many of their compatriots were fighting overseas, regardless of whether they were behind the war effort or not. The man who stayed behind had to understand that "the more considerable effort he puts at the office, the factory, in stores ... added to the nervous tension and worry that come with the [war] circumstances tax at its maximum his physical resistance and moral vigour." Quebec "offered to those who wanted to recuperate their strength a choice of pleasant and restful holiday regions."[143] More than that, by "counter[ing] these factors of depression," travelling in Quebec would afford "the physical and moral resistance which will make it possible to fight to the end and win the war."[144] Thus, in the 1940s, Quebec became a place to "get away from it all." It would more specifically serve therapeutic, if not patriotic, purposes as well.

After the war and by the 1950s, tourist promotion would, in many ways, revert back to how things had been during the 1930s, all the while revealing significant differences in step with the changes identified during wartime, as well as harbingers of more significant changes to come. Furthermore, in the background, a wider economic context accentuated a sense that the tourism market was increasingly competitive across Canada. Indeed, starting in 1951 statistics revealed for the first time that the country was experiencing a worrisome travel deficit of 53 million dollars with the US.[145] Canadians were starting to travel more abroad with the result that "[a]t an especially low point in 1954, every dollar spent by US tourists in Canada was being multiplied eleven times by Canadians in the United States."[146] Added to this, an increasing number of countries were proving more proactive, sending their tourist advertising to the Canadian press. Officials were also keenly aware that Europe was becoming a formidable rival, as getting there was becoming less and less expensive.[147] Promoters' public pronouncements unfailingly called upon Quebeckers to do all they could to make visitors feel welcome. Georges Léveillé, as director of the Provincial Publicity Bureau, was at the forefront of this hospitality campaign. He never tired of pointing out that "[p]ublicity is not sufficient … In all our relations with tourists and travellers we must always keep in mind, that a traveller unhappy with our province, our city, our villages, a visitor unsatisfied with our railroads, buses, taxis, will become a true subversive propaganda agent when he returns to his *patelin*."[148]

In short, Quebec promoters were spurred all the more to make Quebec stand out yet even further. They chose to do so by more systematically and more forcefully making the point that Quebec was a place of contrasts, where past and present coexisted. Thus, along with commentary pointing to historic sites, government publicity provided more boastful descriptions, unrestrained in their praise of adjoining industrial centres. Trois-Rivières was labelled "the pulp and paper capital of the world,"[149] and the St Maurice River as nothing less than the "highest developed power stream in the world." In the "pristine" Laurentians, tourists were called upon to admire "its mighty hydro-electric plants." Overall, prospective visitors were told that by coming to "La Province de Québec" they would come across "cities and towns as up-to-the-minute as today's newspapers."[150] (See figure 2.7.)

Importantly, by this time, tourist promoters gained a larger profile and a certain autonomy in the government bureaucracy, and their task was to

NORANDA

maque, Cadillac et autres centres miniers importants.

Ici vous franchissez *l'Outaouais* supérieur, pénétrez dans *l'Ontario* et suivez la route 63 jusqu'à *North Bay* et la route 17 jusqu'à *Pembroke*, pour revenir dans *La province de Québec* prendre la route 8 qui mène à *Hull* en passant par une contrée fertile. De *Hull*, vous pouvez vous rendre à *Montréal*, par la route 8 et la vallée de *l'Outaouais*. Si vous désirez retourner par les *Laurentides*, suivez la route 11, en direction de *Maniwaki* et *Mont-Laurier*, ou la route 35, de *Buckingham* à *Mont-Laurier*.

Vous aurez accompli un voyage intéressant, rempli d'aperçus agréables du *Québec* ancien et nouveau.

into the settler country of *le Témiscamingue*, leaving behind you, to the far north, another colonization belt where farmers' sons from all over *La Province* are hewing out new frontiers and wresting more and more farm from the forest. As you emerge from lakeland, you strike *Notre-Dame-des-Quinze*, set in a country opened earlier than *l'Abitibi*, and you drive on to *Ville-Marie*, a humming little county town set on *Lac Témiscamingue*. This is a spectacular body of water, its shores at points rearing into

27

2.7 | "Noranda," in *La province de Québec, Canada*, 1952.

exclusively develop the tourism industry (as opposed to concerning themselves with wider economic developments). They more frequently made comments – often bombastic – about Quebec's industrial performance and urban modernity. Such changes point to evolving perceptions about the province and the tourist clientele. At the very least, tourist promoters appeared to be more interested in and proud of showcasing a newer Quebec as they turned it into a more marketable asset. And indeed, "La Province de Québec" replaced "Old Quebec" – the previously ubiquitous brand name in brochure titles and single-ad headlines. Rather than tradition, this new label anchored Quebec in the present, and, by making use of French words, tourism promoters were increasingly choosing to highlight its distinctive French culture and language.[151]

This growing willingness to put the modern Quebec face forward could also be a reflection of tourist promoters' recognition that the post–Second War World travelling public was, by then, looking for more than a trip "back in time." Certainly, other differences in Quebec tourist promotion suggest that the TB was aware that additional strings needed to be pulled to lure the postwar tourist clientele, specifically, the consumer string. Indeed, it was at this time that promotional literature began to make increasing references to alluring stores and opportunities to purchase high-quality consumer products in Quebec cities in addition to traditional local arts and crafts. Tourists were told more systematically that in Quebec were opportunities to enjoy cuisine from France. Clearly, tourist promoters were responding to visitors' demands for modern experiences associated with materialistic and epicurean pleasures – consumer oriented experiences available mainly in larger urban settings. These changes suggest that, by the 1950s, tourist promoters concluded that travellers' motivations and expectations could not only be understood as guided by an antimodernist quest. Responding much as did their Canadian counterparts, they were coming to realize that, for the post-war tourist consumer, "holidays had become ... a right to pleasure"[152] and that destinations were yet another commodity.

It is important to keep in mind, though, that promoters had not chosen to rub out the province's old Quebec. Provincial old-world attractions remained in Quebec tourist advertising. In fact, illustrations of elderly French Canadians in traditional occupations, priests and churches, and fishing villages still outnumbered the pictures of ports, power plants, and modern highways, while expressions of old Quebec and the old world continued to pepper the accompanying texts in this publicity. (See figure 2.8.) Tourists could still read about "the historic centuries-old towns and villages"[153] and learn that in Quebec, "amid the upheavals of modern times, we have been able to retain

2.8 | Woman and outdoor oven, in *La province de Québec*, 1952.

the tempo, the true atmosphere of *Old France* in *America*."[154] The cover image of one booklet underscored this statement, as it foregrounded a seated elderly woman doing needlepoint with part of a spinning wheel in front of her. (See figure 2.9.)

This is not surprising, considering that during the 1950s prominent, traditional nationalists continued to be involved in provincial tourist promotion. Indeed, the principles and assumptions underlined by Asselin, reiterated by Tessier, continued to be defended with vigour by Paul Gouin in his capacity as technical consultant to the executive council of the Province of Quebec. He still held to his position that in order "to continue to benefit from [the tourism industry revenue], to increase it, we must become ourselves again, that is re-give to our province its French face [as] it constitutes our principal tourist attraction."[155] National identity should continue to be inspired by tradition and tourism could be harnessed to serve that vision. He explained: "If I am interested in tourism, it is because it constitutes the easiest way, the most logical and also, which is not to be sneered at, the most remunerative means to make our culture stand out, to revitalize our traditions and our customs, that is to say to give back to our province its French face."[156] He even claimed that it was "Providence that made it so that this heritage contains all that tourists look for."[157] In effect, Gouin would continue to consider himself a man on a mission to promote tourism as a safeguard for the French Canadian nation, one that he had so actively worked to define in the 1930s.

2.9 | Cover page, *La province de Québec*, 1952.

He lost few opportunities to speak out on the subject. At the beginning of his appointment, Gouin gave close to a hundred radio talks inviting the wider public to "*refranciser* the road."[158] Gouin's ideas and recommendations had a familiar ring, illustrating some continuity in attitudes and complaints of those involved in government tourism promotion since its early days. Thus, while recognizing that some progress had been made since the 1930s *refrancisation* campaign – particularly in the case of small hotels – he continued to deplore the fact that the province's French face was still "made up, disfigured by an Americanism of doubtful quality."[159] To make his point more forcefully, he also invoked the ever-present disappointed tourist, claiming that, "more and more, the foreigner considers our 'French face' as a publicity stunt."[160] In line with other traditionalists, he continued to understand the need for *refrancisation* in a wider sense, defining this French face as "our traditions and customs, our folklore, our way of thinking, of living, our way of humanizing our countryside, of building, of decorating and furnishing our churches and our houses."[161] As did his predecessors, he also argued that, as French Canadians, "[we need to] become ourselves again, that is to say give our province its true face" because it "constitutes our main tourist attraction."[162] Those who actively collaborated in this ongoing project of "rediscovery" by seeking his advice were congratulated for their "practical patriotic act."[163]

Yet, Paul Gouin was not averse to the advantages of progress. As he put it, the idea was not "to back pedal."[164] He told an audience in 1955 that "I have never asked ... my compatriots to wear as in the past the blue, red or white toque, wool mittens, the *ceinture fléchée* ... I mean to say that we must preserve our cultural heritage while we adapt to it the demands of modern life."[165] He was adamant that "we can without worry entrust to our 'master the future,'" the responsibility "to ensure the survival of the culture, the traditions and the customs bequeathed to us by 'our master the past.'"[166] He came to the conclusion that it was not only crucial "to transport [this folklore]," "to revive it in the theater, the cinema or the public place," but to be inspired by it "to create radio sketches ... ballets, festivals, literary and artistic oeuvres."[167] In other words, it was essential to make use of modern means of communication to disseminate this culture rooted in the past, and it was vital to draw from it when further developing French Canadian culture in the present.[168] While Gouin continued to affirm that the past is our master, he had clearly evolved when defining the relationship between this traditional culture and French Canadians. His attitude towards arts and crafts is telling in this respect. He remained an ardent promoter of French Canadian arts and crafts, and, much as he did in the 1930s, still argued that "[i]t is thanks to [our arts and crafts] that we can reconstitute the French Canadian atmosphere, the patriotic atmosphere of our homes."[169] However, by the 1950s, he also recognized that craftsmen had had to adapt to the demands of modern life as "our artisans do not practice arts and crafts as they did in the past." More specifically, "they do not try to create furniture, knick-knacks, cloths to furnish their own homes or to support their own family. Having become producers of knick-knack souvenirs they look for the tourist clientele." The same artisans were also looking for a French Canadian clientele who would use their crafts in much the same way as did tourists – to embellish their homes. In his view, "our domestic arts have evolved, they have become decorative arts, they have modernized."[170] He had visibly accepted that these tangible markers of the past had grown to be increasingly commodified, removed from their traditional usage. He considered this a positive development since these "modernized" arts and crafts did not preclude them from offering an exemplary manifestation of French Canadian culture.

Thus, the 1950s offered signs of change against a backdrop of continuity. The "Old Quebec" slogan was replaced by the more present-minded label of "La Province de Québec," and Paul Gouin, one of the prominent tourism promoters of the period, was able to endorse some features of modernity. And while it remained that the tourist publicity and tourist promoters continued to present Quebec's difference as essentially founded on a traditional national identity, modern Quebec and newly emerging consumer-oriented expectations of postwar tourists were given more attention. As developments in the 1960s make clear, change would increasingly be the order of the day.

3

KNOWING QUEBEC BEFORE
GETTING THERE

Public debates over how best to advertise the province both reflected nation-alist tourism promoters' concerns over what stood for the authentic Quebec and their assumptions of what prospective tourists expected and hoped to see during their travels. Promoters were at the same time aware that publicity itself could foster expectations. Thus, detailed information about the content of government publicity offers some insight into visitors' expectations. At the same time, however, simply assuming that this information reveals what travellers knew about the province and why they wanted to visit is not the whole story. According to those who study advertising, little can be said with assurance about the overall impact of publicity on consumer behaviour. Some argue that, "because beliefs and attitudes are firmly ingrained in people, ad-vertising has little effect in changing them." Instead, "advertisements reflect social values rather than create them."[1] In fact, scholars contend, "once we grasp that the consumer is the ultimate author of the meaning of an adver-tisement, the intentions of the makers become of secondary importance."[2] This being said, while few believe that ads can "inject certain attitudes and ideas into the minds of audience members," they nonetheless "acknowledge the power of frequently repeated media images ... in establishing our frames of reference and perception."[3] Viewed from this perspective, exposure to tour-ist advertising would likely reinforce some of Quebec visitors' pre-existing expectations.

This observation certainly falls in line with the findings of those who have studied tourists' motivations and the construction of memory. Overall, knowledge about a destination is acquired from a myriad of sources, often only indirectly related to the destination in question. These sources help tourists decide what is worth seeing, and provide criteria needed in order to draw meaning from their experiences. More specifically, tourists acquire entrenched notions about the history, ways of life, and culture of their hosts and attractions to expect before departure. In short, travel destinations are constructed at home.

Pointing in this direction, the pioneer in tourism studies Dean McCannell noted that "[u]sually, the first contact a sightseer has with a sight is not the site itself but with some representation thereof."[4] Others since have made similar points, arguing, "people have a portrayed image of a destination,"[5] meaning, more specifically, "[their] relationship to the sight is ... always culturally detailed and mediated."[6] John Urry later coined a concept to encapsulate these insights, arguing that travellers of all stripes arrive at their destination with a particular tourist gaze. He eventually specified that "there is no single tourist gaze ... It varies by society, by social group and by historical period." And it is shaped by feelings of anticipation, "constructed and sustained through a variety of non-tourist practices" that distinguish themselves from publicity. These "non-tourist forms of social experience and consciousness" include exposure to "film, TV, literature, magazines, records and videos, which construct and reinforce that gaze."[7] Scholars also emphasize the importance of travellers' backgrounds to account for their expectations and reactions. This is how Sylvain Simard made sense of the French elite's reactions to Quebec during their travels from 1850 to 1914. He argued that they had formed "mental images" of the province before reaching their destination establishing that "those who visit the country do so almost always in a subjective manner [as] they see and bring out, according to their religious, political and social assumptions, the aspects of Canada that captivate them; their trip to Canada confirms their view of things."[8] More recently, postcolonial and cultural studies scholars explore the repercussions of travellers' imperial eyes, and its impact on the imperial periphery.[9]

Currently, the notion that predeparture experiences together with an individual's social, gender, and cultural background shape the travel experience is considered commonsensical. Just as Cecilia Morgan concludes that various sources "inspired [the] fantasies of what should be visited, how it should be viewed, and why it was significant ... among late 19th and early 20th English Canadian travellers to Europe,"[10] it can be assumed this was the case of those who visited Quebec. Furthermore, knowing that the sources available to American, English Canadian, and French Quebec visitors were not always the same, reveals all "the culture-specific and individual patterns of perception and knowledge which every traveller brings to the travelled world."[11] For travel writers of Quebec more specifically, this can prove particularly instructive.

Similar to ordinary tourists, travel writers also arrived in the province informed by their own expectations, often resulting in a predisposition to recount and present their experiences in a certain way. For English North American travel writers, there is no doubt that they came across a wide range of sources of information about the province well before arriving, in addition to the Quebec government's publicity. What these sources were and how they influenced expectations and reactions is, in many ways, speculative. Most travel writers of the period did not mention these sources in their accounts. And those who did, rarely pointed out those that most coloured their expectations. In this respect, they were like most people who travel – rarely fully aware of the influences they were subject to let alone able to identify those that shaped their views most significantly. However, it is possible to imagine aspects of the cultural context from which these travel writers emerged and identify a few "non-tourist practices" that may have shaped their tourist gaze. This involves examining novels, visual art, and school readers. The influence of some of these sources, regardless of their "date of birth," may have influenced the attitudes of travel writers in similar ways over a span of several decades. Thus, travellers who wrote about Quebec in the 1960s could very well have been exposed to many of the same sources as those who had visited Quebec in the 1920s.

Before turning to these, however, it is possible to offer some generalizations about the hopes and expectations of travellers across the board, regardless of nationality and time period. Scholars who have studied why people travel have grappled, from the outset, with the issue of authenticity. More specifically, they establish the extent to which tourists are motivated to travel by a desire to experience authenticity. Dean MacCannell – one of the first to initiate the debate in the early 1970s – offered a sweeping generalization, to the effect that "touristic experience is motivated by its desire for authentic experiences." This meant that "sightseers are motivated by a desire to see life as it is really lived, even to get in with the natives,"[12] because "for moderns, reality and authenticity are thought to be elsewhere; in other historical periods and other cultures, in purer, simpler lifestyles."[13] Since, scholars have qualified this interpretation, agreeing with Philip Pearce and Gianno Moscardo, that his "assertion that tourists seek authenticity in all experiences is probably an oversimplified approach to tourist motivation."[14] For Erik Cohen, not all tourists are seeking authenticity nor are they willing to pursue it to "the same degree of intensity."[15] Jennifer Craik, for her part, argues that tourists "think that they want authenticity," but in reality they "revel in the otherness of destinations, peoples and activities because they offer the illusion or fantasy of otherness, of difference and counterpoint to the every day."[16] Be that as it may, as noted by scholars Pierre van den Berghe and Charles Keyes, the "problem of authenticity" is particularly relevant when considering the motivations of those who partake in "ethnic tourism."[17] This is because those tourists desire an "authentic encounter with other [and t]he greater the otherness," the "more satisfying the tourist experience."[18] And furthermore, most would agree with Nina Wang that the sense that tourists have experienced authenticity is socially constructed, "a *projection* [sic] of [their] own beliefs, expectations, preferences, stereotyped images and consciousness particularly onto toured Others."[19] Such insights offer a helpful lens through which to analyze Quebec travel writers' expectations, extending well into the 1950s.

Desire for an authentic experience may have been shaped by an ambient cultural climate of antimodernism alluded to earlier, most apparent in the 1920s and 1930s, emerging by the end of the nineteenth century, a time when middle-class North Americans were dismayed by what they considered to be the artificial, unreal, and over-civilized nature of their urban working environments.[20] Part of this stemmed from a desire to "rekindle possibilities for authentic experience, physical or spiritual." In their view, "regeneration" was possible "through pre-industrial crafstmenship and a pastoral 'simple life.'"[21] They "idealiz[ed] manual labour," extolled through "the virtues of life on the land."[22] This idealized folk represented the "antithesis to everything they disliked about modern urban and industrial life."[23]

Like other regions in North America, Quebec could boast of having its own folk. Donald Wright points out that, between the 1880s to the end of the First World War, many English Canadians viewed the French Quebec *habitants* through this antimodernist lens. Just as folk people elsewhere, they were considered "pre-modern, pre-commercial."[24] By the 1920s, antimodernism gradually developed into a set of responses made to help bourgeois city dwellers better adapt to modernity through contact with the folk and experience farm life, turning antimodernism from a type of dissent into a "therapeutic world view."[25] This world view endured, continuing to influence the way in which many reacted to French Quebec sites and people. More specifically, many English-speaking North American travel writers were predisposed to react positively to a soothing encounter with *habitants* as they inspired a comforting nostalgia for a supposedly simpler time. Indeed, one such traveller, Sally Bennett, reflected in 1940 that, "the best refreshment to nerves and souls is the habitants, for they are peaceful folk who want nothing but their river country and their traditional ways."[26] Thus, antimodernist sentiments could have tinted the travel gaze of some travel writers, predisposing them to view the people of the Quebec countryside as the authentic folk people of Quebec – feeding their hopes that they might encounter them by visiting the province.

LITERATURE

English-speaking travel writers, both Canadian and American, were influenced by novels. These would have primed them to view the authentic Quebec as old. In fact, novels were what travel writers referred to most often when they mentioned a source from which they gained information about the province. In many ways, this is not surprising. As Sylvain Simard put it, "reading novels becomes ... an excellent way to know the image" of a country during a certain time period.[27] What stands out is that travel writers specifically mentioned titles of historical fiction, published in the late nineteenth and early twentieth century. More significantly, the majority of these novels were set in New France or at the time of the Conquest. Several portrayed well-known New France historical figures, including brave and adventurous French explorers, daring military heroes, and colonial governing elites. Many travel writers would have been exposed to this particular genre of novel as a result of their enduring popularity. Indeed, literary scholars point out a special preference among many North American English-speaking novelists – notably those writing in the late nineteenth century – for the period of New France as a topic. Life then was considered more romantic, eventful, dramatic, and colourful than in later periods of North American history.[28] And in the case of English Canadian writers, more particularly, this tendency is interpreted as "an attempt to appropriate the past of French Canada in order to provide a longer genealogy to the Canadian nation."[29]

The novel travel writers mentioned most frequently was William Kirby's *The Golden Dog (Le Chien d'Or): A Legend of Quebec*.[30] The others are Gilbert Parker's *When Valmont Came to Pontiac*, *The Lane That Had No Turning*, and *The Seats of the Mighty: A Romance of Old Quebec*; and Duncan Campbell Scott's series *In the Village of Viger*. Willa Cather titles also appeared occasionally. While some travel writers only referred to these in passing, others recommended them as reliable, historical accounts of life in New France. Again, this is not entirely surprising. As English Canadian novelist Guy Vanderhaeghe points out, "many readers look at the historical novel as being a genuine historical experience. As readers, they feel that they are inhabiting that time, that place and they are getting a sense of how individual lives were lived in a personal fashion."[31] A case in point is English Canadian W.P. Percival, one of many travel writers to recount conflicts between the dishonest and corrupt Intendant Francois Bigot and Nicolas Jacquin Philibert, a merchant of the 1700s, which is portrayed in Kirby's *Golden Dog*. He informed his readers that the Quebec City home of this brave merchant was marked by a tablet placed on what had been his store and added: "To grasp the full import of the enigmatic tablet one should read the very interesting account of life in old French Canada ... Though the author plays loosely with his facts, the story can still be classed as an historical tale ... The characters and places named in the story give the reader a very good idea of life in Quebec in those primitive days."[32] At times quotes from these novels substituted or complemented their prose. Stanley Helps, for instance, borrowed words of Gilbert Parker to describe Percé Rock,[33] while W.P. Percival uses the same novelist to describe the qualities of British General Wolfe's "burning eye" which reflected "resolution, courage and endurance, deep design, clear vision, dogged will and heroism lived."[34]

We need not be concerned with the accuracy of the facts or the reliability of the historical interpretations of these novels. What is of interest is how their engaging plots and characters may have influenced what travel writers considered worth visiting. One can assume that they would have swayed travel writers to consider the time of New France as the most significant and exciting period in the province's history and sparked an interest to see the associated sites. They could also have convinced travel writers that by reading these novels, they were acquiring a general understanding of Quebec's political history: for example, that the Catholic Church was an omnipresent and powerful institution or that the habitants were innocent victims of a despotic and corrupt French imperial power. Some storylines would have inclined them to believe that as a result of the Conquest, French Canadians were saved from their unworthy, tyrannical French masters and placed under a just, principled, and benevolent British authority. These would have also suggested to them that the Natives, notably the Iroquois from the perspective of the French, were particularly cruel and uncivilized "savages" much to be feared. In the case of English, North American travel writers of British descent (perhaps more so for English Canadians), the reading of these novels could have also fed a pride for being related to their "civilized" and victorious ancestors.

But these travel writers also read or were aware of novels with contemporary plots. The one they brought up most frequently was Louis Hémon's *Maria Chapdelaine: Tale of the Lake St John Country*.[35] It was also valued as a trustworthy source of information. For writer J.M. Donald, *Maria Chapdelaine* was "a true story of the pioneers, the sturdy *habitant* farmers who broke the land."[36] In fact, the novel was to them revealing about contemporary Quebec society. Indeed, in George Pearson's opinion, *Maria Chapdelaine* was a story "best representing the present, even though the author … was not a French Canadian."[37] Another assured readers that "Maria Chapdelaine country … was still worth a visit for here continues and will continue one of America's last frontiers."[38] They would likely concur with what Hémon famously wrote, that this was a place where "nothing has changed. Nor shall anything change."[39] More specifically, one which the author represented as traditional, where loyalty to family and homeland came first, and where devotion to French Catholic beliefs and practices were paramount. This representation would have appeared in historical continuity with the Quebec they had encountered in novels about New France. Brought together, all these stories would have fed expectations that they would find the old Quebec advertised by the provincial government.

These feelings were likely further reinforced by reading Henry Drummond's (1854–1907) popular collection, *The Habitant and Other French Canadian Poems*. According to historian Daniel Francis, "these are some of the most popular poems ever written by a Canadian."[40] The collection brings together a series of tales recounted by fictional stock characters from the Quebec countryside, in what Drummond presents as their distinct French Canadian vernacular. From the tale "The Habitant," readers would also learn of their outlook on life. Speaking of harsh weather, this *habitant* prototype explains:

> You t'ink it was bodder de habitant farmer?
> Not at all – he is happy an' feel satisfy,
> An' cole may las' good w'ile, so long as de
> Wood-pile
> Is ready for burn on the stoves by an' bye.[41]

Certainly English Canadians believed Drummond's "invented" dialect of "fractured English" "was completely authentic to the speech patterns of French Quebeckers."[42] This was made particularly obvious among the travel writers who recounted their voyage much as one would in a diary. They made use of Drummond-like vernacular when transcribing exchanges with the *habitants*.[43] Others such as J.M. Donald's husband "hummed the refrain of [his] poem."[44] The fact that it was extremely popular for decades makes it likely that many more were aware of it.

Furthermore, as with *Maria Chapdelaine*, "The Habitant" poems give an impression of being a source of sociological information. Indeed, in the collection's preface, Drummond explained that, through these tales, he was attempting to help English Canadians better understand their French-speaking countryside compatriots. This was necessary in his view because "the English-speaking public knows perhaps as well as myself the French Canadian of the cities yet they have had little opportunity of becoming acquainted with the habitant."[45] Drummond provided cameo portraits of the *habitants*, the reliability of which may have seemed all the more convincing, certified as they were by the prominent French Canadian poet Louis-Honoré Fréchette, who was known to many in the English Canadian intelligentsia.[46] Fréchette contributed the collection's laudatory introduction, expressing his admiration for Drummond for taking "a poor illiterate" and "present[ing him] as a national type … making of him a kind, *doux*, amiable, honest intelligent character … without allowing the most subtle of critics the opportunity to detect any evidence of caricature." While such comments speak more about Fréchette's elitism, travel writers likely would only remember that he considered these poems the work of a "good citizen."[47]

Another example is Adjutor Rivard's *Chez Nous (Our Old Quebec Home)*, a collection of nostalgic reminiscences of growing up in the Quebec countryside during the late nineteenth century.[48] While directed at French Canadians, the book developed a noteworthy following among North American Anglophones, translated into English in 1924 by W.H. Blake, and, by 1926, it was reprinted five times.[49] It was filled with admiring declarations for his "brothers of the soil" (the *habitants*), whose "hearts are of gold,"[50] in his view, and who deserved such praise as they remained true to the best of old French Canadian values: a dedication to hard work on the land, unwavering Catholic beliefs, and a steadfast attachment to home and family. As with the characters of *Maria Chapdelaine* and Drummond's happy-go-lucky *habitants*, English-speaking readers were encouraged to consider Rivard's reminiscences as a faithful representation of the reality of the Quebec countryside. How else could they have interpreted the "Translator's Note," in which W.H. Blake assured that "there is no surer guide-book to the ways and manners of Quebec than *Chez Nous*"?[51] Readers might very well be expected to take the translator at his word. Some clearly did. A greater leap still was made by a few who came away thinking that, in essence, the authentic French Canadian was the one living off the land: full stop. It should be noted that his reminiscences were also intended to alert his own compatriots that the *habitant* way of life was dangerously close to disappearing. Echoing many of the pronouncements of his fellow traditional nationalists, he warned that the *habitants'* survival was being threatened by modernity and the rural exodus to the cities.[52] This may have led travel writers to think that they best hurry to visit Quebec before this "real" Quebec disappeared altogether. T. Morris Longstreth appeared to have shared Rivard's forebodings, advising his readers to read *Chez Nous* "to learn what they [French Canadians] have given up."[53]

If English Canadians and American travel writers read the same novels, differences emerged between the two as well. English Canadians referred more frequently to literary sources and were more likely to invoke a varied selection, tending to use more quotations and refer more often to names of fictional characters. This is not surprising as they would have been more exposed than Americans to novels that included descriptions of French Canadian culture. Their points of reference were, therefore, bound to be more numerous and more varied. This, in turn, makes it possible that their preconceived ideas about Quebec would have been as well. At the very least, they arrived in Quebec with more developed images and expectations than their American counterparts.

For French Quebeckers, invoking fiction was less useful as a means of highlighting the province's attractions, as the literature was widely known. As a result, few literary references are found in their travel accounts. When they did mention authors, those were chosen from a select few respected Quebec notables. This is particularly true at the beginning of the period. More specifically, those who, in the late nineteenth century, had written travel accounts of their own or literary reminiscences lauding the beauty, charm, and picturesque qualities of the Charlevoix or Gaspé regions.[54] These include journalist Arthur Buies (1840–1901)[55] and the reputed intellectual figure Judge Adolphe Basile Routhier (1839–1920), who admired the Charlevoix area.[56] By virtue of their reputation, French Canadian travel writers could add credibility to their own accounts by quoting these authors. What mostly stands out, though, is that only the beauty of the scenery is referenced, while little mention is made of the Charlevoix or Gaspé inhabitants or the local culture. An exception to this are occasional references to *Maria Chapdelaine*, though the title was most often used as a short-hand expression to identify the Lac St-Jean region and nowhere did they explicitly recommend the novel for its enlightening insights on its inhabitants. Alluding to the novel may simply have been a means to entice readers to a region that inspired a novelist they knew and loved. At the same time, a perception existed among many traditional nationalists that *Maria Chapdelaine* offered a faithful portrayal of French Quebeckers who still remained true to the nation's authentic and admirable way of life. It is entirely possible that by making references to the novel, a few travel writers may have been suggesting indirectly that in the Lac St-Jean region, visitors could expect to come across fellow French Quebeckers who maintained a traditional life style.

3.1 | Krieghoff's happy-go-lucky *habitants*
in *Fiddler and Boy Doing Jig*, 1852.

VISUAL REPRESENTATIONS

Beyond the written word, English-speaking North American travel writers
would have been exposed to depictions of Quebec. Many famous artists had
built reputations on painting the province. Because of this, they were widely
known and available to the general public. This was the case with Cornelius
Krieghoff (1815–1872). The many references to him confirm a familiarity
with and admiration for his work, which appeared in a wide range of venues
including textbooks and postcards. Krieghoff, a prolific nineteenth-century

3.2 | Horatio Walker, ca. 1920.

painter, "essentially devoted his time to represent French Canadian farmers and the Native peoples living on the margins of the important contemporary currents."[57] His *habitants* were timeless archetypes, easily recognized by their traditional dress, way of life, customs, and dwellings. Their disposition was also unrelentingly jolly, enjoying the simple pleasures of life in the countryside. (See figure 3.1.) His work was particularly appealing to the English-speaking elite of the period and their descendants, deep in the throes of industrialization and rapid change. They would have been willing and reassured to believe in the existence of a more slow-paced, bucolic past still alive and in their midst – especially for those imbued with an antimodernist sensibility. The fact that none referred to his depictions of the Natives further speaks to travel writers' assumptions that the authentic Quebec inhabitants were those of French ancestry.[58]

The antimodernist mental image of the province and its inhabitants appears to have also been shaped by Horatio Walker (1858–1938), who was, during his lifetime, "one of the most fashionable artists of his generation," particularly in the US.[59] From Ontario, Walker lived for many years on the Île d'Orléans, painting its pastoral landscape, featuring the hard-working

3.3 | Horatio Walker, *Oxen Drinking*, in
Quebec, Montreal and Ottawa, 1933.

habitants he so admired. (See figure 3.2.) Certainly those who travelled there
often brought up his name. In fact, Gordon Brinley mentioned that she had
actually "met [him] on one of his occasional visits to New York."[60] And a few
included images of his paintings alongside their accounts, such as T. Morris
Longstreth.[61] (See figure 3.3.) Because he was painting in the same time period as these writers were travelling, Walker's art could have appeared almost
as photographic as contemporary representations. Travel writers certainly
attributed photographic qualities to the work of Clarence Gagnon, a contemporary of Walker (1881–1942). His paintings of the Charlevoix region
most famously represented bucolic scenery and the traditional *habitants*.[62]
For Amy Oakley, Ste-Anne-de-Beaupré was "a Gagnon water color come
to life."[63] Thus, it is a reasonable assumption that these painters' soothing
evocation of simpler times coupled with their supposedly photographic skills,

reinforced in Quebec literary sources, further sharpened travel writers' sense that they knew what the authentic Quebec looked like – one where nothing had changed.

For French Quebec travel writers, the impact of art, similar to that of literature, on their expectations is less clear, as there is no mention of visual representations of the province in their accounts. As was the case with novels, they clearly did not believe that invoking art would be of use to convey what visitors should expect to see. Although, in the case of Krieghoff, his absence may also be reflective of attitudes held early on by members of the French-speaking bourgeoisie towards the way he represented their compatriots. As art historian Denis Reid suggests, in the nineteenth century, "there must … have been embarrassment for educated Quebeckers in [his] patronizing view of the jolly habitant as the typical native of the province."[64] Be that as it may, French Quebec travel writers had less need to rely on canonical artists' visual representations of Quebec to imagine what to expect. They could rely instead on photos and learn from family, friends, or acquaintances about the visual attributes of their homeland – more reliable sources than any painter could hope to be.

SCHOOL TEXTBOOKS

While no mention is made of them in their travel accounts, one can be sure that all these writers had read history textbooks in school. Since these were generally perceived by the wider public as imparting reliable information, having been officially sanctioned by the state, a brief look at what they taught about Quebec opens another window onto what travellers likely knew or thought they knew about the province. While there is a general consensus that textbooks leave a mark on young readers' minds, differing points of view emerge as to what extent and in what way. In his study of French Canadian representations in English Canadian high school readers of the 1940s and 1950s, José Igartua finds that it is "impossible to ascertain what students – and teachers – came to believe of what they read."[65] Yet, he recognizes that "it is highly improbable that the depictions of Canadian society they encountered in their texts did not leave an imprint."[66] Other scholars find that accompanying images or photographs further reinforce a textbook's power of persuasion, which "help to better fix to memory the contents that are associated to them."[67] Indeed, historian Pierre Savard reminds us that "during the pre-television era … [the] literary and iconographic images contained in school readers from the catechism to the atlases had much more impact than today on the young."[68] Generally speaking, most end up agreeing that textbooks essentially have a "reinforcing effect" that is "secondary to a predisposition created outside school and its teachings."[69] These offer interpretive frameworks, which individuals may use to fit in knowledge and attitudes about the past and the present garnered from other sources in order to understand the world around them.[70] For travel writers, these frameworks accommodated some of the information they gathered about Quebec from other nontourist practices.

Those visiting Quebec between the 1920s and 1960s were exposed to textbooks published roughly between the 1900s and early 1950s. While it is obviously impossible to identify precisely those used in their school, a brief content analysis of a select few confirms a representation of the province's past and its French-speaking population which remained fundamentally unchanged throughout this period. As far as Americans are concerned, one can assume that a fair number would have read David S. Muzzey's *An American History*. First published in 1911, with its last printing in 1961, it was "the most widely used American history textbook," in some years, outselling "all others combined."[71] French Canada is brought up in a twenty-page chapter on "The Rise of New France." The chapter stands, in effect, as a reiteration of the famous American historian Francis Parkman's (1823–1893) interpretation of the French in North America. This means, among other things, that young Americans would have been taught that the French colonists were much to be pitied compared to their counterparts in the British territories, as "[i]n place of self-rule enjoyed by the English settlements on the Atlantic seaboard there prevailed in Canada the system known as 'paternalism,' which treated the inhabitants of the colony like irresponsible children under the firm paternal hand of the its governors."[72] It follows that the Conquest stood as a blessing, leading "to the eventual substitution of free institutions, trial by jury, religious toleration, and individual enterprise in place of the narrow, paternal absolutism of the Bourbons."[73] Did this interpretation trickle down to shape American travel writers' views? The least one can say is that a few of them were familiar with Parkman as they referred to him or quoted him directly in their accounts.

As for French Canada and French Canadians after the Conquest, by reading Muzzey, Americans would not have learned much, as French Canada received barely a mention beyond that fateful event. However, children might have gained some insight into what life was like for the ordinary French Canadian in another type of school reader. These were more sociological in nature and clearly meant to introduce relatively young American students to the history and contemporary life in Canada including Quebec. While it is not possible to evaluate how widely distributed and read these were, their

3.4 | Mary Graham Bonner, *Canada and Her Story*, 1942.

content is of interest as it echoed novelists and painters' representations of the province and its inhabitants.[74] Reflective of this is the fact they focused much of their attention on present-day French Quebeckers who lived in rural areas – the contemporary *habitants*.

From certain passages, students could very well have expected to encounter, at least in the countryside, a people untouched by urbanization and industrialization, who "ride to church in ox-cart, or horse-drawn wagon or in an old car."[75] Or perhaps more astonishing for them would have been that on the Île d'Orléans, many "do not know by experience what a moving picture is" but instead "supply their own amusement by telling tales, singing folk songs and dancing."[76] Photographs of traditional *habitants* regularly accompanied such passages, making the information all the more convincing. (See figure 3.4.) The tone is unmistakably patronizing: the happy and endearing disposition of the *habitants*, along with their perennial *joie de vivre*, was conveyed by their unshakable love of singing. Indeed, "on name days and feast days the young people gather for taffy pulls, or square dancing to the tunes of a fiddle and an accordion. Many of the farm families now have radios also, but they think homemade music is best on such occasions. The countryside rings with singing and laughter. Oh, there is plenty of fun on an habitant farm."[77]

Though signs of modernity are occasionally presented, more often than not these were referred to in passing and essentially to confirm the enduring ways of by-gone days. For instance, a photograph's caption featuring a woman at her spinning wheel explained that "although Quebec has huge modern factories, many articles are still made by hand in village homes, such as that of that Gaspé woman." And while learning that "the highways have made a great difference to the habitants who live along the tourist routes," they would also learn that this modernization had only made access to tradition easier. Travellers could see "quaint, colourful hooked rugs ... sold from the clotheslines beside the farmhouse."[78] And while the city of Montreal was described as "the Paris, London and New York of Canada,"[79] and recognized as "the industrial heart of the land,"[80] "the second largest French city, a great financial centre,"[81] readers were reminded that the past is never far behind. Montreal also "looks like a city of churches. [It] is a beautiful and modern city, yet, like Quebec [City] it reflects the past."[82]

In short, Americans (including travel writers) were introduced to the province in school, gaining an awareness of Quebec's urban life but mostly of the contemporary *habitants*, who still lived as their ancestors, knowing more about New France than any other period. Further, they learned that thanks to the British, French Quebeckers now enjoyed rights and liberties of a more advanced and civilized society – one closest to their own. In other words, these memories offered them an interpretive framework in which they could very easily have situated other comparable representations of the province available – including those of William Kirby, Henry Drummond, Cornelius Krieghoff, or Horatio Walker.

English Canadian textbooks provided a comparable framework.[83] Though there was more information of Quebec's past throughout their primary and high school education, a survey of a select sample of these textbooks suggests, nonetheless, that students attending school in the first sixty years of the twentieth century were exposed to a fairly similar portrayal of French Canadians, both past and present.[84] For one, English Canadians could also conclude that the history of New France was a particularly significant and exciting time in French Canadian history, as proportionally more importance was given to this period than to nineteenth- and twentieth-century Quebec. Beyond this, French Canadians were mentioned at times of conflict and in relation to great events that emerged in the post-Confederation period and when discussing the Canadian population more generally. As with their southern neighbours, English Canadian students read about the intrepid explorers, New France's heroic elites, and grand continental wars. And, as in the US, Francis Parkman's interpretation of events was supported, as his writings were directly quoted in Canadian texts.[85] For example, in an introduction to an early textbook, readers were told that it was specifically intended to tell "of French failure through the folly of absolutism, monopoly and feudalism; of British success through the wisdom of self-government, freedom and equality."[86]

Decades later, English Canadian pupils were taught much the same thing, notably that their French Canadian compatriots "were the first to taste that larger liberty which is the characteristic of the British Empire and the secret of its success – the liberty to be themselves." Readers, in fact, were assured that the period following the Conquest was nothing less than a "happy time" during which French Canadians "made the delightful discovery that the British, whom they had feared as terrible enemies, were really excellent fellows."[87] Whether primarily attributable to their schooling or not, some English-speaking travel writers certainly made it clear that French Canadians were lucky to have been conquered. So much so that, according to W.P. Percival, "when ... the humane conduct of the victors became known, many who had left the city [of Quebec] returned."[88] When Brian Meredith asserted that "the geographical, political and religious solidarity of the French Canadian is a great example of the beneficial effect of a little casual persecution," one can safely assume that Parkman was not far behind.[89] New France was also the favoured period when these textbooks turned to social history, focusing more than anything else on the life of the *habitants*. The information was infused, either directly or implicitly, with assumptions of British (and Protestant) superiority, echoing the patronizing characterization of American textbooks. Great emphasis was placed on the influence of the Catholic religion. Well into the 1950s, English Canadian students learned that "[t]he Roman Catholic Church remains the supreme influence in the province."[90] And doubtless, in contrast to his British contemporaries, the New France *habitant* "had very few ambitions."[91] In a condemnation of the Catholic Church, the constantly poor *habitants* relied on a priest to "explain things to them and advise as to what they should do" and this "made life simple," but it "was not perhaps, very good for them as it gave them no training in thinking things out for themselves."[92] And there appeared to be a consensus that they were poor farmers. Indeed, "their lack of education led to ignorant and lazy farming."[93] Also highlighted were specific traits of the *habitants*: they were blessed with an endearing carefree temperament; were "cheery, high spirited and very fond of sociability";[94] and, of course, "loved to sing."[95] Indeed, "whenever two or three Canadians were gathered together ... they were sure to burst into song."[96] José Igartua's conclusions with respect to later textbooks apply here: French Canada was represented as "a static community, still largely rural and exotically gregarious, that remained extraneous to Canadian society."[97]

However, English Canadian textbooks were more likely to draw links between life in New France and contemporary Quebec, where pupils were

3.5 | George Bourinot, *The Story of the Nations: Canada*, 1897.

taught that, along the St Lawrence, they could "find the villages, the farm houses, the language, and the traditions of France – not so much of the modern France that has so broken with the church but the older France." In fact, as one author put it, many aspects of life in New France "endure to this day."[98] Interestingly, while George Bourinot's early twentieth-century reader made similar claims, his last chapter was devoted to contemporary "French Canada," reading as a compendium of sociological observations that might be made by a "tourist."[99] What might jump out at young English Canadians was the extent to which these observations echoed those made about the *habitants* of New France. Thus, faithful to their ancestors, "both old and young are very sociable in their habits, and love music and dancing." And their present-day way of life also recalled pioneering days as "the loom is still kept busy in some villages ... The habitant also wears in winter moccasins and a *tuque bleue* ... in which he is always depicted by the painter of Canadian scenes."[100] (See figure 3.5.)

English Canadian textbooks were also distinguished from American ones by suggesting additional sources available as a means to further enrich their understanding of French Quebeckers. Not surprisingly, they included the works of Francis Parkman but also popular novels quoted in some travel accounts[101] such as William Kirby (*The Golden Dog [Le Chien d'Or]: A Legend of Quebec*); Louis Hémon (the author of *Maria Chapdelaine*) who was a "genius" who "caught the spirit of French Canadian country life." Judge Rivard (*Chez Nous*) was also on the preferred list, credited with "reveal[ing] the beauty and charm of many of the commonplace aspects and incidents of French Canadian rural life." As for W.H. Drummond, he was singled out as a great poet who wrote his wonderful tales using "the English dialect of the French Canadian with great success."[102] Given official authority, it is no wonder that some travel writers referred to the novels as reliable sources of information – after all, their teachers said they were.

Further, by the 1940s, history textbooks in English Canada began to pay more attention to nineteenth- and twentieth-century agricultural modernization, as well as industrial and urban expansion in the province. Students were taught that "even with traditions so enduring there is change."[103] In fact, they would learn that "the province is no longer predominantly an agricultural community" as "sixty-three per cent of the population is now urban."[104] As for the "the French Canadian farmer [he] now lives in the present as well, and is rapidly becoming a skilled modern agriculturalist."[105] Particular attention was given to Montreal's industries and seaport, as well as Northern Quebec's paper industry, expansion of hydroelectric power plants, and new mining operations. These differences suggest that English Canadians travel writers – at least those travelling in the late 1950s and early 1960s – may have had greater awareness than their Americans counterparts that the province was modernizing, albeit relatively recently.

Not surprisingly, French Quebec history textbooks imparted a very different representation, focusing almost exclusively on French Canada. But these were also written as a history of their readers' ancestors – making use of possessive pronouns: "our" people, "our" nation. While it is true that, just as in English North America textbooks, pride of place was given to New France, the message and teaching objectives behind this focus could not have been more different. New France was upheld as the "heroic" period of French Canadian history. Well into the 1950s, young French Quebeckers read of valiant exploits of explorers, missionaries, and unrelenting and painstaking work of their pioneering ancestors. Such figures were of interest to young English North Americans, but for French Quebeckers, learning about them was meant to instil a specifically French Canadian patriotic pride, highlighting "the purity and nobility of our origins."[106] Just as importantly, history lessons provided students with religious education. The significance of events and historical figures were, in part, measured according to their success at propagating and defending the Catholic faith.[107]

Furthermore, students were entreated to admire the bravery of heroic figures who fought the British, specifically during the period of the Conquest.

They were also encouraged to view the Iroquois as cruel "savages" bent on victimizing the valiant missionaries through torture. Not surprisingly, references to Parkman were nowhere to be found. On the contrary, students were taught that tragically "the magnificent dream of a French empire in America was broken forever" before the Conquest.[108] And, more ominously, England's goal was to "Anglicize" "the French Canadian-nation" – specifically "to ravish (*ravir*) her religion, her language and her customs." Far from conferring new rights on the conquered French, this military catastrophe threatened those they already had. It was made clear that the French in America had been forced to dedicate their energies to fighting for survival. Presented more positively, French Canadian superiority was evident by the fact that the English failed to destroy them, thanks to "the steadfastness of the clergy and the explicit willingness of the people to remain Catholic and French."[109] French Quebeckers, then, who became travel writers would likely be particularly inclined to value and recommend places that evoked their past, whether statues of revered heroes, places of worship, or battlefields. While English North Americans would likely develop an interest in these sites, as well, for French Quebeckers, such excursions would be viewed instead as pilgrimages of sorts, affording an opportunity to be reminded first hand of ancestral achievements and inspiring a fundamentally different type of national pride.

The *habitant* figured prominently in French Quebec school readers, however, in contrast to English North American textbooks, they were certainly not presented as "other." Instead, a very direct filiation was established between the *habitant* and young readers. The rural population steadfastly held onto the French language, Catholic religion, and a way of life on the land, insuring survival of the French Canadian nation as a whole. The message was clear: their way of life offered an ideal rampart against assimilation and the most threatening aspects of modernization. As a result, they were held up as role models for French Quebec pupils and not simply as worthy of interest for those studying the French Canadian past. Contemporary *habitants* were not considered reminders of the past. This being said, one is struck by the fact that some textbooks portrayed aspects of *habitant* temperament in much the same manner as English North American authors. Indeed, young children learned that *habitants* had essentially been a happy people, that with them "everything is a pretext for rejoicing." Well into the 1950s, they were taught that "[our] ancestors had a base of unwavering gaiety explained by their French blood. They would visit one another on feast days and on Sundays to rejoice, to dance, to eat. Houses that did not have a violin were rare … The habitant, in the midst of the most difficult work, loved to sing."[110] However, similarities would end there. Such statements were meant to inspire admiration. Pointing to this rejoicing was a way to underscore the extent to which the *habitants* were a contented people that had faced adversity without self-pity and discouragement. Their traditional way of life was fulfilling and well worth imitating as it produced a contented people

And if it is true that, as with their English-language counterparts, French Quebec textbooks drew links between the *habitants* of yesteryear and their modern-day descendants, the idea was clearly not to highlight the extent to which French Canadians' way of life was a dated throwback to the days of New France. Instead, the point was to understand this continuity as most beneficial. On the one hand, pupils were informed that thankfully, one could "still find in our cherished rural areas" some "patriarchal mores."[111] But most of all, their compatriots had admirably withstood the threatening on-slaughts of modernity, and many today were still actively seeking to remain true to their French Canadian roots, most visible among those settling in the province's northern regions. In line with an emphasis on continuity, before the Second World War, French Quebec textbooks spent relatively less time discussing urbanization and industrialization. In fact, still in the 1950s and early 1960s, occasional reference was made to the potentially detrimental influence of modernization on the French Canadian way of life. Thus, in 1960, high school students would learn that regretfully "the ancient virtues of *prévoyance*, of sobriety, of abnegation, and even honesty and respect for authority had been put to a rude test and were in general decline."[112] Clearly then, while future French Quebec travel writers might have wanted to visit some of the same historic sites as their English North American counterparts and come across what would remind them of the habitant pioneers or meet with their present-day incarnations, they would have done so for very differ-ent reasons.

What also is clear is that traditional nationalists were right to assume that American and English Canadian tourists expected and hoped to come across an old Quebec. In addition to government publicity, they would have had any number of non-tourist-related sources from which they could have developed the view that the authentic French Quebeckers were people of the soil, en-during Catholics content with their simple lives, faithful to the traditions of their New France ancestors. As will become clear, nationalist promoters may have been less aware that American and English Canadian tourists read the Quebec landscape through distinct gazes but such distinctions did not detract from their claims that to resurrect the ways and values of their ances-tors made for a sound marketing strategy to increase tourist traffic. Thus, not only was it good for business, it was an excellent way to ensure the survival of the French Canadian nation as they defined it. It seems, as well, that the province's tourist promoters had a solid understanding of what French Quebec travellers wanted to see. It was not to discover an old Quebec peopled with seventeenth-century French *habitants* but historical sites and beautiful scenery along with some information about the province's impressive economic progress.

In the end, for a better part of the century, English Canadian travel writers would have shared many of the same expectations as their American colleagues. All could have concluded that Quebec was, in many ways, still anchored in the past. However, more so than their American counterparts, English Canadians travel writers, over time, would have been made aware of urban and industrial developments, suggesting that they may have had a more multifaceted view of the province. As for French Quebeckers, promises of time travel were less likely to be taken seriously by those living in a "new" Quebec – best not demand too much of the imagination of those travelling "at home."

4

IN SEARCH OF THE AUTHENTIC QUEBEC

Ils burent un apéritif, Piazza Navona, comme
les touristes qu'ils étaient, puis traînèrent dans
les rues à la recherche de clichés.[1]

Finalement ce que recherche avant tout les amateurs
de voyages de découvertes, c'est une <u>confirmation</u>
de ce qu'ils ont pu lire dans leurs guides.[2]

As with tourists generally, English North American and French Quebec travel writers arrived in Quebec with preconceived notions about what they would find, at times unconsciously, but it remains to be seen if they found what they expected to see. One should keep in mind from the outset that these travel writers were "self-conscious" observers,[3] most of them paid to provide information that would attract visitors. Indeed, they had either been hired or volunteered to act as discerning arbiters, deemed to be qualified to establish the authentic Quebec, what tourists should look for to discover it, and where they should go to find it. However, it is safe to assume that these professionals believed, in good faith, that the information they were providing was accurate and the impressions they shared genuine. In other words, one has to entertain the idea that they did not simply act as mouthpieces for their paymasters, regardless of whether it can be confirmed that their accounts were in accord with the Quebec government's propaganda.

Thus, the question becomes, what did these "authenticators" choose to highlight as the real and most worthwhile attributes of this destination, and to what extent did these correspond to their likely preconception of it?[4] There is enough evidence to suggest that, during the first half of the twentieth century, travel writers' understanding of Quebec's authenticity, whether American, English Canadian, or French Quebeckers, remained essentially unchanged. In many instances, however, each group did end up reacting to what they saw in significantly different ways, reflecting their distinct nationally tinted tourist gaze.

AMERICAN TRAVEL WRITERS

From the start, American travel writers stand out in the extent to which their observations consistently echoed information they may have accessed from a wide array of available sources. Readers were told that going to Quebec was the next best thing to going to France, a point reiterated again and again throughout the period. The province was "a land as foreign as France"[5] or simply "the France across Our Border."[6] At first blush, such an association between France and French Quebec is of little significance. It was unmistakably French. To say nothing of the fact that being travel writers, they would have been well aware that English North Americans were particularly attracted to things "French."[7] However, the influence of external sources is difficult to ignore when travel writers claimed that, by coming to Quebec, visitors could also expect to travel back in time. "Entering Quebec" was like "pass[ing] the portals of New France,"[8] to see for themselves what life was like during that time period.[9] The province was interchangeably referred to as Old France[10] or Old Quebec.[11] At times these labels lead to perplexing comparisons. Amy Oakley, for one, noted that the province was "not New but Old France ... pre-revolutionary France."[12] This imprecise labelling brings to mind Gordon Brinley's convoluted description that puzzled her husband. Regardless, it is clear that writers chose to specifically associate the province with a historical period they and their readers were most familiar with and learned to find particularly exciting.

These labels provided travel writers some historical wiggle room as well, as they carried with them rather "elastic" views of the distance back in time travelers would go when heading for Quebec – views they had come across elsewhere, including the province's tourist publicity. For many, it evoked seventeenth-century Normandy. For others, regions such as the Gaspé "remained practically unchanged" since "the discovery of Canada."[13] Readers were essentially meant to believe that by coming to Quebec they would find a place loosely defined as New France, steeped in an appealing "pastness" – evocatively yet loosely defined as old Quebec. Many travel writers' descriptions of the province's Canadian Pacific Railway (CPR) hotels offer a telling illustration of how this "indefinite consumable past" conjured up multiple and overlapping time periods. Quebec City's Château Frontenac hotel, for one, built in 1893 and modelled on the Châteaux de la Loire architecture, was unfailingly portrayed as an old European castle, standing on the grounds of the Château St-Louis, the former residence of New France's governors.[14] But it could also recall much earlier times. For Helen Augur, it filled "out the medieval profile of the Rock."[15] As for the CPR's Manoir Richelieu hotel, located in the Charlevoix region it was likened to "a Norman chateau with turrets and pointed gables." Its proximity to "little French villages, the devout and gentle *habitants* [who] till the fields, drive their oxen, and [where] the women spin and weave," "complet[ed] the picture" – a picture that might serve to illustrate any number of rural pasts.[16] All around then, these pseudocastles easily fit into travel writers' predeparture mental image of an old Quebec.[17]

However, the potency of predeparture influences is most strikingly revealed by American travel writers' sustained fascination with the *habitants* during this whole period. Indeed they produced many lengthy accounts describing life in rural areas. Several entreated readers to go beyond the confines of towns and cities. Instead, visitors should head out to the countryside. Stella Burke May claimed simply that "it was the rural French Canada we had come to see."[18] The message was clear: the more visitors came across these "simple unspoiled natives," the more they would consider their trip a success. As we have seen, the Quebec government tourist promoters had certainly recognized this attraction from the outset with their projects to increase road access to the more remote countryside, their beautification campaigns, and modernizing initiatives. Such testimonies also confirm that traditional nationalists were right to argue that tourists were keen to see an old Quebec.

This predilection for rural areas has much do with the fact that travel writers viewed the *habitants* as the incarnation of what they considered to be the authentic French Quebeckers. This is hardly surprising considering the literature, art and school textbooks, to say nothing of the government tourist publicity, which gave particular importance to the *habitants*. It stands to reason then that American travel writers would have been predisposed to view them as the true French Canadians. Many made this point explicitly. Amy Oakley did so by substituting her words for those of Adjutor Rivard who had written that "the habitant ... is the true *Canadien*, the one who has made the country and who is its guardian still."[19]

It was only the rare writer who proved more perceptive when commenting on *habitant* identity. For example, Pat Morgan explained that "in French Canada [the term *habitant*] carries a sting and means only the most old fashioned farmer." She added that "the foreigners ... use it for farmers and townspeople alike ... denot[ing] to them the simple unspoiled natives."[20] These so-called genuine French Canadians were also worth seeing because they offered an appealing contrast to American city dwellers' way of life. This is not simply inferred from travel writers' comments. Many are explicit about what encountering the *habitants* meant to them on a personal level. They mostly felt that seeing them offered a comforting contrast to their hectic lives in the city. Encountering the *habitants* allowed travel writers to engage in a form of "therapeutic tourism" – appealing to people who viewed the modern world through an antimodernist lens.[21] Helen Augur's musings could be interpreted as those of someone who considered herself fortunate to have met a folk people: "[T]he habitants have always managed without modern industry, and that makes them the luckiest people north of the Mexicans. We of the States would like to recover some of the old-time simplicity ... French-Canadians have never lost those days."[22]

Such reactions were inspired by nostalgia for a simpler time and people. As with those in search of the folk of Nova Scotia, the *habitants* were "an essential abstraction, in which an ideal was materialized." On the other hand, it would never have occurred to them to become more than wistful spectators and embrace the *habitant* lifestyle back home. They could make such blanket statements precisely because they knew so little about them in any meaningful way. Their reactions were informed by a sense that they had had to march lockstep with progress. Such is the fate of modernized societies. Contact with the *habitant* simply inspired them to measure the sacrifices they had made along the way and allowed them to escape, ever so briefly, their exacting/ stressful lives.[23]

It stands to reason, then, that travel writers saw themselves as guides to places of encounters with the *habitants*. Leon Dickinson rated the area between Quebec City and Cap Tourmente as "the genuine French-Canadian homeland ... where the inhabitants continue [to use traditional] language, customs and dress of bygone days."[24] Several years later, Byron Steel also found that the Île d'Orléans best represented the "continuation of seventeenth century life" of Quebec.[25] However, more often than not, travel writers singled out the Gaspé as the place to "find the true, unburlesque *habitants* scratching a hard but happy living from forest clearings."[26] Both the Gaspé and Île d'Orléans could, in many ways, convincingly be touted as unspoiled by the modern world. After all, both had only been made easily accessible to the wider motoring public since 1929 and 1935, respectively. Here were destinations that stood the chance of offering ordinary American travelers the thrilling, and all too rare, privilege of reaching a "frontier to the simple life" beyond which very few had ventured. Travel writers made these areas more alluring still for those in search of the authentic old Quebec by pointing out that the time to see them was now; as early as 1930, some warned: "Go [to the Gaspé] before the simple charm is robbed off by thoughtless tourists who

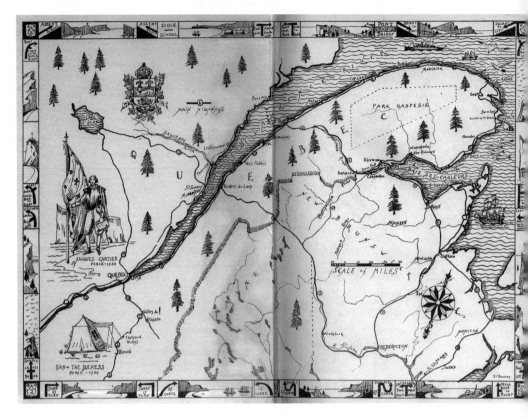

4.1 | Trip itinerary – Gordon Brinley, *Away to the Gaspé*, 1935.

usually spoil the sympathy of any country and the friendliness of natives, after a while."[27] (See figure 4.1.)

Travel writers also acted as authenticators by identifying what it was, specifically, that made all the *habitants* genuine French Canadians. In some respects, such professional obligations lead them to read their surroundings anthropologically. This comparison is a useful one, to the extent that, until the late 1950s, several Americans alluded to the fact that they had lived among the *habitants*, who gave them privileged access to their private lives. Although this foot in the door was not the prerogative of the travel writer, the underdeveloped tourist infrastructure in the Quebec countryside in the first half of the twentieth century made such experiences more common than not (to the great displeasure of hotelkeepers as we have seen). Travel writers often alerted readers that they might end up sleeping in a *habitant* home. In the Laurentians, for instance, "though the district has several first-class inns and modern hotels, by far the greater part of the visitors are cared for in the homes of the habitants." Overall, travel writers made the point that tourists should not hesitate and, in fact, should look forward to knocking on an *habitant's* door, as it could very well provide the opportunity to actually experience what it was like to live among genuine French Canadians whether it was to enjoy an authentic *habitant* meal or be offered other entrées into their world. As an example, Stella Burke May and her travelling companion, who had been asked to join a picnic and observe a *corvée* in the vicinity of Montreal, watched a group of *habitants* helping a neighbour rebuild a burned-out barn.[28]

The way a few American travel writers recounted their experiences could have further convinced prospective tourists that they would be stepping into a world very few had had the chance to encounter. Some conveyed this message using rhetorical conventions typically adopted by travel writers in the past who had published their experiences as stories or diaries. More often, these were the few who wrote detailed guidebooks.[29] While they contained valuable, practical information, these accounts were also meant to entertain, with authors turning themselves into characters in an adventure novel. The Brinleys' account of their three-month trip to the Gaspé is a case in point. The way Gordon Brinley recalled their decision to travel there clearly stands as a narrative device to confer authenticity to her recollections. By framing their expectations and experiences as those of a couple and by transcribing the exchanges they presumably had with each other, she was, in effect, strengthening readers' sense that they were privy to actual personal recollections and more importantly, as would-be tourists, being given information they could rely on to make enlightened decisions as they considered where to take their holiday.[30] Brinley cast their travels as an exciting adventure into the unknown, with amusing anecdotes and colourful depictions of the province's attractive sights – all clearly delightful to those ready to occasionally veer from the beaten track. The fact that she and her husband had decided to camp their way through the region made the writing of such an adventure guidebook that much easier. For one, she made it clear throughout that they had had to "rough it" but only to the extent that they were entering into a territory devoid of many modern-world amenities. It is certainly true that they could not count on a developed camping infrastructure, as until the early 1960s camping tourists to the province had to rely on the willingness of local inhabitants to make their property available to those pitching tents. Indeed, Brinley informed readers that "it is generally the gas station that provides the camper with a safe, watered, lighted, and convenient place to set up a tent for the night."[31] However, she peppered these reassuring asides with light-hearted descriptions of the times when they seemingly had to tough it out. To her mind, this had been the case when, on one occasion, "alas and alack" she exclaimed, "the tea room was closed! [and] only two cups of water in a thermos jug remained for bathing, drinking, and Sunday morning's coffee." Thankfully, spared dehydration, they had just enough water to "carry us till the tea room opens." Concerns about running out of gas or having car trouble punctuated her account as well. At one point, Gordon Brinley entreated her husband to "get some gas [as] there is no telling how much we shall use up before we find a place to spend the night."

As these "adventures" make clear, never did she report situations that had marred the trip in any truly unpleasant way. Should travellers, for instance, forget something back home, using themselves as an example, Gordon Brinley assured that this would not be a problem. Indeed, realizing that Mr Brinley had not brought along proper attire, they had "corduroy trousers" shipped from Quebec to the Matane post office, ensuring that, as Gordon Brinley put it, "now he is ready for any adventure!" Such incidents were clearly meant to convey that travelling in the Gaspé was a sure way of enjoying an exciting trip safely. This being said, at the same time, many of these light-hearted and positive accounts were shot through with unmistakably derogatory value judgments. She did not, for instance, hesitate to use the word "uncivilized" when contrasting the countryside with the cities. Thus, in her view, "the nine miles that stretched between the bridge and Quebec [City] seemed mellow and civilized after our week in the rough."[32] They "celebrate[d their] return to civilization" by going to the city's Capital Theatre.[33] But, again, for those in search of safe adventure, such characterizations made the prospect of heading for old Quebec all the more appealing.

More than ten years later, the Oakleys produced a similar type of road-trip guidebook. Also a wife-and-husband team, interestingly enough, their professional profile matched in uncanny ways the Brinleys'. Amy Oakley was also a reputed travel writer and her husband, Thornton, a famous illustrator,[34] and they too reported finding themselves in situations that would indicate adventure had been in the offing. Thus, on one occasion, driving around Lac St-Jean, Amy Oakley recounted that "bears were to form the climax of our lake-encircling tour. We heard a crashing through underbrush and ran uphill, to come suddenly upon a looming form emerging from the forest, coal black, rearing to immense height." Referring to her husband, she wrote, "my foolhardy Illustrator called, continuing to advance, 'look! ... There is another!'" As this exchange makes clear, occasionally, travel writers reverted to what would have been acknowledged as commonsensical gender differences of the period to convey excitement in store for those in search of exhilarating experiences. Hal Burton was another. He positioned himself as the more intrepid traveller when he recounted that while in the Laurentians, "I donned my own skis, boots and poles ... My wife, who abhors the sports, trotted briskly into the restaurant and took a table by the window."[35] However, the number of female travel writers who set off on such "adventures" alone would have reassured women wanting to visit this old and remote Quebec on their own that it was safe to do so. Travel writers were not in the business of discouraging visitors to the province.

Some encounters with the local population also easily suggest that they stood the chance of encountering a land untouched by the outside world. Much as early European explorers, they would occasionally tell of the thrill of apparently being greeted as objects of curiosity. Thus, driving on roads in the Charlevoix region, Amy Oakley recalled, "eager faces appeared at windows to watch our passage," while in the Gaspé "an *habitant* with wife and a dozen children hailed at us at the top of a long hill."[36]

While travel accounts could differ in style and length, all emphasized the notion that travelling to Quebec was to travel in time. This, of course, implied some form of adventure, as well, but it did mean that a more concentrated effort was put into recording what made old Quebec old. What stands out is that well into the 1950s, American travel writers brought out the very same features and character traits of the *habitants* that were represented in sources of information available to them at home. As late as 1948, Byron Steele, for instance, claimed that the *habitant* "seems so utterly oblivious to the twentieth century ... [that] you [the tourist] begin to feel that you are actually living in the 17th century."[37]

As a result, as much as many tried to convey that they were venturing into the unknown, their observations were, in effect, those of travellers who had already seen what they were describing. In this sense, likening them to amateur anthropologists is limited in making sense of their reactions. Their knowledge was not scholarly or acquired in a scholarly manner. They were, in effect, imparting information about the *habitants* that readers could have learned elsewhere and would be keen to see firsthand. This may account for the fact that they rarely expressed surprise or disappointment at what they came across. More often than not, the impression is that they were amazed at the extent to which their encounters corresponded to their expectations. In effect, they were telling readers that they, too, would find a Quebec worthy of a trip, offering adventure opportunities into familiar territory and peopled with familiar "faces."

This may partly explain why they did not seek out (much), or simply ignored, others who could trace their roots much further into the past – namely the province's Indigenous peoples. Travel writers so keen on being transported back in time rarely referred to them. When they did it was typically when providing brief historical sketches of New France history. But these essentially served to highlight the extraordinary experiences of settlers, famous explorers and colourful leaders. The Iroquois – allied with the English against the French – were mentioned most often to underscore the bravery of the *habitants'* ancestors and add an exotic flavour to their accounts. Indeed, these "hostile savages"[38] were invariably portrayed as having been "ferocious"[39] and as a "treacherous tribe of red men."[40] A few who wrote more detailed accounts made the occasional side trip to encounter "Indians" in the flesh, but these remained brief interludes during a trip which was first and foremost intended to encounter descendants of the French of seventeenth-century New France. Thus, Amy Oakley recounted, in less than four pages, their experiences on the "Iroquois" Caughnawaga (Kanawake) reserve near Montreal. Their objective was not to learn about its residents' contemporary way of life. Instead, their "hopes were high that … we might happen upon some form of celebration" – a traditional one. Sure to reinforce their preconceptions about these "warlike people," they were fittingly entertained by a "war dance." However, they did discover some unexpected bits of anthropological information including that the Iroquois were "totemic Indians." The Brinleys, for their part, encountered a few Montagnais Indians (Innu) when recounting their adventures in the Lac St-Jean region as they came upon the Pointe Bleue reserve, which included a Hudson Bay Company (HBC) trading post. It was open to visitors, with a store and exhibits featuring various artefacts and clothing exemplifying the lives of trappers including those of Native descent. Here again, expectations coloured travel writers' gazes as they compared those they encountered with images they carried with them from home. Thus, at the entrance, as Gordon Brinley was faced with "two Indians … a powerful sense of the alien nature of these human beings pierced [her]." Yet, "to her astonishment [she also] heard that the Montagnais have a jolly nature." And when an HBC employee recounted his exchange with a Native trapper which Gordon Brinley had witnessed, he explained that the Indian was reluctant to take a piece of canvas that would help him during his river travels because he "did not understand about waterproofing."[41] This anecdote was clearly intended to amuse readers feeding on the well-ingrained patronizing and racist views about the primitive nature of these people of the forest. Interestingly however, despite long-standing beliefs among white European Canadians that Indigenous peoples belonged to a vanishing race, travel writers did not set out to entice readers to follow in their footsteps in order to catch a rare and perhaps last glimpse of these disappearing Indians. Being travel writers bent on enticing would-be tourists, they recounted their encounters as entertaining anecdotes much as one would when coming across intriguing "specimens" on the way to the truly representative and alluring sites of the province.

4.2 | *L'Île d'Orléans – Pastoral.* Illustration by
Thornton Oakley in *Kaleidoscopic Quebec.*

Travel writers were much more interested in describing the *habitants*' life on
the farm. They were particularly intrigued by their use of antiquated technology. More often than not, they highlighted the prevalence of animal-powered
means of transportation. In fact, prospective tourists could very well have
drawn the conclusion that motorized transportation had not yet reached the
province's rural areas.[42] According to Gordon Brinley, in the Gaspé, "most of

the native vehicles are carts or wagons of some sort."[43] Thus "farmers used ox-teams to plow, young bullocks hitched to homemade wagons to haul proven-der and dog teams for lighter jobs."[44] Moreover, photos accompanying these accounts almost unfailingly were of an *habitant* and his oxen-driven plow. (See figure 4.2.) Only rarely would a writer question these accounts. Inter-estingly, one that did discredit a source of information readers would have encountered before leaving home recognized, indirectly, their power of sug-gestion. In 1946, Herbert Manghan warned, "Some of the more romantic writ-ers, abetted by diligent photographers, have shadowed forth a legend about Île d'Orléans and the Gaspé which causes many visitors to be disappointed … With luck the visitor may see an ox-team, but he will need more than his share of luck."[45] But such reality checks stood out as few and far between.

Among all animal-powered transportation, travel writers were clearly most intrigued by dog carts (so vehemently decried by Albert Tessier). These were singled out as a signifier of old-world ways. However, despite the fact that it would have been common knowledge to travel writers that these carts were very popular with tourists, they expressed clearly heartfelt reservations. Acting as discerning and detached observers, they alerted readers to the fact that, in some cases, these dog carts had been co-opted by the locals to en-tertain tourists, turning a tradition into a very present-minded spectacle. W. Walker pointed out, cynically:

> Dog carts are another sight that will make you laugh your head off.
> The kids up there know that Americans like a farce and pay to be
> amused, so they've taken to dressing their woolly Newfoundland work
> dogs in silly hats and overcoats and horn-rimmed spectacles. The
> ludicrous contraptions stand on many a curve with a bunch of grabby
> children waving a ragged hat and yelling for tourists to take a picture
> (for which you pay of course!)[46]

Gordon Brinley proved even more critical as, on more than one occasion, she expressed concern about the treatment meted out to these dogs and particu-larly those being put on display. She had seen "dogs dressed up in bonnets, being exploited by people with things to sell. The dogs were kept facing the full blaze of the sun … Why they didn't go mad was a wonder; and I found myself wishing they would, to end their misery."[47] (Albert Tessier would have agreed although these dogs would certainly not have made him laugh.)

Such disapproving remarks were certainly not intended to put into ques-tion the possibility of experiencing authenticity in Quebec. More likely, they were attempts to show they, as professional travellers, could be trusted to discriminate between the real and staged Quebec. Indirectly, they revealed an understanding that travel was a business as well as an opportunity to experience authenticity. For the most part, though, travel writers took this reality in stride. In the words of Larry Nixon, the *habitants* "have learned to nod politely to the visiting artist. They hold poses carefully for the candid-camera expert."[48]

Of course, the "toured upon" French Canadian hosts were not exceptional in this respect. Indeed, tourism scholars have argued that the locals have a gaze of their own and they "construct [it] upon previous and numerous encounters with tourists."[49] They will occasionally stage authenticity to meet visitor expectations of encountering a genuine experience.[50] More specifically, according to Pierre van den Berghe and C. Keyes, the "touree" then becomes "the native-turned-actor-whether consciously or unconsciously – while the tourist is the spectator."[51] The ultimate example of this staging was in the Lac St-Jean region, where residents constructed the world of Louis Hémon's *Maria Chapdelaine* – both real and imagined – creating a kind of theatrical performance to satisfy tourists' imagined realities of the *habitant* and of Quebec, in general.

Travellers such as the Oakleys and the Brinleys appear to have been thrilled and willing spectators. Their detailed accounts of their visit to Péribonka offers insight into how the toured upon aimed to meet (and benefit) from tourists' expectations, and it confirms the extent to which American travel writers' predeparture practices made it easy for them to do so. Amy Oakley recounted their welcome at Foyer Maria Chapdelaine and how they enjoyed its "pleasant dining room."[52] (See figure 4.3.) Visitors could understandably think that they had come across the "real thing" as at least one official marker attested to the historical accuracy of this location, notably a monument erected to Louis Hémon's memory by the Quebec Society of Arts, Sciences and Letters. Fact and fiction were made to intersect in less historically verifiable/convincing ways when Gordon Brinley told of their meeting with Éva Bouchard. She lived in the adjoining carriage house and presented herself as Hémon's muse. Travel writers appeared only too keen to be taken in by her performance. They confidently recounted how delighted they were to meet the closest thing to the heroine of a novel they had so enjoyed. In the words of Amy Oakley, their "cup of happiness overflowed when we were welcomed [at the Foyer Maria Chapdelaine] by 'Maria' in person – Mademoiselle Éva Bouchard who possesses the finesse, the mellow beauty of a Provencal Reines des Félibres."[53] As for Gordon Brinley, she was thrilled to be escorted to her room by this reenacted "Maria." And while "Maria" did not speak English, she nonetheless "showed great intuition and several times discovered what

4.3 | Illustration by Gordon Brinley, *Away to Quebec*, 1937.

I was endeavouring to express."[54] Foyer Maria Chapdelaine, then, brought together willing visitor and tourees in a mutually rewarding production on an old Quebec stage.[55]

However, it is an oversimplification to reduce American travel writers' encounters with the *habitants* as a case of locals setting out to meet tourists' expectations and travel writers playing along. It is about reading the landscape with a selective tourist gaze that led them to see what they wanted to see. This is certainly apparent considering travel writers' reaction to the *habitant* appearance and beliefs. While these did not necessarily stand out as markers of the past, their eyes, as lenses of expectation, told them otherwise. More specifically, the sight of contemporary *habitant* attributes matched the historical pictorial representations of artists, such as Cornelius Krieghoff and Horatio Walker in addition to government advertising. Typically, the *habitant* men who were not working the land were portrayed as sitting "on a porch, pipe between teeth,"[56] while women were often described as working on their porches spinning yarn or standing by their family's outdoor bake oven. And travel writers almost always commented on the large number of children in *habitant* families. Harry A. Franck, taken in by a family in the

Gaspé, recounted in the voice of a well-read traveller that "there were only fourteen children in this family which is not a surprising number for this region. French Canadian families may range from 12 to 26 children – though I heard a priest bemoan the fact that 'even they are learning birth control.'"[57] His message was that travellers could count on having their expectations met and more. While pictures that accompany these accounts certainly confirmed that they had come across such *habitants*, it is also safe to assume that they saw many families in rural Quebec that did not reflect this "familiar" *habitant* trait.

When American travel writers drew readers' attention to the *habitants'* beliefs and character traits, they also homed in on those that confirmed an old Quebec affiliation. Readers were unfailingly told of the ubiquitous presence of the *curés* and nuns dressed in their distinctive habits. A majority of accounts include a picture of priests or nuns on their own or involved in some kind of religious ceremony. They invariably mentioned how they were struck by the numerous roadside crosses dotting the countryside. Several highlighted alluring foreignness by invoking other destinations. Seasoned traveller Harry A. Franck also remarked in amazement that, in this same region, "nowhere have I ever seen more crosses by the roadside, except perhaps in Lithuania on the Baltic."[58] Again, this amazement was not inspired by surprise but more likely was a reaction to the extent to which French Quebecker religious life met their pretravel expectation. But their observations were rarely simply descriptive. Their descriptions were occasionally derogatory remarks infused with latent anti-Catholicism. Although travel writers never explicitly disclosed their religious affiliations, their reactions to religious practices could only be those of non-Catholic observers with well-ingrained prejudices. Their observations were particularly coloured by long-standing views among some Protestants that, for the most part, Catholics were blindly submissive to a top-heavy ecclesiastical hierarchy. This assumption was confirmed by the fact that Catholicism was seemingly an overpowering force in French Quebec society. In fact, according to Byron Steele, "nowhere in the world does the Catholic Church wield a greater influence on the everyday life of its members than in Quebec."[59] Some wore their prejudices more visibly, such as Amy Oakley, who contended that "French Canadians have been able to keep their independence of spirit and their inherited form of civilization only by means of an almost fanatical loyalty to religion and language."[60] In other instances, travel writers pointed indirectly to priests' seeming self-importance and to their parishioners' blind and naïve religious subservience. W. Walker, for one, used lightly veiled irony when he remarked that "some [priests] beamed benedictions as we passed, while others frowned indignantly and lifted an eyebrow in ecclesiastical wrath."[61] Such thinly veiled prejudice would not likely have

offended prospective American Catholic tourists. As travel writers' observations suggest, readers were meant to understand that French Quebeckers
followed a dated Catholicism anchored in the past from which modern-day
practitioners could (and did) easily distance themselves.

American travel writers' reaction to the *habitants'* French language deep-
ens the understanding of how predeparture influences coloured views in
distinct ways. They seemed genuinely surprised at the extent to which the
majority of the population was truly francophone, and many observations
suggest an assumption that readers would be as well, if not sceptical. As a
result, texts were filled with comments about hearing people speak French
and in what circumstances they heard them doing so. Their objective appeared to be to persuade prospective tourists that French Quebeckers used
French in their everyday lives, not simply for the benefit of tourists. Charles
W. Stokes remarked that "one thing the American visitor has at last decided
to unlearn – that the French Canadian speaks French because he likes to
be quaint. On the contrary, French is an exceedingly utilitarian language."[62]
Others proved more emphatic, such as Wes Whitfield who declared, "[t]hey
speak French, write French, read French."[63] Just as revealing were explan-
ations provided to account for this state of affairs. Charles Stokes opined,
"Jean-Baptiste uses [French] partly because he prefers it and partly because
the 1867 Act of Confederation reiterated its equality with English gained
in 1763."[64] If this reasoning speaks to a Parkman reading of Quebec history,
it could also be reflective of another American assumption: the English language was the standard language of communication in North America. When
confronted with the fact that in some places this was not the case, it struck
them as extraordinary and worthy of more detailed commentary.

But their more than passing interest in the French language can also be
explained by the fact that Americans viewed it as yet another marker of the
province's old world ways – a notable holdover from the past. What seemed
remarkable to them was that "these people are proud of their Gallic origin
and are absolutely determined to preserve the spirit of New France."[65] Indeed,
by noting that the "Gaspe is *still* [my emphasis] French to the backbone,"
Diana Rice implied that it had resisted modernity.[66] And others referred to
Quebec French as "archaic French," a dialect or a "patois" passed down from
New France ancestors: "French from the farm is very entertaining and full of
colour ... It was good French when it came over with Champlain and Talon
and Hocquart ... and certainly there are meanings so picturesque as to be
poetry."[67] As with religion, where American travel writers showed prejudice
with humorous and mocking asides, these same writers similarly treated the
French Quebec accent and those with a poor grasp of English.[68] In mocking

amusement Morris T. Longstreth noted that "*creatures ... are*, to a French Canadian, not animals but women!"[69] Amy Oakley, travelling in the Gaspé, recorded comical attempts by locals to communicate with tourists in English. They occasionally transcribed inaccurate sign wording for readers' enjoyment: "GARAG, English Aspeaken Troubles Expert."[70] Those who chose to transcribe exchanges with the *habitants* gave their interlocutors an accent many readers would have recognized as supposedly reliable (and comical) Henry-Drumond vernacular. For example, while trying to find access to a boat to Isle-aux-Coudres, the Brinleys were apparently told by "a genial little fellow" that "Oh! ... the *grand bateau*! She is *frappé* – she bust herself on a rock last night during the great wind."[71] This being said, American travel writers reassured readers that under no circumstances should they worry about being misunderstood or be concerned that language would act as a barrier. Some even tried to turn language differences into a plus, as when Joseph West remarked that "it [is] not necessary to polish up your high school French to get by ... [L]anguage is no barrier, but a refreshing attraction."

While available sources make it very difficult to get a sense of how French Quebeckers reacted to the way they were portrayed in American travellers' accounts, occasionally, there are a few insights. Amy Oakley's transcription of a conversation she and her husband had with Maurice Hébert – director of Quebec's Provincial Tourist Bureau – reveals that some at the helm did not want to see the French language mocked as flawed or backward. He made the point of insisting: "There is ... no patois in the province; but the accent varies according to the region in France from which the settlers emigrated. It is no more poor French that [sic] is spoken than in the United States is the English poor – where for a native to speak with an Oxford accent would be the height of absurdity."[72]

Clearly such instances – however rarely made public – confirm that some leading government tourist promoters took opportunities to set the record straight, countering what they felt could tarnish French Quebeckers' reputation or distort what they considered to be distinctive and constitutive of their character. Some tourism promoters were strong supporters of the *refrancisation* campaigns, so it stands to reason that they would not want French to be associated with an archaic patois. Of note as well, Amy Oakley pointed out that she and her husband had this conversation during "our reception in the office of the publicity bureau." This observation stands as another telling illustration of the travel writing genre's multiple attributes. They were sharing firsthand recollections but informed, in some cases at least, by what official promoters wanted travel writers and eventually prospective tourists to understand about the province.[73]

Interestingly enough, while American travel writers took particular notice of the French language, few commented on the presence of Anglophones or French–English relations. (As will become clear later, this was not the case for writers discussing Montreal.) This is not surprising. The majority population in rural areas was French-speaking, and Americans were looking specifically for the *habitants*. It could also be that many Americans would not be fully aware of the distinctive if not complicated relations between Canada's so-called "two founding nations." As a result, they may not have been conscious that these deserved particular attention or be intrigued enough to want to confirm how these relations played out. When they did mention English Quebeckers, it was essentially to make a point about the French population – mostly to highlight their survival. Byron Steele explained, the French Canadian minority "has not allowed itself to be swallowed up by the rest of Anglo-Saxon America."[74] At times, they made a similar point by invoking the past – more specifically, the time of the Conquest. This makes sense, as this was the historical time period that brought these two groups to the forefront and one Americans had been exposed to in school. Their comments also leave no doubt that they had absorbed Francis Parkman's understanding of the event. Readers were consistently made to understand that the British had been most benevolent, notably in 1774, when "the French were recognized on an equal basis with the English."[75] Kennedy informed readers that French Canadians "who at last yielded to the valour of Wolfe on the Plains of Abraham, have remained steadfastly true to race, language and religion, and have conquered the conquerors by sheer tenacity and wrought from them the admiring tribute of complete equality of rights from the Atlantic to the Pacific at the Confederation of the Dominion of Canada."[76]

If the *habitant* way of life, religion, and language could be viewed as evidence that Quebec was not only different but a living museum, American travel writers also claimed that the actual character of the *habitants* could as well. Ascribing to whole populations personality traits of individuals is quite common among travellers, regardless of time period and destination. However, the traits of the *habitant* highlighted by American travel writers corresponded to those they expected and hoped to encounter – the *habitant* of novelists, painters, and textbooks. Equally remarkable, these representations of the *habitant* personality were consistent, well into the 1950s. Not surprisingly then, they claimed, "the French from the farm is very entertaining and full of colour."[77] Gordon Brinley, for her part, remarked in the Gaspé that "all the way along the prevailing type of face we have seen has been intelligent and likeable."[78] *Habitants* were characterized as reliably "happy-go-lucky."[79] As late as the mid-1950s, George Sessions Perry "observe[d] that most of the people I'd seen that day seemed happy."[80] And, faithful, to their reputation, many commented on how the *habitants* loved to sing. Tourists were assured, "the farmer sings at his work and on the road before daylight in winter on the way to market." A few devolved into a more detailed character analysis, as George Frazier who observed that the *habitants'* "needs are modest" and that they are "resourceful … [and] frugal." Some also commented that they "saw surprisingly little drinking," and when they did, it was done "with dignity."[81]

Yet, however much they wished to share their admiration for the *habitants*, American travel writers infantilized them, in much the same way as had novelists, artists, or textbook authors. At the same time, nothing suggests that American travel writers considered the *habitant* "inferior" or primitive, as had been the case, for instance, with British travellers who encountered *habitants* in the late nineteenth and early twentieth centuries. They cannot be compared, either, to nineteenth-century travellers to Nova Scotia who "develop[ed] the theme of 'primitivism' in the countryside." Instead, the reactions of American travel writers were more akin to those who visited Nova Scotia during the 1920s and 1930s. Indeed, McKay concludes that they had read the province's fisher folk through an antimodernist lens as "objects of contemplation," turning them into "an essential abstraction, in which an ideal was materialized."[82] A similar argument could be made in the case of Americans and *habitants*, clearly reflected by George Sessions Perry in accounting for the French Quebeckers' contented disposition. To his mind, "untroubled by hankerings for progress, the French Canadians do not want to see Quebec's peaceful, harmonious ways altered. Just as he is, the habitant is *bien content*."[83]

Such comments indirectly raise questions about American travel writers' views towards modernity and progress in Quebec. For all their nostalgic yearnings for a simpler, older time, it did not escape attention that parts of Quebec outside large, urban centres were "hankering for progress." However, a majority of them clearly believed that these had emerged relatively recently. Thus it was that Quebec could still remain old. More specifically, a few appeared to associate this recent modernization with the impact of the Second World War. According to Helen Augur, writing in 1942, until the war "Quebec was untouched by the French Revolution, little affected by the machine age or by the modern world in general." Only after the war had things begun changing, as it had incited Quebec to turn to the outside world.[84] The view that change was a recent occurrence lasted beyond the war. In 1948, American travel writers, such as Byron Steele, were still confidently claiming, "even those [French Canadians] who unavoidably come in contact with modern ways continue to base their personal lives on the habits and customs of their forefathers."[85] In effect, such reactions suggest that many ended up seeing and reporting what they wanted to see or, at the very least, attributed less importance to what they did not *expect* to see. As Sylvain Simard put it, when analyzing the reactions of French travellers to Quebec in the late nineteenth and early twentieth century, "[o]ne looks only for what we miss and we find only what we look for."[86] Their blindness is particularly striking in their reactions to the Lac St-Jean region. Helen Augur claimed that in the area of the Upper Saguenay – one that was in the midst of remarkable industrial development and mining expansion – "despite the radios and the busy paper mills ... you will hear mostly Norman songs and the native ones created by the fur trappers and voyageurs."[87]

This being said, the few who wrote full-length travel books, such as the Brinleys and the Oakleys, reacted somewhat differently to certain of Quebec's markers of modernity: they seemed to purposefully look for the "new" Quebec while discovering the old. The new Quebec they described was the one highlighted in government-issued publicity. The Brinleys had in hand the provincial guide for the Chicoutimi region, and judging by their route, it closely followed the brochure's itinerary.[88] They recounted pleasures driving through the Saguenay–Lac St-Jean region's industrializing cities for the very reason that they appeared modern: "enjoy[ing] modernity in the country seat of Roberval" and finding Chicoutimi "handsome, modern and attractive." Clearly intent on following the prescribed itinerary, Gordon Brinley exclaimed dramatically, "I can't bear it if we have missed Kenogami and the Shiplaw Development at Racine!"[89] But both couples reserved their most effusive admiration for the town of Arvida – a city heralded as an emblem of North American modernity. Carved out of the wilderness in 1926 to serve the manpower needs of the Alcoa aluminum mining company, it already numbered 15,000 inhabitants by the mid-1930s.[90] While Brinley described it as "a model town with wide streets, attractive homes for the workers, playgrounds and good schools," Amy Oakley baptized it as nothing less than "a New Jerusalem of industrial towns."[91] She continued lyrically: "in the distance twinkled the galaxy of fabulous Arvida – summoned into being by the genie of modernity, world capital of the aluminium industry, where not millions but hundreds of millions are invested."[92] Visibly, then, some American travel writers were prepared to enjoy what made the Quebec countryside both new as well as old. Put differently, antimodernist leanings did not preclude an appreciation for economic progress, particularly when it could equal or outshine American accomplishments.

Nonetheless, this overview of American travel writers' reactions to the province reveals, above all, that they found an old Quebec and represented it as such. To their minds, the Quebec countryside was the authentic Quebec, and its *habitant* population stood as the authentic French Canadians. Having learned to recognize them as such before leaving home, their accounts certainly did not serve to cast doubt on the image readers also likely had of the province. By the 1950s, while it was impossible to overlook the prevalence of modern economic development, some travel writers still tried to reassure readers that "industrial expansion has not marred the Old World French Canadian atmosphere that visitors to Quebec seek."[93]

ENGLISH CANADIAN TRAVEL WRITERS

Keeping in mind that travellers' reaction are, in part, shaped by homegrown expectations, what comes as no surprise is that English Canadian travel writers did not read the Quebec landscape in the same way as their American counterparts. While there is no doubt they reacted similarly, an awareness that they were visiting part of their *own* country combined with distinct predeparture experiences and a relatively more developed knowledge about Quebec meant that significant differences emerge. For one, English Canadian travel writers were much less likely to view Quebec as a transplanted France in North America. They took "ownership" of the province. After all, Quebec was part of their country. Indeed, for someone like Ken Johnstone, "visiting Quebec is like visiting your own birthplace."[94] It was the homeland of their ancestors as well. Descriptions of specific places also evoked a sense that visitor and visited shared common roots. Writing about Quebec City, Eva-Lis Wuorio gushes, "Old Quebec at night is our own past breathing."[95]

However, readers were reminded it was different for many of the same reasons brought out by their American counterparts. Most notably, they too believed Quebec offered prospective tourists an opportunity to time travel. And as with Americans, opinions as to just how far back in time varied quite markedly. On the book cover of travel writer Blodwen Davies's *Romantic Quebec*, the publisher described the province as "essentially unchanged since the 18th century."[96] Homing in on the town of Murray Bay, Constance Cromarty reflected that it "might have been a little village of Normandy away back in the seventeenth century."[97] For Dr W.T. Herridge, Murray Bay was a place where "some of the most chivalrous features of medievalism still survive."[98] In later years, however, English Canadian travel writers tended to date the province's age more vaguely. In the 1950s, for instance, Wallace Ward claimed that "permeating the whole province is the atmosphere of France of nearly four centuries ago."[99] In short, English Canadian travel writers shared with Americans a sense that Quebec was old in equally vague terms, and they carried this impression for several decades.

English Canadians were also particularly drawn to the rural areas and agreed with Americans that visitors would "find [there] the country people, les *habitants* and the small villages ... the most interesting on the continent."[100]

Indeed, "there is no more attractive type in Canada than the *habitant*."[101] As with their American counterparts however nothing suggests that they were eager to encounter Indigenous people. It seems as though they were glad to when Indigenous people were easily accessible, close to the sites the writers had on their priority list. But their accounts offered only briefs observations. Clearly to their minds Indigenous people were less worthy of interest. A few described their experiences at the Indian Lorette reservation (Wendake) outside Quebec City. Mostly though, as with Americans, bringing up Natives was simply an opportunity to provide tourists with some historical background. In no way was the intent to inform readers about the present-day Indigenous way of life. "Indians" served to infuse writers' accounts with a few colourful highlights of New France's exciting history. Thus, they mostly chose to recount legends or fantastical tales involving what would stand for them as Indigenous superstitions and the efforts of missionaries to convert and civilize them. Those in Lorette offered more opportunities to do so as the reserve had been inhabited by the Hurons – French allies and a central focus of French missionaries' conversion efforts. These were not "fierce and savage,"[102] instead they were "peace-loving Indians."[103]

More in keeping with their understanding of what would make for an authentic experience, a few eagerly headed out to Maria Chapdelaine country. While at first F.O. Call feared that the Bédard family members "might disturb the illusion, or rather the reality of the story," he was not disappointed after having been invited to dine with them.[104] Carleton McNaught and his wife stayed at the Foyer Maria Chapdelaine and also spent some time with the family. Just as the Oakleys and Brinleys, they were thrilled and honoured to meet Éva Bouchard, more so, in fact, than their American counterparts – a likely result of their deeper knowledge of the story. They were simply awestruck, and returned home convinced that Louis Hémon's Maria, unlike other characters of the novel, was no "'composite' country maiden of old Quebec." Éva "was unquestionably the inspiration of the story." However, they did experience a "slight shock to [their] sensitivities" when they noticed that Éva had agreed to autograph a postcard with her picture by signing "Maria Chapdelaine." Carleton McNaught remarked, "What sort of woman could it be who would capitalize ... the fame of the book?" However, he benevolently rationalized this behaviour by pointing to her "frank and simple (naïve is not the word) ... submission to the laurels bestowed upon her by fate."[105] (See figure 4.4.) Mostly travel writers, including Jean M. Donald, felt simply that "[it] is fun to meet the heroine of a great book."[106]

Furthermore, English Canadians consistently brought out the same features of the *habitant* way of life, beliefs, and character traits as those identified

4.4 | Éva Bouchard (Maria Chapdelaine), 1924.

by Americans. They invariably pointed to bake ovens, spinning wheels, and other markers of earlier times. They, too, highlighted the *habitants'* traditional animal-powered means of transportation. English Canadians also remark on the presence of dog carts as more evidence of time travel but with equally mixed feelings. Thus, while the Mackenzies "found it interesting to watch the dogs hauling their small wagons," claiming that they "seem[ed] to enjoy and to take pride in [their] elevated position,"[107] Jean M. Donald considered these dogs nothing less than "a disgrace to Quebec." She also heaped scorn on tourists who took pictures with them, sarcastically remarking that, "somehow, a dirty green top hat and a pair of sunglasses tied on the head of a big, patient dog … failed to amuse us."[108]

English Canadian travel writers were also interested in French Canadian Catholic beliefs and responded in much the same way as Americans. For one, they emphasized the Catholic Church's omnipresence and omnipotence. And to them as well Catholic practices essentially confirmed the old-world ways of the habitants. According to Blodwen Davies, "the church [plays] to these twentieth century Canadians the role that the medieval church played in Europe."[109] Such reactions were, to be sure, informed by Protestant prejudice, but a few, including Davies, offered unadulterated bigoted remarks as she also claimed that "[o]nly a people in some ways primitive enough to preserve a religious faith that has dissolved before the realities of industrial life, could be happy here."[110] Furthermore, English Canadians did not hesitate to make the same type of infantilizing generalizations about the *habitant* temperament. Unfailingly, every writer mentioned the *habitants*' apparent unshakable happiness. Recalling American sentiments, Jean M. Donald invoked their seemingly innate love of singing as evidence of this: the *habitants* "do not [work] in silence, looking glum, with an ear for the dinner whistle, but with lusty song the noisy gangs of colourfully clad workmen shout away the hours, laboring mightily."[111] While "ignorant of much," W.T. Herridge pointed out that the *habitant* "is often graced with a wisdom denied the wise."[112] Rarely however did a writer provide an unflattering characterization. And much as with the Americans, English Canadian reactions were often coloured by an antimodernist perspective, which revealed how much they admired the *habitant* or the idea they had of them. While Herridge condescendingly stated the *habitant*, "[a]t heart, is still a child, responsive, obedient, unworldly, fond of pranks," he also mentioned approvingly that the *habitant* was "not weighed down by a multitude of worries, an unconscious rebuke to materialistic business."[113]

But for all the overlaps in the reactions of American and English Canadian travel writers, evidence confirms that the latter cast a distinctive homegrown, tourist gaze on the Quebec countryside. Indeed, English Canadians were less likely to identify the *habitant* as the authentic French Canadian or, for that matter, that the province's countryside was the authentic Quebec. Instead, they were more prone to speak of the authentic *habitant*. For some, "the true French Canadian habitant" lived in the Gaspé.[114] Fraser contended more generally that "on the land, amid his natural surroundings" one can "understand and appreciate the real genius of the habitant."[115] English Canadian travel writers aimed to help prospective tourists come into contact with this specific type of French Quebecker – the most attractive to their minds and the most worthwhile seeing, to be sure, but not one they considered as somehow incarnating the essence of the French people of the province.

What further reflects their distinctive understanding of the *habitants* is that, taken as a whole, their accounts offer diverse, if not contradictory assessments as to the *habitants'* very existence. In 1926, for instance, according to Katherine Hale, the *habitants* "under modern conditions … have undergone such a rapid change that they have now almost vanished."[116] As evidence, she noted that "the spinning wheel has been removed to the attic and the *étoffe du pays* is no longer seen except to be sold to unsophisticated tourists."[117] Interestingly enough, these are the very same words used in one of the Quebec provincial government's first brochures, *Québec, The French Canadian Province: A Harmony of Beauty, History and Progress*, which, as discussed earlier, also included contradictory information as to the *habitants'* rate of survival. Yet, prospective tourists reading the article by George Pearson a few months later and in the same magazine learned instead that "the old habitant type is not disappearing," adding, "[o]ne might as well say the French Canadian race is dying out."[118] Disagreements as to whether the *habitant* represented the authentic French Quebecker can be gleaned from travel accounts into the 1950s. In 1952, for instance, the Mackenzies indirectly questioned the accuracy (and wisdom) of an American travel writer's comments who maintained that life in Baie-St-Paul "sum[med] up the French Canadian way of life."[119] To their minds, "perhaps it does [sum it up], insofar as one isolated spot can be typical of a huge area like Quebec."[120] Reading between the lines, they were, in effect, suggesting that other places in the province could be considered authentically French Canadian as well. Their point of view, in fact, best reflected English Canadians' overall understanding of what the *habitants* stood for. They incarnated the old Quebec these writers were so drawn to, but it is likely that their access to more diversified sources of information back home allowed for a more multifaceted view of the province's French population.

The English Canadian perspective is distinctive in other ways, as they were more interested in discussing French–English relations than Americans. This is perhaps to be expected, as they were likely more familiar with the complicated, at times antagonistic, interaction between the two groups. In fact, they attempted to dispel what they understood to be readers' wrong-headed prejudices and assumptions about French Canadians, including the *habitants*. In this way, they positioned themselves as Canadian nationalist mediators, particularly when they reported their experiences in regions of the province where the French and English lived side by side. Thus, while visiting a village north of Montreal, George Pearson assured that "there is no ill-feeling, and racial trouble of any kind never occurs, the only noticeable antagonism being a tendency for each [group] to favour its own race in its business dealings and social life."[121] Speaking more generally of the border separating Ontario and Quebec, the Mackenzies acknowledged, "from time to time, people have tried to turn this boundary line into some kind of barrier." However, they insisted, "it is no barrier. It is not even a good sized hurdle, unless you are given to making mountains out of molehills."[122]

More specifically, others hoped to prove wrong those who found it difficult to believe that French Quebeckers could be loyal Canadians. William Mac-Millan, who lived in Quebec City, explained that, "while the laws, houses, narrow streets and street names, all are as French as French can be" and that "over ninety-five percent of the people are French," they are "loyal French Canadians nevertheless."[123] While their observations likely reinforced readers' sense that their French compatriots' nationalist inclinations were not entirely in line with their own, they meant to be reassuring. The frequency and intensity with which English Canadians travel writers tried to challenge their compatriots' concerns about their loyalty were intensified by the political context at the time of writing, most obviously so during the Second World War and shortly thereafter – a period particularly fraught with conflict on the home front between French and English Canadians. In 1948, Eva-Lis Wuorio made clear to readers that they would nonetheless be most welcome in Quebec: "This however, in no way diminishes the Quebecer's innate hospitality ... The English and French within Quebec [city] intermingle in service clubs, did their yeoman work together during the war for Victory Loans and speak one another's tongues fluently."[124] Emphasizing good relations is to be expected from travel writers hired to convince prospective English Canadian tourists to visit Quebec who may have wondered if they would be made to feel welcome. However, it would be an oversimplification to reduce their positive portrayal of French–English relations as chiefly motivated by this type of professional consideration. Overall, their views were consistent with the attitudes of many English Canadians who upheld a *bonne ententiste* understanding of ethnic relations in Canada. It was sustained by a conviction that, despite tensions and misunderstandings, French and English had succeeded in forging bonds founded on mutual respect and accommodation and that this *bonne entente* had and *should* continue to endure through thick and thin.

In fact, a few travel writers represented their Francophone compatriots as more admirable than English Canadians. Some made such claims quite forcefully, including William Macmillan who intoned, "there is no place in it [Quebec City] for the superiority-complexed Anglo-Canadian who steadfastly refuses to recognize the Quebecois as his equal."[125] Much in the same line, George Pearson marvelled at their "care for beauty and the art of living," contrary to the English summer residents, whose philosophy of life is "the struggle for dollars, their great achievement is to beat last year's sales record or to take a few strokes off their golf course."[126] Often times, English Canadian travel writers brought up the French language to encourage readers to look favourably on their compatriots. As might be expected, they were less taken aback than Americans by the fact that French Quebeckers were actually French speakers. Novelist Hugh MacLennan did note that Quebec patois could "mak[e] the purist shudder," but it could easily be accounted for by the fact that "French Canada was cut off from its motherland before the Industrial Revolution" and injected with English nouns and verbs.[127] Mostly though, they were more likely to point out Francophones' enviable bilingualism making clear that visitors would be warmly welcomed and in their own language.

Some English Canadian writers were more explicit than others at wanting to repair relations between the "two solitudes." George Pearson, in 1926, was commissioned by *Maclean's* magazine's editor to produce a four-part series on French Quebec as a fence-mending exercise. The editor believed that in English Canada there "exist[s] suspicion against Quebec and the French Canadian," which "arises from the fact that the people of the other provinces know very little about French Canadians." In fact, Pearson candidly admitted that he, too, once harboured such prejudices. Growing up in Ontario, he was told that the French in Quebec were "lazy, ignorant," and he harboured "unfounded prejudice against a dim, far-off mysterious Quebec, and a people of another language and religion, [supposedly] steeped in ignorance and superstition and anti-British prejudice, a sort of ill-conditioned foreigner, not Canadian at all." With the passage of time, he had learned otherwise, and wanted to set the record straight, as he now realized that it was simply "a wrong assumption" to view the countryside *habitants* as the authentic French Canadian. He explained that "this assumption is right only to the extent one wishes to study the ideal French Canadian, the old habitant type." Instead, "if one wishes to study the French Canadian as he is and not as he ought to be, one must study the French Canadian who has effected those contacts with a broader, if not a better life." Yet, for all these good intentions, he included comments that directly undermined his efforts when he affirmed that "the old habitant type is not disappearing" and that to dispute this was the equivalent of "say[ing] the French Canadian race is dying out."[128] The images illustrating his article further entrenched his double representation of French Quebeckers. (See figure 4.5.) To say nothing of the fact that Pearson's depiction of the *habitants* did not significantly depart from the infantilizing one so prevalent elsewhere.

Another self-appointed cultural go-between was Richard Finnie, an acclaimed documentary filmmaker reputed for his work on the Canadian North and the Inuit. He, too, regretted that "English Canadians who do not understand them are sometimes prone to dismiss the habitants ... as backward, primitive folk without a great deal to recommend them." He set out to put to and the woods and the vigor and swing and rhythm of the pioneers and the work the songs were composed for or adapted to old French airs. The most deservedly popular of all, 'Allouette' (The Lark) obviously has its origin in another land where the lark was ever present, but no one who has ever heard it sung at a French-Canadian gathering in Quebec can ever forget it. The Quebecois have made it their own. In France, such of these songs as are still preserved by the common people. In Quebec they belong to all and are sung by all, as much the possession of the educated classes as of the most illiterate farm boy, and a part of the lives of both.

Barbeau has said that it is often difficult for him to secure certain songs for phonograph record because the singers are accustomed to sing them to work which is complementary, spinning, weaving or what not, so closely are the songs and the work of the people related. There are songs for canoeing and work in the woods, songs for beating flax and chopping wood, fishing, beating the wash, threshing the grain, mending sails and mending nets, making snowshoes, moccasins, and curing skins, songs for paddling, songs for rowing, each attuned to the rhythm of its labor. Such songs require no music with them, their background is their work, the soft 'dip dip' of the paddle, the smack of the axe, the steady thrum of the spinning wheel. But for songs of the dance and other jollity there is in the country always, the fiddle, and in the woods, because it is easier to carry and is less spoil for the robber, the mouth-organ and the har-monica.

A Real May Festival

IN THIS year, when the sixtieth anniversary of the federation of the provinces into the Dominion of Canada will be celebrated, un-officially unrelated to that event but peculiarly a part of it, there will be celebrated in Quebec on the twentieth of May, a Folk Song Festival which will introduce anew to this continent, to which they first came three hundred years ago, a complete repertory of these songs, both in French and in singable English translations.

There will be three days of fun and music. To Quebec will come the principal singers of French-Canadian folk-lore, and with them women in picturesque garb from Isle Dorion, Baie St. Paul, and more remote portions of the province, with their spinning-wheels and looms, and they will spin and weave to the accompaniment of the old songs. There will be fishermen from Gaspe who will sing as they mend their nets and sails, and representatives of all the ancient crafts. A complete display of Canadian handicrafts from the National Museum in Ottawa will be shown in order that the handicrafts and the singing, complementary to one another as they are, may be seen and heard together. Each class of handicrafts and songs will have its proper setting. The ancient household arts will be practised indoors in the Chateau Frontenac, and the ruder labor of the men will be staged outdoors before a replica of an old house amid the trees, the St. Lawrence gleaming in the distance.

The close association between folksong and

Upper: *Old Gilbert Marin, of Echouerir. Gaspé, fisherman and authority on the folk songs of his race.*

Centre: *Visitors to the Quebec festival will be able to see the ancient art of spinning, first introduced to New France by the ladies of the seigneuries when they were unable to obtain fabrics from France, owing to the capture of a vessel by the British.*

Lower: *Madame Gedeon Bouchard, who has delighted thousands of French-Canadians with her recitals of old French legends.*

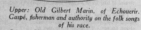

handicrafts will be illustrated by skilled spinners and weavers and other workers and singers from the country districts, who will demonstrate the complete process of making flax into thread and linen, the spinning and weaving of homespun cloth, the hooking of rugs, and the making of the gay colored sashes, *ceintures flechees*, as practised at L'Assomption also will be shown. There will, in addition, be such a gathering of artists and such music on this theme as has never occurred on this continent before, if anywhere. The best musical artists and most distinguished composers of music in Canada will attend to contribute to the occasion and to gather material for compositions that will assist in the hoped-for renaissance of Quebec folk songs. The Basilica choir of Quebec, which has a tradition of singing unequalled in North America, will sing a fully choral Gregorian High Mass as well as old French hymns and other reminders of an ancient musical past. Another equally renowned organization, the *Chanteurs de*

Ste. *Dominique* will render modern compositions of native composers based on the folk music, and the Hart House Quartette, of Toronto, will render new works on the folk theme composed for this occasion, all this against the natural background of the ancient capital of French Canada which is, in its outward aspect, more seventeenth century European than much of Europe.

Charles Marchand, a singer who has made an intelligent study of these songs, and has a genius for them, will depict in his interpretations every type of *habitant* from the coquettish *demoiselle* to the jovial *bonhomme*. The acting of these songs is as important, if not more so, than their singing, and he captures alike their plaintiveness, their rollicking humor and their *joie de vivre*. In his interpretations he is the very spirit of French-Canada.

Groups of boys and girls will sing the *rondelles*, those centuries old children's "rounds" alive with the spirit of the child world. Others will sing the *pastourelles*, *complaintes* and *spirituelles*; narrative poems striking strong notes of vibrant joy or intense sorrow which characterize this music of an ancient race. Phileas Bedard, farmer, and Vincent Ferrier de Repentigny, night-watchman in a Montreal factory, great folk-lorists both, will give the choicest selections in their repertory. These men do more than sing. They act. To see and hear Bedard sing and act his 'Shoemaker's Song', one need not understand French to partake of its uproarious enjoyment as he sits and cobbles an imaginary shoe at an imaginary bench gossiping with and about the village. De Repentigny is in a class by himself. E. Z. Massicotte, the archivist of Montreal, and an indefatigable worker in this field, relates that being desirous of hearing de Repentigny's repertoire, the latter sang for him thirty songs a day for ten days, each one different and all from memory, and even then had not exhausted his repertory. He comes by it honestly. In the days when every French gentleman prided himself on his ability to sing a song relating the love of knight and damsel to his lady, there was a Pierre Legard de Repentigny who is mentioned in the *Jesuit Relations* of the early seventeenth century who was familiar with the French court where these songs were then in great vogue. And in 1705, when the ship which carried the annual supply of Parisian dress materials and frocks to the ladies of New France, was captured by the English, an ancestress, Madame de Repentigny, who was a social leader of that time, organized the great ladies in a body with the purpose of influencing the farmers on their seigneuries to grow flax and sheep, and

Continued on page 70

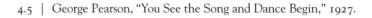

4.5 | George Pearson, "You See the Song and Dance Begin," 1927.

rest his compatriots' prejudices in 1935 by heading for the Gaspé and Anti-costi Island to collect material for a three-part documentary series, *Folkways in Rural Quebec*, which included "Wandering Through French Canada," "Rural Quebec Folk Ways: 17th Century France in 20th Century Canada," and "Feudal Anticosti."[129] He also shared his findings with a wider audience – including prospective tourists – through articles that appeared in popular or specialized Canadian and American magazines.[130] Yet, as with George Pearson, his reading of Quebec's rural areas did not depart significantly from *habitant* representations prospective tourists could encounter in literature, at school, or in government publicity. His films' titles suggest as much, as do his observations. While he clearly greatly admired the *habitants*, all too often he simply reiterated a commonplace and condescending antimodernist re-frain: "In this age of speed we might do well to learn from them how better to enjoy life in a simple, leisurely manner … [though] as yet relatively little affected by modern civilization." Furthermore, by making the point that his "photographic experience with the Eskimos stood [him] in good stead with the *habitants*," he was suggesting that he viewed the *habitants* as worthy of anthropological attention – not primitive, but still not part and parcel of the modern world:

> I had learned that the only satisfactory way to film primitive Eskimos was thoroughly to accustom them to the presence of the camera, sometimes for days, before starting to take pictures, and then they would pay no attention to it. With the *habitants*, however, much less patience was required. While many of them had, like the Eskimos, never before seen a motion picture camera, they were more readily capable of understanding its function and would react accordingly.[131]

Such comments further underscore the extent to which in the eyes of travel writers the Indigenous peoples of the province were in effect the French Que-beckers, and, in the end, Richard Finnie, just as other English Canadians who explicitly set out to alter assumptions and prejudices of English Canadians hoping to encounter the habitants, likely contributed by reinforcing widely circulated cultural stereotypes. (See figure 4.6.)

It remains that English Canadian travel writers proved to be much more interested than their American counterparts in establishing the extent to which modernity had reached the Old Quebec countryside. They concurred that modernity had only recently made its way there – regardless of when they were visiting Quebec – but were more open than Americans to recog-nizing signs of it and clearly more willing to bring up the topic. What best

Setting up a loom preparatory to the weaving of homespun, Baie St. Paul, Charlevoix County.

Madame Joseph Plante at her spinning-wheel; St. Pierre, Island of Orléans.

4.6 | Richard Finnie, "Filming Rural French Canada," 1937.

characterizes this distinctly English Canadian open mindedness is the fact that several alerted readers that they should expect to discover, in rural parts of the province, a world in transition, and they did so early in the period. As Mathew Trill put it, in the 1930s, travelling along the St Lawrence River was to discover "the Old World on the threshold of the new."[132] By the 1940s, and most typically after the Second World War, this double imaging of the countryside became commonplace. G.W. Peter, who remarked that the *habitants* used farm technology that was a "hundred years old," cautioned readers that, "it would be wrong to get the impression that Quebec has resisted the march of time."[133] By the 1950s, English Canadian travel writers' accounts would simply include more such remarks.

This is not to say that some English Canadians would not be taken aback or simply disappointed to discover signs of modernization in the countryside – a constant reminder that their reactions were shaped by predeparture expectations. This was the case with the Mackenzies, who remarked that on the Île d'Orléans a "surprise was in store for us ... A number of the prosperous farms have modern tractors, telephones and electric light."[134] Carlton McNaught and his wife were clearly disillusioned by the "industrial fever" they encountered in Chicoutimi. Having set out to visit their imagined Quebec, they wondered, could "it be, we asked ourselves, that this is the country which produced Maria Chapdelaine?" Yet, in no instance do English Canadian travel writers give an impression that such discoveries marred their enjoyment. As long as the past was in view, signs of modernity could be made to accommodate their predeparture expectations about the countryside. The Mackenzies, for example, reassured readers that on the Île d'Orléans, "farmers have adopted what is good from the present without sacrificing the traditions of their historic past."[135] Echoing the analysis of Helen Augur, Blodwen Davies accounted for the *habitants'* gradual conversion to modernity by situating it in a wider, international context. Writing about the Gaspé, she theorized, "the Second World War [has] brought profound changes to the economic and social life of the Peninsula and one by one old customs are yielding to the awakening of Gaspé to modern life."[136]

Most of those who ventured into the northern mining and power-generating regions of the province expected to encounter modern economic development and wholeheartedly admired it. Overall English Canadian travel writers were impressed by the "tremendous industrial developments" they encountered.[137] On site, their comments were much the same as their American counterparts. Thus, some encouraged readers to seek out areas where modern economic expansion was in full view. And, they were also amazed by Arvida. To their minds, "there is something fantastic about this beautiful city that sprang, full-fledged, from the architects' drafting boards." Clearly then, as with their more varied and contradictory accounts of what prospective visitors might expect to find in the Quebec countryside, English Canadian travel writers were more likely to recognize and admire the province's gradual but undeniable modernization. This surely has much to do with their greater exposure – particularly in school by the 1940s – to detailed information about the province's contemporary economic progress. As adults, they would also have been more aware than Americans of Canadian public debates about their country's modern industrial development, including the one taking place in Quebec. As proud Canadians as well, they may have been less inclined to overly emphasize that some parts of their homeland were completely out of step with the modern world. Put together with their reactions to the *habitant* and modernization in the Quebec countryside, it is clear that, in contrast to their American counterparts, English Canadian travel writers provided a more detailed and multifaceted account of the province. While many of their predeparture experiences predisposed them as well to search for an old Quebec, and to find it, these had also better prepared them to see beyond the old and made it possible for them to represent a many-sided "authentic" Quebec.

FRENCH QUEBEC TRAVEL WRITERS

As one would expect, reactions of French Quebec travel writers to the province's countryside differed considerably from those of Americans and English Canadians. It should be noted that generalizations about their reactions are based on fewer accounts, notably fewer book-length accounts, as fewer were published. Some newspapers, such as *La Presse*, published relatively more travel accounts describing the province's tourist sites, notably in the 1920s.[138] *Le Soleil* tended to publish more articles related to government initiatives or columns and editorials advising ways in which state officials could be more successful tourist promoters.[139]

Not surprisingly, for French Quebeckers, travel experiences would be much less about visiting a foreign land. Reflective of this was the fact that they typically used possessive articles and pronouns when describing sites and landscapes of interest. Travelling in Quebec was visiting their *chez nous*. They essentially drew direct links of belonging between themselves and this destination in ways even English Canadians did not. More significantly, while they did advise their compatriots to head for the countryside or remote fishing areas, they equally touted the province's wilderness areas including the Laurentians. The Gaspé drew a lot of attention, since this was a region that had long been inaccessible to the wider French Quebec public, they too were keen to discover this "region still very ancient, almost unknown, but that we were burning to travel."[140] But contrary to English North American travel writers – and the distinction is significant – they did not claim that travelling to these more remote areas would provide an opportunity to literally time travel to an old Quebec, and they certainly did not claim that visitors would find there their "true homeland." Instead, they would discover the homeland previously occupied by their forefathers, the source of their "ancestral traditions."[141] More to the point, such regions would first and foremost *remind* them of their past, not be places where they could see it fully acted out. Thus, in the 1920s, visitors could discover in the Gaspé "small, old houses in French style [which] evokes recollections of another age."[142] Ten years later it was described as "a land of legends and beautiful stories; a land of memories and mysteries,"[143] with "historical souvenirs, old churches, century old houses, ruins, [which] remind us that numerous generations have succeeded themselves on this corner of earth so deeply *canadien* and French."[144] What also made the Lower St Lawrence worth seeing was that it had been "the witness of the first efforts of the pioneers and the first battles of the French race in America."[145] Into the 1950s, prospective tourists would learn that there the Lévis road "crossed villages steeped in history,"[146] and that other regions in the province could call to mind the past as well. In short, travelling through the Quebec countryside during this whole period would be, for many, the equivalent of embarking on a pilgrimage through a land replete with collective memories shared by writers and readers alike. In this they reacted much as did local residents elsewhere who, as historian David Glassberg points out, "look at the landscape as a web of memory sites and social interactions" whereas non-residents "look for novelty in a landscape, what is not back home."[147]

In line with this distinctive outlook, French Quebec travel writers also invited prospective tourists to gaze at the Quebec landscape as would students of history. According to a *Le Soleil* journalist "tourism must not remain known as simple *vagabondage*, could we say: it should serve to teach the history and geography of our country."[148] The history they were referring to was very much the one they and readers were exposed to in their childhood history classes – more specifically, what they had learned of French Canadian heroic feats. Thus, much attention was given to sites that confirmed they were the descendants of brave ancestors who were mostly explorers, missionaries, pioneers, and defenders of their race. None however was given to places that might have specifically reminded them of their ancestors past relations with Indigenous peoples whether friend or foe. To be sure, some of the sites were the same highlighted by their English-speaking counterparts; however, French

Quebecers viewed them through a different lens and infused them with different meaning. At times, such mediated contact with the past could be a deeply and directly emotional experience in ways not suggested by English-speaking North Americans. In the Gaspé, for instance, "many holiday places are close to three hundred years old and they possess ... an antique character that grips a city dweller at the throat only barely inclined to emotions."[149]

Reactions to Quebec City are telling in this respect as well. While English-speaking travel writers associated it with the seat of New France governors, to a French Quebec author it conjured up memories of the "sublime endurance of the pioneers ... as heroic in front of the vindictive Indian as they were with the New England 'settlers' [sic], all this immortalized by the rock of Quebec; one must tread ... piously, a guide book in hand, in order not to ignore its glorious past."[151] Furthermore, contrary to English-speaking North Americans, French Quebec travel writers could take for granted that French Quebec readers had a more comprehensive knowledge of the province's history. They, therefore, provided more detailed descriptions of the past, peopled with individuals whose reputation did not reach that of well-known figures, such as a Jacques Cartier or a Samuel de Champlain. Thus, for example, they frequently mentioned the names of local seigneurs and curés. Such information could only be of interest to those with a more direct understanding of social hierarchies distinctive to the province or who had an "insider" interest in local history. They also referred to events that, while not requiring the knowledge of an erudite, assumed a solid background in Quebec history. For example, an author reporting on the Richelieu Valley mentioned, in passing, "this Valley is a precious repository of history. The principal episodes of the troubles of 1837–38 took place there."[151] And they obviously assumed that readers had an understanding of the seigneurial system when mentioning the moulin banal.[152]

French Quebec travel writers did recognize that the rural and fishing populations of Quebec had succeeded in maintaining links with past traditions more than any others in the province, but nowhere did they uphold these people as the authentic French Quebeckers. Although traditional nationalists, including some government tourist promoters, such as Albert Tessier, or writers, such as Adjutor Rivard, certainly did, travel writers published in the popular press would likely have been reticent to venture onto the minefield of "identity politics." Doing so, regardless of their own nationalist allegiances, would, at the very least, risk casting doubt on to the national authenticity of city-dwelling readers. Yet, the Gaspé did stand out for them as the area that "reminds the visitor of a corner of earth of the old Normandy."[153] Here the population remained "faithful to the traditions left behind by the

17th century Basques and Bordeaux fishermen."[154] Furthermore, these accounts were often paired with photographs of *habitants* (or fishermen) involved in some kind of traditional activity reminiscent of those illustrating
the accounts of English-speaking travel writers. Together with a text on the
municipality of Les Éboulements, for instance, were photos of an "old oven
still in operation" and "butter day on a farm'" and of people "leaving mass at
the parish church."[155] Such depictions certainly echoed many English North
American travellers' observations, which suggests that, occasionally, French
Quebec travel writers chose to represent an "Old Quebec." But these were
likely meant to grab readers' attention rather than provide evidence that
Quebec was essentially old. Indeed, similarities do not go much beyond this.
French Quebec travel writers were clearly not fascinated by the *habitants* and
they certainly showed no interest in searching for them. In fact, rarely did
they use the term "*habitant.*" They were much more liable to write about "our
farmers" or the "locals."[156] To French Quebec travel writers, those living in
places such as the Gaspé were simply compatriots who held one of several
types of occupations. More significantly, contrary to English-speaking travel
writers, French Quebeckers' descriptions of the way of life of the rural population were few and much less detailed, and they certainly did not figure as
prominently in their accounts. Prospective French Quebec tourists would be
hard pressed to learn much about the way of life of the province's rural or
fishing population. (And, of course, no mention was ever made of the language they spoke.) There was no need: their readers were very familiar with
rural life or fishing, whether it be through friends, family, or other sources, if
not by experience. In line with this distinct outlook, French Quebec travel
writers also very rarely recounted their experiences interacting with the local
population. When they did, it was mostly to point to the gracious hospitality provided. Overall, the *habitants* could be counted on to offer comfort-
able accommodation.

In short, they were in no way textbook antimodernists in search of a
folk. This being said, occasionally, their observations did recall American
and English Canadian writers' condescending characterizations of the happy
habitants. Readers were informed that in places such as the Gaspé, "everywhere life unfolds serenely, smoothly, we would say carefree. It is the charm
of the lower-Quebec society with its simple … life, ignorant of or disdainful of
the trepidations of the big cities and this passive acceptance of happy and unhappy events."[157] However, such infantilizing descriptions stand out more for
their infrequency. These were antimodernists to the extent that they viewed
travelling in the countryside or other nonurban settings as a way to escape
their everyday lives into a restful, pastoral, and picturesque environment or

in wilder forested landscapes. Indeed, French Quebec travel writers made the point that for "city dwellers tired of the city noises and work," the province "can offer absolute tranquility in a scenic decor the wildest and grandiose imaginable."[158]

What stands out more than anything else is that these accounts were also meant to draw readers' attention to the beauty of the landscape. Detailed descriptions of each region's particular scenic attractions outnumbered, by far, references to history or the old world traditions of their inhabitants. Prospective tourists were meant to understand that it was the province's breathtaking landscape that would make their trip so enjoyable/worthwhile. Thus, the Laurentians were of interest, particularly because of the wild scenery – a magnet for those who wanted to hunt and fish. The Saguenay–Lac St-Jean area, too, was primarily lauded for its breathtaking scenery. If it was occasionally referred to as Maria Chapdelaine country, no connections were drawn between it and the traditional society depicted in the novel, and no mention was made of Éva Bouchard.[159] The fact that scenery was brought to the fore when describing the Gaspé is especially telling. To French Quebec travel writers, it was not so much its people that stood as its central drawing card but its picturesque landscapes, its charm "made of so many numerous elements, the panorama's splendour, the beaming sunshine extending a golden hue on the crest of audacious mountains, the sea breeze coming offshore, the immense sea stretching to the confines of the horizon."[160]

Signs of modernity were not ignored, though mostly limited to brief descriptions of the dominant industries in the various regions of the province, drawing reader attention to dairy and sugar maple industry in the Eastern Townships and shipyards in Sorel, for example.[161] As for Quebec City, readers were informed that while it "has conserved almost intact its past *physionomie* ... Quebec is equipped with a most modern port and of all the comforts progress can bring."[162] Unlike English-speaking North American writers, however, they did so more matter of factly, expressing neither surprise nor disappointment. Clearly, modernity did not disrupt preconceived expectations. At best, industrial development and modern economic growth could inspire an understated sense of proprietary satisfaction.[163] Not surprisingly, the Lac St-Jean region was often singled out as deserving of high praise. This was where "one finds oneself in one of the most progressive districts of the province [and] more than anything else" it provided "the satisfaction of noting the fantastic progress of our province."[164]

French Quebec travel writers had the least to say on the issue of French–English relations. Since they did not spend much time discussing people per se, perhaps this should not be entirely surprising. Comments offered were

essentially short asides and arose mostly when describing the Eastern Townships. Invariably, it was to make a *bonne ententise* point that this was where
to encounter French and English populations who lived side-by-side in harmony. As one writer exultingly put it, the region stood out as a "magnificent
bilingual milieu specimen! We meet here the two races, at times mingled and
merged, often distinct in a proximity that respects the integrity of each, or,
more rarely standing separately."[165]

Overall, the reactions of French Quebec travel writers were very much
shaped by the fact that Quebec was their *chez nous*. They were not observ-
ing a people so different and remote that prospective tourists would need
interpreters to make sense of their behaviour. At most, visiting the province's countryside offered an opportunity to commune with their ancestors
indirectly by coming into contact with vestiges of the past. While the country people might, at times, remind them of seventeenth-century Old France
habitants, what attracted them most to the province's remote areas was that
it offered a unique chance to immerse their city-weary selves in a soothing
and beautiful landscape – much as would any countryside regardless of time
and place. As for the modern Quebec, it could only be a source of pride.

Travel writers' reactions to the province, whether they were from English-
speaking North America or Quebec, confirm that theirs were very much
shaped by their respective predeparture expectations whether those were
novels, visual representations, or school textbooks. Reactions also echoed
much of what they would have learned about Quebec in provincial government tourist publicity. It is not surprising, then, that Americans, English Canadians, and French Quebeckers had distinctive perspectives and responded to
the sites and people of Quebec each in their own way. While reactions of
American and English Canadians were often similar, they differed enough
to confirm that different national identities lead to different representations
of the province. Thus, Americans were essentially predisposed to view Quebec as a seventeenth-century New France, and this is clearly what they believed they had found across their border. English Canadians, for their part,
had a more multifaceted view of the province. National pride and a more
extensive knowledge of Quebec's history and achievements better prepared
them to see it as both old and new. As for French Quebec travel writers' reactions, theirs were altogether different. In many ways, they reacted to it as one
would when visiting a cherished childhood home – one that evoked nostalgic
memories of a distant past. But first and foremost they lauded Quebec as a
destination of natural beauty, enhanced, at best, by faint echoes of the past.

5

MONTREAL: A CITY
OF CONTRASTS

"Montreal was frontier Paris,
a Habitant Manhattan."[1]

For travel writers, Quebec's countryside and *habitants* were equally as compelling and popular as metropolitan Montreal – an archetype of the modern urban industrial city in Canada rivalled only by Toronto.[2] And while provincial government promoters, along with their municipal counterparts, primarily imagined the province as old, they simultaneously marketed Montreal as an attractive tourist destination, specifically for its alluring, urban attributes. Promoters praised the city as a centre of tremendous industrial and commercial output and for its various incarnations of modern sophistication – features that were clearly at polar opposites to those represented by a seventeenth-century New France in America. Montreal, therefore, requires separate consideration, as it contradicts in many ways previous conclusions as to what promoters wanted to showcase about the province and why travel writers were drawn to Quebec. How is it that so many prominent French Quebec tourism promoters, propelled as many were by a desire to use tourism as a means to rejuvenate Quebec's traditional French character, reconciled this objective with marketing the attractions of the province's quintessential hub of modernity? Moreover, considering the way in which English-speaking North American travel writers represented the city, their reactions to Montreal offer an opportunity to explore more fully what they understood to be distinctive about French Quebeckers. Many singled out the *habitants*. But what did they make of their city-dwelling compatriots? The reactions of French Quebec travel writers to the city proved much more difficult to come by. This has to do with the fact that so many were, in fact, targeting city dwellers, hoping to get away from places such as Montreal to enjoy the relaxing countryside amenities.

THE MONTREAL TOURIST AND CONVENTION BUREAU

One could argue that provincial promoters, such as Albert Tessier and Paul Gouin, did not need to reconcile their traditional views of French Quebec's authentic identity with Montreal's promotion, as both municipal and provincial promoters, in effect, played a very limited role in marketing the city as a tourist destination. This responsibility mostly fell on the shoulders of the city's English private sector, through the Montreal Tourist and Convention Bureau (MTCB). It had a double mandate: it was charged with convincing prospective convention organizers that Montreal was "the ideal convention city" in which "large, luxurious hotels afford the perfect 'Home, away from home' as well as every scope for meetings."[3] It also acted as the city's principal tourist promoter and would do so well into the late 1950s. In fact, during the mid-1930s, 30 per cent of its budget was spent on advertising, which was "approximately $300,000."[4]

As for the municipal government, by the late 1930s, it provided only a small yearly amount of funding to the MTCB in recognition of its contribution. Evidence suggests that, during this period, this arrangement proved satisfactory. As *Le Canada* observed in 1939, the MTCB "has filled a gap" produced by the "municipal authorities ... and is in effect very efficient," thus, establishing a city office would be a needless overlap.[5] However, some travel writers occasionally remarked upon this exceptional situation, suggesting instead that it was a drawback. Kennedy Crone, for one, pointed out that "Montreal is one of the few Canadian or American cities without a highly organized Publicity Department and as a city does not even issue a map or a street guide, except to local policemen."[6] Regardless, city officials clearly did not think the situation warranted much attention. In 1937, they did create an Office of Economic Development, and, in 1944, it acquired the added responsibility for tourism development. However, the mandate of this new Office municipal d'initiative économique et touristique (OMIET) was very broad and it ended up focusing most of its energies on attracting new industries and encouraging local entrepreneurship.

While the provincial government did not overlook promoting the city, as noted earlier, it had other priorities. Its early forays into the tourism business focused on the countryside, building new roads reaching into remote areas and developing and lending support to local hospitality industries. In Montreal, less involvement seemed to be required. In fact, the city was often used by the newly interventionist government officials as a measure against which to contrast the underdeveloped state of the industry beyond the city's limits. This is not entirely surprising. For one, road access to the city in the early decades of the twentieth century was never the challenge it was for travellers hoping to visit rural areas. Before the growing popularity of car travel this access was provided to many tourists by boat and rail transportation companies. The two largest transportation companies in Canada, Canadian National Railway (CNR) and privately owned Canada Steamship Lines (CSL), had their headquarters in Montreal. Furthermore, these companies and others had developed an impressive hospitality infrastructure, which included well established luxury hotels. And most large companies produced their own widely circulated publicity, to say nothing of the fact that the city was well provided with restaurants and entertainment opportunities.

Further consolidating the private sector's control over the city's tourism industry and promotion was the fact that many well-established Montreal businesses were members of the MTCB. The organization was created at the instigation of the Automobile Club of Canada in 1919 and brought together the likes of Henry Birks and Sons Ltd, Henry Morgan and Co Ltd, CSL, CNR, Hotel Windsor, and Hotel Ritz-Carlton, and was directed by J.R. Douglas, the president of the Automobile Club of Canada, during its first five years of operation. While a few French Quebec representatives from l'Association des commerçants, and a well-established French Canadian retail store, Dupuis frères, were in attendance, it remains that the MTCB was dominated by members of the English Canadian business elite who controlled Quebec's "manufacturing and financial institutions."[7] It raised the better part of its funds "from merchants, hotels and transportation companies." And while the bureau received "a very small contribution from the city of Montreal,"[8] it made the point in some of its promotional material of specifying that it was "not a branch of Federal, Provincial or Municipal government, nor are we in any manner affiliated with a Board of Trade or Chamber of Commerce."[9]

From the outset, the US was its principal marketing target. As Theodore Morgan, then MTCB president, explained, during the 1934 hearings of the Special Committee on Tourist Traffic, "[o]ur policy has been to spend our money as far as possible in the US, where the greatest mass of the tourist business came from."[10] Indeed, during its first year of operation it produced 500 copies of a brochure and tourist map of the city, 90 per cent of which were distributed in the US. By the 1930s, "it distribute[d] yearly some 200,000 pieces of literature in addition to the aggressive and fruitful campaign which employs advertisements and news articles in leading daily newspapers and magazines of the US."[11] There are no indications, though, that the MTCB made any attempt to invite or escort American or English Canadian travel writers to the city. Was this a result of budgetary constraints or did it feel that

Where the Indian village of Hochelaga nestled beside Mount Royal before Columbus found the New World, graceful modern structures now dot Montreal's impressive skyline.

5.1 | Front cover of *Montreal: Ancient and Modern*, 1930.

its own direct publicity, that of its members, and the city's wider reputation were sufficient to draw in tourists? Likely a bit of all three.

What first stands out, in contrast to provincial promoters, is that non-revenue-generating considerations, including ways to imagine the city to satisfy concerns over identity, were clearly not an MTCB preoccupation. More specifically, tourist promotion would not be viewed by the city's English-speaking advertisers as a means to an "existential end" in the way it was for several key French Quebec tourist promoters. This being said, the MTCB's branding choices do allow us to indirectly bring out some aspects of the dominant English business community's sense of identity in a majority French Quebec city. From the outset, the MTCB marketed Montreal as a city of contrasts, "full of places of interest both ancient and modern,"[12] where "history rubs shoulders with modernity ... [where] the old and the new are strikingly blended."[13] (See figure 5.1.) In doing so it was echoing the publicity put out independently by several of its members, notably hotel and transportation companies. Indeed, the CPR also pointed out, "near its skyscrapers are one-storied buildings whose crumbling stones tell of bygone centuries."[14] In fact, on some occasions, identical descriptions of certain sites appeared in both sets of publicity materials. This stands to reason as members of the MTCB, they could hardly be expected to represent the city differently.

What could arguably make this ubiquitous "city of contrast" slogan an identity statement on the part of English Canadian advertisers was their representation of the city's past as embodied by its French-speaking population. Montreal was "different from any other city in the world in that it harbors two distinct peoples ... The French Canadian race, the first to settle here, is responsible for the old, quaint section of the City and, as time went on, the English settlers came and the two races grew side by side. Today they intermingle in all the districts around Montreal but the quaint French district still remains the same."[15] The MTCB's tourism publicity was, in many ways, accurate: the city's first European inhabitants were French and were, thus, by definition, the Montrealers who left behind the city's oldest colonial reminders of the past. However, some "city of contrasts" ads conveyed more than this, suggesting to visitors that some of the city's contemporary French population would remind them of their *habitant* ancestors. The fact that the Bonsecours market – often referred to as the "Bonsecours Habitant Market Place" – was given such prominence in MTCB publicity could very well have served to reinforce the connections it drew between French Montrealers and the traditional *habitants*. (See figure 5.2.) Of all the city's majority French neighbourhoods to choose from, MTCB publicity invariably identified the Bonsecours market as *the* city enclave where visitors could encounter them. The ads did make the point that this market attracted "the country *habitants* [who] flock [to the market] with their little carts and their homespun clothing. Amid the noise of Norman patois over the 'trente sous,' the 'neuf francs' or the 'un écu.'"[16] Yet, prospective tourists could easily be left with an impression that, even in the country's largest metropolis, its French population as a whole remained a people of the past – city cousins to their countryside "relatives": "Even today some of the old two wheel buggies can be seen here. Seventeenth century French is spoken (also English) and if you decide to make a bargain at

Bon-Secours Market the oldest and largest open air market in Montréal, taking its name from the nearby church of Bon-Secours ("Our Lady of Good Help").

LORD NELSON (ON HIS COLUMN) TOWERS ABOVE THIS BUSY SCENE

Visit this crowded and colorful market scene; Habitant vendors bargain excitedly at vehicles and stalls. *Above* is seen one of the typical stalls with one of the pictorial plaques on Nelson's monument in the background.

MONUMENT TO PAUL DE CHOMEDY DE MAISONNEUVE

(*left*) stands in Place d'Armes, facing one of the most picturesque of churches in America—"Notre-Dame de Montréal."

Chateau de Ramezay, ancient landmark, erected in 1705 by the French governor whose name it bears. After the secession of Canada bought by the Crown. In 1775 residence of General Montgomery whose American forces took Montréal. Benjamin Franklin, Samuel Chase and Charles Carroll arrived here in 1776 seeking French Canadian support. Their mission failed, returned to Philadelphia in time to sign the Declaration of Independence.

5.2 | *Come to Montreal,* circa 1928–1930.

one of the interesting stalls you will be thrilled by the vivacious and charming personalities of the 'Canadiens.'"[17] Furthermore, several buildings singled out by MTCB publicity as worthy of interest were those dating back to the time when Montreal had been under French rule, again bolstering the sense that the past belonged to the city's French speaking-population.

And Montreal was also marketed as "one of this continent's richest cities for the churches and cathedrals,"[18] "with more chapels and churches than Rome itself."[19] While tourists were encouraged to visit a few notable Protestant churches, it was made clear that those most worthy of attention were Catholic – those largely frequented by French Montrealers. Of course, their sheer numbers would be reason enough to give them prominence. But the way MTCB promoters chose to draw attention to this unique Montreal attraction was a further reminder of French Montrealers' links to the past. They claimed, "visitors are fascinated by the religious and civic ceremonies which, while of ancient and time honoured origin, are still observed in Montreal – and nowhere else in the Americas."[20] To Catholic English North Americans, this type of information could easily suggest that French Montrealers were unaware of the evolving sectarian practices of their religion. As for Protestants, this characterization would have confirmed latent prejudices towards this "Papist" religion.

To reinforce the depiction of French Quebeckers as traditional people, the MTCB produced another advertising slogan, "Gateway to Beautiful Historic Canada,"[21] showcasing Montreal's surrounding areas as ideally situated destinations to experience Quebec's ethnic ancient-and-modern contrast. The MTCB clearly hoped to capitalize on the appeal of old Quebec. In fact, any number of excerpts drawn from its more detailed publicity confirms that it was borrowing directly from the provincial tourist marketing songbook: "The traveller by highway through rural Quebec finds it easy to believe that 'Je me souviens' (I remember), the motto of the Province, is no meaningless phrase but the expression of the spirit of a people who not only have a deep affection for the 'good old days' but have kept touch with them to a degree unknown elsewhere in the New World." Such advertising highlighted the classic markers of the old Quebec *habitants*' enduring presence, including the ubiquitous spinning wheel and outdoor bake oven. It also pointed to the rural population's ancient religious beliefs. Thus, the wayside shrines which travellers "[would] encount[er] every few miles" stood for "emblems of the simple and unquestioning faith of the French Canadian." In some instances, reader attention was drawn to New France vestiges of questionable authenticity when promoters drew attention to "another odd sight, rarely to be seen elsewhere ... the ancient well-sweep similar to that used in Egypt and the Orient from time immemorial, [and] still in use in many farm yards."[22]

In short, all MTCB advertising, whether about Montreal or sites further afield, associated the past exclusively with the French. In this respect, it suggests that, for English Montreal promoters, what made their city's French-speaking population distinct had not changed with time. This stands to reason, considering that English-speaking North Americans were generally predisposed to assume that French Canadians tenaciously held on to life on the land and their ancestral traditions, while they, in contrast, belonged to a people that embraced modernity. MTCB members learned to gaze upon their fellow French Montrealers in the same way. In fact, their own lived experience could only have made this stereotyping ring true. This was a time when, both professionally and socially, they encountered very few high-ranking French Quebec entrepreneurs. This further strengthened an inclination to view French Quebeckers as a people with little aptitude for business – in short, a quaint people still anchored in the past.

MTCB's representation of English Montrealers in its publicity is much less detailed. In the absence of any articulated justification for this, one is left to speculate. The MTCB may have been again following a basic best practice of tourism marketing, that is to emphasize difference, and French Montrealers, by far, offered it most. Why then allocate time and resources to showcasing a community with which these very same tourists would in all likelihood identify and one to which MTCB promoters belonged?

This being said, the MTCB simply did not bank on attracting prospective tourists or convention-goers by showcasing the city's ties to the past. It was, after all, an organization charged with promoting the business interests of its members who, in turn, hoped to convince outsiders that they offered the latest, up-to-date services. Montreal was first and foremost branded as modern. This explains why the board's more detailed publicity typically started by pointing to Montreal's dominant position as Canada's economic power centre. The idea was to inspire the awe of prospective visitors, potential investors, and convention planners. All were invited to "Montreal … Canada's Business Capital" – a recurring subtitle in most of its publicity brochures. MTCB promoters would unfailingly remind readers that Montreal had the largest population of any Canadian city and was nothing less than "the chief financial, commercial, industrial and transportation center of the Dominion."[23] The port of Montreal figured prominently in this promotion, along with detailed information about the impressive output of the city's main industries. Of course, of more direct value to MTCB members was advertising that offered targeted promotion of their own businesses. While its more detailed brochures did include a few names of hotels, stores, or restaurants, the general text and slogans mostly highlighted Montreal's overall modernity. This was an attribute all could share and guarded the MTCB against accusations of favouring one business over another. Thus, the caption accompanying several photographs of Montreal's large hotels (all owned by English Canadians) read, "A Gay Time for Tourists at any of the fine hotels." MTCB promoters showed here an understanding that city-dwelling Americans would be reluctant to forgo familiar modern comforts when heading for urban destinations. Readers were told that Montreal "has large department stores that would not be out of place in any large American city."[24] Likely to draw their attention even more, the city as a whole was advertised as a shoppers' paradise, where

Hundreds

CROWD THE

OF

Here are shops to suit everyone's taste and purse — small out-of-the-way shops where you poke around to your heart's content. Or large, modern and luxurious stores where you can spend days and days, getting just the things you want at lower prices than you have ever seen at home. Montréal is the very place, if you are shopping for sterling silver, antique or new, for woollen blankets, English haberdashery, furs, diamonds, smart English clothing and hats, Canadian-made specialties as well as articles from all parts of the British Empire. There's a cheery, pleasant feeling everywhere; everybody speaks English—unless you prefer to give your French a little airing.

5.3 | Shopping in Montreal in *Come to Montreal.*

consumers, both men and women, would benefit from more reasonable prices than those charged in the US. (See figure 5.3.)

Of course, MTCB promoters could not hope to lure prospective visitors by simply branding the city as modern and a more affordable American destination. They also foregrounded the appeal Montreal held for those searching unique, urban forms of entertainment and other epicurean pleasures. They invariably made the point that "Montreal is famous throughout North America for its cosmopolitan atmosphere and the vivacity of its night life. Here every taste is adeptly catered to with good food, good wine, good music and good

5.4 | Front cover of *Montreal: The Paris of
the New World* booklet, 1937.

shows."[25] Most reflective of this understanding is the bureau's widespread use
of the "Paris of the New World" slogan[26] – an inspired branding strategy as
the city of Paris had proved irresistibly seductive to American visitors ever
since the early decades of the nineteenth century.[27] (See figures 5.4 and 5.5.)
The MTCB was here again borrowing from the marketing strategies adopted
by some of its members in their own advertisements. Thus, visitors were invited to "make Montreal – the Paris of the New World – your weekend Mecca
and enjoy the amenities of a bustling metropolis in a truly Continental setting." Going there would be "just like going to Paris." Better still, this "Paris
of the New World is just around the corner." Indeed, "Why cross the ocean
to find 'Gay Paree' when Montreal its counterpart, awaits next door?"[28] Here,
as well, the MTCB was echoing an invitation extended by private companies
such as the CNR which asked, "Why go to Europe with a city like this on the

5.5 | Front cover of *Enjoy Historic and Gay Montreal*, 1950s.

American continent?"[29] But similarities end there. MTCB advertisers made it very clear that the Paris travellers would encounter in Montreal was one they could encounter *today* if they visited France, not, for instance, the Paris of the seventeenth century.[30]

Inviting visitors to a New World Paris was to do much more. This "city of lights" had long been seen as a destination for indulging in so-called "bad behaviour." The MTCB was clearly banking on prospective visitors decoding its Paris label with this in mind. In fact, during the first half of the twentieth century, this moniker would have rung particularly true for many. Montreal had long been identified by both English Canadians and Americans as the city in North America where one could act out, in relative anonymity, behaviour that was frowned upon, if not simply illegal, elsewhere. Not without reason it was known as "sin city." Indeed, measured against many standards, there was ample opportunity to sin in Montreal. For one, it was spared the most constraining regulations of the prohibition laws enacted in the late 1910s in other Canadian provinces and, in 1919, at the federal level in the US with the Volstead Act. All these laws, to different degrees and at different times, disallowed or regulated the importation, trade, production, sale, and consumption of alcohol.[31] Contrary to many jurisdictions in North America and parts of Quebec, Montreal opted for temperance rather than prohibition – one of the only large metropolitan centres in Eastern North America to do so.[32] In fact, as early as 1921, the provincial government established a Quebec Liquor Commission regulating provincial liquor sales across the province. Once again, an unprecedented regulatory approach in North America. It stipulated that only government-owned stores could sell bottled alcohol, and only government-licensed restaurants and hotels could serve wine and beer. Spirits could only be purchased in government stores and no more than one bottle per visit was allowed, which could only be consumed in homes or hotel rooms.[33]

Montreal also had the highest number of liquor stores and licensed restaurants in the province and the great majority of alcohol sales were to Americans.[34] And while prohibition laws were, for all intents and purposes, repealed in Canada by the early 1920s and in 1933 in the US, giving way to stringent regulations instead, Montreal still stood as a comparatively open city, unencumbered by various remaining restrictions enacted elsewhere. In the 1940s, "in most provinces ... you couldn't legally consume hard liquor in public, except in a few private clubs. There was no booze to be had in restaurants, no wine with meals."[35]

It was also no secret that Montreal was a lively centre of cabaret life where one could be entertained by the uninhibited talents of famous dancing girls mostly from New York. They, and many other entertainers including jazz musicians, appreciated Montreal's employment opportunities. Indeed, Montreal had more nightclubs than other cities, very much as a result of its more relaxed liquor laws.[36] It could also easily have been marketed as Canada's gambling capital; in other provinces, "virtually all forms of gambling were forbidden" with "no legal casinos or lotteries."[37] In fact, it was estimated that gambling was Montreal's "second largest industry, right behind the manufacturing of women's clothing."[38] To say nothing of the fact that in the early

1920s the city "[was] one of the only cities in North America to have a Red-Light district, that is a neighbourhood with a high concentration of visible prostitution houses."[39] It was also easier to engage in illegal behaviour, as the city's law enforcement agencies were reputedly willing to turn a blind eye to proscribed activities if there was money or other advantages to be gained. For instance, by 1949, "all bars were supposed to stop providing drinks at 2:00 a.m. on weekdays and midnight on Saturday," yet "a great many of them were in the habit of staying open until dawn, with no lack of customers."[40]

Finally, Montreal also had a reputation for being a destination where marginalized groups would be less likely to be harassed or otherwise persecuted for nonconformist behaviour or for being somehow different. Although much less rooted in fact, the pervasive belief that gays and lesbians and Blacks, among others, might find Montreal relatively more tolerant than other destinations in North America only served to further entrench the city's racy persona. Some locations were recognized as relatively "safe," for example, although they remained underground and their patrons were always vulnerable to arrests or other mistreatments.[41] Some bars allowed Black musicians to perform for white audiences relatively unencumbered by standard discriminatory practices found elsewhere.[42] All told, then, by promoting Montreal as the "Paris of the New World," the MTCB homed in on an appealing brand name that rang true.

It remained, though, that the city's business community could not afford to be viewed as condoning illegal behaviour. This may explain why MTCB promoters proved more suggestive than descriptive when featuring attractions of their "sin city." Wording of the short texts in these ads was certainly more elusive than that of texts depicting sites of historic Montreal. For one, the copy consistently specified that entertainment was something they would enjoy at night, which was a clue to what could be expected: "Whether you feel festive or contemplative you can find the environment which to cultivate your mood to the full during every night of your stay in this Paris and Londres of the New World."[43] At times, the text proved more detailed but remained, nonetheless, evocative, merely gesturing to the city's nocturnal sensual and tantalizing appeal: "The French, the Parisian aspects of Montreal become increasingly visible as the sun sinks over Mount Royal and, in peace, the illuminated cross on its crest blazes against the evening sky. Then, in downtown Montreal … electric lights everywhere invite you in to dine & dance & see the latest shows."[44] Prospective tourists would understand, if only indirectly, that the city would appeal to their senses, vaguely defined but unmistakably suggestive of racy epicurean pleasures. It is in this way the MTCB appears to have met the challenge of promoting Montreal's *risqué* Parisian attractions while remaining above reproach. The fact that it could also count on Montreal's preestablished reputation which had long been spread by word-of-mouth and, as far as drinking and nightclubs, very openly in the press likely meant it could afford to be more circumspect.[45]

Comparing Montreal to Paris is illuminating on another front: it offers further insight into English Montrealers' attitudes towards their city's French population. When considering issues of identity, branding Montreal as a North American Paris appears puzzling. The MTCB was, after all, inviting visitors to a place that was French, for both its Parisian allure and for being an "Old French Canadian city,"[46] a city with both traditional old Quebec attributes as well as a racy, sophisticated urbane modernity. Did the MTCB's English-speaking promoters in fact have a less unidimensional view of their French Quebec counterparts? Counterintuitive as it may seem, this double-barrelled invitation does not put into question their essentializing representation of French Montrealers promoted in their "city of contrast" advertisements. What was not said in the MTCB's more detailed publicity helps make sense of this apparent contradiction. More specifically, it did not suggest that French Montrealers' lifestyle, habits, or behaviour contributed to the city's Parisian personality. Instead, prospective tourists were made to understand that French Montrealers' very presence sufficed to give the city a certain Parisian cachet or Gallic charm, very much as would decorative props on a stage. Thus, a so-called intangible "French mentality assure[d] merriment and the pleasures of French and Canadian cuisine."[47] French Montrealers gave "life in Montreal a very Parisian touch."[48] Claiming that Montreal's French population would recall Paris, the MTCB made the case that things French could stand for modernity, while French Montrealers stood for tradition. The only trait French Montrealers shared with Parisians was language. Visitors could expect to "hear French spoken everywhere in shops, restaurants, nightclubs,"[49] as "French is the mother tongue of a large part of the population." Language offered first and foremost a seductive background music. Indeed, "somehow food and drink have an added zest when accompanied by the lilting tones of French voices."[50] Practical considerations came into play as well. The MTCB was clearly intent on foregrounding French Montrealers' bilingualism, a way of reassuring unilingual North Americans of the absence of any communication barriers.

The MTCB's representation of Montreal was not the only influence to colour the tourist gaze. Provincial tourist promoters' views on Quebec's metropolis were also a factor. Although, in the early PTB publicity material, relatively little information is specifically dedicated to the city. Typical in this regard is its 1929 *The Old World at Your Door. Quebec: The French Canadian*

Province advertising booklet, with two scant paragraphs devoted to the city. During this time, Montreal was mostly given visibility as a result of its strategic location on the road grid, as many of the Bureau's travel itineraries were set to begin there. On occasion, it is as if officials felt a need to justify this recurring reference to Montreal, pointing out in one case, "it is ... only natural that the present guide-book should describe Montreal and its main attractions, before attempting to even suggest any excursions into the surrounding country."[51] While not an apology per se, this aside suggests a working assumption that an increasing number of motorized visitors were drawn to Quebec's rural areas. Consequently, not counting instructions on how to get from point A to B, Montreal was given relatively less attention regarding its sites and attractions. Furthermore, although we know that PTB promoters hosted English-speaking North American travel writers with the assumption that they included a visit to Montreal, there is no way of knowing how much care was taken in showing them city sites. Considering the limited attention given to Montreal in their own publicity, it is safe to assume that they spent more time with travel writers in rural areas. Tourists were mostly given general descriptions of the city, often under a "Montreal Facts" subheading, which tended to speak directly to the Roads Department's mandate of fostering economic development, mostly statistics or ranking orders illustrating the city's impressive industrial manufacturing outputs and enviable geographical location for commercial purposes. Typical in this regard, one booklet described Montreal as "the largest city of Canada, the fifth largest city of America and ... the Canadian commercial, industrial and financial metropolis."[52] Here was the seat of "outstanding industries" including "tobacco, paint, textiles, shoes, cement ... a flour mill (the largest in the world)."[53] This marketing approach was most strikingly illustrated in the department's 900-page *Along Quebec Highways: Tourist Guide*, with Montreal as the apex in Canada's economy. The guide detailed in pages filled with tables "the phenomenal annual increase in the exportation of grain through Montreal since 1921" and "the prodigious advance in the value of real estate in the Metropolis of Canada."[54] In typical promotional one-upmanship, the guide often pointed out that Montreal outperformed its American neighbour: "in 1926, 135,000,000 bushels of wheat were shipped from Montreal, as compared with 75,500,000 from New York."[55] In the 1940s, visitors learned that "vivid as any youthful American city in its life and movement, the Canadian metropolis brings you a new flavour, a sense of good living."[56] Overall, readers were made to understand that Montreal "is a typical example of Canada's growth in the past century or so, and of the giant strides made by the Dominion in general, and the Province of Québec in particular."[57]

Thus, to the extent that the Roads Department officials chose to showcase the city as a seat of progress and modernity, they were in sync with their MTCB counterparts. Both took into account visitor interests, either thinking of pursuing some kind of business venture or scouting convention destinations. As for tourists, the MTCB and the PTB also clearly shared a common understanding of English North Americans' hopes and expectations. In line with their English Quebec counterparts, provincial promoters made much of what the city had to offer shoppers, including "fine shoes from Britain's factories, woollens from the looms of Yorkshire, fine Canadian homespuns, blankets of magnificent quality and textures … fragile china, gorgeous furs … French Canadian handicrafts."[58]

However, slight differences emerge. This was especially so when considering how they chose to represent the city's past. From its early days, the city was imagined as a "blend of the old and the new,"[59] going so far as to promote it as "one of Montreal's principal attractions,"[60] where "towering skyscrapers rub … shoulders with centuries-old buildings."[61] Nevertheless, unlike the MTCB's publicity, government promotional material would have made it more difficult for visitors to ascribe the "old" to French Montrealers. Put differently, contrasts between tradition and modernity were essentially divorced from ethnic association – certainly not in ways that would suggest French Montrealers had not kept up with the times.

Indicative of this difference is that the Bonsecours market was given less attention. In fact, some publicity material made no mention of it at all.[62] When it did, it only indicated that this was where "French-Canadian farmers from the outlying townships bring their produce to the city, as their forbears have done for almost three hundred years"[63] or "where the largest market of Montreal now stands,"[64] without suggesting that in this neighbourhood visitors would encounter a mixture of both urban Montrealers and seventeenth-century-like *habitants*. Tourists looking for old Montreal could find it in the city's historic buildings – mostly those dating back to the New France period: "The city of Montreal is replete with history; it is proud of its religious buildings, of the sheltering, educational, financial and industrial institutions which build its power."[65] In fact, some key figures in the tourism promotion at the provincial level discussed the possibility of developing the city's old quarter, the "Vieux Montréal," where some seventeenth- and eighteenth-century buildings still stood. Paul Gouin, for one, voiced strong support to have this area protected and restored. Not only did this "neighborhood … contribute to give Montreal its French character," but it offered the "foreigner a way to know our metropolis in depth, to know its culture, its traditions, its history." But faithful to his view that tourists "appreciate that our artistic culture had not remained static," he also envisaged the city's old quarter as a place where "our comedians, singers and storytellers would present folkloric shows and entertainment modern in inspiration."[66]

As for religion, here as well, the PTB emphasized that visitors would come across it in the built landscape of Montreal's churches: Montreal "is sometimes called the 'City of Churches' due to [its] 250 temples of worship" making it "in some respects more like a medieval French city than a bustling Metropolis."[67] But, in contrast to MTCB publicity, nothing was said about French Catholics' religious practices. In short, prospective visitors relying on government publicity alone in order to understand the differences between English and French Montrealers would have had less reason to think of the French as "old" Montrealers.

Another difference between provincial and MTCB publicity is references to Paris. With rare exceptions, they are absent from provincial promoters' marketing material. Considering it was no secret that English-speaking North Americans were drawn to this city of lights, this appears to be a lost marketing opportunity. Instead, they labelled it "GAY, grand old Montreal"[68] or a place "abounding with a tang of gaiety."[69] Of course, using "gay" as branding was simply code to suggest racy, Parisian-like attractions, as the two terms were often paired. But it also suggests that government promoters were even more wary than their counterparts in the English Montreal business community to appear as though they were promoting the sins of "sin city." "Gay" was more neutral, allowing for a tip of the hat to the city's controversial reputation, without appearing to condone bad behaviour. In fact, official documents attempted to specifically dispel "any possible misconception" by "let[ting] it be clearly stated that the Roads Department never made capital of or otherwise exploited prohibition in the US."[70] Referring to Montreal as "gay" rather than Paris perhaps allowed them to believe that this was the case. Regardless, it remains that provincial promoters were well aware that Montreal's popularity rested in part on its racy attractions.

This being said, during the 1920s and early 1930s, contrary to official claims, provincial promoters were quite explicit, particularly in the US, that Montreal benefitted greatly from prohibition. In the same report claiming they never profited from the city's wide open alcohol consumption policies, officials conceded that, among other factors, the impending repeal of the Volstead Act "threatened to decrease our tourist trade."[71] Their numbers proved right, as decreases in tourist traffic were recorded, notably among those travelling to Montreal for the weekend. Despite the fact that it "is still the city which receives the greatest number of tourists," provincial promoters now spoke of "the difficulty ... [of] keep[ing] these tourists." To address post-1933 repeal challenges, in 1935, the PTB reported having devoted a big proportion "of its publicity to [Montreal] and did not miss a single opportunity of making known the advantages possessed by the Metropolis."[72] More specifically, that year "about one quarter of the advertisements appearing in newspapers, magazines and reviews" were devoted to the metropolis and a new booklet on Montreal–Laurentians was added to a series devoted to distinct regions.[73]

But it remains that they proved cautiously generic when describing what was gay about the metropolis. Visitors could expect to find "numerous theaters giving latest [sic] theatrical successes and hits, as well as classical plays."[74] Ten years later, tourists were simply informed that the city "has a great many theaters presenting latest successes [sic]."[75] It was "a city of bright lights, neon signs, traffic signals, theater marquees, brilliant shop windows."[76] In more targeted publicity, provincial promoters did note that "Gay Montreal" was a city "of tolerance, liberty and cheer."[77] More suggestive still, it had "a large number of world-famous hotels, gay night clubs and cabarets and hundreds of restaurants and boarding houses ... all ready to take care of the hungry traveller and fill the needs of the 'inner man.'"[78] Needless to say, it would not have taken much imagination to figure out what type of tolerance, liberty, and cheer were in store for this "inner man."

Finally, in contrast to MTCB advertising, provincial promoters placed more emphasis on Montreal as a majority French-speaking city, drawing particular attention to the fact that it was "the second French city in the world in point of population."[79] Directed at English-speaking North Americans, they played up this distinctive status: "in some ways Montreal seems a curious city to those who do not know it. Two thirds of its million inhabitants speak French as their native tongue."[80] Visitors would be intrigued by "the children playing about ... prattling in French."[81] Further, this North American city had "French and English universities, five French and three English dailies."[82] Headlines and descriptive texts appearing in newspapers or magazines were typically peppered with French expressions, such as "Bienvenue à Montréal." Some ads featured scenarios, which gave a taste of the pleasurable linguistic encounters in store for visitors. Thus, they could expect that a "cop on the corner calls you M'sieu or Madame,"[83] and where else "does the taxi driver back home suddenly turn aside from his conversation with you to pour out a torrent of French to the cop on the corner?"[84] At the same time, they made the point that English-speaking visitors were able to communicate with the locals in English.

This brings to mind questions of how promoters, both English and French, marketed the city to French-speaking Quebeckers. As far as the MTCB was concerned, these prospective tourists were not a target clientele – it had no

French-language publicity to speak of. As for provincial promoters, they gave the city only a little more importance. In fact, in the PTB's first tourist booklet aimed specifically at Quebeckers, *Voyez Québec d'Abord!/See Quebec First!*, Montreal was hardly mentioned, except as a point of departure for the various itineraries. And even under the "Trip around Montreal Island" heading, information was given about the sights to see in the outlying villages, and no description was given of the city itself. And even during the 1930s, when the PTB was investing increasing resources to attract and retain tourists following the repeal of the Volstead Act, in its booklet, QUÉBEC: *Ses régions de tourisme*, descriptions of the city remained noticeably succinct. When more specific information was provided, it highlighted features that were the same as in English language publicity. Thus, Montreal was summed up as a "City of charms and contrasts, welcoming and gay but at the same time principal financial, industrial and commercial [capital] of Canada; second French language city in the world; sixth American city for its population of more than one million inhabitants; first port of the world for its wheat export, the city of Montreal is unique among the large cities of the universe."[85] And, remarkably, little mention existed of Montreal's connection to the past. At most, visitors learned, "the past blends in to the great pleasure of the visitors."[86] Nor was anything made of the city's English population. And just as striking, little was offered regarding entertainment, including pleasures for the "inner man."[87] Promoters likely assumed that Montreal required less attention, as French Quebec travellers tended to be city dwellers, many from Montreal. Their assumptions did not change much during the following decades.

What this overview reveals is that, taken together, provincial tourist promoters gave Montreal relatively little attention, whether advertising the city for the benefit of English North American tourists or their French-language compatriots. More significantly, PTB promoters were less inclined than their MTCB counterparts to associate French Montrealers with the past, as well as detail the city's nightlife, and more intent on highlighting the language difference.

But such differences may very well speak to larger considerations. Contrary to the MTCB, French Quebec promoters had a distinctive and more daunting set of advertising challenges, having nothing to do with the challenges of marketing a "sin city." Prominent French Quebec tourist promoters who viewed tourism as a means to a traditional nationalist end could obviously not convincingly showcase Montreal as a destination that reflected the province's traditional French character. Quite the contrary, its popularity was directly attributable to what they so deplored about contemporary Quebec or feared would happen to the "real" Quebec. Is it any wonder then that provincial publicity about Montreal was limited or unavailable? The province's most prominent tourist promoters' pronouncements about Montreal confirmed this unease. Albert Tessier, for one, made no mention of the city in his well-publicized report on Quebec tourism, other than to suggest that tourist promoters consider commemorating "the birth dates of our big cities," including Montreal.[88] Édouard Montpetit's detailed analysis of the state of the province's tourism industry only offered a few general comments about the city, to the effect that there were "renovations and reforms to be undertaken" to ensure it lived up to the slogan, "Montreal is the second French city in the world."[89] In fact, those few who proved more loquacious on the subject typically brought up the province's metropolis as a cautionary tale. In contrast with rural areas, Montreal was not under threat of Americanization; it had already fallen prey to its perils. Victor Barbeau, a prolific writer and ardent defender of the French Canadian language, lamented that "the city had lost its soul."[90] The most glaring symptom of this state of affairs was that "this city ... the second French city in the world has an English face."[91] In keeping with the association often made between issues of French Canadian survival and a successful tourism industry, they argued forcefully that "Montreal must become French again by its layout, by its business, by its cuisine. Its inscriptions, its ads, its signs, must make this clear to the stranger who looks for a French city."[92] Such voices could be heard expressing the same concerns throughout the period. Thus, still in the 1950s, commentators deplored that Montreal "looks like an American city."[93] Not surprisingly, Paul Gouin maintained that Montreal was "where Americanization had caused quasi irreparable ravages."[94] More worrisome still was that English appeared to be the language of choice among those who worked in the business – notably in the city's hotels where, according to Gouin, "employees ... only speak English or try do their best to seem as though they do."[95] He and other PTB officials attributed this sorry state of affairs, in part, to a misguided "tendency to believe that the tourists will be flattered if they are offered accommodation in hotels and inns with names that are exclusively English or American, and if they are treated so as to make them feel entirely at home."[96] Gouin was adamant that it be quite the opposite. Those who worked in hotels, restaurants, stores, or theaters should "greet the tourist in French," and doing so would "require them to have a perfect knowledge of French."[97] He entreated Montrealers to give their establishments French names and serve "French-Canadian dishes, written up in French menus, in a decor that will evoke our country, our province and not the United-States." As for Montreal's distinct attractions, such as the city's cabarets, he insisted they should "change [their] atmosphere by entrusting in our locals the task of imagining, executing and interpreting entertainments that will be as spectacular, as captivating, as witty and more original then those that we import in succession from 'Broadway' and 'Harlem.'"[98] Allies of Gouin among representatives of French-speaking hotelkeepers were also outspoken about what they saw as the relatively more advanced state of Americanization in the province's metropolis. As one editorial in L'Hôtellerie/The Hostelry put it, "[t]he greatest need for work is not in country places for, by the grace of God, our best people live there ... but what can we say of Montreal [sic]; a city with an absolutely American appearance."[99] And indeed, more than anywhere else in the province, they argued the city's hotelkeepers could rightly be accused of producing false advertising. More specifically, "when an American tourist arrives in Montreal expecting to see the French City, he surely must ask himself if people are not laughing at him." Sounding a familiar refrancisation refrain, they advised hotelkeepers, "before advertising a country of French culture, to consider first whether this culture is visible."[100]

However, they did recognize that the French involved in Montreal's tourist industry faced unique challenges; after all, not only was the city's tourism promotion controlled by the English-dominated MTCB but the metropolis's most popular and prestigious hotels were also owned by English-speaking businessmen. Was it any wonder that Montreal's face stood out as being English to incoming visitors? As a result, French Montreal hotelkeepers adopted a double-barrelled refrancisation campaign: one aimed at French Montrealers involved in the tourism industry and another meant to ensure collaboration from their more influential Anglophone counterparts. For one, it was imperative to "show our good English friends that it is to [sic] their interest to cooperate with us and give Montreal a French atmosphere" and, at the same time, "commence ourselves to refrenchify [sic] everything we can, and by a sustained effort we shall accomplish our aim."[101] In order to convince all that promoting the city's ethnic side – the French one – was the most effective way to attract tourists, promoters pulled out the economic self-interest card, while tugging at patriotic heartstrings: "[f]rom a business point of view, [the need to preserve the province's French character] is in the best interest of every citizen, not only of our French-speaking population, but of our English-speaking fellow-citizens themselves."[102] It remained that throughout the period, many deplored the grande hôtellerie's unwillingness to change, although it seems that some were optimistic that English Canadians were "not hostile to this idea," maintaining, "[s]ome large English stores of Montreal already understand all the benefits accruing to them from a bilingual trade."[103]

Paul Gouin certainly shared this optimism. While he was adamant that those who worked in the business had to have nothing less than "a perfect knowledge of French,"[104] he nonetheless believed strongly that English Montreal hotel owners were likely to respond well to persuasion rather than coercion. As he put it: "[one] should not demand but suggest, convince the owners of these large hotels that it is in their interest to give to their establishments, at least in part, a French atmosphere … by inviting them to join the competent authorities." Clearly sensitive to the city's often fraught French–English relations, he felt that it was only in this way that "we will demonstrate and that is an essential point, that this is not an initiative dictated by a narrow nationalism but instead a question that concerns all Canadians." He also argued that being too interventionist "would inevitably bring about an unnecessary standardization" that "would lead to the disappearance of local and regional particularities."[105] Therefore, to his mind, the provincial government should limit itself to offering advice on an individual basis to hotelkeepers through its Hostelry Education Service and, on a larger scale, by sponsoring contests or *salons*. These gave opportunities to those involved in the tourism industry to showcase ways in which, for example, to decorate hotels *à la canadienne* with old-style furniture and traditional arts and crafts or serve typical French Canadian cuisine. Several initiatives of this sort were undertaken in the 1930s with the participation of a wide array of institutions including the École du meuble. Gouin was heavily involved in such initiatives, most notably, later in this period, following his appointment as technical consultant to the executive council of the Province of Quebec in 1948. Among others, in 1950, in collaboration with the government's Hostelry Education Service,[106] he participated in the Concours de refrancisation de la publicité de l'hôtellerie in collaboration with Radio Canada, and in 1951 he organized a Salon de l'Hôtellerie.

Furthermore, Gouin demonstrated what he understood to be a productive collaborative approach through his work as cultural advisor for the benefit of a few new hotels, including some of Montreal's English-run *grand hôtels*. Preceded by his reputation as a connoisseur of French Canadian material culture in all its guises and, no doubt, as a result of his well-publicized consulting work with countryside hotelkeepers, he was invited in 1949 by the Ritz-Carlton Hotel to offer his expert advice on how to decorate a so-called *canadienne* suite, meant to showcase the many facets of French Canadian culture and the province's French character. In 1951, he also acted as a decoration consultant for the government-owned Étape hotel in the Laurentians.[107] In 1955, the president of the CNR, Donald Gordon, invited him to join his newly created Decorative Advisory Committee to make recommendations on how best to decorate the new Queen Elizabeth hotel set to open in 1958 – an establishment advertised as the city's largest and most modern luxury hotel.[108] Gordon explained to Gouin that he was "anxious to maintain [in his hotel] an atmosphere essentially Canadian, with special emphasis on a decor distinctive of the city of Montreal and of the province of Quebec."[109]

This invitation was rich with symbolic meaning and promise. It could be read as a sign that at least some members of English Montreal's business elite recognized that things French Canadian could sell. This is certainly how Gouin interpreted it. He claimed that this was nothing less "than the first time in the history of our province that an establishment of this type is concerned with decorating and setting up à la canadienne" and commended Gordon for this "historic event for which you have reason to be proud."[110] Other French Canadians also reacted very positively to this initiative. Even the traditional nationalist newspaper, *L'Action catholique*, congratulated the CNR for having "put the history and art of French Canada to good use: it is a new example which should inspire in future the architecture of large businesses. Still further with this same goal in mind, the bilingual personnel has been chosen with great care."[111]

Overall, the advisory committee recommended what types of French Canadian designs, furniture, art, and textiles were most appropriate. Thus, for instance, its members encouraged the use of *catalogne* designs for rugs planned for the lobby. The committee was also tasked with drawing up a list of famous Canadian historical figures – mostly French – whose names could be used to designate select suites and venues. The committee's preliminary list included Paul de Chomedey de Maisonneuve (founder of Montreal), Jacques Cartier, and Samuel de Champlain. Others were drawn from a roster of military, political, and business elites. Surprisingly enough, Generals Wolfe and Montcalm were put forward, while Wilfrid Laurier was rejected out of hand. The unabated tensions and profoundly divisive debates surrounding the Conquest and the role played by its central protagonists did not appear to have stood as a selection roadblock – at least as reported in the committee's minutes. In the case of Laurier, however, the minutes are more revealing: "the use of [his] name ... might prove controversial because it had been associated with politics."[112] In the end, members of the committee recommended that suites be identified with safely neutral place names directly inspired by an unmistakably old Quebec thematic repertoire, such as Old Montreal, Legends of the St Lawrence, Old French songs, Quebec City, the Laurentians, the Gaspé Peninsula, the Saguenay. In addition to being free of controversy, committee members and CNR authorities were well aware that these destinations were familiar and appealing to would-be tourists hoping to see what they believed to be the authentic French Canada. Thus, while Donald Gordon had instructed the committee that his proudly cosmopolitan hotels should

5.6 | "Hello Montreal." Cover of Irving Berlin's
sheet music, ca. 1928.

adopt "a decor distinctive of Montreal," ultimately, it privileged one that
called to mind traditional Quebec. Gay Paris, the city of contrast, was simply
eclipsed by the old Quebec. Clearly, even at the ultramodern Queen Elizabeth hotel, promoters felt that conjuring up the markers of a North American
seventeenth-century New France remained the most effective way to convey
the enticing difference visitors looked for. Such decorative choices were also
in sync with how traditional nationalists tried to imagine the province as
a whole.

The traditional *refrancisation* initiatives at the Queen Elizabeth hotel raise
questions about the expectations and reactions of visitors headed for Montreal:
would they, in fact, be inclined to showcase the sites and people reminiscent
of old Quebec in the province's largest metropolis? What quickly becomes
apparent is that pinpointing predeparture images travel writers gathered
about the city, other than through tourism publicity, is a significantly more
speculative exercise then establishing those for the countryside. We know

that the press produced articles vaunting the city's unique entertainment opportunities. And its gay reputation was also brought to the fore in popular culture most notably through an American song entitled "Hello Montreal," which became popular in the 1920s.[113] (See figure 5.6.) It remains, however, that travel writers headed to Montreal referred much less frequently to non-tourist-related sources in their accounts. Many factors account for this. For one, less non-tourist-related information, printed or otherwise, involving Montreal was available during this period.

Though information on Montreal was provided in school readers, for example, English-speaking North American travel writers – particularly Americans – learned New France history more generally, with the old Quebec narrative dominating, and little of Montreal. By the 1940s, students were made aware of the province's modernization and contribution to the country's industrial development and that Montreal was front and centre in this economic transformation. However, little was mentioned of the city and even less of its residents. Montreal was mostly painted with a few broad and impressionistic brushstrokes. From their texts, students would have equated the city primarily with ideas of progress and growing prosperity, standing for them as Canada's economic powerhouse. In some cases, they read of the city's modernization and economic dynamism, which was largely attributable to Montreal's English Canadian business elite. Indeed, French Quebec Montrealers were occasionally portrayed as less enterprising or less drawn to modern economic pursuits, just like their countryside compatriots. It is, therefore, easy to imagine that once they reached adulthood, English-speaking North American travel writers were predisposed to view Montreal as somehow "out of character" – an intriguing contemporary modern outlier juxtaposed to a location equated with time travel. For English Canadians more specifically, the discovery in school that Montreal was Canada's economic powerhouse may have made the city an object of curiosity, holding an alluring promise of feeding their patriotism.

Before the 1940s, novels and art did not provide the same insight for Montreal as they did for the countryside, as few English-speaking North American or French Quebec novelists set stories in Montreal, and most painters did not find the city a source of inspiration. After the Second World War, this changed with the emergence of French Quebec novels featuring the urban, industrial face of the province – more often than not that of Montreal. The fact that several of these novels garnered immediate and widespread public acclaim makes it all the more likely that some travel writers were exposed to literary representations of the city. Further, several of these were translated

shortly after their publication. Gabrielle Roy's *Bonheur d'occasion* was published in 1945 and translated into English two years later as *The Tin Flute*.
Set in Montreal's St-Henri neighbourhood and depicting the dreadful living
conditions and struggles facing the French Canadian working class, it was
rewarded with literary prizes at home and abroad. In 1947 alone, it received
the Governor General's Award, the Royal Society of Canada's Lorne Pierce
Medal, and France's coveted Prix Femina. In the US, it "became a selection of the Literary Guild" and, according to the *New York Times*, this would
"assure its having the widest readership in the US of any French Canadian
work since *Maria Chapdelaine*."[114] Roger Lemelin's *Au pied de la pente douce*
(1944), translated as *The Town Below* (1948), also attracted the attention
of Anglophone readers. While set in the late 1930s in Quebec City's working-class neighbourhood of St-Sauveur, it, too, brought to light the hardships
of poor and dispossessed city-dwelling French Canadians. Lemelin's novel,
Les Plouffe (1948), later translated as *The Plouffe Family*, chronicled the trials
and tribulations of an ordinary Quebec City working-class family. With even
more acclaim, it reached a wider audience as a *téléroman* of the same name,
which aired in French on Radio Canada in 1953 and, remarkably, was re-
broadcast on CBC with the same cast the following year. Both series stayed on
air until 1959. In fact, this popular show and its author were rewarded with
an honorary certificate during the meetings of the Association des hôtel-
liers in 1956 "for having awakened the interest of English provinces about
Quebec, by depicting a faithful image of the jovial spirit and hospitable character of French-Canadians."[115] Although it is likely that some travel writers
read these novels and watched this show, their accounts make it difficult to
measure how these shaped expectations. At the very least, they would have
become aware of destinations in Quebec, including Montreal, that did not
belong to old Quebec. More specifically, they would have become conscious
that some French Montrealers were facing the same very contemporary and
harsh struggles as other urban-dwelling English-speaking North Americans.
And a few might have also retained that the working poor in the city were
largely French.

Other prominent novels that featured different Montreals may have provided postwar travel writers with a more multifaceted picture of the city and
possibly a more varied set of expectations. An example is Hugh MacLennan's *Two Solitudes*, for which he won the Governor General's Award in
1945. Partly set in Montreal between the wars, it revealed tensions between
traditional and forward-looking French Canadians, and between French
and English, doubled with class conflicts that went hand-in-hand with the

province's distinct ethnic makeup. The fact that a few protagonists in this novel were also tortured souls confronting challenges of coping with their mixed French–English identities and relationships meant that, in the eyes of many, MacLennan succeeded in representing the uneasy relations between Canada's two so-called founding nations evocatively encapsulated in the title of the book.

Other Canadian authors of distinction depicted groups other than English and French in the city – group targets of overt prejudice and discrimination. Gwenthalyn Graham's *Earth and High Heaven* (1944), for instance, won the Governor General's Award for fiction and, in 1945, became the ninth bestseller in the US.[116] It recounts the fraught relations between a Westmount Protestant woman and a Jewish Northern Ontario male lawyer. Morley Callaghan's *The Loved and The Lost*, which also won the Governor General's Award a few years later in 1951, proved controversial, recounting what would have been then the shocking story of a young, white single woman who dared to socialize with Blacks during a time of deep prejudice. Readers would have discovered Montreal's St-Antoine Street lined with jazz clubs, home to African Canadians. They were also made to see Montreal's class and ethnic divisions, between the Westmount-based Anglophone financial elite and their French Canadian house help, for example. For his part, Mordechai Richler's many highly acclaimed and popular novels were set in Montreal, including *The Apprenticeship of Duddy Kravitz* (1959). It depicted the challenges facing working-class Jews interacting with the "two solitudes" fraught, as they were, with anti-Semitism and social conflict. Here again Montreal was presented as an economically and ethnically divided city, with its wealthy Westmount English, its Jewish St-Urbain working-class, and its French Quebec Outremont middle-class.[117]

Another later postwar fiction genre to emerge – the Montreal-noir novels – could have further cemented in the minds of readers representations of the city they would have come across in the press or through word of mouth.[118] These crime/thriller novels written by Anglophones living in Montreal, featured areas of the city long associated with its *risqué* entertainment opportunities but also its notorious corruption and criminal underbelly. Their cast of characters also brought to life some of the social and ethnic conflicts depicted in more literary novels including the tensions between the wealthy English of Westmount and the French working class.[119] But similar to English North American travel writing depicting life in rural areas, they too "portray[ed] French Canadians ... as childish, naïve, bumbling, colourful, humorous and primitive."[120] Thus, in this case, these novels would have simply reinforced travel writers' preconceptions shaped by fiction of an earlier time.

All this being said, nothing suggests that any of these novels served as a strong impetus to visit Montreal or coloured travel writer expectations – certainly no travel writer indicated as much.[121] The most that can be surmised is that these sources would have constructed an expectation in Montreal visitors that they would experience urban modernity with its appending social hardships and been made aware of its ethnic diversity. They could have also sharpened the city's image as a haven of fun, alluring if not *louche* entertainment.

These urban novels proved controversial among many French Quebeckers.[122] They certainly did among some members of the French Quebec intelligentsia, which, in turn, suggests that they may have affected French Quebec travel writers similarly. There was no escaping that they marked a break from the prevalent *roman du terroir*. As such, many traditional nationalists saw these as yet another confirmation that the real Quebec was threatened by modernization. To others, however, they offered an enriching and realistic representation of the urban-centred Quebec, one familiar to the majority of French Quebeckers. As regards travel writers, for those raised in Montreal or who had visited the city, such novels only pointed out the realities of Montreal, which were not a selling point for visitors.

Irrespective of where they came from, travel writers would have been hard pressed to carry with them a representation of the city directly inspired by visual artists. Well into the 1950s, the better known and most popular painters stuck to rural landscapes and the *habitants*. Although some travel writers might have been aware of painters associated with the Beaver Hall Group, founded in the early 1920s with a studio in Montreal. As a group and as individuals they gained some recognition, notably through their association with the Group of Seven and high profile exhibits including one at the National Gallery of Canada in 1948. While they did paint Quebec countryside landscapes, they mostly represented urban scenes, including industry.[123] There were a few other painters drawn to city life subjects. For example, the work of Adrien Hébert (1890–1967) celebrated Montreal's modernity, with paintings of tramways and the port. Another, Sam Borenstein (1909–1968), represented the city under its various guises. However, these artists had limited contemporary public exposure and, thus, little chance of influencing travel writers' image the city.[124]

While it is difficult to establish with any certainty the extent to which art, novels, textbooks, or publicity shaped travel writers' gaze, they were not arriving in an unknown city. They had multiple ways of conjuring up an image of Montreal before arriving there. However, English Canadian and American travel writers did not gaze upon the city in significantly different ways – certainly not as strikingly as when comparing their observations regarding the countryside. And while the paucity of sources makes it challenging to establish how French Quebec travel writers reacted to the city, enough exist to confirm that, once again, they were reading things differently.

AMERICANS

Generally speaking, it appears that American travel writers clearly took for granted that their compatriots would want to travel to a city that offered the ultimate in the amenities and attractions of a modern cosmopolitan and sophisticated urban environment. And they clearly assumed that the points of reference for such destinations were American cities. Montreal, in their estimation, more than fit the bill. Once they had provided some facts to confirm the city's central position in Canada's economy, they endeavoured to demonstrate that Montreal was in effect just as modern as the great American cities, often using New York as the ultimate benchmark. Amy Oakley, for instance, tried to impress upon readers that "Montreal tends, no less than New York, towards the grandiose, the superlative."[125] And Stella Burke May made the point that "the business sections of Montreal were as progressive as those of New York or London."[126] Others proved more specific by pointing out that "the standard of living is fully as high as, if not higher than, in an equivalent city on the more familiar side of the border."[127] And "culturally too," Byron Steele maintained that the city "ranks high not only in Canada but in all America."[128] In holding up Montreal as worthy of interest by comparing it to their own cities, Americans appeared to suggest that they assumed readers would be surprised to find such a modern metropolis in Canada, all the more so in the "land of Maria Chapdelaine."

This being said, they could not hope to convince prospective tourists that Montreal would be worth the trip if they were simply to end up "at home" abroad. The city's distinctive attributes needed to be highlighted. In line with the MTCB's publicity, they made the point that, first and foremost, "in Montreal, the old and the new are in vivid contrast."[129] However, interestingly enough, to their minds, this contrast appeared to be primarily reflected in the city's architecture. They were less inclined to highlight contrasts among Montreal's population by drawing explicit connections between the French and the past and the English and modernity. Thus, while they encouraged readers to "head for the Bonsecours Market," they did so because this was where they would encounter a "good foreign atmosphere"[130] or where they would "find the real atmosphere of the Old world beyond this city."[131] True, this was where they could encounter "farmers and their spouses – *habitants*," but it seems as though the market stood out more as a generic old Quebec enclave in the city and not a place that would reveal much about the city's overall French population.[132] They were just as likely to bring up Outremont, the neighbourhood in which lived relatively well-off French Montrealers, including lawyers and doctors or businessmen – people not easily identified with the past.

On the other hand, American travel writers showed some interest in French–English relations. One would expect this. Montreal was, after all, a place to observe firsthand the interaction between the country's two solitudes. But more often than not their observations underlined what they viewed as intriguing or surprising. Thus, Amy Oakley explained that "it [had] given me a shock to discover that the English and French speaking citizens had erected different monuments to the World War dead" and "to discover that" referring to the country's residents as "Canadians" in the Montreal context is "not self-evident as all that." She quoted a French Canadian "informant" who exclaimed, "we are the Canadians" as "we settled Canada," and "the others are not Canadians at all. They are English, Irish, Scotch." However, rarely did travel writers go much further to discuss cases of conflict or irreconcilable differences. They ended up adopting a *bonne ententiste* outlook. From Amy Oakley's perspective "when passions are not unduly fanned by special interest – often political – harmony does, on the whole, prevail, although fraternization sometimes stops short of complete appreciation of dissimilar virtues."[133] They also seldom pointed to the city's other ethnic inhabitants. Their apparent surprise in one case and lack of interest in the other may reflect the fact that, before the 1940s, representations of the city and its diverse population in nontourist material were rare. It may also have to do with the fact that both the MTCB and the TB's publicity simply made little of the city's multicultural makeup. As a result, they had little to go by to develop a set of expectations and were less on the lookout for evidence of it. When they did come across some, it was a surprise.

What apparently caught their attention and what, to their minds, most distinguished Montreal from other North American cities was how French it was. All invariably mentioned that "Montreal is ... the second largest French-Speaking city in the world"[134] – echoing the city's promoters' slogan. Especially surprising was that "everyone seems able to speak two languages. French and English – with about equal fluency," recounting occasions witnessing this remarkable bilingualism in action. To one, it came "as a shock to have a sales woman with some other customer in French after she has satisfied one's own wants in perfect English."[135] It begs the question, were such reactions partly inspired by an assumption that a North American metropolis would, by definition, be predominantly English? Their particularly acute sensitivity to Montreal's public French face stands out all the more considering that, well into the 1960s, photos of downtown Montreal revealed the city's predominant English face in a high tourist traffic area. (It seems surprising that they did not point out this incongruity in the so-called second-largest French city in the world.)

Regardless, American travel writers concurred with observers and advertisers, largely English Canadian, that Montreal was the "Paris of the New World" and not simply because it was so French.[136] In contrast to promoters, they proved more forthcoming in detailing its Parisianness. Most notably, they drew greater attention to the city's relatively lenient alcohol consumption laws, particularly during the US prohibition. In 1929, for instance, a travel writer remarked that "one at first notices nothing radically different from one's own city, except that one can a little more openly procure one's self a glass of ale which is by no means 'dear.'"[137] In 1933 – the year the Volstead Act was repealed, but clearly written before it actually happened – T. Morris Longstreth's observations reveal much about how he viewed his own country's response to alcohol regulation. One of Montreal's "charms," he contended, was "its freedom." More to the point, he marvelled at the fact that a man can "drink in public." This, in and of itself, was liberating: "[r]each[ing] her liberal precincts after the weariness of the eternal wrangle over prohibition is like moving from boarding-school to college … The censor-ridden, gang-ridden, law-ridden American who arrives in Montreal for the first time feels naked … He cannot understand the poise, the nonchalance about drink."[138] But, with time, travel writers held up Montreal less and less for the free rein it offered the frustrated drinker. After the Second World War, Fred Coppeland, for one, noted how alcohol was less of a bargain than it had once been: "those who may remember Montreal in the prohibition days will be surprised at the absence of popping champagne corks. Even the full pocketbooks of American tourists do not open with French champagne at $15 dollars a bottle."[139]

Nonetheless, rarely did they venture to detail other reputed pleasures. Longstreth is exceptional for speaking of what he termed the city's dubious "morality," condemning the prevalence of prostitution, suggesting "that omniscience and eternity will be required to settle it."[140] Generally speaking though, well into the 1950s, travel writers relied mostly on suggestive expressions to convey the city's racy attractions, "one of the gayest cities in North America."[141] Those who proved more specific, such as Peter Kennedy, still stuck to generalities: "by day the metropolis offers a full program of sightseeing and shopping while by night its Parisian-style theatres, night clubs and restaurants provide top-rank entertainment."[142] Mostly, though, Montreal's food scene was heralded as being "a galaxy of eating places offering the kind of meals that gourmets write books about."[143]

Descriptions in writers' accounts of Montreal as a shopping destination were clearly intended for female readers. Male writers occasionally mentioned shopping but usually only when accompanied by a woman – typically a spouse – who was brought into the narrative. These were also the few moments when they addressed what they believed would be of particular interests to female travellers. Not only do such assumptions tap into gendered stereotypes, they also offered male writers opportunities to infuse their accounts with moments of levity at the expense of their female companions. Typically, they represented themselves as the patient ones, left with no other choice but to tolerate their wives' compulsive shopping urges. Benedict Thielen, for instance, recalled that "on the way back to *La Normandie* (restaurant), although I had made a point of glancing significantly at my watch, a place called the Linwood Shoppe pulled my wife through its doors as though they were the nozzle of a giant vacuum cleaner ... (claiming claustrophobia), I remained outside."[144]

In book-length travel guides by American travel writers who devoted full chapters to Montreal, it becomes clear that some had visited Montreal a few times. This familiarity coloured the way in which they recounted their impressions. They were certainly not setting out into the unknown. Thus, Amy Oakley pointed out that their "home base in Montreal has varied over the years from the elegance of the Ritz or simpler dwelling-places on residential Sherbrooke to, of late ... the Hotel Windsor on Dominion Square."[145] Furthermore, both the Oakleys and Brinleys, who belonged to the American intelligentsia, frequently alluded to encounters or conversations with Montrealers who often times were members of Montreal's well-established English Canadian elite. Such encounters provided opportunity to share an insider's view of the city – a view belonging to the city's privileged minority.

This was particularly obvious in the case of Gordon Brinley, who often mentioned individuals, name-dropping a list of acquaintances of the city's elite. Going to Montreal, she pointed out, would allow them to "look up that young editor Eleanor King wants us to meet – Brian Meredith."[146] (He also wrote travel accounts of Quebec for both American and Canadian publications.[147]) The Brinleys stayed at his Westmount home and enjoyed the company of "his friend Clifford Wilson, Canadian author."[148] Brian Meredith chauffeured them around Montreal, opting to showcase the city's sites of highbrow culture, including theatres, art museums and galleries, and universities. As they passed in front of the Ritz-Carlton Hotel, in another obvious name-drop, Gordon Brinley remembered, this is "where once the Historical Society of Montreal, Geoffrey Chaucer, and I had a memorable afternoon."[149] These asides reveal that travel writers, at times, worked in concert in unexpected ways, with another writer acting as host and guide. In this way, their exchanges offered readers a view of the province through a "double gaze."

ENGLISH CANADIANS

In fact, in the case of English Canadians, several either were born in Montreal, had lived in Montreal at some point, or were living there when working as travel writers. Furthermore, while most were seasoned journalists, a few were familiar figures to some readers for having acquired a distinguished reputation in other areas of endeavour, more often as novelists. This means, of course, that their gaze would be less influenced by mediated representations of the city and coloured, instead, by direct and intimate knowledge of the place, complete with a distant or active sense of belonging. This explains why, in contrast to the writing style they or others adopted when sharing their experiences travelling through the Quebec countryside, they did not position themselves as outsiders having embarked on a trip of discovery nor were their observations infused with as much of a sense of amazement at what they encountered. This being said, they were all committed to showcasing what they felt made the city different from other destinations, and worth the visit.

English Canadians essentially represented the city and its French residents in much the same way as their southern neighbours. Only slight differences emerge that speak to their different national origins. Thus, instead of trying to establish the extent to which the place was foreign, as when representing the province's rural areas, they tried, instead, to demonstrate Montreal as *more* of and better than what could be found in other large, North American cities. Typical in this respect were observations by Dr W.P. Percival, the Quebec deputy minister of Education: "Montreal has many … claims to greatness."[150] To well-known political scientist and humorist Stephen Leacock, "Montreal in point of natural beauty is excelled by no city in the world and rivalled by only two or three."[151] As might be expected, all invariably made much of the fact that it was the country's economic powerhouse. Not only was it remarkable for being "the fifth largest city on the North American continent,"[152] but, as Percival notes, it was "the wealthiest city and financial centre of Canada" and "the second largest port in America in volume of business and has the supremacy over all ports in North America as a center of grain transport."[153] At the same time, travel writers mostly wanted to promote

Montreal as a metropolis that surpassed all North American cities in terms of modernity and sophistication, with attractions that outshone the best of large metropolises. This was "the Dominion's most cosmopolitan city."[154] Not surprisingly, being Canadian, their observations were often infused with patriotism, rooted in an easily recognizable, English Canadian ambivalence towards their southern neighbour. Percival, speaking for many, stressed that Montreal was as progressive as anything a visitor would find back home – more specifically, in the US: "[with] buildings ... as up-to-date as his own, and the citizens are as business-like as those with whom he is familiar. He can read his New York papers on the streets of Montreal at a reasonable hour on the morning of publication, view in the theatres the newest films produced in Hollywood and meet people who will understand his own idioms and figures of speech."[155] Of course, it was not enough to promote Montreal as worthy or interest for being as, or more, American – particularly if it was to attract Americans. Reflective of Canadians' love–hate relationship with the US, travel writers touted Montreal for being, as Kennedy Crone put it, "amongst the least American-looking Canadian cities," which he presumably assumed to be viewed as a drawing card.[156]

Clearly, English Canadian travel writers decided that the best way to convince prospective tourists of its uniqueness was to home in on many of the same features identified by the MTCB. They, too, promoted Montreal as a city of contrasts, where the past rubbed elbows with modernity. It was "modern in construction but still full of souvenirs of bygone days."[157] However, most, including poet and scholar F.O. Call, emphasized that the modern had gained the upper hand: this "city of contrasts" is a place "where the old and the new war together, the new everywhere prevailing."[158]

Furthermore, like the MTCB publicity, and in contrast to Americans, well into the 1950s, they tended to associate French Montrealers with the old and the city's English population with progress. Such pairings proved particularly convincing coming from highly reputed Montreal novelist, Hugh MacLennan. In Montreal, he remarked that visitors encountered "[h]abitant French, priests in cassocks, wimpled nuns, British looking Canadian magnates alighting from taxis at the doors of private clubs, trudging pedestrians whose dark hair and skin reveal at least a partial Indian ancestry."[159] In fact, at times, English Canadian travel writers' portrayal of French Montrealers echoed the infantilizing stereotypes familiar to those who read about countryside *habitants*. Leslie Roberts, for example, characterized "your French-speaking Montrealer" as "an excellent fellow. He is gay. He is thrifty. He is charming. He is industrious."[160] Morley Callaghan, like other novelists/travel writers, included observations that could very well have reinforced readers' condescending views of French Quebeckers. He quoted "a friend of mine" who claimed that "whatever flavour this town has got, the pea soupers [sic] give to it because they know how to laugh," bringing to mind others' descriptions of the eternally happy-go-lucky *habitant*.[161]

However, some, including Morley Callaghan, offered more thoughtful comments. Recounting an exchange with his wife, who had apparently bemoaned the fact that "too many people visit Montreal and never have a word with the French-speaking citizens," he agreed, adding insightfully, "it is easy to do too. You can visit your friends in Westmount, keep to the strictly English-speaking restaurants, read the *Star* and the *Gazette* and forget that people of another language are all around you."[162] The Callaghans' acquaintances with other writers, including Leonard Cohen, as well as actress Denise Pelletier, suggests that their observations would very likely have been coloured by a privileged access to famous Montrealers – individuals with a distinct, if not contradictory, set of attitudes and points of view.

Some travel writers made a distinction between the French who lived in the countryside and those in the city, often indirectly reinforcing the notion that the way of the future was to become more like English-speaking North Americans. More specifically, English Montrealers informed prospective tourists that, in no uncertain terms, they paved the way to the city's progress. Indeed, for Kennedy Crone, there was no doubt that "the commercial development of the city has been mainly due to the Anglo-Saxon and Celtic elements."[163] Percival concurred, claiming, "with the coming of the English, further great strides were made, and the town began to expand much more rapidly."[164] Further bolstering the idea that French Montrealers had not quite stepped out of the past, travel writers encouraged those who wanted to encounter the quintessential French Montrealer to head for the Bonsecours market. Calling to mind the advice offered by the MTCB, Percival remarked, "no visitor who wishes to get acquainted with French Canadian life should miss [seeing it]."[165] According to MacLennan, "the people who throng it seem to have entered the city from an earlier century."[166] As well, travel writers reinforced the French connection to the past when they brought up the topic of religion, drawing their readers' attention to the city's numerous churches and claiming that the "love of religion in which the city has been born has not diminished a whit in the minds of the French Canadians as the centuries have rolled along."[167]

English Canadian travel writers did not only characterize French Montrealers as reminders of old Quebec or the beloved *habitants*. They were, in fact, more likely to single them out simply for being French-speaking. While taking for granted readers' awareness of this distinction over Americans, they nonetheless expressed amazement at how true this was. Born and raised in the city, one author stated that "[what] strikes you very forcibly when you return to Montreal after so long an interval as I have, and probably strikes a newcomer much more forcibly is to what a remarkable extent Montreal is a French city, and not only a French city but a Norman one." While acknowledging that "I was aware that there were a great many French people in Montreal, and that one heard French spoken very generally in public places," he added, "somehow I had forgotten just how French Montreal is." He speculated, "perhaps it has become rather more French than before or it may be that [it] … is now more evenly blended with the two languages everywhere overlapping."[168] Of course, such "memory lapses" served him well as a travel writer intent on drawing attention to Montreal's distinctive attributes.

What certainly stood out most was the city's "combination of French and English culture" which "create[d] an atmosphere unique on this continent."[169] They were particularly impressed by the extent to which one heard both French and English in the streets of Montreal and how often the two languages appeared on the city's signage. Just as remarkable was French Montrealers' apparent capacity to converse in English or switch to English seamlessly. Of course, some of this had to do with reassuring their readers that they would have no problem being understood but, contrary to travel writers' comments about the French language in the countryside, mostly they were holding up this language "landscape" as a defining and alluring feature of the city. But as English Canadians were likely more aware of the often fraught relations between the "two solitudes," they may have also wanted to reassure that their hosts would be glad to understand them. The topic of language, then, also offered an opportunity for some to editorialize, inviting would-be tourists to admire French Montrealers' bilingualism as an attribute that set them favourably apart from their English Canadian compatriots. Thus, Kennedy Crone claimed that the French Montrealer "usually speaks as good English as he whose language it is, often better English."[170] More critical still, one travel writer referred to the "well known inability of English speaking people to learn any language but their own."[171]

English Canadian travel writers also underscored the city's French connection by referring to the well-worn label "Paris of America." In sync with MTCB publicity, they likely reinforced reader expectations, but, also in keeping with advertisers of all stripes, rarely did they explain in detail what made it Parisian. Put differently, prospective tourists could not rely on their accounts to learn much about the city's "sinning" opportunities, as most writers tended to stick to suggestive descriptions, too, typically referring to its "gay and scintillating" atmosphere.[172] More than likely, such prudishness was self-imposed censorship, though, occasionally, descriptions were direct. Wallace Ward, for example, described Montreal "as Canada's largest and gaudiest playboy," adding suggestively, "night life is gay and practically uninhibited."[173]

Like the MTCB and the provincial government, writers (and their publishers) were loath to appear as though they were condoning or promoting questionable behaviour. By the late 1950s, this silence could be attributed to other reasons, having much to do with the enforcement of anticorruption measures. Indeed, if legislators and policemen had willingly turned a blind eye or directly partaken in the city's sinning opportunities, by the 1940s they had to contend with those who wanted to clean things up. Lawyer Pacifique Plante, for one, collaborated with the Montreal Police Morality Squad, embarking on a mission to eradicate the endemic corruption plaguing the city police and administration. He pursued his efforts in collaboration with another lawyer, Jean Drapeau, during the Caron Inquiry, which held hearings from 1950 to 1954 to unmask municipal officials' involvement in gambling and prostitution. The reformers' efforts proved successful: although Montreal remained more "open" than most, it would no longer be as tolerant of bad behaviour. Morley Callaghan certainly noticed the changes, stating regretfully that Montreal's notorious wild nightlife was "simply not on show any more." He bemoaned the fact that "there is not even a burlesque house in Montreal" and establishments must respect a two o'clock curfew.[174] When describing in any detail the metropolis's epicurean pleasures, travel writers drew reader attention to a less risqué Montreal attraction. Thus, readers were told again and again that the city was the place to dine in Canada. This becomes particularly noticeable during the 1950s – perhaps a reflection of the more consumer-oriented tastes of postwar tourists. Not only did the city support "more eating places per capita than any other city in the world," but, to their minds, "no other Canadian city is so in love with food or devotes so much time, thought and effort to its preparation and consumption."[175] Furthermore, they claimed that Montreal was "gastronomically sophisticated," due to French Montrealers' discerning palate. They "love to eat. For them a meal is not just a necessity but a pleasure and their restaurants are geared to satisfy them."[176] What stands out in this instance is that, contrary to their American counterparts, they commented on what they perceived to be French Montrealers' lifestyle, enmeshed with the "Paris of America" label. Thus, French Quebeckers in Montreal were more than simply a presence that gave the city an alluring French atmosphere. This suggests that English Canadian travel writers held a multifaceted view of their city-dwelling, French Quebec compatriots. Some reminded them of the traditional habitants, while others brought to mind Parisians, excelling in the fine art of sophisticated living.

Further evidence to suggest that English Canadian travel writers' exposure to a wider variety of information about them made those writers less inclined to paint monochromatic portraits of French Quebeckers be it in the countryside or in Montreal; their distinct gaze did not allow them to speak with authority about the "real French Canadian."

More so than Americans, there is no doubt that Montreal inspired English Canadian travel writers to address wider Canadian social and political issues, notably those pertaining to Canadians' fraught French–English relations. Certainly, Montreal stood as an ideal laboratory to observe the evolution of these relations in urban Quebec. To travel writers' minds, prospective tourists could witness here firsthand the extent to which French and English Canadians lived in harmony. Donning yet again the mantle of goodwill ambassadors, they made the point that "no matter whether the ancestors of the present generation be French or English, almost all have a common desire to understand one another – and from this desire springs much of the city's vitality."[177] As was the case when addressing the topic of life in old Quebec more generally, their remarks were clearly informed by the assumption that readers needed convincing and reassurance that they would be welcomed in Montreal. Travel writers who were either past or present Montreal residents may have had an added incentive to represent their city as a seat of *bonne entente*. By doing so, they could indirectly dissociate themselves from belonging to one of the "solitudes," contributing to the city's uneasy ethnic relations. Although they did not entirely ignore existing tensions, they tried to downplay them as best they could. Thus, Leslie Roberts conceded that "[y]ou will discover English speaking Montrealers whose joy it is to fulminate against their French speaking fellow townsmen. You can find French speaking electors who look askance on the English speaking resident of Westmount or Notre Dame de Grace." But, nonetheless, he maintained, "they are exceptions that prove the rule."[178] Overall he argued, "they contrive to live together, not in dutiful, well-bred politeness, but in mutual understanding and harmony – a quality that cannot be reproduced in any other major city in Christendom so far as I know."[179]

As for Kennedy Crone, he granted, "there is no general intermarrying" between English and French, yet he assured readers, "there is generous mixing of the two races in business and social affairs and other matters of interest to the community as a whole."[180] And, they did not shy away from broaching particularly controversial issues. Indeed, Crone tackled head on the intractable Protestant–Catholic divide, claiming that "much more religious and race trouble is credited to Montreal then actually exists." More than that, he soundly rebuked "the ultra-Protestant who wonders how the poor

Protestant minority can get along with the awful Roman Catholic majority," pointing out, "it can honestly be said that the majority is just as tolerant as any Protestant majority has ever been."[181] Percival concurred, assuring readers, "the Protestants frankly admit the generosity that the majority continue to show toward them by consulting their responsible officials before effecting educational changes that touch their interests."[182] As for those inclined to question French Quebeckers' sense of Canadian patriotism, Roberts reassured would-be tourists that "he is a first class Canadian, in whom there is far less of the rebel and the agitator than there is in his English-speaking counterpart, class for class."[183] At times, travel writers also invoked the past – through the eyes of Francis Parkman – to account for what they purported to be the present-day harmonious relations between former enemies. Starting from an ingrained assumption that "British rule proved very mild" following the Conquest, Percival claimed, "the two races saw that if they were to live together in peace they must respect and preserve each other's rights."[184] More specifically, "French Canadians ... had found in British supremacy the guarantee of what they considered to be a real freedom, involving recognition of their language and religious practices."[185] In short, all had been well since, and this would be obvious to all who visited Montreal.

FRENCH QUEBECKERS

Perhaps the most effective way to highlight the extent to which national origin determines reaction to a travel destination is to examine how French Quebec travel writers gazed on their province's metropolis and what they believed would incite their compatriots to visit the city. Doing so, however, is much more challenging, as evidence is hard to come by. One can only deduce from this that the city did not inspire the few who published travel accounts to share impressions about the city or identify what would make the city worth the visit. The paucity of Montreal publicity coming from the MTCB and the provincial government destined for French Quebeckers further confirms that Montreal was far from being front and centre among those who wrote with prospective tourists in mind. In many ways this stands to reason as, throughout the period, a significant proportion of the province's population lived in Montreal, and, presumably, a large proportion of French Quebeckers were less inclined to use holiday time to "visit" their home town. For most, the countryside would stand as a much more alluring destination.[186]

This was clearly the case with editors of the Quebec City newspaper, *Le Soleil*, which rarely featured Montreal. Meanwhile, during the mid-1920s, in a series of articles entitled "Ce que la Province de Québec offre à ses habitants et à ceux qui la visitent," Montreal's *La Presse* showcased various tourist sites of interest in regions across the province, a few of which pertained to Montreal. These articles completely differed from accounts of their English North American counterparts. What stands out is the fact that these mostly pointed prospective visitors to the city's historical sites, as well as those in adjoining communities worth the trip, and suggested the most scenic routes to get there. While summary information was provided underlining its status as "the large financial, industrial and commercial center of Canada" and "where the past mixes with the present for the great pleasure of our visitors,"[187] there was no obvious attempt to present Montreal as an opportunity to see an up-to-date, modern, and sophisticated city, let alone an American one. Nothing of note was said either about the city's mix of French and English inhabitants, save for the occasional reassuring *bonne ententiste* comment to the effect that in Montreal "French and English language Canadians live as a mass, side by side in perfect harmony, in friendly emulation."[188] Thus, just as in the countryside, Montreal travel accounts tended to focus on tourist sites that encouraged a reconnection with and remembrance of their past – yet another trip down memory lane.

This examination of English North American travel writers' accounts of Montreal, if nothing else, confirms the extent to which these writers were not simply in search of an old Quebec with its New France *habitants*. While many spent more time in and wrote more and lengthier accounts of their time in the countryside, they were nonetheless visibly attracted to the province's most modern and sophisticated metropolis. More to the point, they all took for granted that readers would be drawn to Montreal's quintessentially urban attributes. Such findings require a qualification of general assumptions about the pervasiveness of an antimodernist outlook among travellers to Quebec during the first decades of the twentieth century. They call to mind Cecilia Morgan's conclusions that, with respect to late nineteenth-century English Canadian visitors to Britain, having discovered that they showed a keen interest in "signs of imperial progress in Britain," "[this finding] should caution us against labeling all tourists who were interested in history and historical sites as antimodern."[189] The same thing can be said of those who visited old Quebec and the Paris of the New World during the first half of the twentieth century. Put differently, a better understanding of why travel writers found Montreal worth visiting confirms what may very well be obvious: regardless of time period or destination, those who travel seek to enjoy a wide range of experiences however incompatible they might appear on the surface. In times of accelerated change, this might mean being simultaneously drawn to worlds

feared to be either lost or fast disappearing, one inscribed in a nebulous pastness and another which displayed contemporary modern progress, in which
citizens could take pride. Montreal had the advantage of offering both. The
case of Montreal also complicates what most tourist promoters understood
by the importance of promoting difference. In certain respects, they were, in
fact, underscoring sameness. Indeed, English North American travel writers
assumed that drawing parallels between Montreal and the largest cities in the
US would enhance its appeal. In the case of English Canadians, this speaks to
an inherent American-envy: Montreal offered visitors the pleasure and pride
of experiencing a taste of America at home. For Americans, going to Montreal might very well reinforce the gratifying sense that the ultimate expression of modernity in all things was, by definition, American. Of course, this
is what traditional nationalists deplored, but, in the case of Montreal, they
could in no way hope to shape visitors' gaze as they did in the more recently
accessible countryside. The city had already acquired a well-defined popular and seemingly immutable image mostly through its reputation as North
America's "sin city." All the same, Montreal, as the Paris of the New World,
was certainly held up as different. This reinforced a French connection that
was being emphasized for the province as a whole. A marketing coherence
was also maintained, as both official tourism promoters and travel writers
included in their slogans the words "old" and "new" – albeit in various permu-
tations – for both Montreal and Quebec as a whole. Thus, while the French
population was, for the most part, identified with the past, in Montreal, it
could offer an intangible Gallic sophistication miles apart from what tourists
would see in the *habitants*.

6

FROM *OLD* TO *BELLE*

During the early 1960s, tourism promoters markedly changed the way they represented the province. Instead of foregrounding what was old about Quebec, they changed course, highlighting, instead, distinctly contemporary and modern pleasures. "Old Quebec" and "La province de Québec" were replaced with "La Belle Province." More significantly, Quebec tourism itself was divested of the role many traditional nationalists ascribed to it in order to revitalize a French Canada, where "naught shall suffer change." This rebranding can only be understood by taking into account the context in which it occurred – a time of remarkable political and social transformation, otherwise known as the Quiet Revolution.

For the tourism industry, the 1960s was the decade during which trends identified in earlier decades accelerated at an unprecedented pace. Those who, in the 1930s, predicted tourism would stimulate economic development were proven right, as tourism continued to be a growing source of revenue beyond the Second World War. In fact, by the 1950s, "mass tourism truly took flight in North America [as] vacations ... came to represent almost everything good about North American culture."[1] During the immediate postwar period in Quebec, the number of visitors tripled, and by the 1960s tourism "stood in third place ... after pulp and mines."[2] Such economic indicators led Department of Industry and Commerce officials to be optimistic, arguing, "the tourism industry deserves to retain our attention all the more as it can ... increase or decrease of our commercial trade deficit."[3]

However, all was not well. Government promoters never ceased to caution that this lucrative industry remained vulnerable, as competition for the tourist dollar was intensifying. While alarm bells had sounded before, by the 1960s new and potentially more threatening developments were emerging. The rapidly growing affordability of international air travel featured high on the list, as it meant that popular European countries, as well as other more exotic destinations, notably Mexico, were suddenly more accessible.[4] Although, by the early 1960s, Canada had succeeded in reversing its travel deficit, those working in the industry were only too aware of how fragile such reversals were, which made such warnings more convincing. More worrisome still was the mounting evidence that Americans from the northeastern states were increasingly heading for closer Canadian destinations, especially Ontario.[5] And US tourist promoters, more than ever, were pulling out all the stops to encourage their citizens to travel at home.[6] In short, Quebec tourist promoters could no longer assume that Quebec's "natural advantages," such as its geographical proximity and its distinct French character, would be sufficient drawing cards for its principal American tourist market.

Tourist-conscious as never before, the Quebec government undertook major changes to meet these challenges. For one, tourism was given a much greater visibility in state bureaucracy, and politicians took on a more proactive role. During the 1960 election, Jean Lesage, Quebec Liberal Party leader, running under the slogans *Maîtres chez nous* (Masters in our own house) and *Il faut que ça change* (It's time for a change), promised to create a Department of Tourism. While far from being an innovative idea, this time it was taken up by a political candidate who became premier and one who kept his word. In 1961, Lesage's first initiative was to turn the Tourist Branch of the PPB into the Provincial Tourist Bureau (PTB), giving tourism a separate administrative identity under the aegis of the Department of the Provincial Secretary. Robert Prévost, appointed PPB director in 1959, stayed on as director of the newly formed PTB. A seasoned tourist promoter and former journalist, Prévost put his public relations communication skills to good use.[7] The same year, the government also revived the Tourist Council to provide guidance on how best to develop the industry, with Prévost named technical advisor. It proved much more proactive than its predecessor.[8]

In 1959, the Tourist Council had already held nine meetings in nine different provincial regions to gauge the overall state of the industry as well as what improvements were required, receiving more than one hundred submissions from a wide range of industry players. The following year, eighteen recommendations were made; most importantly and widely publicized was the creation of a Department of Tourism to better coordinate tourism-related activities in the province. Following suit, in 1963, Lesage's government acted on this particular recommendation, setting up the Department of Tourism, Fish and Game (DTFG), with Prévost as assistant-deputy minister in charge of the department's newly named Tourist Branch (TB).[9]

From then on, Prévost became the prominent public face of government tourism promotion. In contrast to Tessier or Gouin, Prévost viewed the industry foremost as a business, "a source of foreign currency, a money transfusion … [I]t multiplies jobs; it contributes to a large extent to maintaining our standard of living at a high level of pleasure. In sum, it guarantees a certain material happiness to the population."[10] Quebeckers were "the shareholders of the tourism industry" who drew "dividends from it, without exception, even though they do not all come into contact with travelers."[11] More than did his predecessors, Prévost spent a great deal of time discussing marketing strategies, attempting more effective and creative ways to grab the attention of prospective tourists. And, in line with his unrelenting promoter's zeal, he peppered his reports with self-congratulatory claims that his branch was the first to undertake various innovative marketing initiatives. In the same manner, he made presentations to various business organizations directly involved in tourism promotion – many in the US – to convince their members of Quebec business opportunities. These included advertising agencies, chambers of commerce, travel agents, as well as automobile associations and other transportation companies. This stood in contrast to Gouin's approach, who had taken every opportunity to draw the attention of French Quebeckers to possible profits of the tourism industry by better showcasing French language and culture.

In 1960, reflective of this new climate, government funding for advertising campaigns and printed publicity material in newspapers and magazines outside Quebec increased by close to 35 per cent.[12] This being said, the newly elected Liberal government's priorities were elsewhere, as it poured significantly more resources into healthcare reform, exploitation of natural resources, and overhauling the provincial education system. The bureau's (later the branch) total budget did not see a significant rise until 1966 – the year preceding Expo 67.[13] Regardless, tourist promoters expanded the government tourism publicity outreach as never before, turning their sights on English Canadians in hopes of stimulating interprovincial tourism. Previously, Quebec tourist promoters periodically voiced interest in attracting their English-speaking compatriots in larger numbers – principally during the war years. But the more competitive climate of the 1960s propelled government promoters to spur interprovincial tourism with unparalleled resolve. Now was the time to capitalize on this encouraging trend. They were not alone in this endeavour, as the Canadian Tourist Association was also pushing for an increase in east–west tourism as a way to reduce the travel deficit at the national level. Ever the boaster, Prévost claimed that Quebec promoters were the first to wage a publicity campaign to stimulate interprovincial tourism.[14]

At times, he and others portrayed interprovincial trade "as a very precious tool in our collective efforts to unite Canada and to have Canadians know themselves better," but such Canadian patriotic musings were rare.[15] More often than not, they flagged its undisputable economic advantages. And, they certainly put their money where their mouths were. Although funding for publicity in the US continued to receive the largest share of the TB's allocation, the percentage earmarked for Quebec's "sister provinces," increased steadily throughout the period: 8.71 per cent in 1959–60, climbing three-fold to 21.58 per cent in 1961, subsequently increasing steadily.[16] It appears the TB's efforts paid off, as the number of English Canadians entering the province increased by 13.27 per cent between 1960 and 1961.[17]

The Tourist Bureau did not ignore French Quebeckers. In fact, Prévost pointed out that it was time to do more and decided that a dedicated campaign would be initiated to "stimulate interregional tourism, similar to the one in the United States" and Ontario. Like his predecessors, he wanted "Quebec citizens to travel their own province instead of going elsewhere."[18] To this end, in 1960, the TB produced five billboard ads close to Montreal and Quebec City with the slogan "Visitons le Québec d'Abord."

Increasing the size of its publicity material went hand in hand with new marketing strategies. For instance, the dimensions of black and white ads increased threefold, with some publicity taking full-page ads in widely circulated magazines. Also as part of this campaign, in 1960 four-colour ads were inserted in all Ontario and Maritime daily newspapers. In 1961, the TB launched 300 publicity billboards in various provinces along highways close to the American border, increasing these to 400 the following year – a first strategy of this sort in the province's tourism promotion.[19] In 1962, the TB also distributed a film, *Au pays du bon voisinage/Land of Good Neighbours*, that, according to Prévost, may "be considered the first produced in Canada with the specific aim of stimulating interprovincial tourism."[20]

As well, at that time, Quebec tourist promoters eagerly drew attention to the TB's new and cutting-edge marketing initiatives and the extent to which they broke with past practices. Prévost, first among them, was particularly proud that, in 1961, the TB undertook to replace and redesign all its printed marketing material, bringing it up to date, giving it "an impeccable typographical appearance" and "elegance" to better reflect what officials characterized as the "prestige of Quebec," including making much greater use of colour.[21] For the first time, they produced five, new full-page ads using a four-colour process printing. Also in 1961, Prévost proudly announced that in New York's Times Square, prospective American tourists would see an electronic billboard advertisement of 4,000 light bulbs – apparently another first of its kind in Canadian provincial tourism promotion. In fact, some of the government's initiatives, including this one, attracted the attention of the advertising community at large.[22]

The Tourist Bureau also increased its television advertising. The number of ads on American television increased fourfold, from 49 in 1959–60 to 164 in 1960–61. Those targeting the Canadian market increased from 36 to 270, 34 in provinces other than Quebec.[23] True to form, Prévost bragged that, "of all Canadian provinces, it is Quebec that owns the largest number of film copies to ensure its tourist publicity."[24] In 1963, he summed up this first round of initiatives by noting that "Quebec's tourism advertising has passed from the "artisanal" stage to the professional one."[25] What can certainly be ascertained is that in the space of a few years, Quebec tourism promotion became not only a competitive business but also modern and state of the art.

Of more enduring significance, however, publicity content changed, reflecting an emerging understanding of what made Quebec distinct. Shortly before the Liberal victory in 1960, Georges-Émile Lapalme, then Liberal opposition leader, together with the support of provincial tourist promoters, had argued that advertising content should faithfully reflect a contemporary, modern Quebec. Tourist promoters' main concern was to draw in visitors by foregrounding a Quebec that *had* changed and was still changing. To this end, in December 1959, Lapalme proposed a rethink of the province's "publicity" and "propaganda," as it was time to "abandon a few of the clichés that no longer have any significance and present Quebec under a false light. It is the first step one must take."[26] This remarkable reversal is directly attributable to the province's changing nationalist landscape. Indeed, tourist promoters found themselves in sync with a new generation of nationalists, advocating for a more secular nationalism, fully recognizing Quebec as an industrial and urban society. While traditionalists lost ground, the link between tourism promotion and nationalism was nonetheless maintained, but the new cohort of tourist promoters ended up validating and marketing a newly emerging sense of national identity – one very much rooted in modernity.

This transformation was made apparent in several ways. To begin with, visitors were told that Quebec was a place of rapid development and modernity. As early as 1961, the TB added a film, *Le Québec industriel*, to its audio-visual catalogue, claiming "the industrial expansion of the province has attracted a large external publicity and numerous are the tourists who want to see for themselves the accomplishments that have resulted from it."[27] A brochure, *La Province de Québec*, reflecting this campaign, proclaimed, "[i]n recent decades, the province has become rapidly industrialized." Referring to ongoing developments in northern Quebec, the brochure pointed out, "once a vast wilderness, [the area] is now the site of tremendous mining operations." While past government promoters had also suggested that the province's modern economic development might be a tourist attraction, they did not give it as much prominence. In the early 1960s, rural areas could, at most, evoke earlier times. The brochure described "vast rural regions where the farm tradition, despite its adaptation to industrial progress, is a reminder of Old-World France." More telling still, some publicity material included critical assessments of the province's past. Visitors would learn that "gone are the years when the only aim was to survive, and where culture was restricted to the elite." Rather, today, "[f]ree from urgent material needs/worries, Quebec now is heading towards new summits. In full maturity, culture is penetrating all levels of society ... and is giving rise to a veritable blossoming of scholars and artists who carry the prestige of French Canada to the capitals of the world."[28]

But of more direct interest to would-be tourists, Quebec, from then on, was defined by the pleasures it offered the senses. Coming to Quebec was less about time travel than taking time to enjoy a destination where lifestyle and temperament were very much in tune with contemporary pleasures. Tourists were invited to "Take your pick of Pleasures in Québec."[29] The province in its entirety mutated into a "state of mind," a "life style," a "heart that beats."[30] The TB also started to make greater use of drawings, in the belief that this more suggestive representation would "better reflect the French face of Quebec,"[31] as its "difference is not only visual: it is a lifestyle. Such characteristics often elude the camera lens."[32] Visitors were invited to "Come and enjoy LES BEAUTÉS DU QUÉBEC" [sic],[33] and promoters showcased the lifestyle of its people as a temperament. The Québécois were not defined by their loyalty to tradition but by their "joie de vivre."[34] Quebec was "a land where *franche gaïté* is a way of life."[35] And, effectively encapsulating this far reaching reimagining, Quebec was no longer old but *belle*.

It was also a place where tourists could enjoy "mouth watering cuisine." Previously, Montreal had been promoted as a centre of exceptional cuisine, but it was not highlighted as a central provincial attraction, let alone as intrinsic to French Queckers' lifestyle and culture. Newly baptised as *La Belle Province*, promoters positioned Quebec as a food destination.[36] By the 1960s, the promise of a "distinctive cuisine"[37] was prominently featured as a chief drawing card. The declarative "Quebec is famous for food"[38] was specifically highlighted in the ad series *See the Province of Québec Say – Magnifique!*, with one dedicated to *La cuisine*.[39] This increased attention to cuisine also gave new life to the "Grands salons culinaires." These offered chefs from around the province an opportunity to showcase their culinary artistry.[40] The 1964 edition held in Montreal was, in fact, under the auspices of the DTFG. Interestingly, this targeted focus on cuisine caused tourist promoters to become involved in a debate over national identity. More specifically, it raised the question whether this cuisine should effectively be identified with French

Quebec. Tourist promoters, in the past, made attempts to encourage hotel-keepers and restaurant owners, particularly in the countryside, to serve typical, regional French Canadian dishes, inspired by recipes handed down from past generations, but such entreaties were sporadic. In the 1960s, chefs and restaurant owners were also encouraged to use local produce and adapt traditional recipes to the discerning tastes of their patrons. Indeed, the Hostelry Service Branch published a new compilation of typical traditional recipes, "Adventures in French Canadian Cuisine," coinciding with the Grand Salon culinaire of 1966. Yet, for all this, it was understood that the cuisine from France – not Quebec – was the ultimate benchmark of sophisticated culinary excellence and the type of cooking most appreciated by tourists, particularly Americans. For Prévost, the "Province ... must offer an international cuisine, and, more specifically, the one that rallies the most votes from all continents: French cuisine." Certainly, dishes featured at the annual Grands salons culinaires and menus in Quebec City, Montreal restaurants, and other popular tourist destinations gave pride of place to French cuisine. Culinary refinement was judged according to a chef's capacity to emulate this cuisine's reputed dishes, food presentation, and etiquette.[41] The drawing for the ad *La Cuisine – Magnifique!* certainly conveyed this idea of a refined, French dining experience. It featured a sophisticated-looking couple seated at a table with a checkered tablecloth, wine glasses, and an attentive sommelier pointing to "the delicate finesse of French cooking." This being said, the ad also drew tourists' attention to typically local cuisine. It contrasted the "robust onion soup to [the] delicate *crêpe suzette*" and assured readers that both would "flatter the gourmet's palate." (See figure 6.1.) This nod to traditional cuisine reflected Prévost's opinion that "it was important to revalorize Quebec regional dishes." But his endorsement did not necessarily entail wholesale resurrection. As he put it:

> It has often been noted that the stomach of the urban citizen of
> the 20th century would not be able to assimilate with as much ease
> [as] the one of the first pioneers, dishes such as *tourtière, ragoût de*
> *pâtes* etc. Yet, when one takes into account the great ability of our
> chefs, there is no reason to doubt that they will be able to offer their
> clientele lighter versions, more digestible of this cuisine enjoyed by
> our ancestors.[42]

Clearly, promoters felt that traditional cuisine could be marketed as an asset once it was presented as *one* component of French Quebec cuisine (and not the main one) or when it acquired the more sophisticated veneer of its

6.1 | "La cuisine – Magnifique!" Quebec Provincial Tourist
Bureau ad, 1960.

French counterpart. While this was far from a vote of confidence, it was an affirmation that "La Belle Province" could cater to the most discerning and up-to-date connoisseur's tastes.

Not surprisingly, tourist promoters endeavoured to showcase Quebec as a specifically French destination. However, in line with past commentators, many such as *Le Soleil*'s editor deplored that "one still made use of English signs and ads for restaurants, motels, menus." This was not how to "retain our foreign clientele that does not like to find *chez nous* a pale imitation of what it has *en mieux* at home."[43] Such pronouncements concerned with the province's tourism industry also echoed those of their predecessors. Thus, a month before his election, Lesage lamented that "the French fact is not emphasized enough [in the province's tourism publicity] yet it is what distinguishes us from other regions in North America."[44] Prévost clearly shared his superior's outlook. To his mind, revamping Quebec's advertisements was a deliberate effort to "ensure the omnipresence of our French face."[45] To say nothing of the fact that "the French face of Quebec" is "an extremely remunerative asset and very precious for our economy."[46] Echoing their traditionalist predecessors, they, too, worried about the disfigurement of the province's French face.

Indeed, sounding a familiar refrain, Prévost warned an audience of Sept-Îles tourist promoters in the newly developing tourist area of the North Shore not to repeat mistakes of other popular and more established Quebec tourist destinations. He condemned the fact that "roads in these areas appeared as canyons encased between two rows of signs advertising English corporate names, much more representative of Ontario, Florida or Texas." He pleaded, "for Heaven's sake ... [let's not] let the French face of the North Shore deteriorate to the point where it will eventually require painful plastic surgery ... Do not tolerate that ugliness come to mar such a magical panorama."[47] At the same time, he did not share the solutions put forth by many contemporary nationalists who favoured state intervention to encourage promoters and business owners to make use of French signs. In his view, the "task could not be accomplished by a series of government decrees." Instead, he suggested having "intermediary groups," such as local chambers of commerce, *syndicats d'initiatives*, parish councils, and the like set up their own vigilance committees.[48] He would never tire of saying that *refrancisation* would be impossible without the massive involvement of individuals.[49] In this he was echoing points made earlier by Paul Gouin and members of the Tourism Council in 1961, who argued that one should follow "the more democratic formula of public education and persuasion."[50]

But any similarities end there. By the early 1960s, the French language was made a key feature of their marketing strategy. Not only was the province to be referred to as *belle* but text in new ads was interspersed with French words or expressions as never before. Promoters now made more extensive and playful use of French, adopting words that either had their literal equivalent in English or would have been familiar expressions to the majority of Anglophones, such as the TB's 1961 ad series, *See La Province de Québec Say – Magnifique!* But the TB's boldest initiative in this regard, launched in 1962

6.2 | "Prenez des vacances à la francaise." Quebec
Provincial Tourist Bureau ad, 1962.

and repeated in 1963, included ads published entirely in French in *The New Yorker* and *Time* magazines. (See figure 6.2.)[51] Officials were well aware of the risk of this daring initiative, but it apparently worked. At the end of the first year, requests for information from prospective tourists increased by 42 per cent.[52]

While the ads were effective, tourist promoters made every effort to ensure that lacking knowledge of French was not perceived as a barrier. In addition to using easily recognizable French words, it was made reassuringly clear that "the majority of [Quebec's] citizens, while they are of French origin, are bilingual."[53] Addressing prospective English-speaking visitors directly, Prévost invited them to witness "the charm that springs from our bilingual status, one of the characteristics of Quebec's appeal."[54] He also advised those who might be future hosts, "when we address the Anglophone clientele of the continent we do not present Québécois as essentially unilingual. We must reassure them on this point."[55] Furthermore, the province's more detailed publicity became fully bilingual, maintaining a practice of including a glossary of useful words and expressions. Tellingly, by titling the lexicon "Fun with Fonetic French," promoters signalled that English-speaking visitors would enjoy their French immersion.[56] In 1966, they further claimed that, "our English speaking compatriots and our neighbors across the forty fifth [sic] often wish ... to address people they meet in the street or in commercial establishments in French. This gives them the chance to practice the language for which they have sometimes acquired a few elements."[57]

Taken as a whole, the new *refrancisation* marketing strategies of the 1960s provides insight into what tourist promoters understood to be the province's distinctive attributes. While many of their statements bring to mind those of Tessier and Gouin, they reflect, in fact, French Quebeckers' changing sense of national identity – one for which the French language was replacing Catholicism and tradition. By featuring it more prominently in their ads, promoters were, in effect, asserting the emergence of one attribute of the new Québécois identity to the world in a bold, unprecedented way, by demanding a more active recognition from visitors that Quebec was a French destination. (In fact the word "Québécois" increasingly appeared in ads throughout the decade.) Yet, seen from a different perspective, these *refrancisation* efforts stood as less ambitious than those of their traditional nationalist predecessors. Indeed, *refranciser*, by the 1960s, meant just that: to give the French language pride of place in the public sphere, notably on the province's signage. It did not stand as an invitation to French Quebeckers to resuscitate, as well, traditional values and practices based on loyalty to the ancestors, to a rural way of life, and to the Church – the one so neatly encapsulated by the "Old Quebec" slogan. Tourism was divested of the traditional nationalist agenda. The modern-day Québécois were no longer encouraged to embark on such significant "behaviour modification" in order to be authentic.

Other than asking them to speak French, the only time tourist promoters invited French Quebeckers to modulate their behaviour was to be welcoming, courteous, and friendly – essentially to be good hosts. As Prévost stated, more than anything else "it [was] incumbent on each one of us to do his part so that, in the minds of our visitors, the words 'hospitalité' and 'Québec' be synonymous."[58] It should be said that French Quebeckers were not alone in the need to be welcoming hosts. As historian Karen Dubinsky points out, across Canada, at a time of increasing travel deficits, "an expanded notion of the importance of courtesy became a fundamental tenet of the post-war tourist industry, applicable to service industry personnel and 'civilians' alike." Thus it was that tourist promoters across the country took initiatives to promote collective good manners, the most involved being education campaigns.[59] But officials at the TB worked particularly hard to convince visitors that the province's population was *more* hospitable than neighbouring competitors. While in previous decades, publicity material had certainly noted French Quebeckers' friendliness, by the 1960s, *hospitalité* was touted as one of their defining personality traits, and Quebec was branded as "the province where Friendliness is a way of life."[60] A new slogan, "Hospitalité Spoken Here," would become ubiquitous in government publicity for several years to come.

Tourist promoters also addressed prospective French Quebec tourists. They essentially tried to sell the travel experience as something fun, very much in line with advertising to English Canadian and American tourists. In fact, the first time the word *belle* appeared on a tourist ad was to capture French Quebeckers' attention. A "Visitons la Belle Province" slogan was first issued in 1954 by the Association des hôteliers de la Province de Québec to encourage French Quebeckers to travel in Quebec.[61] Government officials in the 1960s viewed it as effective and worth encouraging. By 1966, they cooperated with private-sector promoters to produce and distribute an official publicity panel, "Visit, Visitons *la belle province*." Of note, rarely did government promoters invoke patriotic duty per se or tout travel as an opportunity for them to embark on a trip "down memory lane." Clearly having urbanites in mind, these ads invited Quebeckers to explore their home province and visit regions unknown to them, notably the province's scenery, as well as small, rural or coastal communities.

Government tourist promoters did not completely dispose of the past as a means to draw visitors, but, by then, it was simply represented as one among many of the province's attractions. Old Quebec was no longer systematically mentioned in all ads, and references to traditional ways of life and historical figures were gone from slogans and most widely circulated ads. Some echoed the "city-of-contrast" representation of Montreal, inviting visitors to "An 'Old World' in the New!"[62] Others specified, "*La belle province* is an intriguing blend of modern vigor and *Old World* charm."[63] This was most obvious in the ad *L'atmosphère – Magnifique!*[64] showcasing Quebec's past. However, by pairing it with "atmosphere," the message was that Quebec now mostly offered tourists the opportunity to *feel* the past. It morphed into a sensual magnet rather than an opportunity to time travel or gain historical knowledge. From a marketing perspective, such representations were all of one with the overriding message of Quebec's tourist publicity: even the past was to be experienced through the senses and could easily coexist with the image of a modern Quebec and not undermine the new *La Belle Province* brand.

Nonetheless visitors were still told they would encounter a few regions that evoked old Quebec. However, time travel to seventeenth-century France in North America was nowhere suggested. A telling illustration of just how things had changed can be found in the Quebec government's 1966 Bureau d'aménagement de l'Est du Québec report making recommendations to further develop the Gaspésie tourism industry. It proposed *reconstructing* (my emphasis) old Quebec with the "creation ... of a fishing village similar to those of the early [20th] century." Such a site would attract visitors who "want to see how simply live those who have not yet been contaminated by urbanisation."[65] Clearly promoters believed that tourists now would gladly content themselves with a make-believe past, informed by an unstated recognition that antimodernist hopes and expectations had greatly faded over the years.[66]

This new reading of the Quebec rural landscape also inspired a semantic change. Promoters mostly referred to "agricultural" communities, an "agricultural parish," an "agricultural center,"[67] or an "agricultural ... industry"[68] – all terms which spoke to these regions' economy rather than a lifestyle. Even the Île d'Orléans, previously singled out as a pristine old Quebec preserve, was now "noted for its strawberries, its delicate cream cheese and other agricultural products." The best tourists could hope for if they wanted to experience old Quebec directly was coming upon vestiges or reminders of it that had survived including historic manor houses, churches, and monuments, despite extraordinary modernization. Thus, what remained old on Île d'Orléans were "traditional Quebec farmhouses of stone with steep-pitched roofs."[69] As for Charlevoix's Isle-aux-Coudres, it stood as "a mid-river museum of old-time French Canadiana." Indeed, "on this peaceful island are the typical farmhouses with three-foot-thick stones walls and steeply-pitched roofs, the conical stone windmills of olden days."[70]

Most striking is how very little promoters made of people living in rural areas. When they were mentioned, little was said about their way of life. More to the point, no longer were tourists promised that they would encounter descendants of the seventeenth-century *habitants*, faithfully keeping alive the old-world traditions of their ancestors in contemporary Quebec. In fact, the term *habitant* appeared to have been edited out of the publicity material altogether. On Île d'Orléans tourists were told, "the ancient stone farmhouses [were] now owned by city people."[71] As for the Gaspé, they would simply encounter "the land of a people who add to proverbial Quebec friendliness a wealth of historical traditions."[72] Further details of these traditions were not provided nor that any of these traditions were part of their everyday lives. Catholic religious practices were also given little text. Visitors would learn simply that "the Province of Quebec is ... different because of its many famous shrines, by the profusion of its ways of the cross and roadside chapels which are evidence of a deep attachment to the faith of the ancestors."[73] In short, religion deserved attention when it appeared in stone.

This new representation of the past had further repercussions. For instance, scant attention was given to Maria Chapdelaine. Promoters for the Lac St-Jean region did not invoke its erstwhile, popular heroine. Péribonka now was simply the place where "a French novelist, Louis Hémon ... had shared the laborious existence of its settlers, made [it] the scene of its celebrated novel *Maria Chapdelaine*." As with other regions which only offered reminders of the past, "Hémon's memory is recalled by a monument which was erected by the Société des Amis de Maria Chapdelaine in 1963 [sic], as well as a museum and a house which was occupied by the author."[74]

The way promoters marketed arts and crafts also indirectly sent a message that Quebec offered few opportunities to witness living history. If, by the 1950s, these artefacts had been increasingly held up as decorative objects, by the 1960s this view of arts and crafts was to dominate with products show-casing a sophisticated level of artistry among Quebec craftspeople, losing any pretension of utilitarian value. Thus, visitors would "know [the atmosphere] has transcended time as you view the works of Quebec's *avant-garde*."[75] Arti-sans in Charlevoix, such as "the weavers, the wood carvers and the others are themselves artists in the media of wool, wood and linen."[76] In representing artisans in this way, promoters were reinforcing Quebec's image as a dynamic and highly sophisticated society. Prévost summed up this new perspective by looking back and making the point that "until a quarter of a century ago, arts and crafts in the province of Quebec, boiled down to hooked rugs and representational sculpture. We have in this field gone beyond a remarkable stage and the accomplishments of our artisans are often comparable to those of reputed European masters."[77]

Another indication that tourist promoters in the 1960s understood the past very differently from their predecessors comes out in the more detailed publicity material where less emphasis was given to certain historical events and more to others. For one, less attention was paid to the heroism of the New France period. Explorers, missionaries fighting the "cruel" Iroquois, and civilizing the New World lost prominence. Indeed, while readers learned that before the Conquest, New France was a "vast empire" and that Quebec City was the "ancient capital of French Canada," tourist promoters were clearly more interested in conveying the extent to which Quebec was "a French land for more than four centuries."[78] Interestingly enough, more information was provided about French–English relations, including constitutional laws enacted by Britain to govern Quebec following the conquest. Such topics were rarely mentioned in earlier tourism publicity. In tune with this shift in focus, visitors were encouraged to visit various English–French battle sites. The accompanying texts or captions occasionally included a nationalist reading but one very much in tune with the more assertive nationalism of the time. Thus, for example, the site of the battle of St-Charles was described as the "scene of a tragic episode in French Canadian history. In 1837, wearied of its demands for constitutional rights, the population rebelled against the government ... Government troops marched on *Saint-Charles* where the Patriots were badly crushed."[79]

Yet, throughout this publicity material, the point was made that, in the end, "[t]he British ascendancy brought little change."[80] This was not meant to suggest that French Canadians' way of life after the Conquest remained the same whether economically or in the composition of the population. Instead, the objective was to underscore the longevity and rootedness of French Canadians in North America. This is eloquently reflected when the subject of the Conquest is brought up directly – a topic rarely alluded to in previous decades. Tourists would learn that it "has always been viewed by scholars as one of the major turning points in the story of western civilization."[81] Yet, if the authors were ready to concede that "the events of 1759–1760 may represent the dramatic high point in Quebec City's history," they hastened to add, "they by no means overshadow the achievements of peace in the centuries that were to follow." [82] In effect, visitors were encouraged to be impressed "by the prevalence of the 'fait français,' which bears witness to an indisputable desire to survive." Visitors might very well find it "hard to understand how 60,000 French settlers, destitute and isolated by the handing over of Canada to England, have increased their numbers a hundredfold in ten generations." In fact, "it is a true paradox that these workers deeply rooted to the soil, understood the value of their French heritage and had jealously preserved it, while many other subdued nations lost their cultural ties forever."[83] Thus, historical information became a means to affirm the long-standing and secure presence of French people in North America, in tune with a changing sense of national identity.

Amidst all these changes, the impact of Canada's Centennial celebrations cannot be ignored. In 1962, Montreal was officially declared the host of the 1967 Universal and International Exhibition – referred to simply as Expo 67.[84] A highlight of Canada's 100th birthday celebrations, Quebec would host sixty-three countries. Significant costs were involved: while 50 per cent was to be paid by the federal government, 37.5 per cent was covered by the Quebec provincial government, and 12.5 per cent by the City of Montreal.[85] Organizers planned to attract 10 million visitors who would, it was hoped, make, on average, three trips, for a total of 30 million paid entries between

28 April and 27 October. Great hopes were placed on attracting the largest proportion of European tourists ever to Canada, Quebec, and Montreal. In 1964, Gilles Tremblay of Expo's Business Development Bureau pointed out, "going back ten years, the major purpose for Europeans travelling to North America was business." In 1962, studies confirmed that "70% of all the Europeans visiting the US and 80% of all the visitors from Europe to Canada travelled alone." But that was expected to change by 1967: "because of higher incomes [they] can now afford to take vacation trips abroad."[86] And, Expo 67 stood as an untold opportunity to further develop the industry and promote to the world the new "La Belle Province" brand. The overarching objective that informed so many initiatives in the few years preceding Expo, and with much greater focus in 1966 and 1967, was to convince the expected surge of visitors to Montreal to extend their stay and visit the province. To this end, provincial promoters put out slogans inviting tourists to "Visit Expo 67, then discover la belle province." Expo was an enticing hook to attract tourists to enjoy Quebec's "BEAUTÉS."

In this exceptional context, the federal government, who had, since the 1930s, taken charge of promoting Canada as a whole abroad and at home, through the Canadian Government Travel Bureau (CGTB), stepped up in 1967 to foreground the province.[87] Thus, it called upon prospective tourists to "This year, visitez le Québec, Canada. Il est unique." Prospective visitors were to understand that Expo 67 was the jewel in the crown of the country's "100th birthday."[88] Prévost, appointed to sit on a Centennial Commission's advisory committee on information and promotion, ensured he was well aware of his federal counterparts' objectives and was likely to raise concerns should Expo 67 promoters' initiatives duplicate or run counter to those of Quebec.

Events post-Expo were also front of mind. In fact, officials and observers of all stripes held up 1967 as a make or break year, as both the province and Montreal–Quebec faced a "vital test: The fate of the tourist industry in Montreal–Quebec over the next five to ten years is going to be settled in the city and in the province in the next six months."[89] Indeed, the minister of the DTFG, Gabriel Loubier, often intervened to remind the public that, "Expo 67 can be a trampoline or an abyss for the future of tourism." And, although the minister recognized that "the great number of visitors who will come to Quebec during Expo 67 might create a certain nervousness, a certain irritation among the population," this should not preclude Quebeckers from being hospitable, sounding the oft repeated refrain to be "courteous, polite and agreeable."[90] In fact, a vast publicity campaign was launched in the early days of the event under the "Dites Bonjour" theme. During July 1967, department officials even went so far as to travel the province, identifying fifty individuals who stood out as particularly good hosts. Ads were then published identifying "Quebeckers who topped our list this week for their outstanding *hospitalité*." These lucky ones "were invited, along with two friends of their choice to spend a day at Expo 67 ... all expenses paid."[91]

More than ever, officials at the TB also became particularly proactive in reaching a wider pool of what they clearly saw as surrogate propagandists, including travel writers, as well as radio and television journalists and film directors. For one, the TB expanded its long-established marketing practice of sending out prewritten travel accounts complete with photos directly to newspapers or magazines. As specified in a TB annual report, "these texts are prepared exclusively for publications which have requested them" and "sometimes we supply information to editors who wish to write their own stories." This was certainly a way to save money. Indeed, in its 1965 annual report, officials indicated that the "total value of the space obtained free of charge was established at close to $1,200,000 ... almost double the total reached the preceding year."[92] But, it also allowed them to "suggest to journalists excellent topics they could showcase" or, more specifically, to give pride of place to regions or sites they wanted promoted.[93] In fact, promoters also sent ghostwritten reports directly to travel writers. In 1963–64, approximately 150 travel writers received "illustrated reports that the Tourist Branch prepares with great care."[94] All these marketing strategies were deemed particularly effective as "contrary to paid ads ... [which] the reader peruses with a certain scepticism precisely because they come from *propagandistes,* signed reports carry with them an undeniable cachet of disinterestedness that catch the attention."[95] Furthermore, TB officials claimed that this was particularly true, as "such reports are signed by well known writers."[96]

Furthermore, increasing energy was put into courting travel writers one-on-one, by extending multiple invitations to encourage them to visit the province, accompanied by hand-picked hosts, mandated as guides to sites they wished to promote. After all, "these people's very work is to offer tourists suggested destinations." In 1966, no less than 536 writers came to Quebec, not including those in groups.[97] Most notably, the intent was clearly to convince them – and by extension their readers – that Quebec was no longer old. As to be expected, Prévost was on the front line of this effort, engaging with these potential marketing allies, both inside and outside the province. True to form, he did not shy away from hyperbole. Addressing an audience of American travel writers in Delaware, for example, he impressed on them that "Quebec is becoming an industrial giant, the hub of western industrial development." But while insisting that Quebec was "shifting from an agricultural to an industrial economy," he also assured, "we do not believe that this situation will influence Quebec's Gallic charm and Old world atmosphere, for our traditions are very deeply rooted. It is and will remain a charming an-achronism in a twentieth-century setting." His description of the Gaspé offers a clear illustration of such attempts to square a marketing circle. Indeed, they should find there that "most of the [fishing] boats used have a look of medi-eval France, but their masters have added the thump of auxiliary diesel to the homely creak of sails and blocks." Old Quebec had drawn visitors for decades, and it was best not to airbrush it out altogether.[98]

Of course, government promoters did their utmost to ensure travel writers enjoyed their stay. Such courting paid off, as a "journalist [will] then report having had an enriching experience," which can only but "arouse his audi-ence's sympathy."[99] In fact, to TB officials, "the resulting publicity is always excellent."[100] Although they were confident this strategy was effective, they also recognized, "because of the large number of newspapers, magazines and other publications," they could not have a full picture of how the province was being represented nor full control over what was being written about it. In other words, despite their attempts to spoon-feed travel writers and their assiduous courting initiatives, the TB recognized that these key players in the tourism promotion business could not be automatically counted on to showcase the province as *belle*. Leaving no stone unturned, it thus hired "two specialized agents" to collect as much information as possible on what was being written about the province. This would, at the very least, allow offi-cials "to take the pulse of the interest tourism journalists had for Quebec."[101] Yet, for all tourist promoters' attempts to rebrand the province, in the eyes of some government officials they were not adapting their publicity material fast enough. For example, public servants at the Department of Industry and Commerce – charged with promoting the economic development of the prov-ince – occasionally requested from their colleagues at the TB promotional material to add to their own in order to make the province more attractive to potential foreign investors.[102] At times, it seems to their dismay, some of the TB's representation was incongruous with the image of Quebec that suited their purposes. This state of affairs was brought to light in the *Rapport sur les communications du Gouvernement du Québec*, produced by the company Inter-Medi Inc., which had been mandated to study the government's over-all communications strategies and offer recommendations. The report con-cluded there existed a lack of clear coordination between departments and that this could lead to "contradiction." It specifically pointed to the contrast-ing information produced by the Department of Industry and Commerce and the TB's publicity: "While the Department of Industry and Commerce was making laudable efforts to convince foreign investors of Quebec's modernity and dynamism, tourism [*sic*] was conscientiously inviting American visitors to come to ... covered bridges." In essence, the problem was that, while "tourist publicity has always banked on the historic character of Quebec to attract tourists ... its archaic and quaint side," other government publicity was working to "stimulate economic development." Such objectives could only be reached by projecting an image of Quebec as dynamic, aggressive, and modern, conveying well-being as well as *joie de vivre*. More critically, the report stigmatized the TB's advertising for "overlooking the government's global objectives ... [and its] corporate objectives." What is more, according to the consultants, "it would have been easy to reconcile the two."[103]

There is no way of knowing how TB officials reacted to this report. However, no doubt some would have considered such criticism unwarranted, if not unfair. After all, the evidence was indisputable: they had completely revamped government tourism publicity precisely to showcase the province's modernity, and they literally emphasized its *joie de vivre*. It was *belle* for all to see. Although, in retrospect, Prévost conceded that critics' "remarks inspired a certain level of caution when choosing [advertising] themes" and that, despite this, his office did not always succeed in steering away from past Quebec representations. He recalled, in fact, that the first four-colour ads published in 1960–61 raised some eyebrows "with a few high ranking civil servants responsible for Quebec's industrial boom." While "the principal [one] represented a *Québécoise* dressed in modern attire," she was nonetheless "sitting in front of a wood oven ... surrounded with domestic arts and crafts." Prévost acknowledged, "a few considered this ad as too quaint ... unrepresentative of a modernizing State."[104] In fact, the great majority of TB brochures included a few illustrations of "classic" Quebec archetypes. The cover page of the 1963 booklet *Inviting ... La Province de Québec Vous Accueille...*, for example, was a drawing of an old-time fiddler with pipe in mouth, and inside were photographs of an old *habitant*, again with a pipe, older women spinning or by a bread oven, and horse-drawn farm machinery.[105] (See figures 6.3 and 6.4.) Thus, up to a certain point, the consultants' conclusions had some purchase on reality, as *La Belle Province* had not entirely eclipsed the old.

This raises questions as to how it was that tourist promoters chose to use some of the iconographic repertoire of their traditionalist predecessors? Were they loath to relinquish what had, for so long, marked them as distinct and popular with tourists? Perhaps this enduring reliance on an old Quebec stock of characters was in conformity with how tourist promoters in the 1960s viewed the province's past. It was one of several attractive features of

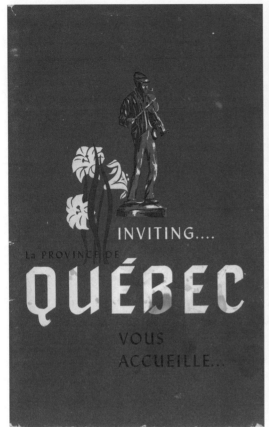

6.3 | Front cover of *Inviting ... La Province de Québec Vous Accueille ...*, 1962.

6.4 | View of the St Lawrence River with a *habitant* photo insert in
Inviting ... La Province de Québec Vous Accueille ..., 1962.

Quebec's personality, yet not the central one. Just as an old family snapshot conjures up memories of times past, these images were a message that in the *belle province* it was still possible to encounter memories from a distant past.

TRAVEL WRITERS' ACCOUNTS

Knowing that, on occasion, government promoters made use of ghostwritten accounts, and judging by official documents more so than in the past, it becomes more challenging to establish whether travel accounts are reliable enough to establish visitors' reactions. Indeed, there is no way of making the distinction between government officials' "in-house" accounts and those written at arm's length.[106] Yet, evidence confirms that travel writers had minds of their own and shared unmitigated reactions. The most vivid evidence of their editorial autonomy is indirectly revealed by Prévost's reaction to a 1968 Maclean's magazine article, "The Little Town of Saintly Miracles," sent to him by Gilles Charron, the deputy minister of the DTFG, one of five articles showcasing distinctive tourist sites of interest across Canada.[107] In Quebec, readers were invited to visit the village of Ste-Anne-de-Beaupré with its famous shrine. The four photographs accompanying the text featured various religious subjects. In other words, the long standing "Old Quebec" representation – in this case, a devoutly Catholic one – was on display. (See figure 6.5.) Charron was particularly irked by the images of "cows with cathedrals in the background and pictures of the eternal religious souvenir shop." Not only did Charron feel that this "is enough to make someone concerned about producing well orchestrated publicity nauseous," he also concluded that "if this is modern Quebec, let's not expect to be invaded by foreign investors in Quebec industry and commerce."[108]

Prévost could not have agreed more, yet he tried to reassure his colleague that this article was nothing more than "one of the rare jolts of an old prejudice." This type of article was to be considered a thing of the past, and he apprised his colleague of the TB's marketing approach. He pointed out, for one, that the publicity issued by tourism promoters now, often to journalists hosted by the TB, "reflect[s] a change in attitude towards the 'quaint old Province.'" Prévost further explained that part of this transformation could be attributed to "the orientation that our advertisements, our brochures and our public relations have taken already several years back." Adopting a slightly defensive tone, he insisted that "for every article in which the author talks about a Quebec entrenched in retrograde habits, there are one hundred that do not refer to this formula long ago expired … presenting instead 'la belle province.'" He pointed out that the "regrettable exceptions … don't justify drawing general conclusions" about his department's overall publicity. Nonetheless, he certainly shared the intense frustration expressed by his colleague, as he also felt that "some of these feature reports loaded with a malodorous dust of yesteryear" inspired nothing less than "nausea."[109]

What this exchange makes clear is that tourism promoters in the 1960s were not always successful in reimagining the province, despite their best efforts to convince travel writers to replace ubiquitous, quaint "Old Quebec" with a more up-to-date representation of a modern and dynamic Quebec. Maclean's magazine and other such accounts associated French Quebeckers with what they viewed as a world of the past, a society whose lifestyle and values they could not identify with and, indeed, one they rejected. The

The little town of saintly miracles

Pastures run to the St. Lawrence River at Ste. Anne de Beaupré, near the famous "miracle" Basilica.

Religious souvenirs and summer refreshments are offered together. At right, Stations of the Cross.

A group of nuns enter the forecourt of the Basilica on their way to morning mass.

6.5 | Images accompanying "The Little Town of Saintly Miracles," 1968.

YOU DON'T HAVE TO believe in miracles to enjoy Ste. Anne de Beaupré. This Romanesque shrine, dedicated to the Mother of Mary and tended by the Redemptorist Fathers, nestles on the flats of the St. Lawrence River, 20 miles below Quebec City. Pilgrims, religious or secular, should avoid the neon-lit commercialism of Highway 15 and follow Route 15b through lush farmland and picturesque Lower Canadian villages. Bilinguists might echo Jacques Cartier's 400-year-old comment, *"Quel beau pré!"* (What a lovely meadow!), and realize how the area got its name.

The shrine itself, sometimes called the Lourdes of the New World, is a few hundred feet beyond the town. It's likely to be crowded, especially during the peak July-August period (nearly a million visitors come every year), but there is a mood of quiet reverence and the fathers prohibit organized tours. Legend has it that the shrine was founded by three Breton sailors who, caught in a storm, vowed they would build a chapel for their patroness Saint Anne if they lived.

Whether this is true or not, it *is* known that the first wooden chapel was erected in 1658. Church records show that during the building a settler crippled with rheumatism laid three stones and was miraculously cured of his ailment. A replica of the original chapel now stands opposite the Basilica, easily the main attraction of Ste. Anne de Beaupré. This magnificent structure has twin 300-foot towers, a great stained-rose window, a forest of columns, pilasters and arches and superb frescoes and interior stations of the cross. Among the Basilica's relics are what is reputed to be the forearm of Saint Anne, sent from Rome in 1960 by Pope John XXIII, the fragment of a finger of the saint and her wrist bone.

Nearby is a shrine-run wax museum that, in sets combining sound and light, tells the story of Saint Anne in both languages. Some of the wax figures are so lifelike that they seem to be watching *you*. Upstairs is an art gallery and reliquary, open July and August only. Another item of major interest, especially for children, is a 45-foot-high, 360-degree Cyclorama showing Jerusalem at the time of Christ. It took four years to paint and was completed in 1886.

There are several hotels strung out along Highway 15 and more austere lodgings operated by the Basilica itself. If you like eating in communal style, try the dining room of the Franciscan Missionaries, commonly known as the White Sisters. Lunch, which is anything but frugal, costs $1.75. Visits might be timed to coincide with one of the main pilgrimages. They begin in May and end September 8, with Our Lady's birthday. The essence of Ste. Anne de Beaupré is a procession of pilgrims, their torches creating a luminous pattern in the summer evenings, climbing the hill opposite the Basilica to reach the Chapel of Ecce Homo.

vehemence of Prévost's and Charron's reactions to the article leaves little doubt that their quarrel with the traditional branding of Quebec was not only born out of professional frustration but was also a very personal response to what they perceived as an affront.

Certainly, English Canadian and American travel writers of the 1960s still often represented the Quebec countryside and smaller communities as old Quebec, although differences between the ways in which both groups of writers imagined the province were less significant. Both measured rural Quebec's appeal with a similar set of criteria as those writers who came before. In some cases, this can be accounted by the fact that some writers were writing about the province during both decades. It can also be explained by predeparture expectations. In view of information they likely acquired before leaving, the similarities are not surprising. After all, travel writers in the 1960s had access to the same novels, art, perhaps even textbooks, as those travelling in earlier decades, which affirmed French Quebeckers' traditional rural Catholic identity. On the other hand, they were obviously familiar with the government's redesigned advertising material, and some may have also noticed the work of a new generation of contemporary French Quebec novelists. Although the most famous of these novels only came out in the mid-1960s, these opened a window onto a very different Quebec. Generally speaking, their plots involved characters propelled by a Québécois nationalist identity. High on the list is Hubert Aquin's *Prochain épisode*, 1965 (*Next Episode*), which recounts an imprisoned Quebec independence revolutionary fighting an oppressive English Canada.[110] Marie-Claire Blais's *Une saison dans la vie d'Emmanuel*, 1966 (*A Season in the Life of Emmanuel*), posits French Quebeckers turning away from the Catholic Church and its behavioural strictures, redefining what traditional elites singled out as their distinctive national traits.[111]

Regardless of whether travel writers kept up to date with the latest Quebec novels, one can take for granted that they read newspapers reporting the province's social and political upheavals.[112] A question on the minds of so many, including journalists, academics, and other pundits, was "What does Quebec Want?"[113] The province appeared unrecognizable, an enigma of sorts, begging for explanation. Keeping these multiple and contradictory predeparture influences in mind, one would expect English-speaking North American travel writers to be both predisposed to encounter features of old Quebec, while on the lookout for signs of change.

The most likely to bring these up were "insiders" – notably English Canadians who lived in Quebec. Although few in number, their credibility was enhanced, as they could position themselves as privileged observers living side-by-side with the locals. These travel writers clearly set out to make the point that Quebec was modernizing, making their travel accounts less an-thropological and more sociological: they were not describing a people steeped in the past but rather one in tune with modern society. Hugh MacLennan stands as a case in point as he had written about Quebec prior to the 1960s in conformity with observations of other travel writers at that time. After that, however, he represented Quebec as a place where "[e]nergies kept frozen for two centuries have thawed out, and French Canadians have learned and are learning science, industry, engineering and business administration." He argued that this change started after the Second World War and was then coming to fruition. What makes his account particularly interesting is that he explicitly articulated English Canadians' views about the other "solitude." More specifically, he contended that "[they] have been forced to revise their notion of the senior province." Quoting English Quebec acquaintances, he reported one who remarked that "[w]e always took it for granted that the French Canadians were poor. We grew up thinking of them as *habitants* – as hewers of wood and drawers of water ... But it's not that anymore." To his mind, Quebec now "has become prosperous." In fact, "[t]he sons and grand-sons of farmers are dining out on Parisian menus. They're driving fast cars and going to art shows and the theater."[114]

But at the same time, English-speaking North American travel accounts of the 1960s also typically reflected past descriptions of the province as a sur-rogate for France.[115] More specifically, links between the countryside and old France, situated in a vague "pastness." They echoed the well-worn refrain of Quebec's "towns and villages" being "steeped in the traditions inherited from 17th century Normandy and Brittany." The Gaspé, as earlier, struck a few as "so inherently French that many of its customs have remained since Jacques Cartier planted the fleur de lys there in 1534."[116] Wrote John Maclure, "things that happened one or two or three centuries ago are spoken of as though they happened one or two days ago."[117]

However, rarely did travel writers go beyond such generalizations and provide detailed descriptions of these old world-traditions or customs, and they had little to say about the previously ubiquitous and unfailingly popular *habitants*. In fact, the term *habitant* almost disappeared from their lexicon. When it was used, it was generally as an adjective pointing, for instance, to the "*habitant* flavour" of a place or of "*habitant* architecture."[118] Only occa-sionally were locals described as *habitants*. For example, John Keats, travel-ling on the North Shore, characterized its people similarly to travel writer Helen Augur in the 1940s: here "lives a population not yet entirely awak-ened from a centuries-long sleep. You will find characters from children's fic-tion in the forest ... trappers, loggers, the lonely priest travelling through wilderness country to serve his isolated parishioners."[119] And visiting the Isle-aux-Coudres, Jacques Coulon remarked that, while "teams of oxen have almost disappeared ... most of the island's farmers are still content to gather seaweed and dead fish from the shore for fertilizer."[120] But even in such cases, seldom was detailed information provided about farmers' daily lives, whether at work, home, or play.

Similarly, writers rarely made generalizations about attitudes, values, and religious beliefs nor to what their predecessors termed as the "French Canadian character." Fewer still wrote of the countryside as a place to find "real" French Canadians nor did they claim that contact with these French Canadians would cure modernity's ills. Travel writers' inclination to essentialize had clearly waned and, with it, a tendency to infantilize French Canadians in condescending terms. In fact, travel writers assured tourists that finding the *habitants* would be challenging. John Maclure, for example, anticipating reader expectations, forewarned that in the Gaspé, "oxen, its outdoor ovens and its two-masted schooners, photographed so often and written about so much that they were like trademarks, have virtually vanished."

Mostly, visitors should expect to encounter *reminders* of traditional French Quebec way of life. John Keats spoke for many when he explained that "[n]ot all the old skills or ways are lost, nor all the memories, but you have to keep looking deeper below the surface to find them."[121] Of course, travel writers still suggested that Quebec was worth the trip. The countryside still offered visitors unique and enticing opportunities to glimpse the past, and they were the ones best suited to point visitors in the right direction. Charles Lazarus clearly took to this role when he described Christiville, as "one of the few remaining Laurentians communities that still looks the way it did a half century ago."[122]

But what was made clear was that what remained of this old Quebec was fast disappearing, suggesting not only that it was worth coming to Quebec but that one had best do so soon. While most clearly came to terms with this reality, a few expressed disappointment. Mostly, they deplored the ways in which people of the countryside had abandoned traditional ways of life for the contemporary amenities and, predictably, not for the better. Robert Carson, for one, bemoaned the fact that now "power and telephone lines adorn the countryside and TV aerials the roofs of the houses, which are frequently of imitation brick."[123] John Keats forewarned, "there are still dog carts in the Gaspé but there are more tractors. Some bread is baked in some stone ovens, but most of it is the familiar, tasteless stuff manufactured in anonymous bakeries."[124] In expressing such disappointments, they broke from past practices. Rarely, if at all, had travel writers previously criticized the sites they were meant to showcase. Of course, travel writers had, occasionally signalled their regret that modernity was intruding on the old Quebec landscape, but, by the 1960s, a few suggested that it was taking over. Such expressions of dissatisfaction reveal the resilience of the familiar "Old Quebec" representations. Carson remarked that he "failed to discover the advertised picturesque qualities or any unreclaimed, simple peasantry … Farmers, far from ploughing with yokes of oxen and sharpened sticks, use tractors."[125] John Maclure shared his feeling of thwarted expectations, when he observed that the Gaspé's "ploughmen have tractors, housewives buy bakery bread, the fishermen have diesel-powered draggers."[126] Although a rare occurrence, some went even further to denounce the fact that the ways of life and traditions that appeared to have survived were nothing less than evidence of crass commercial ventures, obviously meant to cater to visitors in search of authenticity. Ken Lefolii, for instance, even alleged that "Canadian folk customs" are displayed for the visitor "on calculated occasions," and are "soon packed when the festival tents are folded, and the part time *habitants* return to hand-tailoring the hills and catering with zest and skill to the multitudes who play among them."[127]

Of note as well, these travel writers, more so than their predecessors, blamed the tourism industry itself for compromising visitors' chances of experiencing old Quebec. Some, such as Keats, deplored the fact that "impersonal motels have destroyed forever the possibility – which existed in my childhood – of stopping for the night at a lonely farmhouse to enter a world of food, manners and accommodation three centuries old." And he regretted that, in the Gaspé, the "peasant … is giving way to the smooth-faced shopkeeper who wears American leisure clothes and smiles commercially in the villages."[128]

In a great moment of irony, travel writers became more conscious of and resentful of the growing number of tourists they encountered. In fact, the presence or absence of tourists – being *touristy* or not – became an added rating criterion. Some destinations were thus lauded for having escaped tourist onslaughts. St-Jean-Port-Joli, for example, was singled out as "one of those sleepy spots that, although it has been discovered by the outsider, still manages to retain its simplicity and peace."[129] And a trip from Tadoussac to Murray Bay "offers a rare opportunity to savour what driving used to be like before the hot dog stands, motels and basket emporiums made most roadsides look alike."[130] In other cases, destinations previously vaunted as "must sees" inspired more qualified praise. The village of Percé, in Benedict Thielen's opinion, "pays for its fame by being overrun with sight-seers and the inevitable hotels, motels and souvenir shops that spring up in their wake."[131] The Koellers concurred, as they, too, found Percé "a bit too resort-y," lamenting, "motels, restaurants, gift and souvenir shops and all the rest of what goes

with an overabundance of such establishments in resorts everywhere are clus-
tered along the road," regretfully informing readers that "what must at one
time have been a great deal of natural beauty has been regrettably, pretty
much eclipsed."[132]

In many ways, these reactions were not surprising. Travel writers in the
1960s had not only been exposed to "Old Quebec" representations of the
province but Quebec's countryside was changing. While in 1951, "the rural
population represented one fifth of the total population ... ten years later," it
"accounted for only 11 per cent."[133] And by then there was a decreasing need
to rely on *habitant* hospitality for accommodation. Visitors could now avail
themselves of more numerous campgrounds or take advantage of the growing
number of affordable motels.[134] Expectations versus realities aside, it remains
that government tourism promoters were successful at encouraging travel
writers to showcase "La Belle Province," as there were striking similarities between the TB's content and travel writers' representation of the countryside.
Both TB publicity and travel accounts shied away from promising visitors that
coming to Quebec was an opportunity to time travel – one in which they
would encounter descendants of the seventeenth-century *habitants* still living
as had their ancestors. Descriptions of rural people's work life, customs, and
daily occupations also had lost pride of place in both official publicity and
travel writers' accounts, with both ending up making the point that the most
Quebec's countryside could offer were reminders of a past way of life, mostly
through its lifeless built landscape. But it could also be that both government
promoters and travel writers were somehow responding in the same way, consciously or not, to a cultural shift among tourists at this time. They may have
sensed that visitors were now less interested in encountering people of "Old
Quebec." Travel writers may have also simply come to their own conclusion
that showcasing the *habitants* with their seventeenth-century traditions, deep-
rooted Catholic beliefs, and happy-go-lucky disposition, was, in effect, tan-
tamount to producing false representations. Contrary to TB promoters, their
observations ended up tampering with their readers' expectations; visitors
should look forward to coming across reminders of the old Quebec. This
could be disappointing but well worth the trip. If the TB and travel writers did
not always see eye to eye – as the *Maclean's* magazine article made more than
clear – overall, both ended up representing the province in very similar ways.

While French Quebec travel writers also accepted the TB's invitation to
visit "La Belle Province," as in previous accounts, their reactions were significantly different from their English-speaking counterparts. The Gaspé was
still a place to find "souvenirs of the past."[135] It also was still a place equally
prized for its beautiful scenery with its "rustic charm." But French Quebec

travel writers made much less of the Gaspé as a site of memory. They did not laud the region by making references to specific vestiges of the past, be they ways of life, historical events, or specific ancestors. Grande Rivière, for example, was simply a "quaint village typical of the Gaspé,"[136] while others were only "authentically French Canadian."[137] They clearly judged that this would be enough to pique readers' curiosity, as French Quebec readers would know these references and appreciate that the accounts spoke to them directly. Such characterization would bring to mind a traditional French Canadian way of life.[138] But, in greater contrast to past accounts, more was made of new multiple-entertainment opportunities on offer in various communities, activities organized mostly by local tourism promoters or entrepreneurs including, for example, a Grande-Rivière lobster festival (organized by the chamber of commerce), an annual fishing contest in St-Siméon, and a "day of the salmon" in Carleton.[139] Much was made of the fact that the Gaspé was by then becoming very popular with young tourists, offering as it did modern entertainment, including *discothèques* and *boîtes à chansons*. For older tourists there was "peace, life and nature," rides to " picturesque locations in *calèches*" and "boutiques."[140] Highlighting the region's entertainment opportunities over its inhabitants' way of life was in line with a "La Belle Province" representation.

Travel writers also wanted readers to partake in activities that would increase awareness of the province's economic development – another sign that they were in tune with the TB's desire to feature the province as modern. Visitors were encouraged to head for the city of Thetford where they could "visit an asbestos mine," under the aegis of the Asbestos Corporation,[141] and an "Asbestos museum" thanks to the efforts of municipal promoters and the Canadian Johns Manville Corporation.[142] In contrast to their English-speaking counterparts, French-speaking writers were less likely to comment negatively on modern life's encroachment in remote regions. Thus, "for those who have not seen the [Gaspésie] for a few years," they will discover that "[i]t was "profiting … from the province's economic development" "although [the author concedes] more slowly."[143] As for the Isle-aux-Coudres, its "population has assimilated modern comforts without losing … the very special character that it had created for itself by living in *vase clos* for 10 generations." And while they also regretted that the tourism industry was, in some cases, marring the countryside, they nonetheless managed to point their readers in promising directions.

The 1960s were a time of social and political change. An ever-increasing number of French Quebeckers embraced a new sense of national identity less defined by the legacies of the past and more adapted to a secular, urban, and industrialized Quebec society. Quebec government tourism promoters' deliberate initiatives to revamp the province's publicity make this clear, as tourism promoters were not immune to these wider social transformations. Thus, while earlier traditional nationalist promoters viewed tourism as a means to counter the perils of Americanization with a spur to revitalize an "Old Quebec," a new cohort of promoters, partly inspired, as well, by nationalist considerations, used tourism promotion to showcase and celebrate a modern Quebec instead. The province was a sophisticated society, distinct for offering visitors a myriad of pleasures very much rooted in the present. In short, tourist promoters were more satisfied than their predecessors with the product they had to sell. Unlike those who came before them, they aimed to promote the province as it was rather than as it should have been and took unprecedented initiatives to get travel writers on side.

It is difficult to establish how much they contributed, but there is no doubt that English-speaking North American travel writers recognized that the province, notably its rural areas, could no longer be represented as a seventeenth-century New France in North America. For some, this was disappointing but did not make Quebec less worth a visit. They made it clear to readers that they could expect to find only vestiges of a vanishing old Quebec, and they would be the ones to point them in the right direction. Thus, prospective tourists would understand that Quebec was still worth the visit but no longer for time travel. As for French Quebec travel writers, they had no need to spend as much time recounting what their readers should not expect to see as their knowledge of the province was more up to date. Instead, they focused on what the province had to offer. These were first and foremost opportunities to be entertained and surrounded by natural beauty.

7

THE NEW MONTREAL

Situating Montreal in this wider context reveals that the transformations of the Quiet Revolution also had a significant impact on the way the city was promoted. However, Montreal did not experience a clear-cut "Old Quebec"–"La Belle Province" promotional shift. This stands to reason, as Montreal was, from the outset, recognized and promoted as modern in many ways. Nonetheless, by the early 1960s, promoters expressed a strong dissatisfaction with the way the city was marketed and engaged in an unprecedented campaign to rebrand the metropolis. Several factors came into play to account for their new energetic marketing efforts. A few were in line with the province's wider revamping of tourism publicity, but the better part of these were attributable to Montreal's unique circumstances.

There is no doubt that by the late 1950s and early 1960s, Montreal was under increased scrutiny giving way to a net increase in public criticism, mostly directed at those responsible for the city's tourism promotion. These critics did not all agree about the most pressing issues, but they all concurred that change was in order. Of course, Montreal had long been the subject of concern, but, by the 1960s, the spectrum of critics increased in significant ways, and the nature of their criticisms was more diverse. There were still those who echoed the traditional nationalist elites' concerns with the city's Americanization and made use of familiar metaphors to make their point. Jean-Paul Desbiens, an outspoken public defender of the French language otherwise known as Frère Untel, lamented the fact that Montreal had an American face.[1] La Presse journalist and author Alfred Ayotte, for his part, explained that this "disfigured French face" was all too obvious when considering the "number of English signs that could or should be French, [and] of the English sounding names of restaurants, hotels or stores."[2] His colleague Roger Champoux, also of La Presse, summed up an overriding exasperation, asking rhetorically, "And the French character [of Montreal]? A great joke."[3]

7.1 | *The English Face of Montreal, St Catherine St West in 1961.*

(See figure 7.1.) In direct line with Albert Tessier from decades previously, they sounded the well-rehearsed refrain, linking a successful tourism industry to the preservation of the province's French character. They too argued that "the more Quebec becomes French, the more it will attract tourists!"[4]

But by the 1960s, a consensus also emerged that the city was poorly equipped to attract visitors. They felt that officials in charge of tourism promotion were not doing enough and blamed the municipal government for having neglected the upkeep of key services required to ensure a successful tourism industry. For one, Montreal needed better access roads and increased numbers of welcoming publicity billboards located at US and provincial borders, as well as more helpful signs to guide visitors to the tourist sites of interest. All concurred that there was an insufficient number of information kiosks.[5] Was it any wonder then that Montreal appeared to be a "forgotten city" by the tourists when it was so neglected?[6]

Commentators regularly compared Montreal and Quebec City, where, in their view, municipal authorities had always effectively promoted the capital, perceived as better equipped to showcase its tourist attractions, e.g., winter carnival, *calèches*, the fortifications.[7] For writer Roger Champoux, "Montréal is not a tourist city. It is a place no less and no more banal than another; a stopping ground before reaching the city of Champlain or heading out for the Laurentians."[8] They deplored that Montreal had little to occupy visitors, as writer Paul Coucke noted, "so far we do not have much to offer them."[9] They bemoaned the paucity of museums and other venues to attract heritage tourism visitors.[10] Such complaints were common though surprising, considering Montreal's long-standing reputation as the Paris of the New World with its vaunted opportunities for entertainment.

Montreal's municipal authorities' inaction was the likely cause of this reaction and in tandem reflected strong reservations about the quality of the English private sector's tourist advertising – namely the work of the MTCB. Many deplored that tourism promotion was entrusted to an organization whose main project was to encourage visitors to patronize its members' restaurants, shops, and hotels. Critics were particularly irked that this English-dominated business organization did little to highlight Montreal's French character, charging that the MTCB "ignored [it] deliberately," advertising exclusively in English.[11] When it did showcase French Montreal, it seemed to have no bearing on reality. Champoux wrote that Montreal's "atmosphere of a Paris of the New World" was nothing but "a pretentious slogan that corresponds to nothing at all." One would do better to "leave Paris where it is."[12]

What clearly annoyed these critics the most was the stereotyping of the city's French population in tourism publicity as traditional reminders of the past. For instance, one journalist was incensed with an ad that spoke of the "rugged pioneers of old" and how "the city has been transformed, but is still a city where churches and sanctuaries are plentiful."[13] To their minds, city officials needed to take charge of tourism promotion to counter misleading and demeaning advertising. More to the point, French Montrealers' control of city hall could ensure tourists would be presented with a less self-interested and more accurate representation of the French-speaking majority. At the very least, "American tourists could find other things than English ads."[14] For her part, Lysianne Gagnon of La Presse homed in on the information provided to American tourists by private tour bus companies (notably Murray Hill and Gray Line). These visitors "will ... see two aspects of Montreal: the English [one] which looks like the United-States" and the French one "that the guides reduce to a picturesque," "folklore," and "vulgar caricatures," learning that "French Canadians spend their lives between a clothes' line and an exterior staircase in the 'French slums' [sic] that the driver-guide will have shown them gloating with pleasure."[15]

Members of the Chambre de commerce du district de Montréal (CCDM) were the most relentless and vocal critics of Montreal's tourist promotion. Echoing ongoing complaints, they brought together a wide range of highly regarded members. While the CCDM did include English-speaking, private sector members, it mostly represented the interests of the French-speaking business community. Its spokespeople were French Quebeckers and official pronouncements were predominantly in French. The chamber's tourism-promotion interests and concerns were such that it had created a tourism committee in 1957 to study the health of the tourism industry, with three subcommittees: for Montreal, Quebec, and at a federal level. While these committees mainly consisted of business owners, they also included members both from the private sector and those directly involved in public sector tourism promotion.

Lucien Bergeron, for example, was appointed *rapporteur* of the CCDM tourism committee and president of its federal tourism subcommittee. He knew the business community well: in the 1940s he had worked as liaison officer for the Chambre de Commerce de la Province de Quebec (CCPQ) and as news director of *Commerce Montréal* – a CCDM publication. But Bergeron was also active at the municipal level, appointed chief-of-staff to the president of the executive committee of Montreal where, since 1958, he worked as an economist at the OMIET. As a member of the province's Tourism Council in 1961, he was also well apprised of the challenges and issues facing those promoting tourism at the provincial level. He was quite critical of the province's limited Montreal marketing initiatives. To his mind, it "stubbornly refuses to recognize the primordial importance of tourism for the economy of the province."[16]

Clearly aware of the advantages of having such experienced and well-connected members, the CCDM invited Paul Gouin to join the Tourism Committee. As a key figure in tourism promotion at the provincial level, he had demonstrated on multiple occasions his concerns for Montreal's tourist appeal. In fact, not long after, he was appointed to Montreal's OMIET in 1958. Clearly members of the chamber understood the benefits of establishing close relationships with those who could speak to power.[17]

The CCDM's well-connected tourism committee produced a series of articles and briefs addressed to the mayor's office. The first, in 1959, related their central concern that "the City has not preoccupied itself enough with ... the tourist situation in Montreal in the last few years and ranks far behind the other large cities in Canada and the United States as far as the per capita budget devoted to this domain."[18] In the OMIET's 1958–59 budget, a meagre $69,095 was earmarked to fulfill its mandate, $48,787 of which was for salaries, with continuing similarity for the next three years.[19] In 1960–61, Robert Hollier, director of the French government's Tourist's Office in Canada, addressing the CCDM, pointed out that "Paris spends $1 million per year simply on publicity abroad." In 1960–61, Montreal spent $14,600 for tourism publicity.[20] The CCDM's report concluded that the office "play[ed] primarily and above all a role of industrial prospector," as was evident in Montreal, which "rank[ed] far behind the other large cities in Canada and the United States as far as the per capita amount spent on attracting tourists." Leading to the obvious conclusion that "Montreal deplorably lacks tourist activities and that its tourist attractions are not sufficiently showcased."[21] In light of this dire situation, the CCDM argued that the "City has a unique and greater responsibility than the private agencies in the area of tourism … [thus] the information and official propaganda must come from the City … It will only be impartial, objective and complete if it is distributed or controlled by the City."[22] Thus, it recommended the creation of a municipal body exclusively devoted to developing the tourism industry – a municipal department of tourism and a municipal advisory commission.

Although not stated explicitly, the CCDM was in effect demanding that tourism promotion be taken away from the English-dominated MTCB. There is no doubt that MTCB officials felt directly targeted, to the point of officially and very publicly objecting to the CCDM's main recommendation and expressing greater concern still that Montreal was actually entertaining this option. In September 1958, the MTCB president, J.R. Fisher, voiced the board's "unshakable opposition" in a twelve-page letter addressed in French to Mayor Sarto Fournier and members of City Council.[23] The letter's tone left little doubt that members of the MTCB were shocked and appalled by the CCDM's recommendation. Fisher claimed that "no other body, municipal or public" could accomplish the quality of work they were doing to promote Montreal as a tourist destination, and the MTCB had accumulated forty years of experience, spending funds it received from its generous 450 members. To say nothing of the fact that each one advertised their own establishments and, thus, indirectly, the city as well. The MTCB distributed 500,000 pieces of publicity each year, adding the questionable claim that its publicity was "bilingual."[24] As an alternative, Fisher recommended the creation of a Tourist Liaison Committee, which would ensure cooperation and some coordination between all groups working on Montreal's tourism promotion. As for the city, its energies would be better spent creating more tourist attractions, such as festivals and historical pageants.

CCDM members promptly responded to this opposition with astonishment and reiterated their views that tourism should be a civic responsibility. Their reactions underscore the ethnic tensions that fuelled this debate, as the CCDM pointedly remarked that the new municipal body should "showcase the French

7.2 | Front cover of *Montréal*, brochure, early 1960s.

character of our city … for which the MTCB has had very little concern over the last few years." The MTCB's September letter "was an eloquent testimony of the little importance this organization gave to the French language."[25]

MONTREAL MUNICIPAL TOURIST BUREAU

Faced with this barrage of criticism, municipal authorities were quick to conclude that the status quo was untenable and that they should, indeed, assume a leadership role. Setting aside the MTCB's objections, they followed instead the recommendations of the CCDM. Thus, in 1961, municipal authorities created the Montreal Municipal Tourist Bureau (MMTB) – a body solely dedicated to tourism promotion with its own staff and budget and with Lucien Bergeron appointed director.[26] The MMTB promptly cut what little funding the city provided the MTCB and bought its information kiosk on Dominion Square – a clear signal it was assuming leadership from the private sector. (From then on the MTCB would focus on attracting conventions.) In 1962, the MMTB opened new information kiosks along highways bordering Ontario, New Brunswick, and the US, produced a new city map, complemented by a quarterly calendar of events, and published new publicity brochures. (See figures 7.2 and 7.3.)

How can one account for such quick responsiveness? More than a desire to better serve tourists, these new initiatives illustrated a pattern of power shifting in the political and social climate of the 1960s. This was a time when French Quebeckers, inspired by the emerging new nationalism, were pushing to take control of state power at multiple levels. The creation of the DTFG stands as an example. French Quebeckers, generally, were also asserting their French identity more forcefully by ensuring the French language was given pride of place in all aspects of their lives. In this wider context, city officials were more willing to take greater responsibility for tourism promotion and to find more effective ways to showcase its French character.

But other factors came into play as well. Montreal's hosting of Expo 67 also had a great effect. While all levels of government and a wide range of institutions and associations were involved in the planning and promoting of this event, City of Montreal authorities had considerable influence in establishing local tourism promotion policies and initiatives. They viewed Expo 67 as an extraordinary, singular opportunity to address numerous issues and concerns raised by tourism critics. At this time, Montreal attracted "an estimated 3,000,000 visitors annually spending about 100 million dollars," two thirds of whom were Americans, whereas Expo 67 planners expected approximately 30 million visitors from around the world.[27] Viewed as a "cash

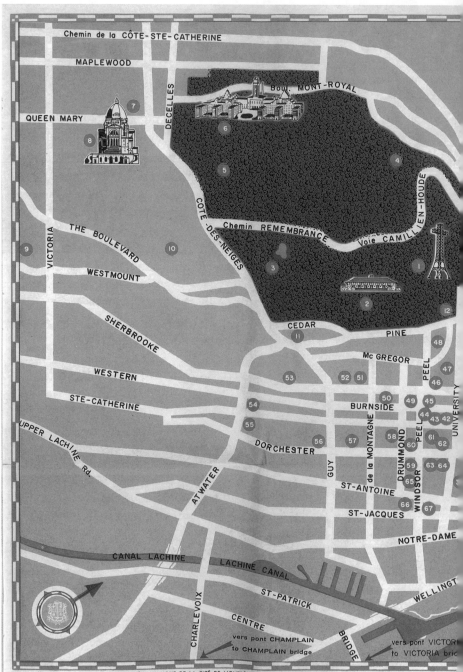

Chemin de la CÔTE-STE-CATHERINE

MAPLEWOOD

Boul. MONT-ROYAL

QUEEN MARY

DECELLES

7

8

6

5

4

VICTORIA

THE BOULEVARD

WESTMOUNT

CÔTE-DES-NEIGES

Chemin REMEMBRANCE

Voie CAMILLIEN-HOUDE

9

10

3

1

2

12

CEDAR

PINE

SHERBROOKE

11

McGREGOR

48

PEEL

47

46

WESTERN

53

52 51

50

49 45

44 43 42

UNIVERSITY

STE-CATHERINE

BURNSIDE

de la MONTAGNE

54

55

56

57

58

DRUMMOND

PEEL

61

60

62

UPPER LACHINE Rd.

DORCHESTER

GUY

59

63 64

ATWATER

ST-ANTOINE

WINDSOR

65

66

67

ST-JACQUES

NOTRE-DAME

CANAL LACHINE

LACHINE CANAL

CHARLEVOIX

ST-PATRICK

WELLINGT

CENTRE

BRIDGE

vers pont CHAMPLAIN
to CHAMPLAIN bridge

vers pont VICTORI
to VICTORIA bric

CARTE PRÉPARÉE PAR L'OFFICE D'INITIATIVE ÉCONOMIQUE DE LA CITÉ DE MONTRÉAL • MAP PREPARED BY THE ECONOMIC DEVELOPMENT BUREAU OF TH

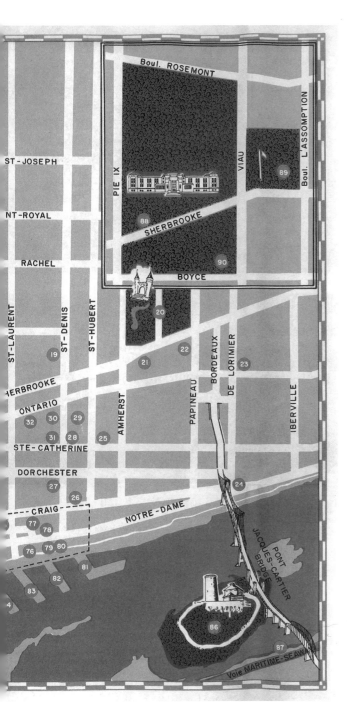

7.3 | Map prepared by the Economic Development Bureau, City of Montreal, in a Montreal Municipal Tourist Bureau booklet, early 1960s.

cow" by municipal authorities, Expo was an opportunity to erase Montreal's stigma as a "forgotten city."

JEAN DRAPEAU

Two of the most influential and dynamic public figures to take advantage of this new turn of events were Montreal's flamboyant mayor Jean Drapeau, elected in 1960 for a second term, and the MMTB's new director, Lucien Bergeron. From the outset, Drapeau's agenda made clear that significant change was in order. Montreal required rebranding that departed substantially from the marketing strategies privileged by the MTCB. To begin with the mayor planned promotion on a much grander scale. The city had to become an international destination, attracting larger numbers from all over the world, most notably Europe.[28] He envisaged Expo 67, using a religious metaphor, as "a kind of international consecration of Montreal."[29] In a 1964 letter to CPR president N.R. Crump, asking for a $15,000 donation to a promotional initiative, Drapeau wrote:

> How often does one see the Eiffel Tower? The Arc de Triomphe?
> The Tower of Pisa? The Pyramids? And many others? Montreal must
> penetrate into the subconscious of hundreds of thousands of people
> who will speak of it instinctively even if they have never been there.
> Within a very short time Montreal must be mentioned repeatedly in
> all conversations, in all the newspapers and on all stations and tele-
> vision screens.[30]

Montreal's tourism industry would no longer rely only on US and Canadian markets, ceasing to be only a crossroad to other destinations. Instead, it would become *the* destination of choice, all set in motion in time for Expo 67.

Confirming Drapeau's determination, in 1964, the city published a high-end monthly magazine, targeting, among others, national and international governing elites likely to influence public opinion.[31] As he put it to a *Gazette* reporter, "Montreal [was] going into the public relations business."[32] The publication, whose first news director was Michel Roy, a highly reputed *Le Devoir* journalist, was composed mostly of glossy photographs accompanied by explanatory text in five languages. Demonstrating his keen understanding of marketing best practices, Drapeau explained to Crump, "The images, in words and pictures must be presented repeatedly in a variety of focus and aspects in order to engrave on the minds of the readers a living portrait of our city and thereby make it more attractive to them."[33] The magazine often included messages or quotation's penned by Drapeau, revealing what he considered Montreal's primary assets, as well as how he believed these should be publicized. Most of all, the metropolis, he insisted, should be first and foremost showcased as the epitome of modernity, a city "about to enter the ranks of the great metropoles of the world."[34] Always with Expo 67 in mind, he made the point that the "image of the modern Montreal that we are trying to present to the world by this monthly revue" was the image that Montreal aspired to.[35] In this, he was of one mind with Premier Jean Lesage who proclaimed that "Expo 67 is an excellent opportunity to demonstrate to the world that Quebec and its metropolis of Montreal are in tune with modern times."[36]

In doing this, though, Drapeau was clearly aware that such objectives meant rebranding the city. As it stood, the available publicity material had not caught up with the city's changing personality. Starting in the early 1960s, the MMTB began promoting the city's new persona, a Montreal "imposing itself more and more on the whole world as one of the most progressive cities,"[37] "undergoing now the most exciting period in its history."[38] More specifically, that it had "detached ... from the past to engage ... with a dynamism and a confidence forever renewed."[39] As a result, it was clear to Drapeau that "the same old centres of attraction" should not be highlighted, deploring that "a few years ago the Canadian metropolis ... offered tourists only the top of Mont-Royal, Notre-Dame church, the wax museum and l'Oratoire St-Joseph [and] that once these four places were visited, there was nothing else left to see. As a result, Americans did not feel the need to come back."[40] He argued that their interests had changed and "that the present clientele favours great achievements" such "as the Place des arts, the permanent structures on Expo 67 grounds, Place Victoria, Place Ville-Marie and the new Bonaventure center" and soon the metro and the growing "underground" shopping below the city – all heralded both nationally and abroad as icons of architectural modernity.[41] More significantly, these sites were embraced by French Quebeckers as emblems of a *French Quebec* modernity. (See figures 7.4 and 7.5.) And when visitors arrived on Ile Ste-Hélène – the site of the exhibition – the hope was that "[t]he Quebec Pavilion ... will reveal to the visitors of the universal Expo of 1967 the true face of Quebec. Its representations will put into relief the dynamism of a people at work, the unrelenting activity of men and women."[42] It followed as well that no longer would the historic and the modern be ascribed respectively to French and English populations. Drapeau articulated this during Expo 67: "Quebec intends to demonstrate by its innovations and successes that the French fact is not simply a set of touching traditions and folkloric songs but that it can be a series of initiatives and productive accomplishments, adapted to the 20th century in the field of ideas

7.4 | Place Ville-Marie, Montreal's first skyscraper,
under construction, September 1961.

as well as facts."[43] Going forward, only rarely did the city's tourism publicity allude to differences between the French and the English. Most often, it was to point to widely circulated, generic stereotypes, those often attributed to the two cultures wherever they happened to live. And while some references were made to its supposed "Anglo-Saxon reserve and Latin effervescence,"[44] more often than not, when cultural differences were brought up, it was to highlight the city's previously ignored cosmopolitan character. Montreal was

7.5 | Place Bonaventure (front) and the Château Champlain
under construction, 1966.

now a "[m]eeting place of all peoples" representing "30 ethnic groups." Indeed, the mayor never tired of pointing out to prospective visitors that "our
cosmopolitan City enjoys different cultures manifesting themselves in many
ways."[45] So much so that Montreal "appears to the immigrant as a kind of
promised land, a land where he has the choice to integrate into one or the
other of the two great ethnic communities but also to remain himself"[46] – a
new brand for a new Montreal.

All this being said, however much the goal was to promote the city's ultramodernity, this didn't mean the city's past was to be entirely eclipsed, as visitors were made aware of the city's historical character. Yet, this past was clearly circumscribed, surviving "in the monuments and the ancient buildings that we want to preserve, [located in the] 'Vieux Montréal' where everything recalls the heroic origins of our city."[47] In this regard, he shared Paul Gouin's long-held convictions that efforts should be made to develop the old quarter for the benefit of Quebeckers intent on asserting the city's French character and for tourists looking for a certain degree of contrast. Under Drapeau's tenure recommendations turned into concrete measures and much was done to protect Montreal's surviving built heritage. Major intervention was certainly required, as, over time, many historic buildings had been torn down,[48] and those remaining required significant repair or had been made to serve commercial interests.[49] In tandem with this deterioration, the old quarter's vitality had gradually died down, and the economic centre of the city had gravitated to the newly built up area of Place Ville-Marie. In 1962, city council established the Commission Jacques-Viger presided over by Paul Gouin, charged with reporting and advising the City Planning Department on the restoration and preservation of Vieux Montréal. Two years later, the provincial government officially recognized it as an *arrondissement historique* – a protected patrimonial area inside the city's boundaries placed under the jurisdiction of the Commission des monuments historiques.[50] Cordoning off this historic Montreal, clearly separated from the new version, meant that no longer would Montreal be heralded as a city of contrasts where the old shouldered the new throughout the city.

But relying mainly on modernity and multiculturalism in a North American context would not be enough to attract visitors, as American cities offered similar attributes. *Montreal* magazine explicitly told prospective tourists that the city had the alluring attractions of an American metropolis, but only the most appealing ones: its soul is "not New York's despite its sky scrapers." Instead, it "is more that of [a] New World city that has been able to spare itself the cold and clinical materialism of the other big North American cities."[51] In short, unlike its famous competitors, it was seductively modern but not plagued with their all-too-common afflictions.

Still, such distinguishing features would not be enough to upend the competition. What of Montreal's French character and its reputation as "the second French city in the world," a reputation in which past promoters had put so much stock as a way to differentiate the city? Considering that critics and the newly emerging nationalists did not think enough was being done to promote the city's Frenchness or assert the French language, one would have expected promoters such as Drapeau to make it an integral part of the new branding. He certainly had friends in high places intent on showcasing the city's French character. No less than Premier Jean Lesage declared that "the Provincial government is ready to join forces with municipal authorities in an all out campaign to make French the 'real priority language' in Montreal ... the government's intention to make Montreal live up to its reputation as the second largest French-speaking city in the world."[52] Drapeau certainly parroted the well-worn slogan of Montreal as "the second largest French city in the world." In fact, he claimed that the "French character of Montréal is no doubt its main attraction."[53] Yet, despite this, he never missed an opportunity to caution advertisers that this French character "could not act alone" as a tourist attraction.[54] They had only to look to Toronto – a city with "a linguistic character shared by all American cities,"[55] which hosted a considerably larger number of tourists than did Montreal.[56] But decisions as to how to showcase Montreal's distinctive linguistic identity raised other problems. For some, the problem was that Montreal was *too* much like Toronto and that vaunting Montreal's French character could easily be revealed as false advertising. Those working to promote Montreal struggled with this. Indeed, in the first issue of *Montreal* magazine, readers were told that although "the French element dominates in a proportion of two thirds," visitors might notice that "one of the two fundamental cultures [English] is perhaps, in the city center, more apparent or, so to speak, more visual than the other." In a clear attempt to preempt complaints while standing by their promotional claims, they spun an undeniable reality, pointing out, "this should not mislead the experienced tourists." In fact, English predominance "likely makes many things simpler for those whose knowledge of French is limited."[57]

The fact that Drapeau did not want the city's French character promoted as it had been was made clear. He wanted promoters to discontinue the Paris connection, insisting Montreal's soul was not "that of Paris despite its French language population."[58] Previously, provincial promoters had shied away from the MTCB's vaunted "Paris of the New World" brand, and 1960s municipal promoters would follow suit. In the nationalist climate of the decade, Drapeau wanted it established that Montreal was French in its own unique way. However, other than the trope, Montreal as the largest French city in North America, the way Drapeau felt about the city's French character and how it should be marketed is not easy to determine. As will become apparent, and contrary to earlier days, in the 1960s encapsulating the city's distinctive French character in a catchy slogan proved a challenging enterprise.

LUCIEN BERGERON

By examining the attitudes and initiatives of the MMTB director Lucien Bergeron, it is possible to better understand how these rebranding challenges played out on the ground. He had been specifically hired to promote Montreal as a tourist destination. Not surprisingly, Bergeron and his employer, Drapeau, shared many concerns and objectives. He, too, counted on Expo to revitalize Montreal's appeal. The city would "acquire … a new stature that will make of it one of the most attractive cities of the world,"[59] making it, hopefully, the "tourist capital of the world,"[60] and, "when Expo ends, the city will have the tourist equipment *par excellence*."[61] While insisting the tourist industry make "*inouïs* efforts" until Expo, long-term goals were to be built into these initiatives.[62]

Bergeron was well positioned to align the city's promotional efforts with Expo organizers, as he was invited, in 1963, to sit on the Centennial Commission's advisory committee on information and promotion.[63] Among other initiatives, he hired two experienced journalists to head tourism publicity – professionals who understood communicating to diverse audiences.[64] As was the case with provincial government tourist promoters, those in Montreal also significantly increased efforts to court travel writers, guiding them through the sites of the city. Bergeron explained to reporter Jean-Claude Germain, "as Director of the MMTB I must receive two or three hundred foreign journalists per year. Most are specialists of the tourist pages in large magazines or large newspapers."[65] Bergeron felt that Montreal "gets better publicity through travel writers." To illustrate his point, he explained that one American travel writer cost his office $100 to entertain and, in turn, produced $100,000 worth of publicity (two articles and two syndicated columns for twenty-five American dailies).

In the following years, in anticipation of Expo, opportunities to reach out to these "specialists" were multiplied, and by 1966 the MMTB had hosted a record 700 journalists, travel writers, agents, and dignitaries.[66] In addition to ensuring face-to-face exchanges, the MMTB published and distributed hundreds of texts to 548 journalists and 376 travel writers in Canada and the US and to embassies and travel companies.[67] Further, "the personnel at the office corrected numerous publicity texts that international transport companies, for instance, were planning to publish."[68] To further facilitate the work of these writers, municipal officials also compiled, more systematically than before, collections of Montreal photos for distribution, many of which "served to illustrate articles on artistic and commercial life of Montreal." Certainly, in the eyes of the CCDM, "the office thus helped to present a better face of Montreal."[69]

The MMTB, of course, communicated directly to tourists. To critics of
Montreal's dearth of tourist offerings or lack of showcasing what was on offer,
in 1962 the bureau began publishing a quarterly calendar, listing theatre pro-
ductions, art galleries, and *boîtes à chansons*. Ten thousand copies were published and distributed in a wide range of American and Canadian cities.[70]
While the MMTB increased access to Montreal's sites of interest with the
city's first official municipal tourist map and new information kiosks,[71] it also
looked further afield, increasing efforts to promote Montreal in markets previously ignored or overlooked; for example, it put up the only Canadian kiosk
at the 1962 International Tourist Exhibition in Nice and distributed material
published in several languages, all in line with Drapeau's goal of internationalizing the city's tourist clientele.

In accordance with provincial promotional objectives, the MMTB also
undertook new initiatives to tap into the English Canadian market. As
numbers confirmed more could be done. In 1962, Bergeron reported that 80
per cent of Montreal's tourists were from the US and only 13 per cent from
Canada, principally from Ontario (73.7 per cent).[72] By 1965, he sounded
optimistic, noting that "Montreal attracts more and more foreign tourists."[73]
Turning inwards, MMTB officials devoted unprecedented energy to convince
Montrealers that the success of the tourism industry depended greatly on
their hospitable and courteous behaviour. In particular, and not surprisingly,
more so than had the MTCB, they expressed concern that tourism workers
not exploit visitors – a concern more easily voiced publicly than by private
sector promoters. More often they urged businesses to make it clear what
clients could expect to pay for each service. In this endeavour, as of 1963,
authorities were given more clout via the provincial Hotels Act, "to make
sure that the physical characteristics of the establishments met with certain
standards," and the TB hired more than thirty inspectors. It also established a
"Provincial Lodging Service for Expo 67 … in order to find rooms in private
homes and in apartment buildings" in Montreal – signalling their seriousness
about hospitality and an understanding that it could not simply be fostered
through moral suasion.[74]

Tourist promoters had always encouraged the public to be welcoming of
course, but during this period, a concerted campaign was launched at many
levels. While the provincial TB had its "*Hospitalité* Spoken Here" and "Dites
Bonjour" campaigns, for Montreal promoters the need appeared greater and
more urgent. Several factors came into play. First, all Montrealers needed
training for the challenge of hosting an unprecedented influx of tourists
during Expo. For Bergeron, many would find themselves, for the first time,
having "to welcome a different type of habitual tourist, the Canadian and
American one." Conversely, Europeans will "have a different mentality than

that of the American tourist," although he did not specify what he meant by this mentality.[75] As well, abusive behaviour could severely tarnish Montreal's reputation, possibly irreparably, on the international stage. Other agencies, for example the CCDM's Tourism Committee, also promoted public awareness of the importance of being exemplary hosts. Its most notable initiative on that front was a yearly Tourism Education Week, initiated in April 1961, meant to encourage Montrealers to make every effort to help tourists and embellish the city. In 1966, the MMTB, CCDM, and the provincial TB also cooperated with the Canadian Travel Association to organize a ten-day colloquium, "Projet Hospitalité," to educate tourism industry workers.[76]

However there loomed more worrisome threats, which seriously imperilled any hopes of convincing visitors to enjoy Montreal's unique *hospitalité*. Beginning in March of 1963, multiple violent attacks from the separatist group the Front de libération du Québec (FLQ) plagued the city, and continued over the remainder of the decade with more than 200 violent incidents, mostly bombings. Targets were those viewed as signs of English colonialism, including the Canadian Army Recruiting Centre, the Stock Exchange, and mailboxes in the wealthy English-speaking Montreal neighbourhood of Westmount. Such violence made the headlines across North America, all the more so as the FLQ was viewed as one with other decolonization movements including those in Cuba, Algeria, and Vietnam. Not surprisingly, these events spread concern among city promoters, and particular efforts were made to preserve Montreal's reputation as a safe destination. MMTB officials made public declarations reassuring visitors and took pains to point out that reliable evidence confirmed that many travellers simply overlooked concerns. In 1963, Bergeron claimed with confidence "that this Spring's wave of terrorism has not frightened off the tourists." Statistics collected by the MMTB indicated that the number of tourists had actually increased compared to the previous year. He credited "the superior value of the American dollar, the publicity done by the provincial and municipal governments, the choice of Montreal as the host of Expo 67."[77] However by 1965, initial optimism gave way to growing concern as reports indicated a 25 per cent drop over the previous year in the rate of Montreal's hotel occupancy.[78] Changing his tack, Bergeron tried to dispel any misgivings tourists might have in coming to Montreal by blaming "the bad publicity given by the Canadian and foreign Anglophone press to the separatist 'manifestations.'" He bitterly remarked that "the facts were greatly overblown to the point where people who wanted to visit la Belle province did not risk it for fear of being caught in the middle of a revolution."[79] At times he clearly found it difficult to contain his annoyance, pointing out that "Americans don't give a hoot for our separatism; it is our province they like to visit and we should be flattered."[80]

Worry, however, was manifest in other quarters. Those directly involved in organizing Expo's exhibit felt the need to develop a well-rehearsed public relations strategy in view of the increasing number of journalists who often enquired about "the FLQ and Quebec's desire to separate from the rest of Canada" and the risk of "possible demonstrations at the opening of Expo 67." Officials were instructed to issue a reassuring official response to the effect that:

> Every growing and vigorous state or part of a state is likely to develop
> a group which is carried away by its enthusiasm over the development
> people see going on around them. They become over enthusiastic or
> extreme in their approach. Canada's problems in this regard are less
> serious than in most other vigorous nations in view of the fact that
> Canadians in general tend to be conservative in their approach.[81]

Quebec politicians also voiced guarded concern. In 1963, a journalist, quoting René Lévesque, minister of Natural Resources, reported that he "saw in these [FLQ] acts a pretty bad publicity." To his mind "Americans view with a different eye than ours this wave of terrorism to which they lend proportions almost identical to those of Algerian terrorism."[82] In its 1965 annual report, the DTFG showed statistics confirming that tourists were discouraged from coming to Quebec; its officials recognized that Quebec was experiencing "tension" and that the tourism industry could greatly suffer. But they, too, essentially blamed "the negative publicity" rather than the tension itself for reduced tourist turn out. The solution was to fight fire with fire, and to do so quickly. In response, the provincial TB had to "at all costs intensify [its] propaganda or otherwise see our tourism industry suffer a set-back." More precisely, what seemed "just and reasonable [was to increase by] 10% ... the amount invested this year in the neighbouring republic."[83] With Expo 67 upon them, such measures appeared all the more urgent.

Such then were the challenges of promoting Montreal in the 1960s. The question remains: what Montreal would the officials at the OMIET choose to promote in its publicity? Not surprisingly they opted to follow Drapeau's overall branding vision. However, Bergeron's comments and internal debates among city officials reveal that identifying alternate representations of the city was not straightforward and could lead to spirited debate. In contrast to Drapeau, who, in view of his position, could not afford to be as candid, Bergeron expressed publicly and forcefully his displeasure at Montreal's representation by the private sector.[84] By way of example, he impatiently insisted, "we have to do away with savages, forests and sleds when we speak of Montreal."[85] This is not a city where, as one ad purported, "on Jacques Cartier place one can meet the habitants and the Indians selling their products in typical costumes."[86] But he also took aim at some French Montrealers' representations of the city. Speaking to a *Montreal Star* reporter, he said that the St-Jean-Baptiste parade had to reject floats "with Indians in bare feet – and mickeys of cognac in their back pockets – [these] just don't do any more."[87] Such comments clearly reflect how promoters rejected what they viewed as a dated and condescending representation of French Montrealers, but they also reveal how they understood Indigenous peoples' place in the overall history of the city. Being still looked upon as "uncivilised" by the colonizers' descendants, Natives appeared particularly out of place at a time when promoters were intent on representing their city and its French population as progressive.

Promoters also balked at ads inviting tourists to the old quarter pretending it retained its old-world heritage and atmosphere. If truth be told, Bergeron countered, the buildings that "dated back to the 17th and 18th centuries served now as warehouses." He was not rejecting the possibility that the area be renovated. To his mind, it "should eloquently illustrate the French heritage of Montreal – not just for visitors but for us all – as this is certainly the neighbourhood where one finds the vestiges of the French period of our history."[88] He was a strong supporter of the work of the Viger Commission tasked with finding ways to restore and preserve the sector. Despite the disrepair of "Old Montreal," in 1964 the MMTB produced its first publicity material devoted to the historic area, a brochure entitled "Walking Tour of Old Montreal/Promenade dans le Vieux Montréal," by Paul LeDuc.[89] It was a clear recognition that however exaggerated some publicity claims might be promoters still recognized the area's attractiveness to visitors.

Underlying Bergeron's misgivings about claims made of the Vieux Montréal was his deeply held conviction that promoters needed to present to "visitors an image of Montreal and of Montrealers that reflects reality."[90] Rebranding was about representing the city in its current state, though defining what that should be was, of course, in the eye of the beholder. For Bergeron, "tourists do not come to see old Montreal but to simply visit a big city."[91] He believed he knew what visitors wanted to see, but, being subjective, it could be a case of what he thought visitors *should* want to see. Regardless, judging from the MMTB's most widely distributed publicity, officials decided that Montreal was first and foremost a big, modern city. The cover page of its first guidebook, with a panoramic view of the city's skyscrapers, made clear that the days of Montreal as the City of Contrasts were over. The publicity overall showcased how Montreal could attract visitors with diverse interests, "[s]ome want to see her historical places, to enjoy the charm of her cosmopolitanism, the dynamic and colourful tempo of her intellectual and artistic activity." Promoters also took every opportunity to reinforce that Montreal had changed. Indeed, they informed prospective tourists that "[m]any also want to study the tremendous industrial and commercial developments that have characterised Montreal's phenomenal growth in recent years."[92] Ads that labelled "Montreal: the Unexpected" suggested the city would surprise visitors. Thus, not only was the new supplanting the old but tourists could feel privileged to witnesses this transformation firsthand.

Further underscoring this marketing makeover were more numerous references in promotions and advertising of the city's multiculturalism. Certainly, Bergeron's public pronouncements suggested he thought more should be made of the city's ethnic diversity. A *Gazette* journalist reported that for him, "the true, the essential change in the Montreal tourist business is unlikely to materialize fully unless the city brings out more of its cosmopolitan flavour." He pointed out that "we've got 100,000 Italians here, 50,000 Germans and then there's the Greeks, the Czechs and the Poles ... [T]here should be many more places identified with these nationalities."[93]

While the city was reimagined as "New Montreal," a long-standing question remained: "How can one prove that Montreal is not an American city?"[94] Bergeron, during an appearance on CKAC radio, detailed this challenge more fully, stating that the difficulty with promoting Montreal as a unique North American destination was that it "only partially has the appearance of a French city and does not resemble ... either an American city." Yet, "it is mostly by these two cultural currents, that enrich themselves mutually ... that Montreal distinguishes itself."[95] In the end, MMTB officials concluded that promoting the city's French character was the way to set Montreal apart. Speaking for tourists, Bergeron reasoned, "the stranger likes Montreal because it is a different city as a result of its French *mentalité*,"[96] though this characterisation left *mentalité* undefined. Bergeron was better at articulating how this "Frenchness" should *not* be represented. Thus, he rejected out of hand what had been the private sector's most ubiquitous and enduring publicity slogan. In other words, "Montreal isn't really the Paris of North America," positing "all that stuff is a publicity stunt."[97] As with Drapeau, and other commentators, he believed that Montreal had nothing to envy Paris over, endowed as it was with its own unique French personality. Yet, clearly, relinquishing the deeply embedded and ubiquitous Parisian connection was difficult, as an early MMTB ad gushed that Montreal is "a gay city, full of vigour, where night clubs with the seductive accents of some left bank singer or the banter of Broadway and Las Vegas comedians harmonize to the rhythms of Miami and Hollywood's agile dancers."[98] And there were times when Bergeron himself found it difficult to avoid Paris references. In an interview with the *Gazette*, for example, it was reported, "he'd like to see at least one big night club set up in Montreal." "One [he said] that would give the opportunity for a guy ... to see some beautiful girls. Not every night but at least once as they do in Paris – give them something to remember us by."[99] More positively he noted that the city had lost the reputation it had acquired during the days of American prohibition, attracting Americans who came to "s'envoyer de l'eau-de-feu derrière la cravate often in disreputable establishments." While he did recognize that the city had "night clubs – some of which are a disgrace ... due to the bad quality of their shows or due to the bad reputation of the women of mauvaise vie that frequent them," he pointed out that today, American shows in general have been eclipsed "almost everywhere by the chanson d'ici."[100]

However, city promoters did not hesitate to showcase the French association when publicizing Montreal's cuisine. While acknowledging that the city's publicity should certainly publicize French Canadian cuisine, Bergeron clearly hoped visitors would, first and foremost, think of France. Echoing Robert Prévost, he warned that "if a tourist ate real French Canadian food for a week – things like salt pork, baked beans, pea soup and head cheese – he'd die."[101] As a result, it was suggested that Montreal's French Canadian cuisine be promoted as essentially French, as it had "the advantage of being able to draw upon the origin of the French [from France] cuisine, the superiority of which is universally recognized." Adopting the bombastic rhetoric of tourism advertising, the MMTB crowned Montreal as "the gastronomic capital of the country."[102] It reinforced this image in multiple and ever increasing ways; for instance, tourist could access a bimonthly guide, Montréal à la carte – Guide de/to Montréal. Its first section, devoted to wine and advice on wine pairings, was an attempt to further bolster Montreal's reputation as a centre of discerning and sophisticated taste – a French one.

But, as reported in the Gazette, Bergeron surprisingly was adamant that Montreal should no longer be referred to as "the second French City of the world." Here, to his mind, was yet another "publicity stunt."[103] Again if one reads his statements from a nationalist perspective, this dismissal stands to reason. It must be viewed as Bergeron's indictment of the city's deteriorating French face. This slogan would be a worthy title if only it were true. Echoing earlier tourism promoters as well as contemporary commentators, he declared that "the French face of Montreal must become a reality rather than a myth ... [M]ake it a more perceptible reality." As things stood now, such claims were nothing but false advertising.[104] What city promoters' pronouncements confirmed is that, regardless of their denunciations of the private sector's branding strategies, they clearly found it challenging to relinquish past marketing practices and showcase their vision of the New Montreal.

Further underscoring what may be viewed as the specifically nationalist undertones of these challenges is the fact that some of Bergeron's initiatives and candid pronouncements did not always sit well at City Hall. Indeed, his spirited exchanges with Municipal Councillor Fernand Drapeau, reported in *La Patrie* in 1964, confirm that the MMTB's initiatives hit raw nationalist nerves. Drapeau apparently reproached Bergeron for producing bilingual advertising that gave equal space to French and English an initiative, it should be noted, Bergeron, was very proud of as it was "fair for everyone." The councillor went further to argue that Americans "are resigned ahead of time not to understand many things because it is said or written in French." And "this is what makes the charm of their visit." As things stood, tourists, he claimed, came back from Montreal "very disappointed, after having read so much English and seen so many English signs." Getting more personal, he also suggested that Bergeron was intentionally compromising attempts to showcase Montreal as more than an American city. Likely in reaction to Bergeron's attempts at highlighting the city's cosmopolitanism, Drapeau advised him to "put less synagogues in the Church columns and put a bit more Catholic churches. That will give a bit of a French face to the *métropole*. Take all that is French and make it the subject of your advertisement. That is what Americans prefer in fact ... you are a host ... You are not at the service of tourists to the point of preventing them from discovering that Montreal is the second French city in the world."

This debate brought out two conflicting marketing approaches: on the one hand Bergeron's, who felt that one should shy away from a marketing label showcasing a Montreal that was on display, however deplorable that reality might be, versus those who wanted to retain the title of "second French city" as a bulwark against linguistic disfigurement. Drapeau's reprimands put Bergeron on the defensive, and his responses confirm that more profound identity issues were at play. While, in the end, the MMTB director was willing to concede, "perhaps it might be better to give French a two thirds share," he felt he needed to specify that "I am quite a nationalist as well and maybe more than you" indicating disagreements were more than arguments over marketing best practices.[105]

Setting aside these debates, it remained that, by the 1960s, a consensus had emerged that advertisements should showcase the city's modernity. Tourists should no longer expect to find contrasts between the old and the new throughout the city. Instead, the past in Montreal could be found in clearly circumscribed areas. At the same time, the metropolis's modernity had to be branded as distinct from the homogenizing American version. While there was a general agreement that this could be accomplished by emphasizing its unique French Quebec character, how this should be done was less obvious. As in the past, tourism branding could not be divorced from nationalist debates. This helps explain why promoters believed in ending the private sector's long-standing North American–Paris representation – Montreal could stand on its own. And the conflicting reactions to "the second French city in the world" label can best be explained by the enduring and more heated debates of this period over the fate of the French language.

ENGLISH-SPEAKING NORTH AMERICAN TRAVEL WRITERS

One can assume that travel writers had limited interest in the reasons and debates guiding municipal promoters' decisions on how to publicize the city. They were aware, however, of Montreal city promoters' attempts at foregrounding a new, modern, and dynamic metropolis, as the MMTB took particular pains to court and host them or, in some cases, even ghostwrote their accounts. This once again, puts in question whether travel writers' reports reflected unmitigated reactions or constituted the equivalent of quasi-official municipal tourism promotion. Whatever the case, their accounts do allow us to establish to what extent these "outsiders" contributed to reinforcing city promoters' branding efforts and establishing whether they drew more attention to some attributes of the city than others.

One thing is clear: more so than before, the differences between English Canadian and American accounts are unremarkable – so much so that they are hardly worth mentioning. English Canadian and American travel writers all remarked that Montreal in the 1960s was "new" – an adjective meant to underscore that the city had changed to become fully modern. But none felt the need to specify what they understood by this modernity nor what they specifically valued about it and why. This stood in contrast to earlier travel writers' reflections about the province's past and its old Quebec character. While their historical points of reference were often vague, they had nonetheless often narrowed this sense of the past to an imagined New France. In contrast, modernity, by definition, referred to tangible, ubiquitous, and current developments. Perhaps this explains why travel writers could assume that their readers would tacitly share their understanding of modernity, which in turn would account for the absence of distinct national observations.

The fact that English-speaking North Americans showcased above all else the modern Montreal means they were very much in sync with how promoters had chosen to rebrand the city. No longer labelling it "The City of Contrast," they referred to it as the "New Montreal."[106] (See figures 7.6 and 7.7.) Over and over, their accounts stressed how much the city was changing in extraordinary ways and at breathtaking speed – largely for the better and largely because it was modernizing. As one headline declared, "Montreal Is Bursting at the Seams."[107] According to Charles Lynch, "[t]oday more than ever it is the most exciting and stimulating of cities – nowhere else is the hum of progress and prosperity so apparent."[108] Jean Drapeau could not have

A 'NEW' MONTREAL

City Will Present a Different Face To Visitor During Coming Season

A 'New' Montreal

City Has Undergone Some Changes In Preparation for Expo 67

7.6 | Charles Lazarus covering Montreal for
The New York Times, 1963 and 1967.

hoped for better publicity. In fact, more than a few gave him credit, including Charles Lazarus who explained that "the changes in the atmosphere and the spirit of Montreal ... have been stimulated by Mayor Jean Drapeau, who envisions this city as a metropolis destined to achieve greatness like Paris, New York and London."[109]

What appears to have impressed travel writers most was the city's extraordinary "real estate boom." They represented this "building frenzy" as a drawing card. More specifically, they assured would-be tourists that they would be awed by the stunning avant-garde architectural design of these buildings, being erected in the city's downtown.[110] As one put it, "strolling around this area is like walking through a city of the future."[111] Place Ville-Marie attracted the most lavish praise. One journalist claimed that a "top item on Montreal's list of sightseeing attractions at the moment is its new Place Ville-Marie" and that "45,000 visitors go there daily."[112] Travel writers echoed the promotional priorities of the MMTB, as they said relatively little about the old Montreal. They shared Lucien Bergeron's point of view about the area. Indeed, W.P. Percival explained that "the modern visitor to Place Royale must use his imagination if he is to conjure up anything of the Romance of old Ville-Marie." He described it as a "poor little square ... situated on a busy, downtown waterfront, almost smelling of water rats."[113] However, as the decade progressed

TRAVEL | By The Star

PINE AVE.-PARK AVE. INTERCHANGE
Nearly 31 million vehicles use it each year

The New Montreal —*It's a weekend wonder*

42-STOREY ROYAL BANK BUILDING
It towers above quaint ball-like lamps of plaza

A VISIT TO Montreal today tells you at one glance why they call it "Canada's metropolis."

It's enough to make a Torontonian bug-eyed with envy.

A MASSIVE REAL ESTATE BOOM has reshaped its downtown section and heightened its skyline.

A FABULOUS NEW thruway boulevard rushes traffic almost the entire length of Montreal island from east to west in minutes. And vigorous redevelopment is swiftly making way for a long-awaited subway.

TORONTO DOESN'T take a back seat in transportation. But in structural redevelopment and planning, Montreal is beginning to give its closest Canadian rival a small-town look.

TOP ITEM on Montreal's list of sightseeing attractions at the moment is its new Place Ville Marie—a structure in the form of a cross that dominates the Montreal skyline.

Some 12,000 people work in its 42 levels; another 45,000 visitors go there daily. Together they give to Place Ville Marie a population greater than that of any but a dozen Canadian cities.

New Plans

Cost of this colossus ran to $83 million. And already its developers are planning their next multi-million dollar project immediately to the north.

The entire downtown area is a study in architectural reform. In the next five years or so a total of $500 million will have been spent on structures ranging from 15 to 50 storeys—including several new hotels.

Montreal makes for a rewarding weekend holiday any time of year. And it doesn't have to be expensive.

ASSUMING YOU ARRIVE there on a Saturday morning and leave late Sunday, a couple can stay at a top hotel, dine in the best restaurants and take in some sightseeing for less than $60.

This, of course, does not include fares—$24.35 each round-trip by train; $46 by plane.

Roughly $15 to $20 could be lopped off this figure by staying at a good hotel and eating in moderately priced restaurants. This way you can enjoy bilingual Montreal and its atmosphere to the full.

Price Varies

Quality double rooms vary from $11 at the Berkeley, slightly more at the Laurentian and Sheraton-Mount Royal, to $14 at the Queen Elizabeth and $15 at the Ritz-Carlton. (November is a busy convention month and reservations should be made in advance.)

Doing Montreal on the cheap requires prior knowledge of the city. But a visiting couple could start their weekend in the right French mood by lunching at the Crepe Bretonne on Mountain St.

Here they can choose from 81 varieties of Britanny-style pancakes, served in unmatched decor. One of these constitutes a full meal and costs little more than a dollar.

On the ground floor of the same building is the "bistro," which imitates those intimate bars found in Paris but nowhere else in North America. At the bistro you can enjoy a giant French bread sandwich with a glass of wine for $1.

In all, Montreal has some 5,000 eating places.

For a more expensive supper, a couple can choose between the classic French cuisine at Cafe Martin, the Cavalier Room, Chez Son Pere, Au Pied de Cochon, L'Anjou and many others. In each case, the best meals might run from $4.50.

But your taste may run to places serving foreign specialties. There's the exciting new Casa Del Sol, featuring Spanish food; the German Heidelberg House with its rathskeller atmosphere; the Suki-Yaki Japanese restaurant where diners must remove their shoes and sit on the floor; the Polynesian Kon Tiki; and the Arabic Four Corners of the World, to name a few.

These can hit the budget hard if drinks are included.

IF YOU WANT to watch a show while dining, there are all sorts of places at fairly reasonable prices.

For a treat, try the Cigale au Louvain where only trained musicians are hired as waiters, or the Lutin Qui Bouffe, where supper-club diners see abbreviated operas and operettas. In the Serenade Opera Lounge at Cafe Andre, you'll hear some of the city's finest singers present arias at your table.

SIGHTSEEING in Montreal isn't expensive. You can climb aboard a sightseeing bus for a $2.50 peek at downtown Montreal, including a view from atop Mount Royal. Or you may prefer a leisurely drive to the lookout at the mountain chalet for about $5 in a horse-drawn "caleche."

Guided tours of Place Ville Marie may be taken at 10 a.m. and 3 p.m. daily for 50 cents. But there is no charge for many other top attractions in the city. Among these is the spectacular Botanical Gardens where a special chrysanthemum show is featured until mid-December.

ON THE ENTERTAINMENT front, you can see a live performance for $2 at the Theatre du Nouveau, Monde, Stella, and Comedie Canadienne theatres.

The more expensive clubs include the Bonaventure Room, the Ritz Cafe and the Panorama Roof at the Queen Elizabeth where dancing is featured.

Dancing Girls

Of course, Montreal remains the city in which to find numerous clubs featuring variety shows and the traditional dancing girls.

Now something new has been added. The high-kicking cuties are now sharing the nightclub spotlight with performers right out of the Arabian nights—belly dancers.

They're billed in fun spots all over town. At Lou Black's they present "A Night in a Turkish Harem" with Lila Gamal, Princess Badia ("darling of the shieks") and Princess Aisha. Then, if you care about the grind, you can move over to the Sahara for a look at Fawzia Amir. She was King Farouk's favorite dancer, they say, and she's supported by other harem beauties billed

Drink Of Water Help To Babies

Give your baby a drink of water during take-off and landing in an airplane, advises American Airlines. This helps his ears adjust to pressure changes. Adults know when to swallow or yawn, but a baby doesn't.

Alex Henderson's | TRAVEL ANSWERS

My husband and I have just finished reading a book by a woman (Ethel S. Smith) who took a trip almost around the world on a freighter. This slow way of travel is how we'd like to go when my husband retires two years from now. How does it compare to passenger ships in price? Is it hard to book on these ships? Is it possible at all?—Mrs. F.R., Toronto.

Travelling by freighter is considerably cheaper than on board a passenger ship, and it's a delightful

shillings a night for bed and breakfast, or from five to eight pounds a week for full board.

* * *

I would appreciate your opinion on a trip to Spain and Portugal in February or March on the 17-day excursion plan put up by Canadian Pacific Airlines. To your knowledge is there anything better being offered at a comparable price or would we be wise to go on our own? This is our first trip and neither my husband nor myself speak anything but English. —

which leaves just 15 days abroad. But if you pre-plan your trip carefully to catch all the highlights of London and other areas, you'd be surprised what you can cover in 15 days. This is the best bargain you can get by air, short of a chartered trip, and I would strongly recommend it at this time of year.

* * *

In New York I discovered there are two cut-rate airlines that fly south, west and to the Far East. Typical fares—$35 to

Nap Rooms For Malton

OTTAWA —(UPI)— Airline passengers who like to nap between flight connections will have their wish answered in new terminal buildings under construction in Toronto and Winnipeg.

The transport department said the new terminal will include air-conditioned roomettes complete with washrooms and showers.

"The roomettes will be

The department said both terminals also will include rooms — five at Toronto and three at Winnipeg—"suitable for business meetings of executives and private organizations."

As a final wrinkle, the Winnipeg building will have a nursery complete with a small kitchen. Both terminals are expected to be completed by next summer.

and plans to restore the old quarter were put into action, it gained better press typically heralded "as a permanent, functioning monument to the city's past." Travel writers usually represented it as a built-in museum preserving the vestiges of Montreal's early history. Thus, as in the municipal tourism publicity, they saw the old as being squarely apart from the new.

Only occasionally were the disadvantages of this accelerated pace of modernization mentioned. Thus, one account warned its readers that, "like all changing towns, Montreal has its share of dubious achievements; its insipid office buildings ... and the inevitable string of cheap motels and shopping plazas leading in from the airport." However, the author was quick to add that "these things happen to all cities when something honestly dynamic has been set in motion, and Montreal has been more fortunate than most."[114] A few also complained about traffic jams and lack of lodgings for the ever-growing number of tourists. But such nuisances were taken in stride as the unavoidable growing pains that went hand in hand with an exhilarating and frenetic modernization.

Of note as well, by the 1960s, Montreal had apparently lost any pretence of being labelled Canada's, if not North America's, "sin city." Travel writers greatly reduced or stopped suggesting, however obliquely, that Montreal offered unique opportunities to misbehave, most likely because other North American urban centres had caught up and provided comparable sinning opportunities. Several also made the point that the city had lost the seedier side of its free-wheeling reputation as one of the "toughest cities in North America."[115] Jay Walz specified, "Montrealers in their fifties like Drapeau, grew up in a city that American prohibition had made a notorious base for gangsters ... [where] Bordellos abounded." Now the city was instead euphemistically labelled as "bold and adventurous."[116] When people referred to the "New Montreal" they were not only thinking of its "[b]illion dollar skyline ... Rather they mean reform." Quoting Drapeau, Montreal "has become 'a great respectable city.'"

Travel writers also stopped referring to Montreal as the Paris of the New World, aligning again with Drapeau and Bergeron who had made it clear that such branding was no longer acceptable. They too made it clear that Montreal had no need to piggyback on the success of that destination. *Holiday* magazine published a travel account that made this very point, while discrediting the comparison with New York as well. The author remarked that while "ten years ago even the most tepid comparison of Montreal to New York was comforting to the Montrealer, and the old soubriquet [sic] of 'Little Paris' was accepted as harmless and even pleasing compliment," things had changed: "Montreal has become its own town and the surest sign of its present standing is that a visitor, even one geared to life in lusher corners, is no longer compelled to liken it to anything outside itself."[117] Such words could have come directly from the mouths of MMTB promoters. (Keeping in mind their sustained attempts to reach out to travel writers, perhaps they had.)

Much was made of the fact that Montreal was a majority French city. As one travel writer wrote, the city offered "the perfect counter-point to all American skyscrapers" with its "French bistros, French waiters, French stores, French peace posters, movies, books and girls."[118] The Paris connection only appeared when travel writers commented on the city's extraordinary dining opportunities. Not only did "Montreal suppor[t] more eating places per capita than any other city in the world,"[119] but this was "the one area where comparison to Paris has some point."[120] Emphasis was also put on the sophisticated, high-end boutiques in the city. When travel writers travelled as couples, the accounts, clearly written from the husband's perspective, at times chose to foreground the city's alluring shopping opportunities by way of sexist mocking asides pointing to their wives' apparently unrestrainable and extravagant buying urges echoing their predecessors' complaints. For example, Hal Burton remarked that while he set off to the Radio Canada building, clearly to his mind a worthy initiative, his wife "agonized over hundreds of teacups before buying a wafer-thin specimen from Northern Ireland [at Birks]." She later "succumbed to a $65 mink toque."[121] A few, though, wanting to prove reassuring, noted that unlike the dangers that faced him (presumably in France), a husband should not worry that he would be "ruined by his wife's patronizing of the salons of *haute couture*."[122]

Notably 1960s travel accounts distinguished themselves from past accounts by drawing greater attention to French Montrealers. Gone however were the Bonsecours *habitants*. Instead, travel writers represented French Montrealers as people who stood out for their chic allure – more specifically, one that evoked the stereotypical attributes often associated with things from France in general. Quoting acquaintances who had returned to Montreal after a long absence, Hugh MacLennan reported how one had asked him, "[w]hat on earth has been happening to the French-Canadians while we've been away?" They couldn't believe "how exciting Montreal has become," remarking on French Montrealers' new "general attitude toward living. Their style."[123] And while describing "Montreal after dark," one author remarked, "it soon becomes clear that much of that sophistication comes from the French," adding sardonically that "one gets the impression that the English-speaking people of Montreal are home watching the telly."[124] Some travel writers extended this stereotype to the Québécois overall, invoking his "French heritage" which apparently accounted for the fact that "[h]e shakes hands at every opportunity. He talks and laughs in public places at the top of his voice. He removes his hat entirely from his head in greeting ladies."[125] Further affirming the Latin epicurean stereotype, visitors were informed that for Montrealers "cuisine was a major concern" and accounted for the "extended lunches and four-hour dinner." Further, visitors were told that "chefs achieve the status that bullfighters have in Madrid." While such asides stand as essentializing, they nonetheless speak to a change in perception: travel writers were by then severing links their predecessors had for so long maintained between tradition and French Quebeckers.

They also occasionally made pointed remarks about French Montreal women, deviating again from the focus of writers of earlier decades. This "city of women"[126] inspired authors to indulge in sexist stereotypes about the supposedly distinctive attractive charm of French women; thus, Michael Herr contended, "[o]nce, Montreal's women dressed in clothes that were essence [sic] repressed ... shut tight at the neck and dropping in dismal lines far below the knee." This "[c]hanged, all changed ... The girls have taken over the trick that women in Europe once used, owning a few terrific outfits and wearing them often like signatures."[127] Ian Adams saw much more in them than that. While he too admired their "European clothes," he was also quite taken by their "fat little bosoms bobbing around in bras designed by middle-aged men to provoke, stimulate desire."[128] In many ways, these remarks were meant to further reinforce their imaging of the city as a centre of French sophistication evoking enduring stereotypes of the supposedly less inhibited women of France. And, just as the wives of travel writers, women in Montreal were inveterate shoppers. Indeed, Robert Hollier, when highlighting the alluring shopping opportunities on St Catherine Street "at lunchtime," added that this was when "thousands of pretty young secretaries besiege these emporiums ... and deliver themselves to a buying orgy."[129]

Travel writers in the 1960s paid more attention to Montrealers in different ways as well and, in turn, revealed the emergence of another "New Montreal" – one shaped by the transformations associated with the Quiet Revolution. Thus, in 1964, commenting on the city's upcoming St-Jean-Baptiste Day celebrations, a *Toronto Star* journalist observed that major changes were in store: while in previous years, he claimed, "[t]he rural aspect of Quebec was often stressed ... Not so this time." That summer the theme was "French Canada – a 20th Century Reality."[130] Percival specified, "the purpose [of this change] was to show that French Canada is strong, vigorous and progressive in business and industry."[131] But they proved more sensitive to the emergence of a new nationalism among the French population of the city along with the accompanying fraught French–English relations. More specifically, they appeared to have taken particular note of French Quebeckers' increasing desire to assert their power in the face of English Canadian economic and political control. Such observations were clearly entirely their own. At no time had city promoters such as Bergeron suggested that promotional material should draw attention to these emerging developments. Overall, those who commented on Quebec society appeared to share the view that French Montrealers were succeeding in asserting themselves in unprecedented ways. According to Charles Lynch, "Never, certainly, have her French-speaking people been so much in the ascendency, setting the city's tone in the broad field of culture and exerting her influence as never before in the realm of the counting houses. Their politicians' control in the city, as in the province, at large has been unquestioned in modern times."[132]

V.S. Pritchett noted much the same thing when he remarked that English and French Montrealers "have nothing like a proportional share of economic power" and that "until only a few years ago, they were resigned to this. Now, they are not."[133] Not surprisingly, it was the rare travel writer who suggested that such changes would impinge on English-speaking North American visitors' enjoyment in visiting Montreal. Some emphasized how though in the past "the old [English] Establishment" was "proud of speaking very little French very badly – [this] has begun to change."[134] In contrast to writers in previous decades, they appeared, as well, to have been particularly struck by the fact that "the two people interpenetrate very little. They are like separate currents of two rivers that have been joined by events that happened 200 years ago."[135] Americans appeared more bewildered by this cultural insularity than were their English Canadian counterparts. Not surprisingly, Hugh MacLennan offered more insightful observations about the two solitudes his famous novel had so vividly brought to life. In addition to religion and language, he "[thought] that the greatest barrier has been an almost mystic feeling that their overriding duty is to exist as a separate community." Ian Adams, for his part, went further to suggest that visitors might witness some intercultural tensions; however he did so for humorous effect. He explained reassuringly that "there is a two per cent chance that the visitor may meet a Montrealer who just doesn't like English-speaking people, no matter how reasonably they appear to behave." He added, "so the handy phrases to understand in this situation are ones that will enable you to walk away with dignity. Most common is 'Maudit Anglais' … Another easily recognizable slang epithet is 'Tombez mort!'"[136]

What makes such light-hearted observations particularly noteworthy is that this was the time when the violent acts of the FLQ shook the city and garnered headlines around the world. Rarely though did travel writers broach the topic head on. When they did it was only to reassure tourists there was nothing to be concerned about, and they should not revise their travel plans to Montreal. As Charles Lynch insisted, "the sounds and sights of Montreal are much happier than the flurry of FLQ bombings would indicate."[137] Travel writers in the 1960s essentially followed in the footsteps of their *bonne ententiste* predecessors – even when they brought up the FLQ: "not for a minute should you [the visitor] believe that the succession of violent acts carried out by this small band of fanatics in any way reflected the attitude of the rank and file separatists." They were essentially "nutty."[138] In fact, as early as June 1963, the *Toronto Star* proclaimed optimistically that "the 'FLQ' has been smashed" and that visitors "will find old Quebec as serene as ever."[139] In 1967, American travel writer Michael Herr made the point differently, explaining, "[t]he extremism of FLQ has subsided into *la Révolution tranquille*, the Quiet Revolution."[140] These were, of course, the type of reassuring observations Montreal tourist promoters would have wished for to counter what they perceived to be the alarmist and overblown reactions published in the English-speaking North American press.

Overall, in the 1960s, municipal promoters could not have been more pleased with how their city was represented by travel writers. In contrast to the Quebec countryside, which occasionally did not meet with these writers' expectations – mostly for not being as old as they had expected it to be – Montreal rarely seemed to disappoint. It was no longer banking on its long-vaunted reputation as the Paris of North America, and travel writers clearly took this in stride. They were enthralled by it precisely because it was new in unexpected ways and all the more popular for it. Municipal officials could also congratulate themselves for having finally understood the benefits of taking charge of the city's tourism development. The fact that the city would host Expo 67 clearly spurred them into action. But it is clear that, regardless, they also concurred with their critics that more needed to be done to better showcase Montreal's French character and French modernity. The English-dominated MTCB had not only favoured its own business interests but also had represented the city in ways that would no longer be tenable in the context of the Quiet Revolution with its more assertive nationalism bent on turning its back on tradition. Yet, for all that, as in the past, coming up with a brand which conveyed what municipal promoters hoped Montreal should be – French and ultramodern but not American – proved challenging as the reality on the ground made this at times tricky.

EPILOGUE

PROMOTERS

A close examination of tourist promoters' initiatives over the better part of the twentieth century, whether they were working to market the rural areas or Montreal, reveal how their branding objectives changed significantly over time. More specifically, it confirms the extent to which these mirror the equally significant changes in French Quebeckers' sense of national identity. Not surprisingly, the most striking transformations occurred during the 1960s – the heyday of the Quiet Revolution. But this decade was bookended by Expo 67 – an event closely linked to this period of nationalist affirmation.[1] It is also perceived as a significant one in the history of Quebec tourism. Most concur with Paul-André Linteau's assessment that it had "significant effects for [its] population and for Montreal's image." On the cultural front more specifically it "favour[ed] an opening to the world."[2] Many tourism promoters at the time were convinced that Expo 67 would, as never before, put Quebec, and Montreal in particular, on the radar screens of future tourists from all over the world. As noted, they viewed it as a "do it or lose it" opportunity. And as early as October – the last month of the exhibit – Prévost proclaimed triumphantly that "1967 will go down in the history of our province as a turning point in the development of our tourism industry."[3] A brief overview of developments that occurred immediately after Expo 67 enables us to establish whether Prévost's predictions were proven right.

There is no doubt that, on a few fronts, 1967 deserves such recognition. By any statistical measure there is clearly a "before and after" Expo. For one, observers were quick to report that "Expo 67 helped tip the second quarter balance of travel spending in Canada's favour," with "[e]arly Expo visitors [already leaving a] $120,000,000.00 surplus."[4] Feeding this windfall was, of course, the unprecedented number of visitors, which far exceeded everyone's expectations. Instead of the projected 30 million visitors, no fewer than 51 million made the trip.[5] Further evidence of this remarkable achievement is revealed when calculations confirmed that "US car entries in June [1967] were up by a dazzling 223 percent over the last year."[6] Looking at Quebec more specifically, the 1968 annual report of the DTFG noted, "the extraordinary attraction of Expo 67 combined with the centenary celebrations of Canadian Confederation more than doubled the tourist influx in the 'Belle Province.'"[7] Thus, "instead of the usual 6 million tourist average, Quebec welcomed close to 15 million in 1967 and almost all went to Expo."[8]

However, what stood out most of all for government officials and what represented a particularly gratifying indicator of success is the fact that the province attracted the highest proportion ever recorded of so-called international visitors, by which they meant non-American tourists, primarily from Europe. While this was true for Canada as a whole as "some 55 per cent more Europeans visited Canada in 1967 than the previous year,"[9] in the case of Quebec, "5 times more tourists [came] from other continents, mostly Europe."[10] In short, the success of Expo confirmed what Drapeau and others had been arguing: Quebec had the potential to attract visitors from all over the world. Thus, from a statistical perspective, 1967 stands as a turning point: never before had the province reaped so many benefits from the tourism industry in terms of both revenue and visitors.

These successes spurred those involved in the tourist business to take new measures in the hopes of increasing the flow of foreign tourists during the years to come. European travellers tended to be wealthier, and therefore spent more money and stayed for longer periods of time than did their North American counterparts, which made them all the more worthy of attention. Of course, competition was fierce as other countries and Canadian provinces were keen to reap the benefits of this prized clientele. Added to the mix were the airline companies who continued to significantly decrease their fares and expand the number of their charter flights. Companies such as Air Canada aggressively promoted the numerous destinations they serviced and all tourist promoters understood that getting them on side was crucial. Quebec tourist promoters certainly did and they extended their marketing outreach to travel agencies and airplane companies as never before. They also made greater use of increasingly sophisticated scientific market studies in order to establish, with more accuracy, the specific cities or regions tourists came from, to determine what they were looking for, the amount of money they spent, and on what. The objective was to avoid planning marketing campaigns based on undocumented or dated assumptions. To this end, the DTFG created its own research service in 1968 for this very purpose, hiring among other specialists, geographers, statisticians, and economists.

What became clear early on was that France stood as the most promising international tourist market. During Expo 67 the French made up the largest contingent of foreign visitors.[11] Quebec tourist promoters quickly concluded that looking much beyond France's borders would be a waste of time. From a wider diplomatic perspective and in the context of the heightened Québécois nationalism, their decision to branch out onto the international stage, and France in particular, mirrored Quebec politicians' wider proactive initiatives to assert the province's international diplomatic presence. The most striking example of this was the opening of the Maison du Québec in 1961, which became the Délégation générale du Québec in 1964.[12] Wasting no time, in 1968 Prévost was appointed general commissioner of Tourism with the mission of analyzing the possibilities and the ways in which the province could attract a larger proportion of French tourists and scout out the possibilities of bringing over other European visitors. He produced a report the following year in which he concluded that because of Quebec's undeniable popularity among the French, "[Paris] is the only one of the European capital[s] ... where it would be logical for Quebec to maintain a tourist information counter open to the public ... Everywhere else, it will suffice to have tourist consultants maintain direct contacts with travel agents and transportation."[13] He convinced his superiors and the government established a tourist office in Paris.

However, if one turns to the way promoters represented Quebec as a whole, and Montreal in particular, in publicity material, change was not the order of the day. They remained faithful to the images designed in the early 1960s. There was not much incentive to redesign them in any significant way. This was most obvious in the case of Montreal. Years earlier, Drapeau and Bergeron had worked hard to rebrand the city as "New Montreal," and, just as they had hoped, Expo 67 sealed its "world class" reputation as well as its status as a modern sophisticated city. As far as Bergeron was concerned, Montreal had become "a city with an international character principally because of Expo 67."[14] There was thus a sense of mission accomplished as most concurred that "tourists are coming [to Montreal] because they know that from now on, this city is universal to the same extent as other big capitals of the world."[15] Making a similar point more colourfully, in 1970 MMTB's liaison officer, Benoît Bélanger, recounted that before Expo "we had tourists who arrived in Montreal with skis on the hood of their car in the middle of July but since 1967 tourists arrive knowing what to expect." No longer did they consider Montreal "a bit of a village."[16] What need was there to reassess the city's pre-Expo makeover? Just as previous publicity had, a 1968 brochure informed readers that Montreal was "Canada's metropolis" and "considered by top ranking town planners as one of the world's fastest growing." Post-1967, marketing material continued to showcase the city's avant-garde architecture and other markers of urban modernity, including the metro, high-end restaurants, and lively theatres. Much was also made of Montreal's "three miles underground arcades all weather access" with its abundance of luxury boutiques. And promoters made more of Montreal's cosmopolitan character. If Drapeau and Bergeron had been keen to tout the city's multicultural population as a valuable drawing card, following 1967, Montreal's cosmopolitanism was systematically featured as one of the city's defining markers of modernity and urbanity. Bergeron proudly proclaimed that "the city could now ... rightly claim to have an international character ... with its French culture but also with its inhabitants of various other nationalities."[17] It was as though aiming to attract the attention of the world had made promoters more aware and proud that the world was already in Montreal.

But embracing multiculturalism as tourist-bait did not mean promoters abandoned the objective of emphasizing the city's predominantly French population and character. They remained faced with their predecessors' challenges: how could this be done when Montreal's French face continued to be overshadowed by an English and Americanized one? The minister of Tourism, Fish and Game, Gabriel Loubier, summarized the issue in familiar terms when he declared that "Montreal [wa]s not living up to its reputation as the second largest French city in the world." He also expressed the long-established assumption that "if Montreal were transformed into a really French city, it would benefit the tourist trade." The options facing promoters were familiar as well: either "keep the [city's] present 'prostitute' image and give up on the French city myth or change the image."[18] But by 1967, such well-rehearsed recriminations took on a more pressing significance as language debates – particularly in Montreal – were by now daily front-page news and at the core of extremely acrimonious, loud, and at times violent confrontations.[19] Those on the front lines and observers of all stripes advocated solutions that stood in stark contrast with those offered in the past by people such as Gouin. While he had sought to encourage those involved in the tourist industry to *refranciser* their establishments and offered his consulting services, by then many advocated coercive measures instead. Minister Loubier himself assured, "the provincial government will provide any technical and legislative aid necessary; if Montreal passes legislation to *refranciser* its imagine."[20] The time for persuasion and old style *refrancisation* campaigns was coming to a close. The much-vaunted second-largest French city in the world would be legislated into existence if need be.

Promoters of course could not afford to wait for politicians to take legislative action, but their efforts suggest that they struggled to encapsulate Montreal's cultural identity in pithy slogans. This is hardly surprising: how does one brand a multicultural French city with an English face while asserting its predominant French character? A few of their marketing attempts may have left some tourists baffled. For instance, one brochure offered them "[a] little reminder [that] when walking along the streets of Montréal [they shouldn't] conclude from looking at the signs in front of shops, stores and even restaurants that the owners are all English-speaking. They may be Italian, Greek, Irish, Portuguese and even American." At the same time though, they should realize that "most of them are French-speaking Québécois." In fact, "three-quarters of the population are French-speaking but a good proportion also speak … the language of business."[21] Presumably, English-speaking tourists should at one and the same time understand that they were not to worry about being misunderstood and enjoy the sounds of diverse languages in a majority French environment in which the English dominated the economy. Those more attuned to the ambient linguistic tensions in Montreal might read between the lines and detect a veiled politically charged observation: the English in the city held the economic power leading the ethnic minorities to speak the language of power all the while eclipsing the majority French population. Regardless, here was yet another indication that tourism promoters' marketing strategies were inevitably coloured by current nationalist debates.

Expo 67's limited impact on representations of the province is also revealed in the way promoters marketed Quebec's more rural areas. Continuity unequivocally trumped change. These areas had been severed from the old Quebec characterization and would continue to be so. The publicity drew would-be tourists' attention to these areas' beautiful scenery such as the Gaspé whose "great asset [was] its looks, its wild beauty, its capes and cliffs."[22] This region offered some reminders of the past with its "long established villages, towns and farms [dating] back to the French regime" but as in the early 1960s, this past was first and foremost visible through the built landscape. And if in the surrounding areas of Quebec, visitors would discover that "the old French traditions are still flourishing," no mention was made of what these traditions entailed nor was anything written about the people's lifestyle or character. As suggested in previous publicity, those who lived there were essentially unremarkable. They were not the *habitants* of old, but "farmers"

who, "[a]s in every country, have a deep respect for tradition and their own
cultural heritage."[23]

Was Expo 1967 a "turning point" as Prévost suggested? Clearly not if
one considers how Quebec was publicized as a tourist destination. Rather,
it entrenched patterns already set in motion. At most, it added impetus and
in some ways accelerated the rebranding initiatives of the early 1960s. The
"New Montreal" and "La Belle Province" were in effect revealed for the world
to see during Expo 67 – a crowning moment which cemented Quebec's reputation as a destination worthy of international attention for being in lockstep
with modernity and for the beauty of its scenery.

A better way of making sense of the evolving history of Quebec's tourism
industry is to consider that it was marked by a series of changes. Multiple
turning points punctuated its development since the first few decades of the
twentieth century. Expo 67 was simply capping these off with a splash. The
first noteworthy turning point occurred during the late 1910s and early 1920s
when, for the first time, the Quebec government got involved in the tourism
industry. Granted, this involvement started out rather modestly considering
that the newly formed Provincial Tourist Bureau became an ancillary responsibility of the Roads Department. This pairing made sense since the industry
was still in its infancy and fast developing as a result of the tremendous increase
in car ownership. In this initial phase, the government's undertakings were all
about modernizing the province's tourist infrastructure. The Roads Department embarked on an ambitious campaign of road construction, of upgrading
hospitality services and embellishing the province's rural areas – regions that
were increasingly becoming a favourite among motorized tourists. Although
very popular as well, Montreal did not require such sustained attention as
it was readily accessible, and its reputation and the long standing promotional work of the private sector ensured that its visitors' needs were covered.

PTB officials were also making decisions about what they thought made
the province distinct and particularly attractive to tourists. The fact that the
better part of their initiatives were contributing to setting the "Old Quebec"
stage and that some of its publicity invited tourists to visit a seventeenth-
century France in North America reveal that they endorsed the private sector's early branding efforts. This being said, they occasionally labelled Quebec
the "new–old province." Their more detailed publicity material showcased
areas remarkable for their tremendous industrial development. However, this
double imaging had less to do with what they believed tourists were looking
for than the fact that PTB officials were ensconced in a department whose
overarching priority was to promote the province's economic development.
Its officials had to find ways to brand the province in a manner that would

attract potential investors as well as tourists. This could not be achieved by labelling it exclusively as old. A "new–old" representation could better convey the promise of enticing financial returns to potential investors while catching the attention of those planning to visit.

However, they were not to stay on the branding fence for long. By the early 1930s, it became clear that the tourism industry could be very profitable in its own right and worthy of the provincial state's more focussed attention. This was also a time of increased competition for the tourist dollar as many governments across North America and Europe viewed the tourism industry as a potential antidote to future devastating economic downturns. More significantly, in Quebec this decade was when the tourism industry was embraced by a coterie of prominent and vocal traditional nationalists who were very concerned about the threats posed by Americanization. Thus emerged a second turning point when the responsibility of tourism development was eventually relocated to the Department of the Executive Council. To their minds, a prosperous tourism industry devoted to the promotion of old Quebec would position the province in an advantageous position differentiating it from other destinations, but, more importantly to their minds, tourism held the promise of resuscitating the authentic Quebec – a French-speaking nation steeped in the values and traditions of the ancestors born on the soil. It also offered itself as a unique and auspicious opportunity to inspire French Quebeckers to reconnect with their roots and strengthen their attachment to the ways of old. They backed up these claims by invoking the fact that English-speaking North American tourists were particularly drawn to the province's countryside and its old Quebec attributes. In short, it was a "win win" situation: selling a traditional Quebec made financial sense and could reap traditional nationalist benefits.

The onus rested on French Quebeckers to live up to the brand and avoid opening tourism promoters to charges of false advertising. They would not be left alone in that task. Well respected, traditional nationalists were charged by government decision-makers to create the conditions under which tourism publicity material would reflect reality on the ground. Albert Tessier, for one, offered ways to improve the province's tourism industry in a report in which he outlined how the state could create tourist sites that would reflect Quebec's *valeurs nationales*. Paul Gouin spoke of holding on to traditions to better attract tourists and worked tirelessly to encourage those in the industry to *refranciser* their establishments. Roads Department officials and their successors in other government departments invoked the need to promote the province's French face and character. Among other initiatives, they entrenched the seventeenth-century New France representation of the province in their publicity by foregrounding the traditional *habitants* and proved in-strumental in revitalizing the dying arts and crafts *petite industrie*. In the same vein, the PTB's publicity destined for French Quebec citizens aimed to spur them to visit the sites of their proud heritage. True patriots would welcome the opportunity to visit places that would remind them of their ancestors' heroic determination and inspiring values. Such concerted efforts made tour-ism promotion part and parcel of a wider traditional nationalist campaign.

However, as the case of Montreal makes clear, the connection between traditional nationalism and tourism promotion was not a province-wide affair. Not only did the "Old Quebec" brand simply not apply there but the city was all the more popular for being nothing like it. As one would expect, Montreal was a source of constant worry to traditional nationalists. It stood for what they feared was most threatening about modernity and its anglicizing influence. Their appeals to use tourism to revitalize the values and way of life of the ancestors thus made no sense in the context of this bustling metropolis. Montreal's outlier status was further accentuated by the fact that French Quebeckers had very little say in the way it was being mar-keted. The majority French-speaking municipal government officials had re-linquished tourism promotion to the city's predominantly English-speaking private sector in the hands of the MTCB. As for the provincial PTB, its tepid marketing efforts could do nothing to impose a distinctive and recognizably French Quebec brand. The private sector defined the city in ways that cast the French of Montreal as stand-ins to evoke the city's past and its Gallic charm. It was a city of contrasts between the old and the new. Its French past was highlighted better to reflect the city's dynamism and sophisticated mod-ernity – one largely controlled by its English-speaking residents. Furthermore, the MTCB's attempts to showcase Montreal as "Gay Paris" were not intended to draw visitors' attention to the distinct ways of life of French Montrealers. This slogan conveyed instead a recognizable and appealing European French-ness for tourists in search of the city of lights' vaunted sophistication and naughty entertainment. The fact that the MTCB made few efforts to attract French Quebec visitors reinforced the sense that the city was first and fore-most ideally suited to cater to English-speaking North Americans.

The following decades, leading up to the late 1950s both in Montreal and at the provincial level, offer no clear turning points. For one, the MTCB stayed at the helm and did not make noteworthy changes to its marketing strategies. At the provincial level, the most influential government tourist promoters were in many cases one and the same, including Paul Gouin. He remained a steadfast advocate of persuasive *refrancisation* and insistent that however much traditions should evolve in lockstep with changing times, the province was attractive to tourists for its old Quebec heritage. Those involved in the tourist industry who forgot this did so at their peril. At most, the PTB's publicity in the 1940s and 1950s revealed signs of gradual change. Tourists continued to be assured that they would come across an old Quebec; however, the wartime travelling restrictions of the 1940s also inspired promoters to promise them that they would enjoy a destination that offered sophisticated pleasures associated with France. Furthermore, promoters returned to double imaging pointing to the province's up-to-date economic development. While the old was still very much in view, comparisons to seventeenth-century rural Normandy and New France and its oxen, spinning wheels, and dog carts no longer occupied pride of place. Their increased use of the "Province de Québec" label also speaks to a greater attempt at highlighting the province's French identity. This more multifaceted image of the province would endure into the late 1950s. It tapped into the postwar touring public's increasingly consumer-oriented priorities. The Quebec brand by then combined timeless quaintness with some of the alluring features of contemporary refinement. Such representations were in lockstep with a period during which an increasing number of French Quebeckers were publicly questioning what traditional nationalists claimed made them distinct as a people.

One has to wait for the early 1960s to witness the next turning point and the most transformative one. It is no coincidence that these were the years of the nationalist high-water mark of the Quiet Revolution. By then tourist promoters, along with their fellow French Quebeckers, embraced with open arms the changes that had transformed Quebec society over time into a modern secular society. Traditionalist nationalists' objectives to resurrect their compatriots' authentic values and ways of life by way of the tourism industry no longer held sway. In the 1960s, a new cast of civil servants, including Robert Prévost, took over the reins of tourism promotion in the newly created DTFG. They were proud of the nation that had evolved in sync with modernity. As a result, they revamped the province's tourism publicity to better showcase contemporary Quebec and the newly defined Québécois identity. Thus was born "La Belle Province." The past and history simply became one of the province's alluring attractions, no longer the principal one.

Viewed from a different perspective, tourism promoters in the 1960s had less ambitious objectives than their predecessors. Rather than considering their work as contributing to a wider national reformist movement, they set out to showcase the nation that was already on display. In turn, they were less demanding of their compatriots. They followed in the footsteps of Albert Tessier and Paul Gouin when it came to entreating them to *refranciser* the province but rather than asking them to revitalize the old ways of life, they insisted more forcefully that French Quebeckers should first and foremost distinguish themselves by being outstandingly hospitable.

Tourism promotion in Montreal during the 1960s also underwent remarkable changes reflective of a more assertive new nationalism. The French-dominated city council took over tourism promotion from the English-dominated MTCB and undertook to revamp the city's image by showcasing a "New Montreal." The old was thus eclipsed by modernity and sophistication and showcased for the world to see at Expo 67.

TRAVEL WRITERS

Of course, tourist promoters' evolving marketing strategies do not only reflect changes in national identity. In order for these to be effective, officials had to take into account prospective visitors' hopes and expectations. Traditional nationalists made the case that English-speaking North Americans mostly wanted to see "Old Quebec," while their successors argued that they wanted to enjoy "La Belle Province." An overview of travel accounts published during this period suggests that, in many ways, they were right. Their accounts did laud the province's old-world character and, later, its more modern and sophisticated offerings.

Yet, as noted at the outset, attempting to tap into the thoughts and desires of visitors by way of travel writing is never a straightforward endeavour. The findings in this study certainly give pause to anyone assuming that the views expressed in this material reflect the authors' reactions to the province. Certainly those published by English-speaking North Americans were not always what they purported to be: clear cut, unmediated, firsthand observations. One need only bring to mind the scenario outlined by Gordon Brinley as they set off for the "New France of yesterday." Here stood travel writers commissioned by an independent publisher, setting out with a travel account in hand – one perhaps written by a PTB official – to write one of their own. In fact, there could be a case to be made that travel accounts stand as just another form of government tourist propaganda. Indeed, public documents, both at the provincial level and later in the period at the Montreal City Council, bring to light that officials made a practice of commissioning travel writers to produce articles showcasing the beauties and attractions they deemed worthy of attention. They even sought out reputed writers to better enhance the credibility of these articles. (There is less evidence to suggest that they hired French Quebeckers who presumably knew what their homeland had to offer.) They also compiled dossiers of pictures and other publicity material for their benefit. The distinction between propaganda and travel writing is blurred even more knowing government officials also sent out unsigned travel accounts to the most widely circulated or prestigious magazines and newspapers and that publishers never noted their provenance. This marketing strategy, initially proudly touted in the 1930s as clever and unorthodox, becomes standard practice over the years as more and more travel writers are solicited to undertake this "undercover work."

Further muddying the waters, provincial and municipal government promoters also offered their guiding services to travel writers whether hired by them or not. By the 1960s, they also made the point of attending their professional gatherings, inviting them by the hundreds to the province, all the while providing them with reports and offering them editing services. Such face-to-face encounters obviously gave promoters the chance to shape travel writers' representation of the province and its people in ways that accorded with their own marketing objectives. As a few examples in this study reveal, they made it possible for officials to correct some travel writers' misconceptions or what they viewed as dated or unflattering impressions. In light of this, can one consider the thoughts expressed in travel accounts as an entrée into their authors' impressions, let alone those of ordinary tourists? There are, in fact, many reasons why one can. To begin with, in instances too numerous to discount, travel writers shared disappointments and put forward criticisms of the sites and services showcased in the publicity. Most often, these were regrets at not encountering the "Old Quebec" so prominently showcased in the government publicity. Others pointed to the unfortunate encroachments of modernity or the touristy nature of certain popular sites. Moreover, English-speaking North American reactions can be considered genuine and propaganda-free when one takes into account that before they set out for Quebec, they had many opportunities to develop preconceived notions and expectations about Quebec which would have predisposed them to think of it as old. (Occasionally much to the dismay of government officials in the 1960s intent on proving the opposite.) In fact, it would have been difficult for them not to. Many would have been exposed to novels, art, and most assuredly school textbooks which consistently represented French Quebeckers as a people of the past, incarnated by the happy-go-lucky Krieghoff and Drumond-like *habitants*. In the first few decades of the period, this preestablished knowledge would have been further ingrained by a prevailing antimodernist climate. Thus, regardless of whether government promoters spoon-fed travel writers information about the province or not, whether they were being paid or not, officials were not really telling them something they did not already know. Much of that information would have simply reinforced travel writers' preconceptions. This means that they were not simply wilfully parroting provincial promoters' marketing publicity. Their lenses were certainly tinted, and the accuracy of their representations questionable, but their gaze had been honestly come by. Thus, they could have easily and legitimately considered themselves as independent professionals reporting firsthand, unmitigated impressions.

There is more evidence to indicate that they considered themselves so: English Canadian, American, and French Quebec travel writers did not represent the province in exactly the same way. Travel writers had distinct gazes and the differences between them make clear that they were not always singing from the same government publicity songbook. True, English-speaking North American travel writers overall read the Quebec landscape through similarly tinted lenses. But English Canadians held more varied reactions and were more predisposed to view the sites and French Quebeckers themselves as multifaceted. This is not surprising as they had been exposed to more varied information about the province and its people. Contrary to their American counterparts, for instance, they did not systematically identify the *habitants* as the real French Quebeckers. In fact, they did not necessarily agree on who was worthy of that title, nor where they could be found. A palpable patriotism also inspired them to write more positively about signs of modern economic development in old Quebec and much more forcefully so in the postwar period. Finally, as Canadians, a few were moved to act as goodwill ambassadors, a role for which Americans had no inclination. They took it upon themselves to debunk some of their fellow English Canadians' prejudices and emphasize French Quebeckers' loyalty to Canada and their favourable disposition towards their English Canadian compatriots. As for French Quebeckers, not surprisingly they reacted to the province in very different ways. What set them most apart were their reactions to the Quebec countryside and the *habitants*. At no time did they encourage their readers to seek them out; in fact, they hardly mentioned them at all. And while some of their reactions echoed the same features highlighted in the distinct French-language government publicity, their reactions evolved over time. Initially, they were eager to explore the foyer of their people and be reminded of their ancestors' glorious past. By the 1960s, their observations reflected the desires of travellers simply hoping "to get away" from home, mostly to be entertained and enjoy beautiful countryside scenery.

Looking at decades' worth of travel accounts by a cross-section of authors published in a wide sample of magazines and newspapers makes it possible to establish that their accounts reveal much about their own heartfelt expectations and reactions. By extension, one can safely assume that they also reveal much about how ordinary tourists likely reacted. Travel writers and visitors alike were, in so many ways, subject to the same representations of the province before leaving home. They would have learned to look for "Old Quebec," as well as old and new Montreal. And for the better part of the period they mostly found them. Later they eventually enjoyed discovering "La Belle Province" and "New Montreal." Different time periods predisposed them to do both just as different times had predisposed tourist promoters to represent the province in contrasting ways.

Each on their own then government tourism promoters and travel writers represented the province informed by distinct nationalist allegiances. However, examining them side-by-side, as their objectives and views changed over time, also brings out, in clearer relief, the direct link between the province's tourism industry and Quebec's wider and evolving political culture. There is no doubt that simply taking slogans such as "Old Quebec" and "La Belle Province" as neatly encapsulating French Quebeckers' changing sense of national identity over the better part of the twentieth century obscures some of the multifaceted representations of the province and other slogans that point to more gradual changes. But it remains that the Quebec government chose to completely revamp its tourism publicity and rebrand the province in 1960 on the heels of the election of the Liberal Jean Lesage government. While such rebranding does not reflect an abrupt change in national identity, it does convey how quickly it was seen as significant and how quickly French Quebeckers wanted to showcase it to the world. And following the reactions of American, English Canadian, and French Quebec travel writers further allows us to measure how long it took them to come to accept the new image of "La Belle Province," one they could view as both alluringly modern and authentic.

NOTES

INTRODUCTION

1 Gordon Brinley was Kathrine Gordon Sanger's pen name. Her choice to take on a man's name might suggest that she felt her work would be taken more seriously if apparently written by a man. She would have had no reason to put into question her credentials as she was also "an expert on English writing and language of the 14th century" and "published articles and books on these subjects. During the 1920s she had a successful career touring as a dramatic recitalist of the works of Geoffrey Chaucer." Furthermore, other women were successful travel writers. Her husband, Daniel Putman Brinley, was a successful muralist and painter by profession and illustrated her four travel books. See Archives of American Art, Daniel Putnam Brinley and Kathrine Sanger Brinley papers, 1879–1984, http://www.aaa.si.edu/collections/daniel-putnam-brinley-and-kathrine-sanger-brinley-papers-6830.

2 Brinley, *Away to the Gaspé*, 2.

3 Ibid., 5.

4 "Gaspé: Romantic Eastern Tip of Far Flung Quebec," Provincial Tourist Bureau (hereafter PTB), *Saturday Night*, 1933. At the end of the book she provides a reference to a government issued travel guidebook entitled *The Gaspé Peninsula*, published by the PTB.

5 "See the Old Quebec Province of Quebec, the Cradle of American History," PTB, *Halifax Herald*, 25 July 1936, 6.

6 While during the better part of my period French Quebeckers considered themselves more broadly as French Canadians, in order to make it clear that I am referring to a specific group of French Canadians, those living in Quebec, I will use the term French Quebeckers. The term French Canadian will appear when quoted as such by those living at the time.

7 Holland and Huggan, *Tourists with Typewriters*, xiii.

8 Esman, "Tourism as Ethnic Preservation," 459. Robert E. Wood, for his part, defines ethnic tourism as "a direct focus on people living out a cultural identity

whose uniqueness is being marketed for tourists." Wood, "Ethnic Tourism, the State and Cultural Change in Southeast Asia," 361.

9 van den Berghe, *The Quest of the Other*, 8, 9.

10 See Chambers, *Native Tours*, 80–4, for a discussion of Indigenous tourism more generally.

11 For a glimpse at some latter-day reactions from curious visitors, see the impressions of Jesuit Edmund Keane. Commenting on the state of the reserve, after seeing a "highly-coloured wigwam," in disillusion he noted that "these wigwams were somewhat misleading – bait for the tourist!" and, when he walked further down the main road, he saw "a scatter of timber-built houses that no more suggested Indian braves then the main street of an Irish town." Keane, "I Visit the Iroquois," *The Irish Monthly* 79, no. 934 (April 1951): 180.

12 Little is one of the few to devote some attention to the subject in his article "Travels in a Cold and Rugged Land" when he analyzes C.H. Farmham's reactions to the Aboriginal peoples he encounters. For studies on the subject elsewhere in Canada see Jasen, "Native People and the Tourist Industry in Nineteenth Century Ontario," and *Wild Things*; Little, "Natives Seeing Icebergs"; Phillips, *Trading Identities*; Francis, *The Imaginary Indian*.

13 Studies addressing the emergence of modernity and the related debates over the meaning of the Quiet Revolution are too numerous to list. The following offer a representative sampling of the principal and contested interpretations. Linteau et al., *Histoire du Québec contemporain*; Rudin, "Revisionism and the Search for a Normal Society"; Rouillard, "La Révolution tranquille"; Bélanger, Comeau, and Métivier, *La Révolution tranquille 40 ans plus tard*; Meunier and Warren, *Sortir de la "Grande noirceure"*; Gauvreau, *The Catholic Origins of the Quiet Revolution*; Bouchard, "L'imaginaire de la Grande noirceure et de la Révolution tranquille."

14 In my research, I found only one book-length history (Prévost, *Trois siècles de tourisme au Québec*), which covers three centuries of the history of tourism in Quebec, written by a former director of the PTB and the first assistant deputy minister of the Department of Tourism, Fish and Game (hereafter DTFG) during the 1960s. While the book's scope is impressive and provides a broad and useful overview of events and facts pertaining to the Quebec government's involvement in the tourism industry, it remains both uninformed by in-depth primary source research and lacking an engagement with the existing historiography. For a review of this book see Neatby, "Notes bibliographiques."

15 Owram, "'Quaint Quebec,'" 90.

16 Simard, *Mythe et reflet de la France*. Luc Bureau produced an anthology of thirty-four texts written by well-known personalities, mostly French and American novelists and thinkers, who travelled to Quebec during the nineteenth century. Bureau, *Pays et Mensonges*.

17 See, for instance, Bélanger, Desjardins, Frenette et al., *Histoire de la Gaspésie*; Dubé, "Deux cents ans de villégiature" and *Charlevoix*; Guénette and Hétu, "Le tour du bout du monde."

18 The American anthropologist Richard Handler was one of the early scholars interested in this development in Quebec. See, among his extensive body of

research, "In Search of the Folk Society" and *Nationalism and the Politics of Culture in Quebec*. Others include Wright, "W.D. Lighthall and David Ross McCord"; Murton, "La 'Normandie du Nouveau Monde'"; Little, "Travels in a Cold and Rugged Land."

19 Ian McKay has been an inspirational scholar in the Canadian context with his nuanced and multifaceted examination of antimodernism in relation to tourism in Nova Scotia. See *The Quest of the Folk*; "Tartanism Triumphant"; "Handicrafts and the Logic of Commercial Antimodernism"; "'Cashing In on Antiquity'"; and, with Bates, *In the Province of History*. For the reactions of tourists in other parts of Canada see the work of Ed MacDonald, "A Landscape ... with Figures"; Monica MacDonald, "Railway Tourism in the Land of Evangeline"; MacEachern, "'No Island Is an Island'" and "Discovering an Island"; MacRae, "The Romance of Canada"; Michael Dawson, *Selling British Columbia*. For the United States see, among others, Lears, *No Place of Grace*; Becker, *Selling Tradition*; Brown, *Inventing New England*.

20 They have mostly focused their attention on visitors' impressions of Quebec City. See Gordon's "What to See and How to See It" and "'Where Famous Heroes Fell'"; Little, "In Search of the Plains of Abraham" and "Like a Fragment of the Old World."

21 Lambert, "'Québécoises et Ontariennes en voiture!'" What makes her study particularly interesting is her comparative approach as she studies similar developments in Ontario. More recently, in her regional study on the Gaspésie, Jacinthe Archambault provides a meticulous study of travellers' written and visual accounts. Archambault, "'Much More than a Few Hundred Miles'" and "'Near Enough to Be Neighbours.'"

22 Notable exceptions are Aubin-Des Roches, "Retrouver la ville à la campagne"; Dagenais,"Fuir la ville"; and Drouin, "Le tourisme dans le Vieux-Montréal."

23 Geographical studies include an early PhD thesis by Roger Brière, "Géographie du tourisme au Québec" and "Les grands traits de l'évolution du tourisme au Québec"; Cazelais et al., *L'espace touristique*; Gagnon, "L'émergence de l'identité rurale," *L'échiquier touristique Québécois*, and "L' intervention de l'État québécois dans le tourisme entre 1920–1940"; Géromini, "Québec dans les discours des guides touristiques, 1830–1930" and "Permanence paysagère et consommation touristique." Several architectural historians have also studied links between the built landscape and tourism. See Vanlaethem, "Modernité et régionalisme dans l'architecture au Québec"; Morisset, "Voyage au pays de l'identité" and "Un ailleurs pour l'Amérique"; Villeneuve, *Paysage, mythe et territorialité*.

24 Serge Gagnon refers to a "mise en scène" (tourist staging) to underline the idea of construction. Gagnon, "L'émergence de l'identité," 24, 28. Lucie Morisset writes of a "paysage construit" (built landscape) and of a "mise en tourisme" in "Voyage au pays de l'identité," 216 and 225.

25 Morisset, "Voyage au pays de l'identité," 218–19.

26 Prince Edward Island tourism scholars, for instance, raise comparable questions. Thus, Ed MacDonald points out that "[i]t is difficult to measure how much Islanders' sense of themselves is shaped by tourism imaging." MacDonald, "A

Landscape ... with Figures," footnote 61. See also MacEachern, "'No Island Is an Island'"; and McKay, *The Quest of the Folk*, 274–311.

27 One of the first historians to study this question in any detail was Alain Roy in his MA thesis, "Le Vieux Québec, 1945–1963."

28 See Durand, "Essai d'analyse de la pratique de l'artisanat au Québec"; Hamel, "Coordonner l'artisanat et le tourisme," *Notre maître le passé, notre maître l'avenir*, and *La Collection Coverdale*; Gauthier, *Charlevoix où la création d'une région folklorique*; Nurse, "The Best Field for Tourist Sale of Books"; Murton, "La Normandie du Nouveau Monde"; Handler, "In Search of the Folk Society."

29 Villeneuve, *Paysage, Mythe et Territorialité*.

30 Gagnon, *L'Échiquier touristique québécois*, 256.

31 Historian Michael Dawson, for instance, has made a very revealing use of such sources to reveal the reactions of visitors to British Columbia between 1890 and 1970. He looked at a wide range of accounts by "local residents and journalists anxious to publicize the province [and] visitors from afar keen to detail their experiences for the magazine buying public." This body of material, from several types of sources, made it, as he put it, "possible to get a sense of why people toured BC in the early part of the twentieth century." Dawson, *Selling British Columbia*, 15.

32 Kröller, *Canadian Travellers in Europe, 1851–1900*, 7. See also Koshar, "What Ought to Be Seen"; Gilbert, "Long in All Its Glory."

33 Morgan, "*A Happy Holiday*," 28, 29, and "A Choke of Emotion."

34 Cronin, "Fellow Travelers," 62.

35 Publications of note on the Gaspé were written by American palaeontologist John Mason Clarke, including *Sketches of Gaspé* and *The Heart of Gaspé*. Although, as we shall see, English Canadians did have access to the Government of Quebec's tourist publicity on the region.

36 Scholars, many of them inspired by the work of Edward Said, consider "travel writing as a symptom of ethnocentric and colonialist thinking." Bédard, Augustin, and Desnoilles, *L'imaginarire géographique*, 1, 46.

37 Holland and Huggan, *Tourists with Typewriters*, x–xi.

38 Thompson, *Travel Writing*, 11.

39 Korte, *English Travel Writing from Pilgrimages to Postcolonial Explorations*, 9. See also Holland and Huggan, *Tourists with Typewriters*, 8.

40 Lyndsay, *Contemporary Travel Writing of Latin America*, 11. Barbara Korte contends that "as far as the text and its narrative technique are concerned, there appears to be no essential distinction between the travel account proper and purely fictional forms of travel literature." Korte, *English Travel Writing*, 10.

41 Gordon, *Time Travel*, 7.

42 Gordon, "What to See and How to See It," 81, 83.

43 Gordon, *Time Travel*, 8. The American *Holiday* magazine, first published in 1946, stands as the best example of this development. It proved to be an instant success as the following year "circulation had climbed to over 800,000." Richard Popp offers a detailed analysis of the context of *Holiday*'s launch, marketing strategies, and content. Popp, *The Holiday Makers*, 49 and, especially, 37–52.

CHAPTER ONE

1 "Old Quebec: Niagara to the Sea," advertisement for Canadian Steamship Lines (CSL), *New York Times* (NYT), 6 May 1926, 51.

2 "Vacation in Old Quebec," advertisement for the Canadian Pacific Railway (CPR) Château Frontenac, NYT, 2 May 1926, sect 8, 18.

3 See the Canadian National Railway (CNR) ad for Murray Bay, Ste-Anne-de-Beaupré, *Montreal Gazette*, 4 July 1930, 2.

4 Advertisement for the newly opened Log Lodge Hotel, Lucerne in Quebec sponsored by the CPR, NYT, 4 May 1930, 16.

5 "Jaunts Through Normandy in Historic Quebec," advertisement for the Château Frontenac, NYT, 19 June 1926, sect 18, 8

6 "Explore! ... North America's Normandy," ad for the Château Frontenac, NYT, 26 June 1926, sect 17, 16. For a fully developed analysis of CSL advertising initiatives see Murton, "The Normandy of the New World."

7 For a detailed overview of similar promotional patterns see Dawson, *Selling British Columbia*; McKay, *In the Province of History*; M. MacDonald, "Railway Tourism in the Land of Evangeline"; and MacRae, "The Romance of Canada."

8 A "good roads movement" had emerged in the last decade of the nineteenth century with some provinces founding their respective Good Roads Associations including l'Association des bons Chemins de la Province de Québec in 1895. This development led to the creation of a National Good Roads Association, which held regular conventions bringing together officials from different provinces to discuss, among other things, the latest paving methods, safety regulations, and conformity in road regulation. See S. Gagnon, *L'Intervention de l'État québécois dans le tourisme*, 3–6, and "Du cheval au rail." For a detailed overview of the Quebec government's initiatives in road development see Faugier, "De la codépendance à l'indépendance" and chapter 2 in Lambert, "À travers le pare-brise," 49–106.

9 Occasionally, in certain documents, the department is also referred to as the Quebec Highways Department. Speech given by J.L. Perron, minister of the Roads Department at a banquet in St-Jovite, date and occasion unknown, reported in *L'Hôtellerie*, 31 November 1927, 16.

10 Of those 16,000 miles however only "about 2,500 miles are hard surfaced; the balance are in gravel." The Senate of Canada, *Report and Proceedings of the Special Committee on Tourist Traffic* (hereafter *Senate Report on Tourist Traffic*), 85.

11 See Prévost, *Trois siècles de tourisme*, 66, 86, 89.

12 "Les Laurentides et la Rive Sud du St Laurent," *La Presse*, 19 June 1930, 2. See also Leon Dickenson, "Open Roads in Old Quebec," NYT, 20 July 1930, sect 19, 7.

13 *Province de Québec Province, Ministère de la Voirie/Roads Department, Rapport de 1923/Report*, Quebec: Rédemption Paradis, King's Printer, 87 (hereafter *Minister's Report-Roads*). In 1926, the department's report includes the first "Tourist Traffic" subheading.

14 Jackle, *The Tourist*, 169.

15 Dawson, *Selling British Columbia*, 43. Davis, "Dependent Motorization: Canada and the Automobile to the 1930s," 109. See also tables 1 and 2 in Prévost, "1900–1929: Affirmation du Québec comme destination touristique," 17.

16 Shaffer, *See America First*, 137. Jackle, *The Tourist*, gives particular attention to the growing importance of car travel in the United States.

17 Jackle, *The Tourist*, 12, 128.

18 Ouellet, "Nos routes se couvrent de touristes," 242. It should be noted that scholars systematically underscore that calculating exactly how many tourists came to Quebec has been a perennial challenge for both government agencies and tourist promoters. This is because, at different times, visitors were counted by different bodies using different measures. Thus, the Quebec Department of Roads, year after year, consistently confirmed sharp rises in the number of cars entering Quebec by taking into account interprovincial tourism. At the federal level, the Bureau of Statistics and, later, the Canadian Tourist Bureau, starting in the mid-1930s, were charged with establishing the number of travellers who came to Canada and the revenue they generated. Their methods of calculation, however, were directly linked to the fact that they "defined [tourism] as a cross border phenomenon" and associated "tourists ... with their automobiles," accounting compiled by custom officials. This meant that the Canadian government had no comparative method for tracking interprovincial, domestic tourist movements. More than that, "this early limitation was that the tourist frequently figured as 'American' simply because it was the tourist most easily counted." Apostle, "Canada Vacations Unlimited," 34, 91.

19 Dubinsky, *The Second Greatest Disappointment*, 118.

20 Ibid., 119.

21 Popp, *The Holiday Makers*, 13–22.

22 See among others, Dawson, *Selling British Columbia*, 5; Wrobel and Long, *Seeing and Being Seen*; Baranoski and Furlough, *Tourism, Consumer Culture, and Identity*.

23 Ibid., 5, 7.

24 Popp, *The Holiday Makers*, 13–22.

25 Ibid., 13.

26 *Minister's Report-Roads*, 1926, 37.

27 Dubinsky, *Second Greatest Disappointment*, 151.

28 *Minister's Report-Roads*, 1927, 49. In 1934, Assistant Deputy Minister of Roads Arthur Bergeron provided another set of numbers when reporting to the Senate Special Committee on Tourist Traffic. Breaking these revenues down by time period, he informed the committee that from 1915 to 1918 these totalled $4.4 million; from 1920 to 1927 they had climbed to $130 million; from 1928 to 1932 they were at $262,500,00 [sic]; by 1933, $35 million. *Senate Report on Tourist Traffic*, 86.

29 By the mid-1920s, its revenues were close to double those of the mining sector. See Ouellet, "Nos routes se couvrent de tourists," 251.

30 Conference given by J.L. Boulanger to the Municipal Union in Halifax, quoted in "Ministère de la Voirie," *L'Hôtellerie* 2 (31 July 1928): 7–9.

31 In 1926, a publicity bureau was established and evolved into a bona fide Provincial Tourist Bureau. For more than thirty years it was headed by Maurice-L. Hébert, a highly reputed French literature scholar with a well-known interest in Quebec's heritage. See Prévost, *Trois siècles de tourisme*, 85–6; Gow, *Histoire de l'administration publique*, 107. The bureau also opened information offices in Quebec City and Montreal in 1932. It should be noted that the Quebec government emerged relatively early as an active player in tourism promotion. Several other provincial governments became fully involved later in the 1930s. Thus, in 1923 the Nova Scotia provincial government established a Tourist Association of Nova Scotia which stood as the "the first province-wide attempt to create a viable state presence in tourism." Starting then it "would always employ bureaucrats charged with monitoring and improving the 'tourism plant.'" However, it only took a truly proactive role in the 1930s under the leadership of Premier Angus L. Macdonald. In British Columbia, the government set up a Bureau of Information, which was charged with "promot[ing] tourism and immigration" but "involvement was sporadic." Here as well, it truly stepped in the 1930s. This pattern is replicated in Prince Edward Island, as it provided some government funding to the Prince Edward Island Publicity Association founded in 1924 but became a key player in the late 1930s. McKay, *In the Province of History*, 270; Dawson, *Selling British Columbia*, 81; MacRae, "The Romance of Canada."

32 *Minister's Report-Roads*, 1927, 49; *Minister's Report-Roads*, 1928, 45.

33 Brown, *Inventing New England*, 205. Several other scholars have made similar observations concerning the new types of travelling experiences made possible by car travel. Jackle, *The Tourist*; E. MacDonald, "A Landscape...with Figures"; Lambert, "À travers le pare-brise."

34 So much so that those who worked in the hospitality industry in Montreal would, by the early 1930s, start to complain about a decline in business. Indeed, "[a] striking feature this year, according to observers, is that tourists are attracted more and more by the rural sections." Quoted in the context of reporting comments by the deputy minister of highways, Col. J.L. Boulanger, "Tourist Traffic in Province Greater than last season," *Montreal Gazette*, 9 July 1930, 9.

35 Morisset, "Voyage au pays de l'identité," 222.

36 See note 26 in introduction, 9.

37 Zurkin, *Landscapes of Power*, 16.

38 Although it should be noted that the road construction along the shores of the Gaspé Peninsula began in 1920 under the Department of Colonization to "open up that region to settlement, and thus allow it to develop along normal and reasonable lines." *The Gaspé Peninsula*, 23.

39 Bélanger et al, *Histoire de la Gaspésie*, 595, 616. Serge Gagnon also notes that "during the 1930s, one will find along the Perron Boulevard the highest density of *cabines* in Quebec" – 331 to be exact. Gagnon, *L'Échiquier touristique*, 268.

40 Louis Hémon (1880–1913) was a French author who travelled to Canada spending most of his time in Quebec. He eventually was hired as a field hand by the Bédard family in Péribonka in the Saguenay for a few months in 1912. Inspired

by his surroundings he wrote the novel in 1913. It was first published in serialized form in France in 1914, then in Canada in 1916 as *Maria Chapdelaine: Récit du Canada français* (Montreal: J.-A. Lefèbre, Godin Ménard Ltd, 1916). It appeared in an English translation by William Hume Blake (1861–1924) in 1921 as *Maria Chapdelaine: A Tale of French Canada* (Toronto: MacMillan, 1921).

41 Éva Bouchard was a schoolmistress, sister-in-law of Samuel Bédard. A certain controversy surrounds her with some disputing her claims. Literary scholars contend that Maria Chapdelaine is much more likely to have been a composite character inspired by several women. It should be noted that other members of the family could also have easily felt a certain kinship with the characters in the novel, as a few did have the same first names as its main protagonists. For instance, Samuel Bédard and Samuel Chapdelaine were both fathers. For more on the life of Éva Bouchard, see Racine, *La légende de Maria Chapdelaine*; Achard, *Le Royaume du Saguenay*, 199; Bouchard, "La maison Samuel-Bédard"; and the introduction by Michael Gnarowski in the reissue of *Maria Chapdelaine*, trans. W.H. Blake, 21.

42 McKay, *In the Province of History*, 80. For a detailed study of the "Evangeline Phenomenon" see the book's chapter 2 and M. MacDonald, "Railway Tourism in the 'Land of Evangeline.'" Ian McKay has wondered if "the 'Land of Evangeline' [was] the first major eruption of literary tourism on the American continent?" While studies so far make it difficult to provide a clear answer, he notes nonetheless that "[i]t seems possible." McKay, "Cashing in on Antiquity," 461.

43 See Squire, "Ways of Seeing, Ways of Being"; Fawcett and Cormack, "Guarding Authenticity at Literary Tourism Sites."

44 *Minister's Report-Roads*, 1929, 87.

45 They started to do so in 1929. A total of 1,615,872 pounds was delivered free of charge to 10,500 people. Ibid., 91.

46 For a more fully fleshed out overview of the Roads Department embellishment campaign, see Lambert, "À travers le pare-brise."

47 See C. Michael Hall's reflections on the objectives of such strategies. Hall, "Packaging Canada/Packaging Places," 199–213.

48 Report on the speech given by Minister of Roads Department J.L. Perron at a banquet in St-Jovite, Grey Rocks, *L'Hôtellerie*, 30 November 1927, 16.

49 "Une campagne d'Hygiène, et d'Embellissement pour la Province de Québec," excerpts of a speech given by J.L. Perron in June 1927 during a banquet in his honour by the Comté de Terrebonne in thanks for a road built in their county, *L'Hôtellerie*, 31 July 1928, 5.

50 In 1914, the government had passed the *Loi de l'inspection des hôtels et des maisons de pension*. Initially, it was meant to meet the demands of travelling salesmen. Two inspectors were mandated to ensure the salubriousness and comfort of these establishments. See Gow, *Histoire de l'administration publique*, 107. Over the years, the Hostelry Service would belong to different home departments including the Department of Revenue and, by 1936, the Department of Municipal Affairs, Industry and Commerce.

51 *Minister's Report-Roads*, 1927, 55.

52 "L'hôtellerie qu'il faut à nos touristes," *La Presse*, 5 June 1926, 57.

53 This was still the case in 1930. By that time, of a "total of 6,595 establishments servicing visitors … 85% were run by French Canadian families and located outside large urban centers." Percentage provided by the Hostelry Service in 1930. Garceau, *Chronique de l'hospitalité hôtelière du Québec de 1880–1940*, 19.

54 Founded in 1926, in 1931 it became a bilingual publication, *L'Hôtellerie/The Hostelry*. It widened its mandate, as it was "devot[ing itself] to the interests of Hotels, Clubs, Restaurants, Boarding Houses and for the development of Tourist traffic in Canada." As far as the English hotels discussed in the magazine were concerned, the focus was placed on city establishments, most notably those of Montreal. In 1938, the Association des Hôteliers de Campagnes (AHC) created *La revue hôtellière*, which dealt more directly with issues pertaining to country-side hotels. In 1940, this publication worked closely with the government's Hostelry Service and by 1943 effectively become its mouthpiece.

55 *L'Hôtellerie*, 31 October 1927, 9. The department continued to offer the services of these lady lecturers well into the 1940s. In 1943, two teaching housekeepers "visited 381 hotels, making a stay of one or more days at each place, teaching hygiene, cleanliness, good Canadian cooking, ways to prepare menus, etc." Annual report of the Ministry of Municipal Affairs, Industry and Commerce 1943, 34. With time, those responsible for managing the tourism industry would increasingly rely on offering courses on various aspect of hotel management including construction, cooking, interior decorating, and publicity through a Hostelry Education Service. Garceau, *Chronique de l'hospitalité hôtelière*, 18; Gow, *Histoire de l'administration publique québécoise*, 217–18.

56 *L'Hôtellerie*, 30 September 1927, 4.

57 "Nouvelles de l'Association des Hôteliers de Campagne," *L'Hôtellerie/The Hostelry* 89 (31 January 1934): 11.

58 "Canadian Good Roads Association," *L'Hôtellerie/The Hostelry* 97 (30 September 1934): 11.

59 "Tourist Camps Is [*sic*] a Menace," *L'Hôtellerie/The Hostelry* 107 (31 July 1935): 13.

60 In 1928, under the aegis of *L'Hôtellerie*, visitors could avail themselves of a 200-page Hotel Directory. Although incomplete, the aim was to eventually produce a list of all Quebec hotels. In 1930, the Revenue Department began the distribution of a free bilingual directory entitled *Guide Officiel Prix des Chambres dans les Hôtelleries avec ou sans repas/Official Guide of Rates of Rooms in the Hostelries with or without meals*. It listed hotel room rates, types of meals served at the hotels, etc. Hostelry Service, 1930.

61 "Booklet Describes Trips for Tourists," *Montreal Gazette*, 10 June 1930, 12.

62 *L'Hôtellerie*, 29 February 1929, 11.

63 Excerpts of the 1927 Official Report of the Minister, Departments of Roads. *L'Hôtellerie*, 31 January 1928, 7.

64 Rodrigue Langlois, director general of the AHC, quoted in "Hôtellerie à la campagne," *Le Soleil*, 24 May 1930, 13.

65 Le Ministère de la Voirie: Extraits du Bulletin Officiel, *L'Hôtellerie*, 31 July 1928, 3.

66 Thus, for instance, the value of gold production between 1910 and 1930 jumped from $3,000 to $2,930,000, copper from $112,000 to $10,426,000, and asbestos from $2,556,000 to $8,390,000. Dickenson and Young, *A Short History of Quebec*, 211.

67 Ibid., 203.

68 By 1933, for example, "almost half of Canada's total electric capacity ... was located in Quebec." Ibid., 208.

69 *Québec, The French-Canadian Province: A Harmony of Beauty, History and Progress*. The bureau described it as a "brochure de luxe." Ministère de la voirie, Extraits du Rapport officiel pour l'année 1927, *L'Hôtellerie*, 31 January 1928, 5.

70 *Québec, The French-Canadian Province*, 5.

71 Ibid., 6, 7.

72 Ibid., 6, 8.

73 Ibid., 39.

74 Ibid., 19, 27.

75 Ibid., 36.

76 *4, 5, and 6 Days in Quebec, Canada* (1928). That year 65,000 copies were printed. *Minister's Report-Roads*, 1928, 49. The following year, the number rose to 100,000. *Minister's Report-Roads*, 1929, 81.

77 *4, 5, and 6 Days in Quebec, Canada* (1928), 51, 35.

78 Ibid., 6.

79 *4, 5, and 6 Days in Québec, Canada* (1929), 30.

80 *4, 5, and 6 Days in Quebec, Canada* (1928), 28, 12, 26.

81 *The Old World at Your Door, The French Canadian Province*, 3.

82 *Québec, The French-Canadian Province*, 39.

83 *Along Quebec Highways, Tourist Guide*. See the Department's *Minister's Report-Roads*, 1929, 83.

84 Ibid., 51, 823, 45.

85 *Québec, The French-Canadian Province*, 39. *Along Quebec Highways* made a comparable point with respect to Quebec's "labouring population" when it stated that it is "absolutely impervious to the theories of socialism." *Along Quebec Highways*, 45. Historians John Dickenson and Brian A. Young note that companies would also characterize the French Canadian labour pool in this way to attract investors. See Dickenson and Young, *A Short History of Quebec*, 187.

86 *Voyez Quebec d'Abord!/See Quebec First!*, 5.

87 *Minister's Report-Roads*, 1926, 39.

88 Shaffer, *See America First*, 30. A campaign that is also referred to in Dawson, *Selling British Columbia*, 45.

89 *Voyez Quebec d'Abord!/See Quebec First!*, 101.

90 A term often used by French Quebec city dwellers themselves but not one likely to be used in official government promotional material aimed at the whole Quebec population.

91 Ibid., 37.

92 Ibid., 96, 97–8.

CHAPTER TWO

1 Jean Bruchési, "L'aveu d'une faute," *Le Terroir* 14, no. 12 (May 1933): 13.

2 Camille Roy, "La refrancisation: Un témoignage," *Le Terroir* 14, no. 12 (May 1933): 15. Camille Roy (1870–1943) was a priest and noted literary critic and, among other prestigious university appointments, served as rector of Laval University for four terms between 1924 and 1943.

3 Abbé Albert Tessier, "Vieilles enseignes," a talk given at the annual meeting of the Société du Parler français at Laval University, 31 January 1933, 13, Paul Gouin Fond (PGF) (P190), File "Hôtellerie-Documentation," 1983 03-038/72, BAnQM.

4 Bélanger, "L'antiaméricanisme et l'antimodernisme," 514, 518. See also Lamonde, *Histoire sociale des idées au Québec*, 299–311.

5 Bélanger, "L'antiaméricanisme et l'antimodernisme," 517.

6 From 1930 to 1937, the Quebec government spent $26 million to establish settlers in Northern Quebec. See Linteau et al., *Histoire du Québec contemporain*, 47. However their efforts proved unsuccessful as many more French Quebeckers headed south to the New England states eager to take advantage of factory employment opportunities. "Between 1840 and 1930, close to 900,000 people left Quebec for the American republic, almost two thirds of them to New England." Roby, *Les Franco-Américains de la Nouvelle-Angleterre*, 11.

7 Montpetit, "Prends la … route," 940 (reprinted in the *Revue trimestrielle canadienne*, December 1939, 23).

8 Roy, *Le Vieux Québec*, 27.

9 Alphonse Désilets, "Pour le tourisme," *Le Terroir* 13, no. 1 (June 1932): 3. He was the director of the conservative *Le Terroir* periodical. See also Lebel, "Quand *Le Terroir* faisait rêver les citadins," 24–6.

10 Roy, *La refrancisation*, 12.

11 See, for instance, McKay, *The Quest of the Folk*; Dawson, *Selling British Columbia*, especially 17–20; Brown, *Inventing New England*. For a more complete list of studies on antimodernism in Quebec see this volume, introduction n19.

12 Zuelow, *Making Ireland*, xxx. For a European context, in her study of Scottish tourism, Haldane Grenier argues that the tourist industry "helped to assert a distinctive identity for Scots, while also answering their customers' expectations." Grenier, *Tourism and Identity in Scotland*, 6. Zuelow makes the same argument in *Making Ireland*. For the US, see Shaffer, *See America First* and "Seeing America First," 166.

13 McKay, *The Quest of the Folk*, 28, xv.

14 Désilets, "Pour le tourisme," 3.

15 According to T.R. Enderly, general manager of the CSL, "[t]he tourist traffic of Canada has dropped from $300,000,000 in 1929 to about $125,000,000 in 1933," *Senate Report on Tourist Traffic, 1934*, 106. This being said, in the United States – Canada's principal source of tourists – the industry "rebounded quickly and proved almost immune to the 1937 recession." Popp, *The Holiday Makers*,

12. Others also confirm that tourist spending during the Depression was maintained. Berkowitz, "A 'New Deal' for Leisure." In BC a wide range of decision makers upheld tourism as a way to promote economic recovery during the Depression. Dawson, "'Taking the "D" out of Depression.'"

16 *Senate Report on Tourist Traffic, 1934*, v. Tourism was a shared federal–provincial responsibility under the British North America Act, sections 91 and 92.

17 He was a former journalist and head of the New Brunswick Bureau of Information. He became the central figure in Canadian tourism promotion for more than two decades. For an in-depth analysis of Leo Dolan's understanding of tourism's positive role in promoting national unity, forging international relations, and its major contribution to economic development, see Dawson, "A 'Civilizing' Industry: Leo Dolan."

18 During some parts of its tenure, "[e]verything from building the Trans-Canadian highway, choosing the location of new national parks, campgrounds, airports and resorts to solving the accommodation shortage of the war years fell within the Bureau's purview." Alisa Apostle also provides a detailed analysis of the CGTB's instructional films produced between 1947 and 1959. Apostle, "Display of a Tourist Nation," 180. See also Brégent-Heald, "Vacationland: Tourism, Film and Selling Canada."

19 Apostle, "Display of a Tourist Nation," 193.

20 Although, the CGTB did not escape criticism from its provincial counterparts, they mostly complained about not being given equal or enough publicity. Alisa Apostle makes this point with regard to their responses to the bureau's films. Apostle, "Display of a Tourist Nation," 193. For their part, BC officials objected to the "federal bureau ... promoting the nation's national parks." Dawson, *Selling British Columbia*, 105.

21 See Apostle, "Canada, Vacations Unlimited," for the most detailed analysis of the federal government's involvement in the tourism industry from 1934 to 1959.

22 J.E. Perrault, "Le tourisme est notre meilleur revenu," *Le Canada*, 13 December 1932. Such confidence would only grow and, by 1935, during a talk at a banquet of the AHC, Émile Vaillancourt, director of the Tourist Bureau, was able to claim that "it was recognized that tourism immediately after wheat and flour and before wood and pulp, as a source of hard currency is classified as second in capital generation which each year increase the currency of Canada." Émile Vaillancourt, "À propos du tourisme," *L'Hôtellerie/The Hostelry*, no. 105 (31 May 1935): 13.

23 The council was reorganized and held six meetings over the following thirty months. But in large part due to the war, it fell off the radar screen. According to Robert Prévost, its only notable initiative was to launch a photography contest in 1940. Prévost, *Trois siècles de tourisme*, 86.

24 *L'Hôtellerie/The Hostelry*, no. 88 (31 December 1933): 17. As Maude-Émmanuelle Lambert details in her study, save for three, they gradually disappeared for lack of funds. Lambert, "À travers le pare-brise," 228–9.

25 Morisset, "Voyage au pays de l'identité," 228.

26 Speech by Adélard Godbout (in English) at the first National Tourist Congress, Château Frontenac, Quebec City, 1943, P172, file 3, loc 34/4-3505 B, BAnQQ, 2.

27 He had worked as a journalist for *Le Devoir* and *La Patrie*.

28 The other two were the Cinéphoto and Government Publicity.

29 Robert Prévost mentions in his history of Quebec tourism that "the Premier acted in many ways as would a Minister of Tourism." Prévost, *Trois siècles de tourisme*, 123.

30 The Société launched its campaign in *Le Terroir*. See Lebel and Roy, *Québec: 1900–2000*, 42–6.

31 "Le Tourisme avantageux à Rimouski," *Le Soleil*, 8 May 1930, 23.

32 Garceau, *Chronique de l'hospitalité hôtelière*, 197.

33 Anonymous letter from Ste-Foy, Québec to the editor of *La Presse*, lauding the *francisation* campaign, *La Presse*, June 1930, 6.

34 See letter from Joseph Ferland to Mr Horace Philippon, 11 December 1933. PGF (P190), BAnQM.

35 He had a hand in innumerable French Canadian nationalist causes and organizations. Among other things, he founded the Ligue nationaliste canadienne (1903) and was president of the Société Saint-Jean-Baptiste (1913).

36 Olivier Asselin, "Sur une organisation du tourisme," *Le Canada*, 7 December 1932.

37 Ibid.

38 At this time, he was préfet des études at the Séminaire de Trois-Rivières. In 1937, he was appointed visiteur général des Écoles ménagères supérieures. In the same year, in recognition of his contribution, he was appointed to Laval University's Chaire en Histoire, replacing the famous conservative historian Thomas Chapais.

39 For more on Tessier the filmmaker, see Mackenzie, *Screening Quebec: Québécois Moving Images*, 4, 113; Poirier, *The Clergy and the Origins of Quebec Cinema* at http://www.ameriquefrançaise.org/en/article-367; and Le Pan, "Les images d'Albert Tessier."

40 In "Tessier fait de la photographie et du cinéma à ses frais: Non aux frais du Gouvernement!," 11 January 1941, Séminaire de Trois-Rivières, E16/181 7C37 2603A, BANQQ. The provincial government bought several of his films, extolling the traditional rural lifestyle of the province's rural communities.

41 Albert Tessier, "Vieilles enseignes," 12.

42 Ibid., 13.

43 Jean-Marie Gauvreau, *Rapport général sur l'artisanat* (Quebec: Minister of Municipal Affairs, Industry and Commerce, 1939).

44 Tessier, *Rapport sur le tourisme*, 3.

45 Ibid., 23.

46 The fact that it was later published by the Comité permanent de la survivance française en Amérique meant it likely reached a wide audience. Tessier, *Les valeurs nationales et économiques*.

47 Ibid., 4.

48 Ibid., 51.

49 Tessier, *Rapport sur le tourisme*, 4.

50 Tessier, *Les valeurs nationales et économiques*, 4.

51 Tessier, *Rapport sur le tourisme*, 6.

52 Édouard Montpetit had used similar terminology, defining Quebec's greatest tourist asset as its "capital-traditions," brought to life in French Canadians' "religion, culture, language, mores." Montpetit, *Prends la … route*, 10, 23.

53 Tessier, *Les valeurs nationales et économiques*, 4.

54 Seemingly overtaken by a spirit of missionary zeal, Tessier went as far as to suggest that "this irresistible attraction would bring strangers to our faith" as "Catholic Quebec will almost resound as the call of a Holy Land." Ibid., 21.

55 Ibid., 20.

56 Ibid., 24.

57 Reproduced here is a still of the CNR. "Ce que la province offre à ses habitants et à ceux qui la visitent," *La Presse*, 31 July 1926, 25. See a photograph of a young child in a cart pulled by a dog near Quebec in *4, 5 and 6 days in Quebec, Canada* (1928), 19.

58 His father, Lomer Gouin, had been Liberal premier from 1905 to 1920 and justice minister under William L. Mackenzie King from 1921 to 1924. Paul Gouin also had a short, albeit unsuccessful and disappointing, stint in provincial politics. For more information on his political career, see Ferland, *Paul Gouin*.

59 From 1955 to 1961, he was president of the Conseil de la langue française en Amérique whose motto was *Conservons notre héritage*. He was appointed president of the Commission des monuments historiques de la province de Québec from 1955 to 1965. For a more detailed overview of his accomplishments in the field of cultural development, see Hamel, *"Notre maître le passé, notre maître l'avenir."*

60 Paul Gouin, "Une forme pratique de Patriotisme: Le Civisme (1)," a talk given to members of the Association des retraitants de la paroisse du St-Nom-de-Jésus, in Maisonneuve, 1 May 1938, reprinted in *Servir*, 209.

61 Paul Gouin, "La Refrancisation de la province," *L'Action nationale*, April 1933, reprinted in *Servir – 1. La cause nationale*, 39.

62 Paul Gouin, "Noms français et meubles 'esperantos,'" *Le Progrès du Golfe*, 27 May 1932, reprinted in *Servir*, 11.

63 In fact, he acted out his commitment to French Canadian culture on a more personal level by becoming a reputed collector of French Canadian antiquities, which included handicrafts, silverware, ceramics, and furniture. In 1946, he opened a gallery (Beaumanoir) in Montreal, showcasing his compatriots' talents as artisans and selling their work. It closed in 1949, and Gouin sold his antiques collection to the government in 1951. See Hamel, *"Notre maître le passé, notre maître l'avenir,"* 47–59, and Ferland, *Paul Gouin*.

64 Rodrigue Langlois in "Nouvelles de l'Association des Hôtels de Campagne," *L'Hôtellerie/The Hostelry*, no. 92 (30 April 1934): 11.

65 "Campagne de refrancisation," *L'Hôtellerie/The Hostelry*, no. 96 (31 August 1934): 9.

66 *L'Hôtellerie/The Hostelry*, no. 105 (31 May 1935): 1.

67 "Industrie hôtelière," editorial, *La Presse*, 12 May 1936.

68 Between 1932 and 1935, the province's hotel industry revenues were cut in half and countryside hotels were especially badly hit. Garceau, *Chronique de l'hospitalité hôtelière*, 16. And still, in 1935, some lamented, "Alas! The crisis still lasts!" Editorial, *L'Hôtellerie/The Hostelry*, no. 106 (30 June 1935): 1.

69 Passed in the US Congress in 1919 to enforce prohibition in line with the 18th Amendment.

70 Editorial, *L'Hôtellerie/The Hostelry*, no. 91 (31 March 1934): 1.

71 In Quebec, local handicraft promotion was not initiated by French Canadian nationalists. The first to call for a renaissance of traditional arts and crafts were middle-class Anglophone women in Montreal, who founded the Women's Art Association of Canada in 1896, which later became the Canadian Handicraft Guild in 1906. Among other initiatives, they organized exhibits to showcase the artistry of local craftsmen and women. Furthermore, this push to revive dying traditional home-based handicrafts can be seen as a homegrown off shoot of an international Arts and Crafts movement, which took root most notably in Nova Scotia, outside of Quebec and in New England, in the US. See Hamel, *Coordonner l'artisanat*, 99; Harvey, "De l'économie familiale à l'artisanat"; Rouleau, "La fille du gouvernement," 23–7; McKay, "Handicrafts and the Logic of Commercial Antimodernism."

72 Hamel, *Coordonner l'artisanat*, 99.

73 See Durand, *Essai d'analyse*, 271.

74 Paul Gouin, "Les arts domestiques," a talk given at the Congrès de la Société Saint-Jean-Baptiste de Montréal, 10 March 1938, in *Servir*, 193.

75 Gouin, "Nom français et meubles 'Esperanto,'" 12.

76 Gouin, "En marge du féminisme (1)," talk given at the Club Wilfrid Laurier, 3 December 1934, in *Servir*, 137. As noted by historian Jane Becker, in the 1930s, calls for reviving traditional handicraft production could be heard in the US as well. However, in contrast to the entreaties made by French Canadian nationalists, such calls were provoked more by the severe economic hardships of the Depression and were in tune with the ambient, antimodernism cultural context. More specifically, they were "derived from [an] idealized national past," which "served as a crucible of simplicity and self-sufficiency – ideals that might guide a unified nation through difficult times." Becker, *Selling Tradition*, 15.

77 Ibid., 138.

78 Gouin, "Les arts domestiques," 198–9. See also Gouin, "La femme de la campagne: Son rôle (1)," talk given on CKAC radio, under the auspices of the Ligue des droits de la femme, 10 March 1933, in *Servir*, 57. And, although it never saw the light of day, in line with his desire to offer expert advice on cultural matters, he recommended the creation of an "esthetics commission," which would, among other things, offer advice to institutions, commercial establishments, and individuals on how best to give "to the whole province a worthy French Canadian character," "without coercitive measures." Gouin, "L'architecture et l'hôtellerie," *Le Canada*, 4 August 1932, in *Servir*, 18, 19.

79 He began his fieldwork in 1914 and worked for most of his professional life at the Museum of Man in Ottawa. See Gauthier, *Charlevoix ou la création d'une région folklorique.*

80 Barbeau, "Gaspé Peninsula," 92.

81 *L'Action nationale* 17, no. 2 (February 1941): 133, 134; Barbeau, "Gaspé Peninsula," 79.

82 Notably in 1927, 1928, and 1930. For a more in-depth look at Barbeau's work with the CSL, see Nurse, "Tradition and Modernity"; Murton, *The Normandy of the New World*; Handler, *Nationalism and the Politics of Culture in Quebec*; McNaughton, "A Study of the CPR-Sponsored Quebec Folk and Handicraft Festivals"; Hamel, *"Notre maître le passé, notre maître l'avenir."*

83 Andrew Nurse makes the point that Barbeau was keen to have some of his work more widely disseminated which is why he agreed to write a guidebook entitled the *The Kingdom of the Saguenay*, available to CSL passengers. His *Canadian Geographic Journal* article would stand as chapter 5 of this publication. It foregrounded the *habitants* and included detailed descriptions of their customs and traditions. Thus, travellers could read the landscape and the people they came across through the lens of someone who believed old Quebec was the authentic Quebec. Barbeau, *The Kingdom of the Saguenay.* Nurse, "The Best Field for Tourist Sale of Books."

84 *Minister's Report-Roads*, 1929, 81.

85 B.L.P., "Avons-nous réellement cessé d'être français qu'il faille nous refranciser?," *L'Hôtellerie/The Hostelry*, no. 94 (30 June 1934): 13.

86 *Minister's Report-Roads*, 1933, 122 and 123.

87 *Minister's Report-Roads*, 1932, 91.

88 Pierre Homier, "La vie courante: Campagne de refrancisation," *Action nationale*, 1 January 1933, 59–60.

89 J.-E. Perrault, "Le Tourisme est notre meilleur revenu," *Le Canada*, 13 December 1932.

90 The idea for this contest came from Abbé Albert Tessier. Document "Concours d'enseignes artistiques. Le Syndicat d'Initiatives de la Mauricie," Syndicat d'Initiative de la Mauricie, sous le patronage de l'Office provincial du tourisme, Trois-Rivières, Québec," PGF (P190), Dossier "Hôtellerie – Documentation," 1983-03-038/72, BAnQM.

91 *Minister's Report-Roads*, 1933, 125. In the 1930s, the provincial government became proactive in its support of handicraft revival. Among other initiatives, it founded several specialized schools to train artisans. These included the École Provinciale des Arts domestiques in 1930, the École du Meuble de Montréal in 1935, and the Atelier de céramique at the École des Beaux-Arts de Montréal, as well as a binding section at the École Technique de Montréal. In 1945, it founded the Office provincial de l'artisanat et de la petite industrie to promote arts and crafts. Natalie Hamel provides an in-depth analysis of this development, revealing the extent to which the traditional techniques were in fact invented or "improved upon" in order to better lure tourists. Hamel, *Coordonner l'artisanat et le tourisme*, especially 99.

92 The 1935 annual report included a chart compiled by the French monthly publication, *Le Mois*, listing various destinations and the revenue they generated. Canada came in second after France. Based on revenues, the province's officials calculated that Quebec came "in 6th place among nations of the world." *Minister's Report-Roads*, 1935, 99. More references in the minister's reports on the state of the tourism industry are a telling indication of the PTB officials' increasing concerns.

93 For the first time, in 1933, the minister's report included the heading "Advertising in newspapers, reviews and magazines." More precisely, ads were sent to forty-five dailies and three magazines in the US and Canada. *Minister's Report-Roads*, 1933, 139, 141.

94 Marchand, *Advertising the American Dream*, 5, 7.

95 "See the Old Province of Quebec, the Cradle of American History," PTB, *Halifax Herald*, 25 July 1936, 6.

96 "Lazy, Unhurried Days, through the Quaint, Picturesque Quebec Countryside ...," PTB, *Saturday Night*, 10 June 1933.

97 "Old Quebec ... Where the Spirit of the Past Lives Again," PTB, *Saturday Night*, 7 July 1934.

98 "Bienvenue à Montréal," PTB, *Halifax Herald*, 23 May 1936, 10.

99 "Visit the Old Province of Quebec, Land of Legend and Romance," PTB, *Halifax Herald*, 27 June 1936, 7.

100 "Lazy, Unhurried Days."

101 "It Happened in the Old Province of Quebec – The Age of Miracles Is Not Dead," PTB, *Halifax Herald*, 13 June 1936, 11.

102 "Lazy, Unhurried Days."

103 "Gaspé: Romantic Eastern Tip of Far Flung Quebec," PTB, *Saturday Night*, 1933.

104 Williamson, *Decoding Advertisements*, 12.

105 These "sectional booklets" promoted "Montreal, Québec, Trois-Rivières, the Eastern Townships, the Gatineau, Pontiac and Lièvre, the Laurentians west and north of Montreal, the St Maurice Valley, the Laurentian National Park, Chicoutimi, Charlevoix and Saguenay, and the Gaspé Peninsula." *Senate Report on Tourist Traffic*, 88. While not all regions got their own booklet, those selected varied over time, though the intent to highlight specific regions remained constant.

106 The same can be said of the new *Tours in Quebec, Canada*.

107 This new label was not given much visibility as it appeared only on the back cover of the brochure. *Quebec the Good Roads Province*.

108 Ibid., 2.

109 *Montréal and the Laurentians*, 17.

110 *Hunting and Fishing in La Province de Québec*, 25, 47, and 41.

111 Dawson, *Selling British Columbia*, especially chapter 5.

112 *Minister's Report-Roads*, 1932, 97.

113 The bureau made sure "that no other such prizes should be offered in Canada." (The winner was a Col. L.S. Powers of Hawsville, Kentucky.) *Minister's Report-Roads*, 1932, 97.

114 *Minister's Report-Roads*, 1931, 71.

115 Ibid.

116 Reporting on the campaign of 1934. *Minister's Report-Roads*, 1935, 149–50.

117 Ibid., 149.

118 Wilfrid Bovey, "The Gaspé Peninsula Wonderland," *National Geographic* 68 (2 August 1935): 209–30. However, a *National Geographic* photographer provided the accompanying images. The fifteen colour photos were grouped under the heading "Remnants of Royal France in Canada." *Minister's Report-Roads*, 1935, 113.

119 *Senate Report on Tourist Traffic*, 89. It should be noted that this marketing approach was not unique to Quebec. BC promoters, for one, made use of such marketing strategies. Dawson, *Selling British Columbia*, 59. Interestingly enough, the federal government also eventually endorsed this marketing strategy as revealed in the deliberations of the Senate Standing Committee on Tourist Traffic of 1948. The director of the Canadian Travel Bureau, Léon Dolan, reported that he had been in touch with Mr Patrick – the editor of the US *Holiday* magazine – to point out that his magazine had not published the type of article he would have liked to see on Canada. He reported having given him the names of travel writers Patrick could hire to write accounts on Canada. He mentioned Miss Wurio for Ontario, who had also written about Quebec (see chapter 4, notes 95, 118, 124), and an unnamed writer for Quebec.

120 *Minister's Report-Roads*, 1935, 149.

121 The most they would say is that the bureau had the responsibility to educate the public "on the necessity of showing the Province as it really is, and not as it would seem, judging by disparaging buildboards and posters." Ibid.

122 It also advertised in all French papers distributed in the US (twenty-two of them). *Minister's Report-Roads*, 1933, 141.

123 Ibid.

124 "Allez en Gaspésie … Le Paradis des inoubliables vacances …," Office provincial du tourisme, Ministère de la voirie, *La Presse*, 13 June 1936.

125 "Québec … Pays du tourisme idéal," Office provincial du tourisme, Québec, *La Presse*, 11 June 1938.

126 "Allez en Gaspésie … Le Paradis des inoubliables vacances …"

127 "Québec … Pays du tourisme idéal."

128 Ibid.

129 Canadian Steamship Lines ad in *La Presse*, 13 June 1934.

130 Reissued in 1935.

131 *Québec: Ses régions de tourisme*, 1st ed., Office provincial de Tourisme, Ministère de la Voirie, 1934.

132 Ibid., 5.

133 Ibid., 15.

134 Ibid., 12.

135 "Discover a New Vacation – A French Canadian Vacation," *Halifax Herald*, 5 June 1940, 8.

136 "Contrast … Atmosphere … Gaiety … A French Canadian Vacation," *Halifax Herald*, 24 July 1940, 12.

137 "Refreshing ... Different ... A French Canadian Vacation," *Halifax Herald*, 17 July 1940, 4.

138 See Dawson, *Selling British Columbia*, 126–8. At the start of the war in 1939, the estimated value of foreign travellers to Canada was $164 million; by 1942, this was down to $81 million. Information taken from a letter of 14 March 1945 from Canadian Travel Bureau to J.L. Ilsley, Department of Finance re: War Appropriations for CTB. LAC RG 20, vol. 55, File 19131-B, Title: War Appropriations – Canada Travel Bureau 1945–46.

139 "Une intéressante causerie de M. Boulanger sur le tourisme," *Le Soleil*, 12 July 1940, 20.

140 "One American's Opinion: A Daily Interview with a Tourist from South of the Border," *Montreal Gazette*, 10 June 1940, 18.

141 *La Province de Québec, New France in Canada*, PTB, date unknown. It appears that Quebec officials voiced their worries to federal authorities. The Quebec representative at the National Tourist Advisory Committee of the Department of National War Services – a body which brought together representatives from provincial tourism boards or departments and representatives from various industries – the Honourable Paul Beaulieu, minister of Commerce and Industry, expressed some exasperation at the fact that "[s]tories have come out of Quebec by individuals and through newspapers who are interested chiefly in politics and not always in facts." He added, "the people of Quebec are not all supernationalists [*sic*] as some of you would believe." LAC RG 20, vol. 6, File 12292, National Tourist Advisory Committee of Department of War Services, 1944–46.

142 "Have You Had a French Canadian Vacation?," *Halifax Herald*, 12 June, 11.

143 "Des Vacances? Mais certainement," Office du tourisme de la province de Québec, *La Presse*, 20 June 1942.

144 "Vacances de guerre," Office du tourisme de la province de Québec, *La Presse*, 27 June 1942.

145 "Leo Dolan nous parle!," *L'Hôtellerie/The Hostelry*, May 1951.

146 This lasted until 1966 – the year before Expo 67. Dubinsky, *Second Greatest Disappointment*, 178. Dawson also provides a brief overview of this new economic context in *Selling British Columbia*, chapter 5. For a fuller discussion of the Canadian tourist industry in relation to the wider Canadian economy, see Apostle, "Canada, Vacations Unlimited," especially chapters 3 and 4.

147 In 1956, Georges Léveillé, in one of his many public talks, warned that "roughly 420,000 Americans and 60,000 Canadians visited the old continent last year." Comments to the Kiwanis Club in St Laurent, reprinted in "Tous doivent s'intéresser au tourisme: M. Georges Léveillé l'a affirmé – 'Être différents': rôle des citoyens du Québec," *La Presse*, 23 June 1956, 13.

148 Ibid., 13.

149 *La Province de Québec, Canada*, 31.

150 Ibid., 38, 21, and 1.

151 Reflective of a greater desire to signal that Quebec was a French-language destination, in the early 1950s, a Tourist Branch guide, *La Province de Québec, Canada*, included two pages with roughly forty useful questions translated into three languages, including French.

152 Dubinsky, *The Second Greatest Disappointment*, 325.

153 "Enjoy Your Honeymoon in Romantic Québec," *Toronto Star*, 15 May 1950, 7.

154 Brochure entitled *La Province de Québec, Canada*, 6th ed., Tourist Branch, Provincial Publicity Office, 1, date unknown but most likely from the early 1950s.

155 "Extraits de l'allocution prononcée par Paul Gouin lors de la clôture du Congrès de la refrancisation," 24 June 1957, PGF (P190), 1983 09 038/35, BAnQM, 2.

156 Presentation by Paul Gouin, most likely in 1952 or 1953, which opens with "Mesdames, Messieurs, Au cours de mes causeries," PGF (P190), 1983-03-038/63, BAnQM, 1.

157 Gouin, "Au pays de Québec," 45.

158 See the printed copies of his "Causeries" in PGF (P190), 1983-0-03/1, BAnQM and in E4 1960-01-483/436, BAnQQ.

159 "Causerie prononcée sur le réseau français de Radio-Canada, Sunday, 5 November 1950, 6 pm par M. Paul Gouin, Conseiller Technique auprès du Conseil Exécutif de la Province de Québec," E4 1906-01-483/436, BAnQQ, 7.

160 Gouin, "Texte Technique," 1951, PGF (P190), BAnQM, 12.

161 Presentation given by Paul Gouin to the Saint-Jean-Baptiste Society of Ottawa on 27 February 1955, 3, PGF (P190), 1983-03-038/72, BAnQM. Paul Gouin would be active in the new *refrancisation* campaigns of the 1950s including the 3e Congrès annuel de la langue française au Canada of 1952 organized by the Société Saint-Jean-Baptiste and the following one, in 1957, which he presided over in Quebec City under the auspices of the Quebec government and the Conseil de la vie française en Amérique.

162 Excerpts of the conference given by Paul Gouin at the closing of the Congrès de la refrancisation on 24 June 1957, PGF (P190), 1983-03-038/35, BAnQM, 2.

163 Letter dated 10 June 1950 by Paul Gouin to Léo Trépanier, cabin owner in Trois-Rivières. Gouin was responding to his inquiry by sending him a list of suggestions of names for his cabins, as well as the names of craftsmen who could build signs for him. PGF (P190), 1983-03-038/61, BAnQM.

164 Presentation given by Paul Gouin to the Société Saint-Jean-Baptiste of Quebec at the Palais Montcalm in Quebec, 1 April 1951, PGF (P190), 1983-03-038/72, BAnQM, 23.

165 Gouin, presentation of 27 February 1955, 2.

166 Gouin, "Au pays de Québec," 45.

167 Presentation given by Paul Gouin, to the Société Saint-Jean-Baptiste of Joliette at the Séminaire de Joliette on 20 October 1953, PGF (P190), 1983 03-038/72, BAnQM, 7.

168 Gouin, *Culture*, 45. For a fully fleshed-out analysis of this interpretation, see Natalie Hamel's nuanced and comprehensive study *"Notre maître le passé, notre maître l'avenir"* on Paul Gouin's contribution to the preservation of the province's heritage and his central involvement in the crafting of its cultural policies.

169 Conference given by Paul Gouin in Chicoutimi, for the Société Saint-Jean-Baptiste on 6 May 1954, entitled "Patrimoine au Foyer," PGF (P190), 1983 03-038/72, BAnQM, 17. During that talk he also gave the Société Saint-Jean-

Baptiste members the same advice he had given them in the late 1930s: encourage them to include in their statutes rules requiring members to purchase crafts at least once a year.

170 Gouin, *Culture*, 46.

CHAPTER 3

1   Lollar and Van Doran, "US Tourist Destinations," 623.
2   O'Barr, *Culture and the Ad*, 8. See also Johnston, *Selling Themselves*.
3   Marchand, *Advertising the American Dream*, xx.
4   MacCannell, *The Tourist*, 110.
5   Lollar and Van Doran, "US Tourist Destinations," 624.
6   Rojek, "Indexing, Dragging and the Social Construction of Tourist Sights," 70.
7   Urry, *The Tourist Gaze*, 2, 3. Several others came to the same conclusion coining concepts of their own. Thus, Myra Schackley writes of a "destination image [which] begins with the development of a mental construct based upon a few impressions chosen from a flood of information." Schackley, "The Legend of Robin Hood," 319.
8   Simard, *Mythes et reflet de la France*, 11, 40.
9   Pratt, *Imperial Eyes*.
10 Morgan, "A Happy Holiday," 78. See also MacEachern, "'No Island Is an Island,'" 40.
11 Korte, *English Travel Writing*, 6.
12 MacCannell, "Staged Authenticity," 597, 592.
13 MacCannell, *The Tourist*, 3.0. See also his article "Staged Authenticity," 589–92.
14 Pearce and Moscardo, "The Concept of Authenticity in Tourist Experiences," 130.
15 Cohen, "'Primitive and Remote,'" 31. More recently, Chris Rojek and John Urry claim that "the quest for authenticity is a declining force in tourist motivation" and go so far as to claim that tourism "involves a search for the inauthentic." Urry and Rojek, eds, *Touring Cultures*, 12.
16 Craik, "The Culture of Tourism," 115, 114.
17 van den Berghe and Keyes, "Introduction: Tourism and Re-recreated Ethnicity," 345. Nina Wang makes much the same point when she argues that "authenticity is relevant to some kinds of tourism such as ethnic tourism, history or culture tourism which involve the representations of the Other or of the past." Wang, "Rethinking Authenticity."
18 van den Berghe, *The Quest for the Other*, 8.
19 Wang, "Rethinking Authenticity," 355.
20 For studies pertaining to antimodernism in the North American context as it emerges at the turn of the twentieth century see the introduction, n19.
21 Lears, *No Place of Grace*, 57.
22 Ibid., 74.

23 McKay, *The Quest of the Folk*, 4.

24 Wright, "W.D. Lighthall and David Ross McCord," 139.

25 Ibid.

26 Sally Bennett, "The Grand Style at Murray Bay," *Travel* 75 (May 1940): 37.

27 Simard, *Mythe et reflet de la France*, 19. The sociologist Maurice Halbwachs, recollecting his first visit to London, makes the point eloquently. Noting that he did so without a guide, he remarked that "I cannot say that I was alone" as "many impressions ... reminded me of Dickens' novels read in childhood, so I took my walk with Dickens." Halbwachs, *The Collective Memory of Maurice Halbwachs*, 24.

28 See Gerson, *A Purer Taste*.

29 Coates and Morgan, *Heroines and History*, 44.

30 William Kirby's *The Golden Dog (Le Chien d'Or)*. Translated into French by Pamphile Le May as *Le Chien d'or: Légende canadienne* (Montreal: Imprimerie de L'Étendard, 1884).

31 Interview with Guy Vanderhaeghe, "Making History," 27. Literary scholar Renée Hulan notes further that, "the reading of historical fiction has been and continues to be one of the ways Canadians collectively imagine the past." Hulan, "The Past Is an Imagined Country," 591.

32 Percival, *The Lure of Quebec*, 42. Many include the inscription word-for-word, including Mackenzie and Mackenzie, *Quebec in Your Car*, 136, and Donald, *Quebec Patchwork*, 103–4.

33 Stanley Helps, "An Eastern Canadian Wonderland," *Canadian Magazine* 64, no. 1 (February 1925).

34 Percival, *The Lure of Quebec*, 102.

35 Hémon, *Maria Chapdelaine* (1921). The translator, William Hume Blake, came from an Ontario family of lawyers and politicians who had vacationed in the Murray Bay area since the 1870s. A lawyer, he was a great admirer of the province's countryside, landscape, and language. See Simon, "William Hume Blake."

36 Donald, *Quebec Patchwork*, 224.

37 George Pearson, "My Friend Jean-Baptiste," *Maclean's*, 1 November 1926, 19.

38 Unnamed author, "World Travel Notes: Eastern Canada," *Living Age* 336 (August 1929): 236.

39 Hémon, *Maria Chapdelaine* (1948), 171.

40 Henry Drummond eventually toured Canada, the United States, and Britain giving poetry readings. See Francis, *National Dreams*, 99.

41 Drummond, *The Habitant*, 4.

42 Francis, *National Dreams*, 99.

43 The accounts of Donald, *Quebec Patchwork*, 30–2, and Oakley, *Kaleidoscope Quebec*, 13–14, are typical in this regard.

44 Donald, *Quebec Patchwork*, 13.

45 Drummond, *The Habitant*, xi.

46 Louis-Honoré Fréchette (1839–1908). He also wrote prose, founded two newspapers, and became the Liberal Member of Parliament (1874–78) for Lévis, Quebec.

47 Louis Fréchette, in the introduction, Drummond, *The Habitant*, vi and ix.

48 See Douglas MacKay, "Some Fresh Glimpses of a Familiar River," *Canadian Geographical Journal* 1, no. 4 (August 1930) and Pearson, "My Friend Jean-Baptiste," 19.

49 The book was first published in French as *Chez Nous* (Québec: L'Action sociale catholique, 1914). The English version was entitled *Chez Nous (Our Old Quebec Home)* (Toronto: McClelland and Stewart Publishers, 1924).

50 Rivard, *Chez Nous*, 148.

51 W.H. Blake, in *Chez Nous*, 15–16.

52 Adjutor Rivard (1868–1945) was also a judge and prominent linguist, a defender of the French language in North America. Among other things, he is noted for having founded the Société du parler français au Canada in 1902. He was the principal organizer of the Premier Congrès de la langue française au Canada in 1912.

53 Longstreth, *Quebec, Montreal and Ottawa*, 133.

54 See "Places et Plages d'été de la région du Québec," *La Presse*, 3 July 1926, 46.

55 In his *Chroniques, humeurs et caprices* (Quebec, 1873) and *Petites chroniques pour 1877* (Quebec 1878), he recounted his summer stays in the Malbaie.

56 Others were historians Abbé Jean-Baptiste-Antoine Ferland (1805–1865) who wrote about his trip along the Gaspé coast in "Journal d'un voyage sur les côtes de la Gaspésie," *Littérature canadienne*, 1863; Faucher de Saint Maurice (1844–1897), *Promenades dans le golfe Saint-Laurent – Une partie de la Côte Nord, l'Île aux Oeufs, l'Anticosti, l'Île Saint-Paul, l'archipel de la Madelaine* (Quebec: Typographie de C. Darveau, 1879).

57 Cook, "L'observateur empathique," 145–6.

58 See Gagnon, "Un regard sur l'Autre," 207–33.

59 Géronimi, "L'émergence des lieux du tourisme et de la villégiature," 220.

60 Brinley, *Away to Quebec*, 226.

61 "Oxen Drinking," in Longstreth, *Quebec, Montreal and Ottawa*, 147.

62 Another painter a few may have come across is Canadian W.M. Mitchell (1879–1955), who painted many miniatures of rural Quebec. Maude-Émmanuelle Lambert also reveals how provincial tourist promoters themselves were inspired by some of these painters, including Clarence Gagnon and Horatio Walker. Lambert, "À travers le pare-brise," 128–30.

63 Oakley, *Kaleidoscopic Quebec*, 140.

64 Reid, "Cornelius Krieghoff," 35. However, François-Marc Gagnon puts into question the legitimacy of some French Quebeckers' pejorative views by reinterpreting Krieghoff's depiction of the *habitants*. Gagnon, "Un regard sur l'Autre," 207–33.

65 Igartua, *The Other Quiet Revolution*, 12.

66 Igartua, "The Genealogy of Stereotypes," 107. For his part, Christophe Caritey concurs that despite everything, "the contribution of the textbook is very real." Caritey, "Manuels scolaires," 137, 162–3.

67 Caritey, "Manuels scolaires," 155.

68 Savard, "Les 'caractères' nationaux," n1, 205.

69 Raimer Riemenscheider quoted in Caritey, *Manuels scolaires*. Family members are identified as central in shaping people's understanding of the past and museums, documentaries, television, and novels also come into play to varying degrees. For others who have studied the relative influence of school textbooks in the Quebec context, see Létourneau and Moisan, "Young People's Assimilation of a Collective Historical Memory," 109–28.

70 Caritey, "Manuels scolaires," 137.

71 See Gary North, "Textbooks as Ideological Weapons," at http://www.lewrockwell.com/north/north461.html.

72 Muzzey, *An American History*, 73.

73 Ibid., 88.

74 This overview is based on a random selection of these readers, mostly chosen on the basis of their availability.

75 Harris and Harris, *Canadian Ways*, 46.

76 Ibid.

77 Carpentier, *Canada and Her Northern Neighbors*, 180–1.

78 Ibid., 188.

79 Bonner, *Canada and Her Story*, 44.

80 Carpentier, *Canada and Her Northern Neighbors*, 29.

81 Graham Bonner, *Canada and Her Story*, 44.

82 Harris and Harris, *Canadian Ways*, 26, 27, 33.

83 The fact that the textbook publishing companies, located in Ontario, were officially approved by several provincial Departments of Education throughout the country and over several decades means that one can speak in general terms about the imprint these publications could have left among English Canadian travel writers as a whole. See Igartua, *The Other Quiet Revolution*, 12.

84 For an in-depth analysis of history textbooks used in English Canada and Quebec see the 5th Study commissioned by the Royal Commission on Bilingualism and Biculturalism. Trudel and Jain, *Canadian History Textbooks*.

85 He was also included in sections of suggested readings. See Wrong, *The Canadians*, 115.

86 Duncan, *The Story of the Canadian People*, v. See also Clement, *The History of the Dominion of Canada*, 89. Under the subtitle "The Canadian Contented," students learned that "the rule of the British officers was mild and conciliatory." Ibid., 91.

87 Burt, *The Romance of Canada*, 137, 139. See also Brown, *Building the Canadian Nation*; Dorland, *The Romance of Canada*, 69, 111.

88 Percival, *The Lure of Quebec*, 96. See also his lengthy Parkman quotation on page 38.

89 One could also argue that these views about French rule help to better understand the striking appeal of Kirby's novel. Canadian travel writer Blodwen Davies is a case in point. While referring to "the unscrupulous Bigot," she editorializes, "[i]t was the criminal irresponsibility of her own leaders that was largely to blame for her fall." Davies, *Romantic Quebec*, 67. Brian Meredith,

"Laurentian Prospect: An Aperçu of French Canada," *The Fortnightly*, January 1938, 97

90 Dorland, *Our Canada*, 356.
91 Brown, *Building the Canadian Nation*, 95.
92 Dickie, *The Great Adventure*, 98.
93 Wrong, *The Canadians*, 63–4.
94 Ibid., 95.
95 Dorland, *Our Canada*, 78.
96 Burt, *The Romance of Canada*, 92.
97 Igartua, "The Genealogy of Stereotypes," 125.
98 Wrong, *The Canadians*, 423, 98.
99 Bourinot, *Canada*, 428. Reissued several times, it was last published in 1922. Sir George Bourinot was a historian and writer, cofounder of the Canadian Royal Society, and chief clerk of the House of Commons between 1880 and 1902. He had a cottage in the Gatineau Hills which, much like W.H. Blake and Horatio Walker, made him a member of an English Canadian elite who summered in the province and enjoyed it for its "Old Quebec" attributes.
100 Ibid., 436, 435.
101 Duncan, *The Story of the Canadian People*, 387–94.
102 McArthur, *History of Canada*, 494, 489, 502–3. George Wrong's section on "Literature and Arts" notes that W.H. Drummond's "Habitant" and his "Voyageur" were "merely Everyman in a French Canadian setting." Wrong, *The Canadians*, 360.
103 Wrong, *The Canadians*, 423.
104 Ibid.
105 Dorland, *Our Canada*, 356.
106 Laviolette, *Histoire du Canada*. For a full analysis of French Canadian textbook content in the 1960s, see Trudel and Jain, *Canadian History Textbooks*.
107 This is not surprising in view of the fact that, until the early 1960s, the Catholic clergy had a monopoly as teachers and on the content of teaching material. The Clercs de Saint-Viateur, for one, distributed a series of history textbooks in 1917, which were reissued several times. Quebec historian Micheline Dumont provides a brief and evocative overview of their content and how they shaped her historical memory in "Growing up in … /Grandir en …," 141–52.
108 Laviolette, *Histoire du Canada*, 193.
109 Ibid., 79, 70.
110 Ibid., 129–31.
111 Rutche and Forget, *Précis d'histoire du Canada*, 57.
112 Filteau, *La civilisation catholique et francaise au Canada*, 376.

CHAPTER FOUR

1 Benaquista, *Quelqu'un d'autre*, 203.
2 Houellebecq, *Plateforme*, 225.
3 Morgan, "*Happy Holiday*," 23.

4 Redfoot, "Tourist Authenticity, Tourist Angst and Modern Reality," 295.

5 Stella Burke May, "Along Rural Highways in French Canada," *Travel* 59 (June 1932): 33.

6 Larry Franck, "The France across Our Border," *Travel* 75 (May 1940).

7 For a detailed look at Americans' attraction to France see Levenstein, *Seductive Journey* and *We'll Always Have Paris*. For the post–Second World War period see Endy, *Cold War Holidays*.

8 "Canada's Transcontinental Playgrounds," *Literary Digest* 109 (6 June 1931): 50.

9 R.S. Kennedy, "Cruising the Gulf of St Lawrence," *Travel* 61 (June 1933): 47.

10 L.P., "Bit of Old France in Canada," *NYT*, 9 June 1940, sect 10, 9.

11 Leon Dickinson, "Open Roads in Old Quebec," *NYT*, 20 July 1930, sect 19, 7.

12 Oakley, *Kaleidoscopic Quebec*, 145.

13 James Montagnes, "Circling Canada's Gaspé," *NYT*, 16 June 1930, sect 10, 23.

14 Géromini, "L'émergence des lieux du tourisme et de la villégiature."

15 Helen Augur, "New Order in New France," *Travel* 49 (May 1942): 26.

16 Sally Bennett, "The Grand Style at Murray Bay," *Travel* 75 (May 1940): 36.

17 Also referred to as "fetishized monument[s] serving a symbolic function" by Pelletier, Vallée-Tremblay, and Malo in "La function symbolique," 4–5. Put differently, Château Frontenac "represent[s] Quebec city" giving it "imageability." Jackle, *The Tourist*, 273, 284. See also Dominick, "Le développement du tourisme."

18 Burke, "Along Rural Highways in French Canada." In fact, headlines of their articles, published in newspapers or magazines, occasionally included the word "*habitant*" – a clear sign that it was considered an attention grabber. "The Habitant Ho Kays Winter," *Saturday Evening Post* 21 (4 February 1939): 42.

19 Oakley, *Kaleidoscopic Quebec*, 7.

20 Pat Morgan, "Popular Art in the Raw," *Commonweal* 28 (13 May 1938): 71–2.

21 In fact, the way they described the *habitants* is very similar to the way travel writers reacted to the Nova Scotia folk. McKay, *The Quest of the Folk*, esp. chapter 4, 214–73.

22 Augur, "New Order," 36.

23 McKay, *The Quest of the Folk*, 14.

24 Leon Dickinson, "Open Roads in Old Quebec," *NYT*, 20 July 1930, sect 19, 7.

25 Steel, *Let's Visit Canada*, 124.

26 Stokes, "Picturesque Canada," 60. Rarely did they refer to the "locals" as fishermen and their wives – those they likely came across most often in the Gaspé. The term *habitant* appears to have served as a generic one to describe all French Quebeckers involved in some form of work linked to the land and the sea.

27 E.B. Hotton, "Along the Perron Boulevard," *NYT*, 27 July 1930, sect 19, 7.

28 Burke May, "Along Rural Highways in French Canada," 35.

29 In the same vein as the travelogues described by Alan Gordon. The detailed accounts written by a few travel writers during this period can be considered as a distinct type of travel writing, a combination of the travelogue and the more prescriptive guidebook produced by private companies in the late-nineteenth century.

30 Brinley, *Away to the Gaspé*. Their style of travel writing was obviously very popular as *Away to the Gaspé*, originally published in 1935, was reprinted five times the year it came out and, by 1938, had already gone through its tenth printing. It was widely distributed: 1,000 copies were also sent to Canada to be published by McClelland and Stewart. Daniel Putman Brinley and Kathrine Sanger Brinley Papers, 1879–1984, Biographical Material: folder on books by Kathrine Sanger "Gordon" Brinley, 1934–circa 1936, Box 1, folder 28, "Story of the Gaspe Book," page 2, Washington: Archives of American Art, http://www.aaa.si.edu/collections/daniel-putnam-brinley-and-kathrine-sanger-brinley-papers-6830/more. Their interest extended to the province as a whole as a couple of years later they produced *Away to Quebec: A Gay Journey to the Province*, which proved to be very popular as well. Brinley, *Away to Quebec*.

31 Brinley, *Away to the Gaspé*, 71.

32 Ibid., 81–2, 56, 75, 35.

33 Ibid., 36.

34 Amy Oakley (1882–1963) wrote travel articles and more than ten books on wide-ranging destinations including several on France. Her husband Thornton Oakley (1881–1953) was an artist and art teacher who published in highly regarded periodicals and illustrated several of his wife's travel accounts.

35 Hal Burton, "Christmas in Montreal," *Holiday*, 26 December 1959, 56.

36 Ibid., 218, 162, 242.

37 Steel, *Let's Visit Canada*, 136.

38 Oakley, *Kaleidoscopic Quebec*, 33.

39 Brinley, *Away to Quebec*, 78.

40 Oakley, *Kaleidoscopic Quebec*, 33.

41 Brinley, *Away to Quebec*, 131, 134.

42 See Lambert, "À travers le pare-brise," for an enlightening connection between this interest in traditional ways of transportation and increasing automobile touring.

43 Brinley, *Away to the Gaspé*, 99.

44 Diana Rice, "Invasion of Canada," *NYT*, 28 June 1936, sect 10, 1.

45 Herbert J. Manghan, "Unchanging Gaspé," *NYT*, 16 June 1946, sect 2, 8.

46 W. Walker, "Gaspé through a Trailer Window," *Scribner's Magazine* 101 (May 1937): 74.

47 Brinley *Away to Quebec*, 210–11. For a very interesting analysis of the use of dogs in the countryside and how visitors reacted to them, see Lambert, "À travers le pare-brise."

48 Nixon, *See Canada Next*, 70.

49 Maoz, "The Mutual Gaze," 229.

50 Tourism scholars early on show an interest in the behaviour of host societies, starting with Dean MacCannell. He raised the question of potentially detrimental consequences of staging in "Staged Authenticity: Arrangements of Social Space in Tourist Settings" and "Reconstructed Ethnicity: Tourism and Cultural Identity." For a more recent overview of the subject, see Wrobel's introduction to *Seeing and Being Seen*, "Tourists, Tourism and the Toured Upon."

51 van den Berghe and Keyes, "Introduction: Tourism and Re-created Ethnicity," 347. The term was first coined by van den Berghe. See "Tourism as Ethnic Relations."

52 Brinley, *Away to Quebec*, 97.

53 Oakley, *Kaleidoscopic Quebec*, 212.

54 Brinley, *Away to Quebec*, 98. These travel writers did not fully appreciate how lucky they were to meet her, as Éva Bouchard died in 1949.

55 Longstreth is another American who wrote about his visit to Péribonka and with the Bédard family in *The Laurentians*.

56 Brinley, *Away to the Gaspé*, 70.

57 Franck, "The France across Our Border," 17.

58 Ibid., 16.

59 Steele, *Let's Visit Canada*, 46.

60 Oakley, *Kaleidoscopic Quebec*, xii.

61 Walker, "Gaspé through a Trailer Window," 73.

62 Stokes, "Picturesque Canada," 59.

63 Wes Whitefield Walker, "A Survival of Old Normandy in Canada," *Travel* 69 (August 1937): 17.

64 Stokes, "Picturesque Canada," 59.

65 George Sessions Perry, "Quebec City," *Saturday Evening Post* 228 (18 February 1956): 22.

66 Rice, "Invasion of Canada," 1.

67 Longstreth, *Quebec, Montreal and Ottawa*, 132.

68 It may be assumed that those writers with basic knowledge of so-called "standard" French, sometimes referred to as Parisian French, would have stood in contrast to the Quebec French language.

69 Longstreth, *Quebec, Montreal, and Ottawa*, 132.

70 Oakley, *Kaleidoscopic Quebec*, 228.

71 Brinley, *Away to Quebec*, 182.

72 Oakley, *Kaleidoscopic Quebec*, 105.

73 Ibid.

74 Steele, *Let's Visit Canada*, 41.

75 Whitefield Walker, "Survival of Old Normandy in Canada," 17.

76 Kennedy, "Cruising the Gulf of St Lawrence," 47.

77 Longstreth, *Quebec, Montreal and Ottawa*, 132.

78 Brinley, *Away to the Gaspé*, 102.

79 Oakley, *Kaleidoscopic Quebec*, 14.

80 Sessions Perry, "Quebec City," 54.

81 Such surprise may have had just as much to do with the fact that they were coming to a region in North America free of the prohibition laws still in place in the US under the Volstead Act.

82 McKay, *Quest of the Folk*, 39, 225, 14.

83 Sessions Perry, "Quebec City," 54.

84 Augur, "New Order," 25, 36.

85 Steele, *Let's Visit Canada*, 123.

86 Simard, *Mythe et reflet*, 316.

87 Augur, "New Order," 36.

88 In fact, she gives it high praise, remarking to her husband, "It is well planned, and printed in large type so one can read it easily while motoring. My blessings on the tourist bureau [*sic*]." Brinley, *Away to Quebec*, 89.

89 Brinley, *Away to Quebec*, 135, 87, 91.

90 Igartua, *Arvida au Saguenay*.

91 Brinley, *Away to Quebec*, 90, and Oakley, *Kaleidoscopic Quebec*, 205.

92 Oakley, *Kaleidoscopic Quebec*, 185–6.

93 Bill Weintraub, "Canadian Tourism," NYT, 7 May 1950, sect 10, 35.

94 Ken Johnstone, "Holiday Weekend in Quebec City," MM 71 (8 November 1958): 27.

95 Eva-Lis Wuorio, "Quebec: Museum Piece with Muscle," MM 61 (1 April 1948): 49.

96 Davies, *Romantic Quebec*. Blodwen Davies (1897–1966) earned her living as a freelance travel writer and historical researcher. During the 1930s, her many books of travel and history raised the cultural profile of picturesque locations in Quebec and Ontario. She spent many years of her career living in the US but returned to Canada and lived in rural Ontario.

97 Constance Cromarty, "Seignories [*sic*] Weaving Looms and Homespuns: An Article on the Quaint Old Settlements along the North Shore of the Lower St Lawrence," *Canadian Magazine* 63, no. 4 (August 1924): 198.

98 Dr W.T. Herridge, "Murray Bay: A Distinguished Paradox," *Canadian Magazine* 64, no. 8 (September 1925): 228. He was an Ottawa Presbyterian minister who owned a cottage in the Gatineau hills.

99 Wallace Ward, "The Quebec of the Visitors," *Saturday Night* 67 (12 July 1952): 23.

100 Meredith, "Laurentian Prospect," 95–6.

101 Herridge, "Murray Bay," 229. Wright, studying the attitudes of the late nineteenth century, refers to this fascination as the "cult of the habitant." Wright, "W.D. Lighthall and David Ross McCord," 139.

102 Davies, *Romantic Quebec*, 99.

103 Donald, *Quebec Patchwork*, 198.

104 Call, "Country of Maria Chapdelaine," 459.

105 Carlton McNaught, "The Real Maria Chapdelaine," *Canadian Magazine* 83, no. 1 (January 1935): 6.

106 Donald, *Quebec Patchwork*, 228.

107 Mackenzie and Mackenzie, *Quebec in Your Car*, 219.

108 Donald, *Quebec Patchwork*, 175. Jean M. Donald (1903–2005) was a writer and distinguished artist. She was raised in England and immigrated to Canada. She lived in British Columbia for most of her life. She eventually worked as a librarian at National Defense and as a writer and researcher for the CBC. *Quebec Patchwork* was her only travel book. As with a few of her American counterparts, she travelled to Quebec with her husband which allowed her to recount her experiences in a lively manner interspersed as it was with some dialogue.

109 Davies, *Gaspé*, 40–1.

110 Ibid., 8.

111 Donald, *Quebec Patchwork*, 14.

112 Herridge, "Murray Bay," 229.

113 Ibid., 229.

114 "Gaspé – Canada's Riviera," *Saturday Night* 50 (May 1935): 16.

115 T.M. Fraser, "Meet Mr Habitant," MM 32 (September 1919).

116 Katherine Hale, "Legends of the St Lawrence," MM 39 (1 July 1926): 67.

117 Ibid.

118 George Pearson, "My Friend Jean-Baptiste," MM 39 (1 October 1926): 8.

119 The comment they are referring to was written by Sydney W. Morrell, "Canada," *Holiday*, August 1949, 40.

120 Mackenzie and Mackenzie, *Quebec in Your Car*, 162.

121 Pearson, "My Friend Jean-Baptiste," 8.

122 Mackenzie and Mackenzie, *Quebec in Your Car*, 3.

123 William MacMillan, "I Prefer Quebec," MM 46 (April 1933): 42.

124 Wuorio, "Quebec: Museum Piece with Muscle," 48.

125 MacMillan, "I Prefer Quebec," 24.

126 Pearson, "My Friend Jean-Baptiste," 9.

127 Hugh MacLennan, "Canada: The Dramatic North," *Holiday*, July 1953, 46.

128 Pearson, "My Friend Jean-Baptiste," 8.

139 Unfortunately, only silent versions of these films devoid of Finnie's voiceover are available. This may be because he accompanied the showing of these films and provided the commentary on site. See Geller, "Visions of a Northern Nation."

130 Before his *Travel* magazine article "Old France in Modern Canada," *Travel* 77, was published in May 1941, he wrote another article, "Filming Rural French Canada," for the *Canadian Geographical Journal* 14, no. 4 (April 1937), which recounts the same experiences and impressions, in several instances, word-for-word. Here is one of a few examples of Canadian travel writers addressing both Canadian and American audiences, and thus, at times, making the distinction between American and Canadian travel writers less self-evident.

131 Finnie, "Filming Rural French America," 183.

132 Mathew Trill, "Road to Yesterday," *Saturday Night* 53 (11 June 1938): 19.

133 G.W. Peters "Where History Is Candy-Coated," *Saturday Night* 55 (15 June 1940): 24.

134 Mackenzie and Mackenzie, *Quebec in Your Car*, 148.

135 Ibid.

136 Davies, *Gaspé*, 170.

137 "Along Quebec Highways," *Saturday Night* 50 (27 July 1935): 10.

138 Indeed, in a notice entitled "À Nos Correspondants," the editors noted that "[a]lready city dwellers leave town for the sea, the woods, the mountains where the air is purer and more breathable, where life offers pleasure and rest." Thus, "[a]s in previous years, *La Presse* will devote liberal space in its columns to leisure movements, more particularly in our beautiful province of Quebec, and

about this topic we would like to attract the attention of our reporters. They are invited to send us the news and interests linked to holidaying." *La Presse*, 5 June 1926, 50. Of the series of articles, "Ce que la Province de Québec offre à ses habitants et à ceux qui la visitent," one was published each week until 10 July 1926.

139 The fact that it was a Quebec City paper – the province's seat of government – may have had something to do with their focus on the industry per se as opposed to what visitors would discover by travelling at "home."

140 "Lettre de Québec: 'Deux nouvelles routes,'" *La Presse*, 7 June 1930, 32.

141 "La Gaspésie, pays qu'il faut voir," *La Presse*, 13 June 1936.

142 "Vers la Gaspésie ... Pays du tourisme," *Le Soleil*, 8 May 1926, 2.

143 "Gaspésie, pays qu'il faut voir," *La Presse*, 13 June 1936.

144 "Pays aux panoramas majestueux et variés," *La Presse*, 11 July 1936.

145 "Centre touristique des plus populaires," *La Presse*, 20 July 1940, 39.

146 "Cette année, pour vos vacances, choisissez d'abord la Gaspésie," *Le Soleil*, 21 May 1956, 4.

147 Glassberg, "History and Memory," 19–20.

148 "Pour instruire le touriste," editorial, *Le Soleil*, 14 May 1920, 4.

149 "Plages et places d'été de la région de Québec," *La Presse*, 3 July 1926, 46.

150 "Ce que la province de Québec offre à ses habitants et à ceux qui la visitent," *La Presse*, 19 June 1926, 21.

151 "La banlieue de Montréal – Les Cantons de l'Est, régions parsemées de superbes lacs," *La Presse*, 8 June 1940.

152 "Ce que la province de Québec offre à ses habitants et à ceux qui la visitent," *La Presse*, 8 May 1926, 67.

153 "Vers la Gaspésie," *Le Soleil*, 8 May 1926, 4.

154 "La Gaspésie à 120 milles de longueur," *La Presse*, 8 June 1940, 31.

155 *La Presse*, 14 June 1930.

156 "Territoire popularisé dans le monde entier," *La Presse*, 15 June 1940, 44; "Plages et places d'été de la région de Québec," *La Presse*, 3 July 1926, 46. As noted earlier, the term "habitant" carried, in some circles, negative connotations.

157 "Pays aux panoramas majestueux et variés," *La Presse*, 11 July 1936.

158 "Les Laurentides et les rives du Saint-Laurent," *La Presse*, 26 June 1930, 30.

159 Although *Le Soleil* edition of 12 June 1926 did publish a page of photos of the Lac St-Jean area which included one of Éva Bouchard, no reference was made to her.

160 "La Gaspésie, pays qu'il faut voir," *La Presse*, 13 June 1936.

161 "Les Cantons de l'Est," *La Presse*, 19 June 1926, 52; *La Presse*, 8 June 1940, 36.

162 *La Presse*, 8 June 1940, 28.

163 Later in the period, their occasional observations proved more bombastic, reflecting an enhanced pride in the province's tremendous postwar economic development.

164 *Le Soleil*, 28 May 1956, 4.

165 *La Presse*, 19 June 1926, 52.

CHAPTER FIVE

1   George Elliott Clark, *George and Rue*, 20.

2   In fact, government promoters were well aware of this fact, noting in 1935 that "Montreal is still the city which receives the greatest number of tourists." *Minister's Report-Roads*, 1935, 133. As Paul-André Linteau points out, Montreal was the major metropolis in Canada in the early twentieth century and despite the fact that following the First World War it gradually lost some ground to Toronto, it remained a close rival. Linteau, *Histoire de Montréal*, 314, 286–8.

3   *Montreal: The Paris of the New World*. Coronation Year, 1937, Montreal Tourist and Convention Bureau (hereafter MTCB) brochure, Fonds P405, 002554-002580, BANQM, 3.

4   McNamee G.A., secretary treasurer, MTCB, *The Senate Report on Tourist Traffic*, 1934, 50.

5   "Propagande touristique," *Le Canada*, 5 June 1939.

6   Kennedy Crone, "La Ville de Montréal," *Canadian Geographical Journal* 3, no. 1 (July 1931): 4. In one of several cases where travel writers "borrow" from one another, T. Morris Longstreth made the same observation word-for-word a few years later. Montreal, he remarked, "is almost alone among the great cities in being without a highly organized municipal publicity department and as a city she does not even issue a street guide except to her policemen." Longstreth, *Quebec, Montreal and Ottawa*, 238.

7   Bellerose, "L'Office des congrès et du tourisme du Grand Montréal," 24.

8   McNamee G.A., secretary treasurer, MTCB, *The Senate Report on Tourist Traffic*, 1934, 50.

9   *Helpful Information for Visitors to the Metropolis of Canada: Montreal, the Year Round Vacation Center – A guide where to go, what to see or do, where to get it in Gay Montreal*, MCTB brochure, PGF (P190), 1983-03-038/53, BANQM, 32.

10 *Senate Report on Tourist Traffic*, 49.

11 "Artistic Booklet Advertises City," *Montreal Gazette*, 14 June 1930, 3.

12 *Come to Montreal*, MTCB brochure, not dated but likely late 1930s or early 1940s as it includes a welcome letter by the city's mayor, Adhémar Raynault, who occupied the position from 1936 to 1938 and 1940 to 1944. Fonds P405, 001304-001339, BANQM.

13 *Montreal: Gateway to Historic Province of Quebec*, MTCB brochure, 1934, Fonds P405, 002420-002449, BANQM.

14 *Quebec and the Maritimes*, CPR brochure, 1932, 3.

15 *Quaint Montreal*, MTCB brochure, not dated but most likely published in the 1920s or early 1930s. These same words are used in the introduction of the Gray Line bus company advertising booklet, also entitled *Quaint Montreal*, also without a publication date but likely early 1930s as it includes "Greetings" from Fernand Rinfret, Montreal mayor from 1932 to 1934. Fonds P405, 001340-001352, BANQM.

16 *Quaint Montreal*. The same words (although it used "dialect" instead of "patois") appear in the introduction of the Gray Line bus company advertising booklet also titled *Quaint Montreal*.

17 *Montreal: The Paris of the New World*, MTCB brochure, 1937, 20, Fonds P405, 002554-002580, BAnQM.

18 *Come to Montreal*, MTCB brochure.

19 From the 1939 campaign "Let's Go to Montreal." Such words recall Mark Twain's often-quoted comment made during his 1881 visit to Montreal: "This is the first time I was ever in a city where you couldn't throw a brick without breaking a church window."

20 *Montreal: The Paris of the New World.*

21 MTCB campaign slogan of 1931. It is used again in following years with slight variations. (1932: "Montreal Gateway to Historical Province of Quebec," and 1934: "Montreal: Gateway to Historic Province of Quebec.")

22 *Montreal: The Paris of the New World.*

23 *Montreal: Gateway to Historic Province of Quebec.* By 1931, the City of Montreal counted 818,577 inhabitants and by 1951 it had reached a population of just over a million. Linteau, *Histoire de Montréal*, 314.

24 *Come to Montreal.*

25 Ibid.

26 *Montreal: The Paris of the New World.*

27 Harvey Levenstein traces the history behind Americans' attraction to Paris in *Seductive Journey*, and *We'll Always Have Paris.* See also Lusignan, "Comment Montréal est devenu Paris pour les Américains!," 20.

28 Slogans for a 1937 MTCB advertising campaign.

29 "Quebec Canada" brochure, 5.

30 In keeping with their intent to imagine the city as modern, in these Montreal ads the province was more often referred to as a *New* World rather than an *Old* Quebec.

31 See Heron, *Booze*, for prohibition laws in Canada.

32 Half of the province of Quebec in the 1920s was still officially dry.

33 Although no restrictions were placed on those who left the store only to return to purchase another bottle, and in 1941 such quantity restrictions were lifted.

34 In 1922, the Quebec Liquor Commission estimated in fact that 84 per cent of wine and spirits sold in its stores in Montreal was bought by foreigners. These were mostly Americans but Ontarians also took advantage of the city's lax regulations until 1927 when their province repealed prohibition. Prévost, Gagné, and Paneuf, *L'histoire de l'alcool au Québec*, 96. See also Michael Hawrysh's excellent MA thesis on Montreal during the US prohibition era, "Une ville bien arrosée."

35 Weintraub, *City Unique*, 120.

36 By 1948, there were "fifteen of them ... plus about twenty five smaller 'lounges' with more modest entertainment." The entertainers "brought with them an aura of Broadway" and "from the music halls of Paris for the city's French audiences." Weintraub, *City Unique*, 124, 121, 136. See also Bourassa and Larrue, *Les nuits de la "Main."*

37 William Weintraub points out, "the map of the city was studded with establishments that offered horse betting, roulette, blackjack, chemin de fer, baccarat, craps and of course barbotte, the hugely popular dice game unique to Montreal."

Weintraub, *City Unique*, 61. See also Proulx, *Le Red Light de Montréal*, and Brodeur, *Vice et corruption*.

38 Weintraub, *City Unique*, 85.

39 Hawrysh, "Une ville bien arosée," 68. See also Lévesque, "Éteindre le Red Light." The district was closed in 1944.

40 Ibid., 12.

41 For studies on lesbian experiences in Montreal, see Podmore, "Gone 'Underground'?"; Chamberland, "Remembering Lesbian Bars."

42 By the early years of the Depression, for instance, "Black music had found its way into the city's dance halls, nightclubs, and vaudeville theaters." While Black jazz musicians were not welcome in the west end of the city, they did find work "downtown on Antoine St." Gilmore, *Swinging in Paradise*, 47, 53. See also the National Film Board 1998 film entitled *Show Girls: Celebrating Montreal's Legendary Black Jazz Scene*. http://www.nfb-onf.gc.ca/eng/collection/film/?id=33572.

43 "A Pleasant Place to Dine," MTCB brochure, 1937.

44 Ibid. Under section entitled "Montreal at Night."

45 Many of these articles appeared in the 1920s and 1930s, in reputed newspapers or magazines including *The New York Times* and *Life*. Humorous caricatures often accompanied these texts, leaving no doubt in readers' minds that Montreal was a place to enjoy some forbidden pleasures in the open.

46 Advertising of the 1933 and 1934 campaigns.

47 *Helpful Information for Visitors to the Metropolis of Canada: Montreal, The Year Round Vacation Center*, 20.

48 *Montreal: The Paris of the New World*.

49 Ibid.

50 *Come to Montreal*.

51 *Tours in Quebec, Canada*, 4.

52 *4, 5 and 6 Days in Quebec, Canada* (1928), 12. The same text is reproduced in *Tours in Quebec*, 5.

53 *4, 5 and 6 Days in Quebec, Canada* (1928), 13; repeated in *Tours in Quebec*, 5.

54 *Along Quebec Highways*, 71, 74.

55 *4, 5 and 6 Days in Quebec, Canada* (1928), 12.

56 *La Province de Québec Canada: Have You Ever Had a French Canadian Vacation?*, not dated but likely 1941, 21.

57 *Montréal and the Laurentians*, Provincial Tourist Bureau, Department of Roads, Quebec, Canada, 2nd edition, 1935, 3.

58 *Have You Ever Had a French Canadian Vacation?*, 17.

59 *La Province de Québec: Historic-Romantic-Picturesque*, Province of Quebec Tourist Bureau, 1939, 5.

60 *Tours in Quebec*, 7.

61 *Tours in Quebec*, 6.

62 See *La Province de Québec*, not dated but likely published in late 1930s. This held true into the 1950s. See *La Province de Québec Canada*, Tourist Branch, Provincial Publicity Office, 6th ed, 1952.

63 *Have You Ever Had a French Canadian Vacation?*, 19.

64 *Along Quebec Highways*, 60.

65 *The Old World at Your Door*, 5.

66 Gouin, "Technique," 7.

67 *Montréal and the Laurentians*, 3.

68 *Halifax Herald*, 23 May 1936, 10.

69 *Have You Ever Had a French Canadian Vacation?*, 21.

70 *Minister's Report-Roads*, 1934, 79.

71 *Minister's Report-Roads*, 1933, 145.

72 *Minister's Report-Roads*, 1935, 133, 118–19.

73 *Minister's Report-Roads*, 1935, 113. *Montreal and the Laurentians*, 1935.

74 *4, 5 and 6 Days in Quebec, Canada* (1928), 14.

75 *La Province de Québec: Historic-Romantic-Picturesque*, 5.

76 *Have You Ever Had a French Canadian Vacation?*, 19.

77 "Bienvenue à Montréal," ad, *Halifax Herald*, 23 May 1936, 10.

78 *Montreal and the Laurentians*, 12–13. Its 1940s brochure, *Have You Ever Had a French Canadian Vacation?*, did not provide tourists much information, but noted that visitors "should not miss it by night" when they would discover a "fairyland of sparkling lights" and "the great illuminated cross above send[ing] down its benediction to a million souls!" This was "a city in which you may take your ease, find rest and repose," that is "abounding with the tang of gaiety." *Have You Ever Had a French Canadian Vacation?*, 17, 21.

79 *La Province de Québec: Historic-Romantic-Picturesque*, 5.

80 *Montreal and the Laurentians*, 5.

81 Ibid., 7.

82 *La Province de Québec: Historic-Romantic-Picturesque*, 5.

83 *Halifax Herald*, 24 July 1940, 12.

84 *Have You Ever Had a French Canadian Vacation?*, 17.

85 Office Provincial de Tourisme, Ministère de la Voierie, 1st ed., 1934. The other booklet translated in French was the 120-page brochure on the Gaspésie.

86 *La province de Québec, Pays de l'histoire, de la légende et du pittoresque*, Office du tourisme de la province de Québec, 1939, 6.

87 Ibid., 4.

88 Tessier, *Les valeurs nationales et économiques*, 44.

89 Montpetit, "Prends la … route," 24

90 "La ville qui a perdu son âme," *Le Devoir*, 7 April 1937 – an article reporting Victor Barbeau's comments at a conference at the University of Montreal.

91 Jean Bruchési, "L'aveu d'une faute," *Le Terroir* 14, no. 12 (May 1933): 13.

92 Victor Barbeau in "La ville qui a perdu son âme."

93 "Le tourisme et la conservation de nos monuments d'autrefois," *Le Devoir*, 5 December 1950.

94 A talk he gave on "French in tourism and hostelry" on 3 December 1952 during his appearance on a Radio Canada show. He gave the same talk at a meeting of the Fédération Saint-Jean-Baptiste. Title of document: "Radio Canada, le 7

janvier, 1953 – Fédération des Sociétés St Jean-Baptiste," 7. PGF (P190), 1983 03 038/72, BANQM.

95 Lecture given to the Montreal Chamber of Commerce, 4 December 1951, 3.

96 *Minister's Report-Roads*, 1932, 91.

97 Gouin, "Technique."

98 Ibid.

99 "Just a Word about Tourism!" *L'Hôtellerie* 91 (31 March 1934): 2.

100 Editorial, *L'Hôtellerie/The Hostelry* 9 (31 May 1935): 1.

101 Editorial, *L'Hôtellerie/The Hostelry* 8 (31 March 1934): 2.

102 *Minister's Report-Roads*, 1933, 123.

103 Editorial, *L'Hôtellerie/The Hostelry*, 31 May 1935, 3.

104 Gouin, "Technique," 5.

105 His Radio Canada talk on "French in tourism and hostelry," 3 December 1952, 5, 10.

106 For more information on these state-sponsored initiatives, see Hamel, *"Notre maître le passé, notre maître l'avenir,"* 130–2.

107 Ibid., 202.

108 Jean-Marie Gauvreau, director of the École du meuble, was the other French Canadian member of the committee.

109 Letter written by Donald Gordon to Paul Gouin, 18 March 1955, PGF (P190), Reine Elizabeth file, "Montreal," document, 20.

110 Letter written by Paul Gouin to Donald Gordon, 23 March 1955, PGF (P190), Reine Elizabeth file, "Montreal," document, 20.

111 "Ouverture de l'hôtel 'Reine Elizabeth,'" *L'Action catholique*, 17 April 1958. It should be noted that other members of the French Canadian intelligentsia proved much less impressed. Journalists at *L'Action nationale*, for one, organized an extensive lobbying campaign, demanding a French name be given to the hotel. For a brief overview of the controversy see Levine, *The Reconquest of Montreal*, 36–8.

112 Alternatives considered were Simon McTavish or Martin Frobisher. These options proved more palatable as members remarked that they added English names to the list. Decoration Advisory Committee, Minutes of Meeting No. 11 … 14 November 1956, 1, PGF (P190) Reine Elizabeth file, "Montreal," document.

113 Put to music by Harry Warren and written by Billy Rose and Mort Dixon, it was published as sheet music by Irving Berlin in 1928. Several of its lyrics including "And I'll make whoop whoop whoopee night and day" did not leave much to the imagination. Hawrysh, "Une ville bien arrosée," 93–4.

114 Weintraub, *City Unique*, 208.

115 "Inauguration de la Semaine du tourisme: Proclamation de M. Georges Léveillé," *Le Soleil*, 7 May 1956, 4.

116 "Within six months (it) sold 600,000 copies in Canada and the United States" and "was translated into nine languages." Weintraub, *City Unique*, 204.

117 For a fuller discussion of Quebec literature in the 1940s and 1950s, see chapter 9, "Novelists, Poets: New Views of the City" in Weintraub, *City Unique*, 203–23.

118 Examples of these mystery/thrillers also associated with pulp fiction include Ronald J. Cooke, *The Mayor of St Paul* (1950); David Montrose, *The Crime on Côte des Neiges* (1951), *The Body on Mont Royal* (1953); Douglas Sanderson, *Hot Freeze* (1954).

119 For a more fully developed analysis of the genre and how it relates to Montreal's image see Kuplowsky, "Captivating 'Open City,'" chapter 1.

120 Ibid., 73.

121 The American travel writer Amy Oakley stands out as an exception when she informs readers that "Montreal is the setting for two outstanding modern novels by Canadians, dealing with human problems: *Earth and High Heaven*, by Gwenthalyn Graham, which concerns the love of a Jew and a Christian; and *Two Solitudes*, by Hugh MacLennan, whose hero and heroine are a Canadien and an English Canadian." Oakley, *Kaleidoscopic Quebec*, 52.

122 Lise Payette, a journalist, documentary filmmaker, and minister in René Lévesque's Parti Québécois government, resented having their harsh living conditions exposed in such a public manner. She explained that she felt nothing less than humiliated reading Gabrielle Roy's *Bonheur d'occasion*, which depicted the shameful living conditions that prevailed in the neighbourhood in which she had been raised. http://www.milieuxdefavorises.org/serie_C/30.html.

123 Des Rochers, *1920s Modernism in Montreal: The Beaver Hall Group*.

124 Esther Trépanier studied artistic urban representations in *Peinture et modernité au Québec 1919–1939*.

125 Oakley, *Kaleidoscopic Quebec*, 37.

126 Burke May, "Along Rural Highways in French Canada," 33.

127 Unnamed author, "World Travel Notes: Eastern Canada," *Living Age* 336 (August 1929): 456.

128 Steele, *Let's Visit Canada*, 51.

129 Unamed author, "Present Day Adventures," *Literary Digest*, 7 June 1924, 89.

130 Thomas B. Lesure, "Canada's Big Four," *Travel* 105 (May 1956): 16.

131 "Canada Offers," *Literary Digest* 113 (4 June 1932): 36.

132 Oakley, *Kaleidoscopic Quebec*, 35.

133 Ibid., 44, 29, 30.

134 Horace Sutton, "Footloose in Canada," *Saturday Review of Literature* 35 (7 June 1952): 31.

135 Unamed author, "World Travel Notes," 456–9.

136 Lesure, "Canada's Big Four," 16.

137 Unamed author, "World Travel Notes," 456.

138 Longstreth, *Quebec, Montreal and Ottawa*, 238 and 239.

139 Fred Coppeland, "Montreal: A Spring Tonic," NYT, 12 May 1946, 8.

140 Longstreth, *Quebec, Montreal and Ottawa*, 223.

141 Lesure, "Canada's Big Four," 16.

142 Peter Kennedy, "Canadian Honeymoon," *Travel* 100 (July 1953): 10.

143 Lance Connery, "Canada Coast to Coast," *Travel* 110 (August 1958): 15.

144 Benedict Thielen, "Ring around the Gaspé," *Holiday* 35 (April 1964): 32.

145 Oakley, *Kaleidoscopic Quebec*, 36.

146 All indicates that they had met him before. Brinley, *Away to Quebec*, 31.

147 Including Meredith, "Laurentian Prospect: An Aperçu of French Canada," *The Fortnightly*, January 1938, quoted in chapter 4, n100.

148 Brinley, *Away to Quebec*, 42.

149 Here she is likely referring to a research trip she conducted as a Chaucer scholar. Ibid., 45.

150 Percival, *The Lure of Montreal*, 20.

151 Stephen Leacock, "A Tale of Two Cities," MM 56 (1 March 1943): 7. He also wrote two histories of Montreal: *Leacock's Montreal* and *Montreal: Seaport and City*.

152 Percival, *The Lure of Montreal*, 15.

153 Ibid., 20, 15.

154 Gorman Kennedy, "Holiday in Quebec," *Canadian Geographical Journal* 34, no. 1 (January 1947): 22. A journalist, Kennedy was general manager of the Montreal Allouettes from 1957 to 1959 and later served as Expo 67 chief liaison officer in the US.

155 Percival, *The Lure of Montreal*, 3.

156 Kennedy Crone, "La Ville de Montréal," *Canadian Geographical Journal* 3, no. 1 (July 1931): 9.

157 Author unnamed, "Canada's French Province," *Saturday Night* 48 (10 June 1933): 19.

158 Frank Oliver Call was a poet and professor of languages at Bishop's and McGill universities. Call, "Le Chemin du Bon Dieu," *Canadian Magazine*, February 1926, 8; *The Spell of French Canada* (Boston: L.C. Page and Co, 1926) – reprinted in 1927 and 1932.

159 "Montreal," *Holiday*, 16 August 1954, 13. (His wife, Dorothy Duncan, also wrote travel accounts; her most famous was *Bluenose: A Portrait of Nova Scotia*.) Other highly respected novelists were invited to share their impressions of Montreal or other cities in the province including Hugh Garner, famous for his novel *Cabbage Town* (1950), set in Toronto's working-class district, and who wrote about Quebec City. Hugh Garner, "Quebec City: Eye to the Future," *Saturday Night* 72 (2 February 1957).

160 Leslie Roberts, "A Swell Place to Live," MM 45 (15 January 1932): 46. Leslie Roberts attended school in the Eastern Townships; later he was a prolific writer and popular radio commentator (1896–1980).

161 Morley Callaghan, "Holiday Weekend in Montreal," MM 71 (August 1958): 42.

162 Ibid.

163 Crone, "La Ville de Montréal," 35.

164 Percival, *The Lure of Montreal*, 14.

165 Ibid., 40.

166 MacLennan, "Montreal," 14.

167 Roberts, "A Swell Place to Live," 10.

168 P.O'O. (name not spelled out in full), "Montreal Becomes a Metropolis," *Saturday Night* 45 (23 August 1933): 3.

169 B.W. Riddell, "Canada by Night Offers Fun, Food Second to None," *Financial Post* 50, no. 12 (16 June 1956).

170 Crone, "La Ville de Montréal," 37.

171 "P.O'O., "Montreal Becomes a Metropolis," 3.

172 Mackenzie and Mackenzie, *Quebec in Your Car*, 11.

173 "The Quebec of the Visitors," *Saturday Night* 67 (12 July 1952): 23.

174 Callaghan, "Holiday Weekend in Montreal," 42. The curfew had been imposed in 1949, when legally "all bars were supposed to stop providing drinks at 2:00 a.m. on weekdays and midnight on Saturday." Apparently "a great many of them were in the habit of staying open until dawn, with no lack of customers." Weintraub, *City Unique*, 121.

175 Frank Hamilton, "Montreal's the Eatingest Town," MM 64 (15 July 1951): 17.

176 B.W. Riddell, "In Any Season Old Quebec Has Vacation Variety," *Financial Post* 50, no. 12 (26 May 1952).

177 Percival, *Lure of Montreal*, 17.

178 Roberts, "A Swell Place to Live," 46.

179 Ibid., 11.

180 Crone, "La Ville de Montréal," 39.

181 Ibid., 39, 38.

182 Percival, *Lure of Montreal*, 16.

183 Roberts, "A Swell Place to Live," 11, 46.

184 Percival, *Lure of Montreal*, 156, 122.

185 Crone, "La Ville de Montréal," 29.

186 For an analysis of Montrealers' vacationing habits and desires, see Dagenais, "Fuir la ville" and Aubin-Des Roches, "Retrouver la ville à la campagne."

187 "Montréal est une ville unique en son genre," *La Presse*, 15 June 1940.

188 Part of a description of Montreal in "Les Cantons de l'Est," *La Presse*, 19 June 1926, 52.

189 Morgan, "A Happy Holiday," 19.

CHAPTER SIX

1 Dubinsky, *The Second Greatest Disappointment*, 178.

2 A lecture by Robert Prévost, "Tourisme Provincial Expo 67," to Club-Vente. Publicité de Québec, 7 November 1966. Robert Prévost Fonds (hereafter RPF) (P573), File Conférences de Robert Prévost (FCRP), s1, loc 20 004-06-05-001A-01, 1997-04-003/4, BAnQM.

3 In the *Statistical Year Book*, Department of Industry and Commerce (Quebec: Queen's Printer), 543.

4 In 1959, statistics revealed that, for the first time, American tourists spent more money in Mexico than in Canada. Conference given by Robert Prévost at the annual dinner for Guides, Association des marchands de la Place de l'Hôtel-de-Ville, Québec, 16 June 1960. RPF (P573), FCRP, BAnQM, 5.

5 Numbers varied but they all confirmed this trend. In 1958 alone, for instance, Ontario hosted 4,000,000 American tourists while Quebec only attracted 600,000. See "À qui la faute? Les touristes Américains sont 6 fois moins nombreux au Québec qu'en Ontario," *Journal dimanche matin*, 24 May 1959.

6 In 1959, Leo Dolan notes, "sixty-one domestic campaigns in the United States" were launched to this end. Dawson, *Selling British Columbia*, 155.

7 He had worked for several newspapers including *Le Petit Journal* from 1934 to 1951 and *La Victoire* as well as being the director of *Canadiana Review*.

8 In effect, the first iteration of the council, created in 1933, only met on a few occasions and essentially disappeared from view.

9 The department's other branch was responsible for hunting and fishing, with a separate assistant deputy minister. Debates followed as to whether tourism deserved a department of its own. With the exception of PEI, until the mid-1960s, no other provincial government had a department dedicated exclusively to tourism.

10 "Mémoire à M. Arthur Labrie, d. sc., Sous-ministre du Tourisme, de la Chasse et de la Pêche, 19 December 1966 de Robert Prévost," RPF (P573) SI 20 004-07-07-001, BAnQM, 2.

11 Lecture given by Robert Prévost to the Rotary Club of Drummondville, 3 July 1962, RPF (P573), FCRP, BAnQM, 6.

12 Lecture given by Robert Prévost to the "Bureau touristique et économique des Laurentides" – Alpine Inn, Ste-Marguerite, 30 March 1960. RPF (P573), FCRP, BAnQM, 4. The budget devoted to publicity campaigns amounted to $230,000 in 1959–60, and increased to $367,468.70 in 1960–61, reaching $545,751.31 in 1965–66 and $713,154.75 in 1967–68. Numbers taken from annual reports. See table in Prévost, *Trois siècles de tourisme*, 326.

13 The budget for ads was $535,000 in 1960–61 and $550,000 in 1965–66. The funding increased for Expo to $690,000 in 1966–67, then to $713,000 in 1967–68, and to $754,000 in 1968–69. See Prévost, *Trois siècles de tourisme*, 214–15. As always with statistics in the tourism industry, numbers vary from source to source. In Prévost's "Mémoire, sous-ministre adjoint des Finances, Sujet: nos prévisions budgétaires au poste 6–3 (annonces), 6 février 1968," allocations were $945,000 (1960–61); $900,000 (1961–62); $850,000 (1962–63); $884,700 (1963–64); $868,000 (1965–66); $1,125,000 (1966–67); $1,290,000 (1967–68). This being said, in each case, the trend reveals a near static budget until 1966. RPF (P573), SI 20 004 07-07-001A-01, 1997 04-003/6 File "Documents II"), BAnQM, 2.

14 Prévost, *Trois siècles de tourisme*, 202–3.

15 Speaking for Lionel Bertrand, minister of the Department of Tourism, Fish and Game (DTFG), at the "Ceremony Marking the Commencement of Reconstruction of Fort Sainte-Marie," 12 August 1964. RPF (P573), FCRP, BAnQM.

16 *Annual Report–Tourist Bureau, Department of the Provincial Secretary (DPS)*, 1960–61, Tourist Bureau, Department of the Provincial Secretary, 39. E16/1990-03-011/176-2A 021 01-05-005B-01, BANQ. In 1964–65, the budget allocated for Canada increased to 25.17 per cent. *Annual Report*, 1965, Ministère du Tourisme, Chasse et Pêche, Québec, January 1966, 14.

17 *Annual Report – Department of Provincial Secretary (DPS)*, 1960–61, 42.

18 Memo to Guy Langlois, c.a. 29 December 1964, concerning the "New Initiatives, 1965–1966" by Robert Prévost. Nouvelles Initiatives "1965–1966F," RPF (P573), SI 20 004 07-07-001A-01, 1997 04-003/6 File "Documents," BAnQM.

19 Prévost, *Trois siècles de tourisme*, 203.

20 In this half-hour production, contrasts were made between Quebec cities and others throughout Canada. Conference by Robert Prévost "Tourisme interprovincial: Association canadienne du tourisme, Montréal 4 November 1963," RPF (P573), FCRP, BAnQM, 4.

21 "Congrès annuel de la Régionale des Chambres de Commerce du Lac Saint-Jean," Roberval, 20 May 1962, Résumé du travail accompli depuis la réorganisation des services touristiques. RPF (P573), FCRP, BAnQM, 2.

22 In 1962, for instance, the *Marketing* journal selected the bureau's four-colour print ads as one of the top ads produced that year.

23 Lecture given to the Congrès de l'Association canadienne de la Radio et Télévision de la langue française, Toronto, 12 September 1961. RPF (P573), FCRP, BAnQM, 4.

24 Lecture given to the "Chambre de commerce d'Arvida, 16 April 1962." RPF (P573), FCRP, BAnQM.

25 Lecture given to the Association canadienne des éducateurs de langue française at the Université de Montréal, 16 March 1963, entitled "Techniques publicitaires modernes," RPF (P573), FCRP, BAnQM, 5.

26 Quoted in Prévost, *Trois siècles de tourisme*, 103.

27 Rapport préliminaire sur le tourisme à l'honorable Lionel Bertrand, Secrétaire de la Province, Directeur de l'Office Provincial de Publicité, Robert Prévost, 12 July 1960, E4/4960-01-483/436 7C 012-04-04-00113-01, BAnQQ, 24.

28 In the foreword of the Tourist Branch brochure, *La Province de Québec*, 1963, 3–4.

29 Tourist Bureau ad, "Hospitalité Spoken Here," MM, 20 May 1961.

30 See the introduction by Lionel Bertrand, minister of the DTFG, in the brochure *The Province Where Friendliness Is a Way of Life/Province de Québec: L'aimable province*, Provincial Tourist Branch, 1964.

31 Annual report, DTFG, 1965, 14.

32 Annual Report, DTFG, 1966, 14.

33 A slogan given pride of place in the campaign of 1966. *Toronto Star*, 16 April 1966, 20.

34 Tourist Bureau ad, "Les Sports – Magnifiques!," *Toronto Star*, 25 June 1960, 16; Tourist Branch ad, "Come and Enjoy les beautés du Québec," *Toronto Star*, 16 April 1966, 20.

35 "Come and Enjoy les beautés du Quebec," 20.

36 Tourist Bureau ad, "Visit Quebec First," *Montreal Gazette*, 28 May 1960, 21.

37 Tourist Bureau ad, "Hospitalité Spoken Here," MM, 20 May 1961.

38 Tourist Bureau ad, "*La Cuisine – Magnifique!*," *Toronto Star*, 2 July 1960, 15.

39 Ibid., 15. That same year, Belgium's Sabena airlines used the slogan "Le Service Belgique … c'est magnifique!" No information could be found to suggest that Quebec promoters were inspired by this ad. See *The New Yorker*, February 1960, 45.

40 The first such salon event was held in 1913 and only sporadically afterwards, mostly due to the two world wars. Garceau, *Chronique de l'hospitalité hôtelière*, 46–54. See also Annual report, DTFG, 1966, 19.

41 These included "quenelles de brochet, civet de lièvre aux nouilles, canard à l'orange, coq-au-vin à la dijonnaise, le homard à la parisienne, homard Thermidore, coquille Saint-Jacques." Garceau, *Chronique de l'hospitalité hôtelière*, 53.

42 "Dîner-Causerie" for the Association canadienne des restaurateurs, Rond-Point du Québec, 4 October 1966, RPF (P573), FCRP, BAnQM, 3.

43 Editorial, "Une propaganda plus active fera le succès de l'industrie du tourisme," *Le Soleil*, 21 June 1960, 4.

44 Quoted in "M. Lesage promet la création au Québec d'un Ministère du Tourisme," *La Presse*, 27 May 1960, 11.

45 Lecture by Robert Prévost at the Saint-Jean-Baptiste Olivar Asselin awards ceremony to honour Miss Germaine Bernier, in Montréal, 20 February 1962, "Notre visage français, un actif rentable," RPF (P573), FCRP, BAnQM, 11.

46 Lecture by Robert Prévost to the Advertising and Sales Club of Canada, Annual Congress at the Château Frontenac, 26 May 1962, RPF (P573), FCRP, BAnQM, 9.

47 Lecture given by Robert Prévost at the "Premier festival du Caplan-Sept-Île, 31 mai 1964," RPF (P573), FCRP, BAnQM, 2.

48 Lecture given by Robert Prévost to the Quebec Chamber of Commerce, Journée d'études de 1964, Holiday Inn, 12 November 1964, RPF (P573), FCRP, BAnQM, 7, 8.

49 Lecture given by Robert Prévost, "Advertising and Sales Clubs of Canada, Congrès annuel," Château Frontenac, May 26 1962," RPF (P573), FCRP, BAnQM, 9.

50 Tourist Council Memoire, Recommendation #10, E16/1976-00-066/163; 7B014 04-01-003A-01, BAnQQ, 10.

51 Tourist Branch ad, "Prenez des vacances à la française au Québec!," *The New Yorker*, 5 May 1962. See Prévost, *Trois siècles de tourisme*, 212–13.

52 Further, peers in the tourism promotion business recognized the ad's originality, and, in 1964, it was mentioned at the International Union of Official Travel Organizations in Dublin. Annual report, DTFG, 1963/64, 12.

53 *The Province Where Friendliness Is a Way of Life/Province de Québec: L'aimable province.*

54 Lecture by Robert Prévost, "New York, Vermont Interstate Commission on the Lake Champlain Bassin, Stowe Vermont," 27 September 1962, RPF (P573), FCRP, BAnQM, 4.

55 Lecture by Robert Prévost to the Société Saint-Jean-Baptiste, 26 February 1963, RPF (P573), FCRP, BAnQM, 7.

56 This lexicon contained more than 400 sentences or expressions and was included in the Tourist Branch brochure, *Travelling in Québec: La Belle Province*, 1967 and reissued under the title "Travel Fun en Français."

57 Annual report, DTFG, 1966, "Travelling in Quebec," 19–20.

58 Lecture by Robert Prévost to the "Club Saint-Laurent, Montréal, 8 February 1961," RPF (P573), FCRP, BAnQM, 6.

59 Dubinsky, "'Everybody Likes Canadians,'" 340–1. One of a few postwar Canadian Government Tourist Bureau instructional films dedicated to Canadian audiences, including *Welcome Neighbour* (1949). Another, *Tourist Go Home*

(1959), was a satire showing viewers what not to do when encountering tourists. For a detailed analysis of the Canadian Government Tourist Bureau's efforts to increase Canadian tourist revenue through movie production see Apostle, "The Display of Tourist Nation."

60 Tourist Bureau ad, "Hospitalité Spoken Here," MM, 20 May 1961, 2.

61 Garceau, Chronique de l'hospitalité hôtelière, 110.

62 Tourist Bureau ad, The New Yorker, 7 May 1961, 39.

63 Tourist Branch ad, "Hospitalité Spoken Here," MM, May 1 1965.

64 Tourist Bureau ad, "L'atmosphère – Magnifique!," Toronto Star, 16 July 1960, 17.

65 Reported in Jocelyn Lavoie, "Le tourisme en Gaspésie," Le Soleil, 13 July 1966.

66 The bureau did not follow through with the recommendation. In fact, in contrast to many jurisdictions in Canada during the mid-1950s through to the 1970s, most notably Ontario (with Ste-Marie among the Hurons, Upper Canada Village, Fort Henry) and in the Maritimes (with Louisbourg and Kings Landing Loyalist Village), the Quebec government did not show much interest in the creation of living history sites, whether these be in the form of pioneer villages or forts. In view of the new nationalism emerging at this time, bringing to life the everyday world of the New France rural and traditional habitants would have been out of step with Québécois' new sense of national identity. More in tune with the times were projects such as the spectacular and ambitious reconstruction and restoration project of the Place Royale in Quebec City. It started in earnest in the mid-1960s, funded by the Quebec and Canadian governments. The objective was to work on the Place's built landscape. Not only was it slated to be a great draw for tourists but it also served as a symbolic reminder of the deeps roots of the French presence in North America as a powerful colonial power. Not coincidentally, it was located in an urban space – yet another signal that the French of Quebec had been more than simply old world habitants. For a detailed study on the emergence of living history museums in Canada see Gordon, Time Travel.

67 Bas Saint-Laurent et GASPÉSIE/Lower Saint-Laurent and the GASPÉ, Tourist Branch 1965, 3, 32.

68 Under "Picturesque Saint-Maurice Valley" in Inviting... La Province de Québec Vous Acceuille ...

69 Under "The Vicinity of Québec city" in Inviting... La Province de Québec Vous Acceuille ...

70 Under "Charlevoix" in Inviting ... La Province de Québec Vous Acceuille ...

71 Ville de Québec City et/and Environs, Tourist Branch, 1969.

72 Text of a caption for photos on the Gaspé in the Province Where Friendliness Is a Way of Life booklet, 32. In fact, in the Gaspé advertising brochure, a great majority of photos are of old buildings or of various landscapes, mostly devoid of local inhabitants. Bas Saint-Laurent et GASPÉSIE.

73 Province Where Friendliness Is a Way of Life. In the 1960s, visitors could still find a booklet, Sanctuaires de la Province de Québec/Shrines de la Province de Québec, cordoning off the religious from the secular, everyday life, focusing once again on the built landscape.

74 *Visite au/A Visit to the Saguenay & Tour du/A Tour around Lac St-Jean*, 15. The museum had clearly fallen on hard times before then as revealed in a letter written by Damasse Potvin of the Bibliothèque du Parlement du Québec to Paul Gouin in 1952. He wrote speaking of the work of the Société des amis de Maria Chapdelaine which, once it had received "generous funding" to rent the premises, ended up with "the old furniture from Louis Hémon's room" and "an old spinning wheel" where "during a few years an old maid [Éva Bouchard] [had] suffered from the lovely and puerile habit of passing herself for Maria Chapdelaine in person." Letter by Damasse Potvin to Paul Gouin, 20 May 1952, PGF (P190), 1983-03-038/63, BANQM.

75 "See Québec Say – Magnifique! L'atmosphère – Magnifique!," *Toronto Star*, 16 July 1960, 17.

76 Section on Charlevoix in *Inviting ... La Province de Québec Vous Acceuille ...*

77 "Rapport préliminaire sur le tourisme à l'honorable Lionel Bertrand," 24.

78 From the introduction to the guidebook, *The Province Where Friendliness Is a Way of Life*, DTFG, 1964.

79 *Le Sud du Québec/Southern Québec*, Tourist Branch, 7.

80 From the introduction to the guide *Ville de Québec City et/and Environs*, published by the Direction générale du tourisme, Publicity Service, DTFG, publication date unknown, likely around 1969.

81 "Sur la route des pionniers/Heritage Highways," a joint publication of the Quebec Department of Tourism, Fishing and Game and the Province of Ontario, Daniel Johnson & John Robarts, 1968.

82 From the introduction to the guide *Ville de Québec City et/and Environs*.

83 From the foreword to the guide *La Province de Québec*, 3.

84 Conferring on the event yet more prestige was its First Category status – the third such exhibit in the world and the first in North America. This meant that it should first and foremost be educational, informative, and entertaining rather than a showcase to market products. It also required a unifying theme. See http://www.canadienencyclopedia.ca/en/article/expo-67.

85 Yves Jasmin, *La petite histoire d'Expo 67*, 16.

86 Foreword by Gilles Tremblay, Business Development Bureau, in "Estimated Number of Europeans Visitors to Expo 67, Operations Departments, Expo 67, December 1964," LAC, RG71, arc 71/137/12, 2–3.

87 Eventually this increased involvement exacerbated the already fraught Quebec–federal government relations of the time. In previous years, the federal government had remained relatively hands off, interfering very little in the way provinces chose to promote themselves. This changed in 1971 as the Canadian government undertook, on its own initiative, a televised publicity campaign, without consultation – much to the dismay of the Quebec government. For more on these debates, see Prévost, *Trois siècles de tourisme*, 327–30.

88 "This year, visitez le Québec, Canada. Il est unique." Canadian Government Travel Bureau ad, NYT, 16 April 1967, 19.

89 Report, *The Gazette*, 28 April 1967.

90 *Le Soleil*, 9 May 1967.

91 *Montreal Gazette*, 20 July 1967, 4.

92 Annual report, DTFG, 1963–64, 18. On one rare occasion when these reports cited a specific example, it is possible to confirm that government tourist promoters did indeed provide very detailed accounts. In 1960–61, for instance, "a picture story of 11 pages, with 5 in four colors, [was] published on Quebec City in the rotogravure section of the *Los Angeles Times*, at the end of January 1961." Annual report, DPS, 1960–61, Tourist Bureau, Department of the Provincial Secretary, "Publicity and Public Relations," 56.

93 Annual report, DTFG, 1965, 22

94 Annual report, DTFG, 1963–64, 18.

95 Ibid., 18.

96 Annual report, DPS, 1960–61, 56.

97 Annual report, DTFG, 1966, 22–3. In some cases, these annual reports include the names of travel writers, journalists, and filmmakers escorted on tours of the province.

98 Lecture by Robert Prévost describing the multiple attractions of the province at a travel forum (Delaware), RPF (P573), FCRP, BAnQM, 6.

99 Annual report, DTFG, 1963–64, 18.

100 Annual report, DTFG, 1960–61, 56.

101 Annual report, DTFG, 1963–64, 18. Unfortunately, no records of their reports show up in the archival sources consulted.

102 Documents confirm that officials at the Department of Industry and Commerce regularly made such requests to government tourist promoters. See E6, loc 2A 021 01-05-005B-01, 1990-03-011/176, BAnQQ.

103 Excerpts of the *Rapport sur les Communications du Gouvernement du Québec*, vol I, chapter "La Situation des Ministères," written by Inter-Medi Inc., MM. Jean Loiselle and Paul Gros-D'Aillon, 1770, rue Ducharme, Outremont, P.Q., (Undated), RPF (P573), SI 20 004 07-07-001A-01/6, BAnQM.

104 Prévost, *Trois siècles de tourisme*, 205.

105 Of the six photographs on the cover of *L'aimable & Lovable Province de Québec* booklet, four were of an easily recognizable "old Quebec": a wayside cross, woman at a bake oven, haying with horses, an old stone house. Inside the booklet, out of a total thirty-six photos, twenty-nine are of scenery, the majority of which included manors, churches, or monuments.

106 Since none of the names of travel writers listed in the annual reports correspond to writers I have identified in my research, it suggests that those I do quote, at the very least, did not take advantage of the bureau's hosting services.

107 "The Little Town of Saintly Miracles," MM, May 1968, 81, 5, 26–7.

108 Letter addressed to M. Gérald Bossé, directeur général du tourisme, to the attention of Robert Prévost, assistant deputy minister, Department of Tourism, Fish, and Game, from Gilles Charron, deputy minister of Industry and Commerce, 6 June 1968, RPF (P573), BAnQM.

109 Letter by Robert Prévost responding to Gilles Charron concerning the May 1968 issue of *Maclean's*, undated but likely in June 1968. RPF (P573), BAnQM.

110 Aquin, *Prochain épisode*. It was translated as *Next Episode* by Penny Williams.

111 Blais, *Une saison dans la vie d'Emmanuel*. It was translated as *A Season in the Life of Emmanuel* by Derek Coltman.

112 The expression "Quiet Revolution" was, in fact, coined by a Toronto *Globe and Mail* journalist – another type of outside observer.

113 A scan of the titles of newspaper articles, books, and other publications of the period and themes of conferences dedicated to current affairs in Quebec confirm the attention given to the province, and, although English Canadian travel writers, at this time, had long moved on from school, textbooks by the early 1960s were alerting young readers that, after the Second World War, "the province was no longer the simple rural community that some of its romantics loved to picture. It was now highly industrialized … [with t]wo thirds of its people liv[ing] in cities and towns." McInnis, *The North American Nations*, 381.

114 Hugh MacLennan, "French Canada: Portrait of a Proud People," *Holiday* (June 1960): 163, 164.

115 Robert Carson, "The French Touch: Quebec," *Holiday* 35 (April 1964): 72.

116 "Motor Tour of Old Quebec, A Holiday to Remember," *Toronto Star*, 22 July 1961, 12. And as an illustration of writers borrowing from one another or simply "cutting and pasting" observations that had been printed earlier, the following year, another travel account notes, "in the Gaspé region especially, life hasn't changed much since Jacques Cartier planted the fleur-de-lis [*sic*] to proclaim it French." "Were You Ever in Quebec?," *Toronto Star*, 7 July 1962, 14.

117 John Maclure, "Holiday Trails in Canada: The Gaspé," MM 78 (24 July 1965): 19.

118 Ken Lefolii, "The Lavish and Lovely Laurentians," MM 73 (2 January 1960): 13.

119 John Keats, "The St Lawrence," *Holiday* (August 1962): 38.

120 Jacques Coulon, "'A World Apart,'" NYT, 21 June 1963, sect 10, 19.

121 Keats, "The St Lawrence," 102.

122 Charles Lazarus, "Day Excursions to the Laurentians," NYT, 8 May 1960, sect 12, 29.

123 Carson, "The French Touch," 99.

124 Keats, "The St Lawrence," 102.

125 Carson, "The French Touch," 99.

126 Maclure, "Holiday Trails," 19.

127 He singled out the big snow carnival in Ste-Agathe and others when they "bring out old farm sleighs and bell-hung harnesses, for the horses, multicolored *ceintures fléchées* … red tuques and gay old songs." Lefolii, "The Lavish and Lovely Laurentians," 13.

128 Keats, "The St Lawrence," 102.

129 Charles Lazarus, "Canadian Artisans Carve Themselves a Niche," NYT, 9 June 1963, sect 10, 49. See also Maclure, "Holiday Trails," 19.

130 Shirley Sloane and Bob Sloane, "River Resorts Out of History," *Montreal Gazette*, 28 May 1966.

131 Benedict Thielen, "Ring around the Gaspé," *Holiday* 35 (April 1964): 31.

132 Charles Koelher and Margaret Koelher, "Canada Carefree," 60.

133 The speedy decline of the rural inhabitants is revealed more starkly considering that "although the population of Quebec as a whole increased by more that 20 per cent between 1941 and 1951 and again between 1951 and 1961, the farm population fell by more than 5 per cent between 1941 and 1951 and then tumbled dramatically by 24 per cent in the second half of the 1950s." Linteau et al., *Histoire du Québec contemporain*, 238.

134 In 1961, there were sixty-one and ten were government run. In 1964, these increased to 312. Prévost, *Trois siècles de tourisme*, 185, 222. Furthermore, opportunities to "rough it" were considerably diminished. Whereas up to the early 1950s only 20 per cent of hotel rooms outside large centres had washrooms, by 1959, the number had climbed to 71 per cent. Garceau, *Chronique de l'hospitalite hôtelière*, 110.

135 "Le Bas du Fleuve et la Gaspésie, où le present et le passé se côtoient," *Le Soleil*, 3 June 1967, 9.

136 "Le Bas du Fleuve et la Gaspésie … paradis du touriste!" *Le Soleil*, 18 June 1966, 10.

137 "La tournée du Bas du Fleuve et de la Gaspésie: Un voyage à répéter périodiquement," *Le Soleil*, 10 May 1960, 4.

138 "Le Bas du Fleuve," *Le Soleil*, 4 June 1966, 40.

139 All taking place in 1966. "Le Bas du Fleuve et la Gaspésie … paradis du touriste!," *Le Soleil*, 18 June 1966, 10.

140 Marie Parise and Jean-Guy Lauzon, *Gaspésie: Textes-Photos, Guide touristique* (Montreal: Les Éditions 0.25, 1966). One hundred thousand issues were printed, although, this publication was much more than a guide, as it also included a substantial sociological overview of the region, which, above all, emphasized how poor and economically underdeveloped it was. Thus, a fisherman of yesteryear who "appeared to live a captivating life … carries with him the worries over those he has left behind, and does not always enjoy the picturesque side of his existence."

141 "Les touristes peuvent visiter une mine d'amiante dans la région de Thetford," *Le Soleil*, 13 July 1966, 15.

142 "Asbestos cherche à s'attirer le touriste," *La Presse*, 4 May 1960, 27.

143 "La tournée du Bas du Fleuve et de la Gaspésie: Un voyage à répéter périodiquement," *Le Soleil*, 10 May 1960, 4.

CHAPTER SEVEN

1 Reported in "Le Frère Untel l'a dit: Montréal n'a pas de visage français," *La Patrie*, week of 20 to 26 August 1964. He was a Marist priest brought to fame after the publication of *Les insolences du Frère Untel* in 1960, which decried the use of *joual* French and the quality of public education in the province.

2 Alfred Ayotte, "Plus le Québec sera français …," *La Presse*, 19 January 1961. He was an editorialist at *La Presse* and the coauthor of a biography of famed novelist Louis Hémon (published posthumously), with Victor Tremblay, *L'aventure Louis Hémon* (Montréal: Collections vies canadiennes, Éditions Fides, 1974).

3 Roger Champoux, "Montréal: Une ville où l'on passe," *La Presse*, 18 April 1961.

4 Ayotte, "Plus le Québec sera français ..." In the words of yet another *La Presse* journalist, "we must live up to our role. Quebec must appear as French in reality as it does on publicity billboards." Part of a series of articles published by Claude Gendron, all titled "Montréal, ville fermée?," *La Presse*, 15, 16, and 17 April 1961.

5 By 1961 the city had only two kiosks in operation.

6 "Du Boulot pour l'Office municipal de tourisme," *Le Nouveau Journal*, 27 January 1962.

7 All views expressed by Jacques Delisle of *La Presse*, Paul Le Duc of *The Montreal Star*, and in *La Patrie du Dimanche*, 10 September 1961.

8 Champoux, "Montréal: Une ville où l'on passe."

9 Paul Coucke, "Impression sur la ville de Montréal, Montréal doit multiplier ses attraits," *Journal de Montréal*, 8 April 1965.

10 Martin Drouin, of the Département d'études urbaines et touristiques at the Université du Québec à Montréal, points out that the existing museums at the time included "le Musée des beaux-arts de Montréal (1860), le musée du Château de Ramezay (1895), le musée McCord (1921)" and they "exposed their collections side by side other small institutions." Drouin, "Le tourisme dans le Vieux-Montréal," 94.

11 Georges Langlois, "La guerre des Agences de tourisme," *Le Nouveau Journal*, 21 March 1962. A document found in the Paul Gouin fonds reveals the level of frustration some felt towards the MTCB's unilingual publicity. Attached to three MTCB brochures is a note addressed to Paul Gouin: "You will notice by these brochures all the solicitude for the French language of the Montreal Tourist and Convention Bureau – an organization hired by the city." He went further, "Could something be done, perhaps by the mayor [?]" Illegible signature, undated although accompanying documents in the file are otherwise dated 1950–55. File title Tourisme-Document' in PGF (P190) 1983 6036038/53 loc 002 0 004 17 07 04 B01.

12 Champoux, "Montréal: Une ville où l'on passe."

13 "La métropole vue par une agence privée de publicité ...," *La Presse*, 21 March 1962.

14 "Montréal 2e ville française du monde: Il est bon que la chose se sache," *Montréal-Matin*, 14 June 1961.

15 Lysianne Gagnon, "Montréal vue avec les yeux de John Smith des États-Unis," *La Presse*, 28 July 1962.

16 "A qui la faute? Les touristes Américains sont 6 fois moins nombreux au Québec qu'en Ontario," *Montréal-Matin*, 24 May 1959.

17 "Mémoire sur le Tourisme Municipal de la Chambre de Commerce du district de Montréal," Avril 1962 à la ville de Montréal, PGF (P190), 1983-0 6038/15 002 0 004 18 04 002 B01, BAnQM.

18 Highlights of the 1959 brief in "Votre comité de Tourisme de la Chambre de Commerce de Montréal" published in its magazine *Commerce Montréal*, 14 and 17 April 1959, 38. City of Montreal Archives (CMA), Reel #106, 17.121.

19 "Aux Autorités Municipales de la Cité de Montréal, l'opinion respectueuse de la Chambre de Commerce du District de Montréal concernant le tourisme à Montréal," 25–26 April 1959, 3. A second brief was produced in 1962, "Mémoire sur le Tourisme Municipal de la Chambre de Commerce du District de Montréal," April 1962, PGF (P190), E/16 1983-03-03815 0020004 18 04002B-01BAnQM.

20 This fact irked him all the more considering that the city was subsidizing the MTCB to the tune of $25,000. Jean Rivest, "Paris de l'Amérique? Non, Montréal n'a pas d'attrait pour les touristes," La Presse, 20 April 1961.

21 "Votre comité de Tourisme," 1, 121.

22 Ibid.

23 Letter by J.G. Fisher, president, Office Montréalais du Tourisme et des Congrès, to Honorable Sarto Fournier, mayor of Montreal, the chairman and members of the executive council, members of the City Council of Montreal, 25 September 1958.

24 "Tourism Department Opposed," The Gazette, 4 October 1958.

25 Document "untitled," CMA.

26 OMIET was divided in two, leading to the creation of l'Office d'initiative économique and MMTB.

27 Don Newman, Montreal Star, 19 February 1962.

28 For a fuller picture of Jean Drapeau's internationalizing ambitions see Bastien, "Les relations internationales de Montréal depuis 1945."

29 Quoted in "Air France signale la qualité humaniste que le Canada a voulu donner à l'Expo 67," La Presse, 20 June 1966, 12. Indicative of how much Drapeau linked Montreal's prestige with Expo 67, he hoped to be appointed the exhibition's general commissioner. He did not consider the two roles as incompatible. However, the Diefenbaker government saw things differently. Jasmin, La Petite Histoire d'Expo 67, 20.

30 Letter dated 12 March 1964 by Jean Drapeau to Mr N.R. Crump, president, CPR, 12 February 1964, Montreal City Archives (MCA), "Tourisme," Reel #106.

31 Funding was municipal along with private sector donations and subsidies by the Department of Industry and Commerce. The free publication of roughly thirty to forty pages, Montreal '64, was retitled each year to Montreal '65, and so on. The last, Montreal '67, was issued in the fall of that year. Circulation in 1964 was 50,000 per month, sent to embassies, universities, corporations, and all cities with populations of 25,000 and over. See "Montreal to Sound Off With Its Own Magazine," Montreal Star, 14 February 1964.

32 Robert Mackenzie, "City Plans Its Own Monthly Magazine," The Gazette, 14 February 1964.

33 Letter by Jean Drapeau to Mr N.R. Crump.

34 Message by Jean Drapeau, Montréal '64, vol. 1, 1 May 1964.

35 Message by Jean. Drapeau, Montréal '66, vol. 3, 5 May 1966.

36 Gordon Page, "Lesage Pledges Quebec to join City Show Off True French Canada at Expo," Montreal Gazette, 4 June 1966, 1. Furthermore, Yves Jasmin, the director of public relations, information and publicity of Expo 67, recalled

that the magazine "became our spokesperson to the governing classes across the world … and was a precious support in all the countries that we approached." LAC RG71, arc71/42/1.

37 Message by Jean Drapeau, *Montreal*, MMTB brochure, MCA, real #106, 10.72.

38 Message by Jean Drapeau, *Montréal '64*, vol. 1, 1 May 1964, 3.

39 Message by Jean Drapeau, "La ville de l'avenir," *Montréal '65*, vol. 2, 11 November 1965.

40 Oswald Mamo, "Montréal doit être un centre d'attraction," *La Presse*, 5 March 1965.

41 Jean de Guise,"Potential Same as New York," *The Gazette*, 31 March 1965.

42 *Montreal '65*, vol. 2, 9 September 1965.

43 Jean Drapeau, *Montréal '67*, vol. 4, 9 September 1967.

44 *Montréal '64*, vol. 1, 1 May 1964, 26.

45 "Montréal," MMTB brochure published by and for the City of Montreal, date unknown (but before Expo 67).

46 Message by Jean Drapeau, "Meeting Place of all Peoples,' *Montréal '64*, vol. 1, 6 October 1964. This was a clear case of catching up with reality. The city's immigrant population had increased considerably over the years notably during the post–Second World War period. It totalled 12 per cent in 1951 and rose to 17 per cent in 1961. Linteau, *Histoire de Montréal*, 462.

47 Quoted from Drouin,"Le tourisme dans le Vieux-Montréal," 96. Quoted from Jean Drapeau, "Préface" in Clayton Gray, *Montréal qui disparaît* (Montréal: Éditions du Jour, 1964), v.

48 An inventory published by the city's Service d'urbanisme revealed that only eighteen historic houses stood in the old quarter. Drouin, "Le tourisme dans le Vieux-Montréal," 94. And in reality, many buildings dated back to the nineteenth century.

49 Concerns about the area were also expressed by the CCDM. A spokesperson for the organization warned that, "by destroying without any shame our historic buildings, we are taking away from our city one of its best attractions." "Communiqué de presse de la Chambre de Commerce de Montréal dans le cadre de la semaine d'éducation intitulé 'De l'urgence d'embellir Montréal." PGF (P190), 1983 03 038/15 0020004 18 04 002 BOI, BANQM.

50 This, once again, put Paul Gouin at the centre of this revitalization as he had been appointed president of the commission in 1955 and stayed at its helm until 1965.

51 See "Le soir, dans Montréal," *Montréal '64*, vol. 1, 1 May 1964, 26.

52 Quoted in Page, "Lesage Pledges Quebec to Join City Show Off True French Canada at Expo," 1.

53 Jean de Guise, "Potential Same as New York," *The Gazette*, 31 March 1965.

54 Quoted in "'Montréal doit être un centre d'attraction,'– M. Drapeau," *La Presse*, 31 March 1965.

55 "Montréal doit être un centre d'attraction," *La Presse*, 31 March 1965.

56 Presentation by Jean Drapeau at the opening of the Semaine d'éducation touristique. Jean de Guise, "Potential Same as New York." Of the money spent by

Americans in Canada in 1960, 16.9 per cent of it was spent in Quebec and 55.6 per cent in Ontario. "Chambre de commerce du District de Montréal. Mémoire à l'Office fédéral du Tourisme, Mars 1962," PGF (P190).

57 *Montreal '64*, vol. 1, 2 June 1964, 17.

58 *Montréal '64*, vol. 1, 1 May 1964, 26.

59 Lucien Bergeron, "Les atouts du tourisme, hier, aujourd'hui," *Le Devoir*, 19 June 1965.

60 Quoted in Bob Hayes, "Great Tourist Year Forecast," *The Gazette*, 5 December 1996.

61 John Yorston, "Expo Keeps City Tourist Office Busy," *Montreal Star*, 28 December 1966.

62 "Des efforts inouïs seront nécessaires d'ici l'Expo 67," *La Presse*, 12 April 1966.

63 Also included were Prévost and Gérard Delage, president of the Quebec Tourist Council and legal advisor to the Quebec Hotel Association. Collaboration between all levels of governments was seen as key. In that spirit, Bergeron offered members of the committee the MMTB's contact list of 400 travel agents. "Procès-verbal de la troisième réunion du comité consultatif en matières d'information et de promotion, tenue le 24 juillet 1963" à Montréal. LAC RG 69, vol. 130, arc 71/130/3, 5.

64 They were Jacques Delisle, municipal chronicler at *La Presse* (chief of information), and Paul LeDuc of the *Montreal Star* (liaison officer).

65 Jean-Claude Germain, "Il faut classer nos restaurants," *Le Petit Journal*, 23 January 1963.

66 Yorston, "Expo Keeps City Tourist Office Busy."

67 Ninth radio talk show at CKAC for the year 1964, Bergeron, Office municipal du tourisme, 3, MCA, Reel #106, 16.23. (Starting in the late 1950s, every Monday at this radio station, the journalist Claude Bourgeois invited a City of Montreal civil servant to speak of Montreal.)

68 "Mémoire sur le Tourisme Municipal de la Chambre de Commerce du district de Montréal," April 1962.

69 Ibid.

70 Fabienne Julien, "Une tâche difficile pour Mme Archambault: Comment prouve-t-on que Montréal n'est pas une ville américaine?" *Photo-Journal*, 7–14 September 1963.

71 It also published a guide targeted at taxi drivers providing information they should know about the city and pass on to their tourist passengers.

72 "Tourists' Main Worry – Lodgings in Montreal," *Montreal Star*, 21 December 1962. Only 5.8 per cent from British Columbia and 5.3 per cent from Nova Scotia. "Année de progrès au point de vue touristique pour Montréal," *La Presse*, 29 December 1962.

73 Maurice Roy, "A Montréal ville de tourisme international: Trois visiteurs sur 20 ne sont pas Américains," *Le Petit Journal*, week of 15 August 1965.

74 Prévost to Air Canada bureau chiefs, "[m]any regulations … derived from this Act since then, such as the licensing and inspection of camping grounds in 1964

... the control by our Branch of all tourist information counters ... the posting of menus with rates at the door of each dining room of the hotel or of each restaurant." Robert Prévost, "Conférence. Sujet: séjour à Québec des chefs de bureau de la société Air Canada. Château Frontenac – le 6 octobre 1967." RPF (P573), Conférences de Robert Prévost, BAnQM.

75 "'Des efforts inouïs seront nécessaires d'ici Expo' – le directeur de l'Office du tourisme," *La Presse*, 12 March 1966. At the tourist education week in 1965, CCDM officials expressed similar views, noting that in anticipation of 1967, Montrealers needed to be particularly welcoming, acknowledging that "we are not used to this [new] clientele." Yves Margraff, "La Chambre de commerce souhaite faire des Montréalais des hôtes acceuillants," *Le Devoir*, 30 March 1965.

76 "'Il faut créer auprès de nos visiteurs une image juste de tous nos concitoyens' – le maire Jean Drapeau," *La Presse*, 31 March 1966.

77 "'Le FLQ n'a pas nui au tourisme à Montréal' – M. Lucien Bergeron," *La Presse*, 8 July 1963.

78 Renaude Lapointe, "Les sourires suffiront-ils?," *La Presse*, 1965.

79 He added that some had likely delayed their trip to come to Montreal during Expo 67 instead. Paul Coucke, "Les statistiques ont le dos large," *Journal de Montréal*, 21 August 1965.

80 Entrefilet, *Journal de Montréal*, 12 August 1965.

81 "Questions frequently asked about Expo 67," *Expo Journal* 1 2, 6, July 1965, LAC RG 171, 71/16/8. *Expo Journal* was a magazine published by the organizers of Expo 67 every three months in 1964, every month in 1965–66.

82 "M. René Lévesque: Le FLQ risque de compromettre le tourisme au cours de l'été," *La Presse*, 25 April 1963.

83 "Ministère du TCP, Direction générale du tourisme: Nouvelles directives pour 1965–1966."

84 Interview with Lucien Bergeron. "La publicité touristique de Montréal: Pourquoi des agences privées?" *Le Nouveau Journal*, 30 March 1962.

85 Lucien Bergeron quoted in Bill Bantay, "'Montreal Not French City, Only Publicity Stunt' – Tourist Chief," *The Gazette*, 20 March 1962.

86 Apparently, a few sentences of this publicity were removed from a French company's tourist publication, which had submitted its text to MTCB. "Aux touristes: Présenter une image fidèle de Montréal," *La Presse*, 21 March 1962.

87 "City Myths Dispelled by Tourist Director," *Montreal Star*, 20 March 1962.

88 Lucien Bergeron, "Les atouts du tourisme, hier, aujourd'hui," *Le Devoir*, 19 June 1965.

89 An annual tour had been organized by the Société historique de Montréal on 17 May (birth date of Paul Chomeday, Montreal's founder) starting in 1917. See Drouin, "Le tourisme dans le Vieux-Montréal," 94–7.

90 The journalist is reporting back comments made by Lucien Bergeron at a meeting of the Mt St-Louis alumni Association. "Aux touristes 'Présenter une image fidèle de Montréal,'" *La Presse*, 21 March 1962.

91 "Aux touristes," *La Presse*, 1962.

92 MMTB forty-five-page guidebook. Text by Charles Roy and Lucien Bergeron, undated, PGF (P190), 1983-03-038/53, 1.

93 Keith Cronshaw, "Tourist Today: A Different Breed Finds Reporter Keith Cronshaw," *The Gazette*, 22 May 1965.

94 Title of an article reporting more specific challenges by Archambault who was the Coordinatrice des événements spéciaux au tourisme municipal since 1962. Julien, "Une tâche difficile pour Mme Archambault," *Photo Journal*, 7–14 September 1963.

95 "La vocation touristique de Montréal," talk given by Lucien Bergeron, Office d'initiative économique et touristique, 'Au quart d'heure Concordia,' au Post CKAC, lundi le 24 mars 1958 à 10.30 p.m., CMA, #106, #16.5.

96 "Chez vous, tout est Américain sauf … les habitants," *La Patrie*, week of 24 June 1966.

97 Quoted in Bantay, "'Montreal Not French City.'"

98 Taken from a publicity insert reproduced in *La Presse*, 4 June 1962.

99 "Tourist Time … Not Like It Used to Be: But Going Up Up Up," *The Gazette*, 22 May 1965.

100 Maurice Roy, "Que faire la nuit dans la métropole du Canada?," *Le Petit Journal*, week of 17 April 1966.

101 Bantay, "'Montreal Not French City'"

102 *Montréal*, Montreal Municipal Tourist Bureau guidebook, undated, 37.

103 Bantay, "'Montreal Not French City.'"

104 Bergeron, "Les atouts du tourisme, hier, aujourd'hui." Although references continued to be printed calling Montreal the "second largest French city in the world."

105 It should be noted that this exchange also suggests another level of identity politics involving the city's multiethnic makeup, notably the Jews of Montreal. But I found no other evidence that promoters or commentators saw their presence as an issue worthy of concern. "Le Frère Untel l'a dit: Montréal n'a pas de visage français," *La Patrie*, 20–26 April 1964.

106 Charles Lazarus, "A 'New' Montreal," NYT, 5 May 1963, sect 10, 33.

107 Harry E. Mercer, "Montreal Is Bursting at the Seams," *Saturday Night* 75 (23 January 1960): 12.

108 Charles Lynch, "Begins to Resemble New York City. Exciting Montreal Enjoys Building Surge," *The Province*, 26 October 1963.

109 Charles Lazarus in "A 'New' Montreal," NYT, 23 April 1967, sect 10, 16.

110 The number of Montreal's architectural landmarks built at this time is remarkable. They included – other than Place Ville-Marie – Place des Arts, the Bourse, Square Victoria, the opening of the Champlain bridge, and construction of the metro. For a detailed analysis of Montreal's distinct architectural modernization see Lortie, *Les années 60 Montréal voit grand*.

111 No author, "The Idler's Guide to Montreal," MM 79 (3 December 1966): 23.

112 "The New Montreal," *Toronto Daily Star*, 27 October 1962.

113 Percival, *The Lure of Montreal*, 27.

114 "Montreal: The Good Life," *Holiday* 35 (April 1964): 158.
115 Michael Herr, "Expo 67," *Holiday* (April 1967): 74.
116 Jay Walz, "A 'Sin City' No More," NYT, 19 April 1967, 16.
117 "Montreal: The Good Life," 158.
118 Ian Adams, "The Feel of the Place," MM 79 (3 December 1966): 13.
119 Frank Hamilton, "Montreal's the Eatingest Town," MM 64 (15 July 1951): 17.
120 "Montreal: The Good Life," 158.
121 Hal Burton, "Christmas in Montreal," *Holiday*, 26 December 1959, 54.
122 Carson, "The French Touch," 72.
123 Hugh MacLennan, "French Canada: Portrait of a Proud People," *Holiday* (June 1960): 163.
124 Ibid., 162.
125 Carson, "The French Touch," 94.
126 Adams, "The Feel of the Place," 10.
127 Herr, "Expo 67," 74, 78.
128 Adams, "The Feel of the Place," 10.
129 Hollier, *Montréal*, 51.
130 *Le Canada français, réalité vivante*. This point was an overstatement as the themes showcasing tradition had given way to more modern realities since the 1940s. By the 1960s however, the new nationalism putting Quebec and its distinctive linguistic identity forward was more clearly on display.
131 Percival, *The Lure of Montreal*, 104.
132 Lynch, "Begins to Resemble New York City."
133 V.S. Pritchett, "Across the Vast Land," *Holiday* 35 (April 1964): 185.
134 Herr, "Expo 67," 82.
135 Pritchett, "Across the Vast Land," 185.
136 Ian Adams, "Enjoying Montreal without Actually Speaking French," MM 79 (3 December 1966).
137 Lynch, "Begins to Resemble New York City."
138 Carson, "The French Touch," 72–3.
139 "For a Different Holiday Try Quebec," *Toronto Star*, 22 June 1963, 14.
140 Herr, "Expo 67," 82.

EPILOGUE

1 Some go so far as to claim that it served as an "identity catharsis," that led to the "emergence of a new Quebec identity." Currien, "L'identité nationale exposée," 10.
2 Linteau, *Histoire de Montréal*, 539.
3 Talk given by Robert Prévost, "Sujet: séjour à Québec des chefs de bureau de la société Air Canada. Château Frontenac – le 16 octobre 1967." RPF (P573), FCRP, BAnQM, 6.
4 *Montreal Star*, 11 December 1967. The Office National de la Statistique revealed a "$427,000,000 surplus in the international balance of payment in terms of

travel [which set] a record." "Le tourisme a rapporté $1,300,000,000 au Canada en 1967, année de l'Expo," *La Presse*, 20 April 1968.

5 Jasmin, *La Petite Histoire d'Expo 67*, 32. The following year Quebec and Montreal experienced a reduction in tourist traffic, but according to authorities, this could easily be explained by the fact that tourists who had come to Quebec and Montreal in 67 would not likely return the following year.

6 "How Expo 67 Helped and Hurt Tourism," MM, October 1967.

7 Annual report, 1968, DTFG, 7.

8 Ibid.

9 This number was provided by the Organization for Economic Development on 7 October. "1967 tourism up 55 percent," *The Gazette*, 8 October 1968.

10 Annual report, 1968, DTFG, 7.

11 Between 120,000 and 130,000 of them came to Quebec that year. André Boily, "L'Expo a ouvert au Québec la porte du tourisme international," *La Presse*, 7 November 1970. By 1970, of the 4 million tourists who visited Montreal, 60 per cent were American, 30 per cent came from Canada, and 10 per cent came from other foreign destinations. Hilda Kearns, "City Tourists Continue Their Love Affair," *The Montreal Star*, 5 August 1970.

12 Over the course of the decade, Quebec politicians would push for the right to develop independent state-to-state foreign relations in areas of provincial jurisdiction – in line with the so-called Paul Gérin-Lajoie doctrine.

13 Although they did come to appreciate the advantages of spreading their promotional wings more widely, as in 1972 the government appointed two other Quebec commissioners to serve in Chicago and Boston. "Lettre à M. P.-A. Brown, sous-ministre du MTFG de Robert Prévost (sous-ministre adjoint), 16 octobre 1970 sujet: les locaux destinés au tourisme à Paris." RPF (P573) SI, 20-004-7-7-001A-01, 1997-04-003/6 Doc II.

14 "Le tourisme se porte bien dans les grandes villes," *La Patrie*, 16 August 1970.

15 Claude Masson, "Montréal confirme son internationalisme," *La Presse*, 13 May 1970.

16 Quoted in Kearns, "City Tourists Continue Their Love Affair."

17 "Le tourisme se porte bien dans les grandes villes."

18 "City Told to Push French Image," *The Montreal Star*, 21 March 1969.

19 One need only think of the emergence of the McGill français movement, the demonstrations over schooling in the St-Léonard district. For more on language debates in Montreal see Linteau, *Histoire de Montréal*, 475–81, and Warren, "L'Opération McGill français."

20 "City Told to Push French Image."

21 "Québec, oui m'sieur (Yessir)," DTFG, 1971, 14.

22 *Québec, la Belle Province*, guidebook published by the DTFG, 1968.

23 "Québec, oui m'sieur (Yessir)," 12.

BIBLIOGRAPHY

ARCHIVAL COLLECTIONS

Bibliothèque et Archives nationales du Québec

P190 – Paul Gouin fonds.
P573 – Robert Prévost fonds.
E4 – Tourist Bureau, Department of the Provincial Secretary fonds.
E6 – Ministère de la Culture fonds.
E16 – Ministère de l'Industrie et du Commerce/Office du tourisme de la province de Québec fonds.
P405 – Office des Congrès et du Tourisme du Grand Montréal/Montreal Tourist and Convention Bureau fonds.

Archives de la Ville de Montréal

VM131 – Office municipal du tourisme Tourisme Montréal fonds.
VM146 – Office d'initiative économique et touristique fonds.

Archives of American Art

Daniel Putnam Brinley and Kathrine Sanger Brinley papers, 1879–1984.
http://www.aaa.si.edu/collections/daniel-putman-brinley-and-katherine-sanger-brinley-papers-6830/more.

NEWSPAPERS

(April to July: 1920, 1926, 1930, 1936, 1940, 1946, 1950, 1956, 1960, 1966)
The Halifax Chronicle and *Halifax Herald*
The Halifax Chronicle-Herald
The Montreal Gazette
The New York Times
La Presse
Le Soleil
The Toronto Star
The Vancouver Sun

PERIODICALS AND MAGAZINES

Canadian Geographical Journal (1923–70)
The Financial Post (1950–61)
Holiday (1950–69)
L'Hôtellerie (1926–31)
L'Hôtellerie/The Hostelry (1931–35)
Literary Digest (1920–35)
Maclean's (1919–70)
Le Magasine Macleans (1961–70)
Montreal (1964–68)
Saturday Evening Post (1939–56)
Saturday Night (1918–60)
Travel (1931–70)

GOVERNMENT DOCUMENTS
Government of Quebec

Annual reports (1923–35). Roads Department.
Annual report (1960–61). Department of the Provincial Secretary, Tourist Bureau.
Annual reports (1962–68). Department of Tourism, Fish and Game, Provincial Tourist Branch.

Government of Canada

Government of Canada. *Report of Proceedings, Dominion Provincial Tourist Conference.* Ottawa: King's Printer, 1947–51.
Government of Canada. *Report of Proceedings, Federal–Provincial Tourist Conference.* Ottawa: King's Printer, 1952–59.
The Senate of Canada. *Report and Proceedings of the Special Committee on Tourist Traffic.* Ottawa: King's Printer, 1934.
The Senate of Canada. *Report of the Standing Committee on Tourist Traffic.* Ottawa: King's Printer, 1946–59.

TOURISM PROMOTION GUIDE BOOKS AND BROCHURES
Quebec Government

4, 5, and 6 Days in Quebec, Canada. Quebec: Provincial Tourist Bureau, Roads Department, May 1928.
4, 5, and 6 Days in Québec/Canada. 3rd ed. Quebec: Provincial Tourist Bureau, Roads Department, February 1929.
Along Quebec Highways, Tourist Guide. Quebec: Provincial Tourist Bureau, Department of Highways and Mines, February 1930.
Bas Saint-Laurent et GASPÉSIE/*Lower Saint-Laurent and the* GASPÉ. Provincial Tourist Branch, Department of Tourism, Fish and Game, date unknown but likely 1965 or 1968.
The French Canadian Province. Quebec: Provincial Tourist Bureau, Roads Department, March 1927.

The Gaspé Peninsula: History, Legends, Resources, Attractions. Quebec: Provincial Tourist Bureau, Department of Highways and Mines, 1930.

La Gaspésie. Provincial Tourist Bureau, not dated.

La Gaspésie/The Gaspé. Provincial Tourist Branch, Department of Tourism, Fish and Game, late 1960s.

Hunting and Fishing in La Province de Quebec. 6th ed. Province of Quebec Tourist Bureau, June 1940.

Île d'Orléans, Ville de Québec City et/and Environs. Provincial Tourist Branch, Department of Tourism, Fish and Game, 1969.

Inviting ... La Province de Québec Vous Accueille ... Provincial Tourist Branch, Department of Tourism, Fish and Game, date unknown but likely 1963.

Montréal and the Laurentians, 2nd ed. Quebec: Provincial Tourist Bureau, Roads Department, 1935.

Official Guide: Rates of Rooms in the Hostelries with or without Meals. 1st ed. Hostelry Service, Parliament P.O., 1930.

The Old World at Your Door, The French Canadian Province. Quebec: Provincial Tourist Bureau, Roads Department, 1932.

La Province de Québec. Provincial Tourist Branch, Department of Tourism, Fish and Game, 1963.

La Province de Québec, Canada. Tourist Branch, Provincial Publicity Office, date unknown but likely the early 1950s.

La Province de Québec, Canada. 5th ed. Tourist Branch, Provincial Publicity Office, 1950s.

La Province de Québec, Canada. 6th ed. Tourist Branch, Provincial Publicity Office, 1952.

La Province de Québec Canada: Have You Ever Had a French Canadian Vacation? Quebec Tourist Bureau, date unknown but likely 1941.

La Province de Québec, Canada: Beauté/Beauty. Provincial Tourist Branch, Department of Tourism, Fish and Game, 1960s.

La Province de Québec: Historic-Romantic-Picturesque. Province of Quebec Tourist Bureau, 1939.

La province de Québec, Pays de l'histoire, de la légende et du pittoresque. Office du tourisme de la province de Québec, 1939.

La Province de Québec, Some Aspects. 5th ed. W.P. Percival, distributed by the Provincial Tourist Bureau, 1959.

The Province Where Friendliness Is a Way of Life/Province de Québec: L'aimable province. Provincial Tourist Branch, Department of Tourism, Fish and Game, date unknown but likely the early 1960s.

Québec, The French-Canadian Province: A Harmony of Beauty, History and Progress. Quebec: Provincial Tourist Bureau, Roads Department, 1927.

Quebec the Good Roads Province. Provincial Tourist Bureau, Department of Highways and Mines, January 1930.

Québec: Ses régions de tourisme. 1st ed. Quebec: Provincial Tourist Bureau, Roads Department, 1934.

Le Sud du Québec/Southern Quebec. Provincial Tourist Branch, Department of Tourism, Fish and Game, 1960s.

Sur les routes de Québec: Guide du touriste. Provincial Tourist Bureau, Roads Department, 1929.

Tours in Quebec, Canada. 1st ed. Provincial Tourist Bureau, Department of Highways and Mines, May 1931.

Travelling in Québec, la belle province. Provincial Tourist Branch, Department of Tourism, Fish and Game 1966.

Visite au/A Visit to the Saguenay & Tour du/A Tour around Lac St-Jean. Provincial Tourist Branch, Department of Tourism, Fish and Game, late 1960s.

Voyez Quebec d'Abord!/See Quebec First! Weekend Trips and Holiday Suggestions for Motorists. Quebec: Provincial Tourist Bureau, Roads Department, 1926.

Montreal Tourist and Convention Bureau (MTCB)

Come to Montreal. MTCB, date unknown but likely late 1930s or early 1940s.

Helpful Information for Visitors to the Metropolis of Canada: Montreal, the Year Round Vacation Center. MTCB, undated.

Montreal: Ancient and Modern/Cosmopolitan Montreal. MTCB, undated.

Montreal: Gateway to Historic Province of Quebec. MTCB, 1934.

Montreal: The Paris of the New World. MTCB, 1937.

Quaint Montreal. MTCB, date unknown but likely 1920s or early 1930s.

City of Montreal

Montreal. Montreal Municipal Tourist Bureau for the City of Montreal, undated but likely early 1960s.

Montréal '64 to Montréal '68. City of Montreal magazine, 1964–68.

BOOKS AND ARTICLES

Aaron, Cindy. *Working at Play: A History of Vacations in the United States*. New York: Oxford University Press, 1999.

Achard, Eugène. *Le Royaume du Saguenay*. Montréal: Librairie générale canadienne, 1942.

Apostle, Alisa. "Canada, Vacations Unlimited: The Canadian Government Tourist Industry, 1934–1959." PhD thesis, History Department, Queen's University, 2002.

– "The Display of a Tourist Nation: Canada in Government Film, 1945–1959." *Journal of the Canadian Historical Association/Revue de la Société historique du Canada* 12, no. 1 (2001): 177–97.

Aquin, Hubert. *Next Episode*. Translated by Penny Williams. Toronto: McClelland and Stewart, 1967.

– *Prochain épisode*. Montreal: Cercle du livre de France, 1965.

Archambault, Jacinthe, "'Much More Than a Few Hundred Miles of Land or Water …': Témoignages du voyage autour de la Péninsule Gaspésienne (1929–1950)." *Cahiers de géographie du Québec* 57, no. 162 (2013): 479–502.

– "'Near Enough to Be Neighbours Yet Strange Enough to Be the Goal of Our Pilgrimage': Tourisme, consommation et représentations identitaires dans la Péninsule Gaspésienne (1929–1966)." PhD thesis, History, Université du Québec à Montréal, 2016.

Aronzyk, Melissa. "New and Improved Nations: Branding National Identity." In *Practicing Culture*, edited by Craig J. Calhoun and Richard Sennett, 105–28. London: Routledge, 2007.

Ashworth, G.J., and P.J. Larkham, eds. *Building a New Heritage: Tourism, Culture and Identity*. London: Routledge, 1994.

Aubin, Paul, and Michel Simard. *Les manuels scolaires dans la correspondance du Département de l'instruction publique, 1900–1920: Inventaire*. Sherbrooke: Ex Libris col Cahiers du GRELQ, no. 9, 2005.

Aubin-Des Roches, Caroline. "Retrouver la ville à la campagne: La villégiature à Montréal au tournant du XXe siècle." *Urban History Review/Revue d'histoire urbaine* 34, no. 2 (Spring 2006): 17–29.

Aykroyd, Peter. *The Anniversary Compulsion: Canada's Centennial Celebrations, a Model Mega-Anniversary*. Toronto: Dundern Press, 1992.

Backer, Allan R.H., and Gideon Biger, eds. *Ideology and Landscape in Historical Perspective*. Cambridge: Cambridge University Press, 1992.

Barbeau, Marius. "Gaspé Peninsula." *Canadian Geographic Journal* 3, no. 2 (August 1931).

– *The Kingdom of the Saguenay*. Toronto: The Macmillan Company of Canada (for Canadian Steamships Lines), 1936.

Baronowski, Shelley, and Ellen Furlough. *Tourism, Consumer Culture and Identity in Modern Europe and North America*. Ann Arbor: University of Michigan Press, 2001.

Bastien, Frédéric. "Les relations internationales de Montréal depuis 1945." *Relations Internationales* 2, no. 130 (2007): 5–27.

Beaudet, Gérard, et al., eds. *L'espace culturel touristique*. Ste-Foy: Presses de l'Université du Québec, 1999.

Becker, Jane S. *Selling Tradition: Appalachia and the Construction of American Folk, 1930–1940*. Chapel Hill: University of North Carolina Press, 1998.

Bédard, Mario, Jean-Pierre Augustin, and Richard Desnoilles, eds. *L'imaginaire géographiques: Perspectives, pratiques et devenirs*. Quebec: Les Presses de l'Université du Québec, 2011.

Bélanger, Damien-Claude. "L'antiaméricanisme et l'antimodernisme dans le discours de la droite intellectuelle du Canada, 1892–1945." *Revue d'histoire de l'Amérique française* 61, nos. 3–4 (Winter–Spring 2008): 501–30.

Bélanger, Jules, Marc Desjardins, and Jean-Yves Frenette, with the collaboration of Pierre Dansereau. *Histoire de la Gaspésie*. Montreal: Boréal Express, IQRC, 1981.

Bélanger, Yves, Robert Comeau, and C. Métivier. *La Révolution tranquille 40 ans plus tard: Un bilan*. Montreal: VLB, 2000.

Bellerose, Pierre. "L'Office des congrès et du tourisme du Grand Montréal: La plus ancienne organisation touristique du Canada." *Téoros Revue de la recherche en tourisme* 14, no. 2 (1995): 24–5.

Benaquista, Tonio. *Quelqu'un d'autre*. Paris: Gallimard, 2002.

Bendix, Regina. *In Search of Authenticity: The Formation of Folklore Studies*. Madison: University of Wisconsin Press, 1997.

Berkowitz, Michael. "A 'New Deal' for Leisure: Making Mass Tourism during the Great Depression." In *Tourism, Consumer Culture and Identity in Modern Europe and*

North America, edited by Shelley Baronowski and Ellen Furlough, 185–212. Ann Arbor: University of Michigan Press, 2001.

Blais, Marie-Claire. *A Season in the Life of Emmanuel.* Translated by Derek Coltman. New York: Farrar, Straus and Giroux, 1966.

– *Une saison dans la vie d'Émmanuel.* Montreal: Éditions du jour, 1965.

Blanchard, Raoul. *L'Ouest du Canada français, Province de Québec: Montréal et sa région.* Montreal: Beauchemin, 1953.

Blundel, Valda. "Riding the Polar Bear Express: And Other Encounters by Tourists and First Peoples in Canada." *Journal of Canadian Studies/Revue d'études canadiennes* 30, no. 4 (Winter 1995/96): 28–51.

Bouchard, Gérard. "L'imaginaire de la Grande noirceure et de la Révolution tranquille: Fictions identitaires et jeux de mémoire au Québec." *Recherches sociographiques* 46, no. 3 (September–December 2005): 411–36.

Bouchard, Guy. "Dossier: La maison Samuel-Bédard." *Continuité* (Summer 1990): 64–5.

Bourassa, André, and Jean-Marc Larrue. *Les nuits de la "Main": Cent ans de spectacles sur le boulevard Saint-Laurent, 1891–1991.* Montreal: VLB, 1993.

Bourinot, J. George. *Canada.* Story of the Nations series. London: T. Fisher Unwin, 1897.

Brégent-Heald, Dominique. "Vacationland: Film, Tourism and Selling Canada, 1934–1948." *Revue canadienne d'études cinématographiques/Canadian Journal of Film Studies* 21, no. 2 (Fall 2012): 27–48.

– "Primitive Encounters: Film and Tourism in the North American West." *Western Historical Quarterly* 38 (Spring 2007): 47–67.

Brière, Roger. "Géographie du tourisme au Québec." PhD thesis, Geography, Université de Montréal, 1967.

– "Les grands traits de l'évolution du tourisme au Québec." *Bulletin de l'Association des géographes de l'Amérique française* 11 (1967): 83–95.

Brinley, Gordon. *Away to the Gaspé.* Illustrated by Putman Brinley. New York: Dodd, Mead and Company, 1935.

– *Away to Quebec: A Gay Journey to the Province.* New York: Dodd, Mead and Co, 1937.

Brodeur, Magaly. *Vice et corruption à Montréal, 1892–1970.* Quebec: Presse de l'Université du Québec, 2011.

Brown, Dona. *Inventing New England: Regional Tourism in the 19th Century.* Washington, DC: Smithsonian Institute Press, 1995.

Brown, George W. *Building the Canadian Nation.* Toronto and Vancouver: J.M. Dent and Sons, Canada Ltd., 1942.

Buies, Arthur. *Chroniques, humeurs et caprices.* Quebec, 1873.

– *Petites chroniques pour 1877.* Quebec, 1878.

Bureau, Luc. *Pays et Mensongges: Le Québec sous la plume d'écrivains et de penseurs étrangers.* Montreal: Boréal, 1999.

Burt, A.L. *The Romance of Canada: A New History.* Toronto: W.J. Gage and Co. Ltd., 1940.

Burton, Pierre. *Hollywood's Canada: The Americanization of Our National Heritage.* Toronto: McClelland and Stewart, 1975.

– "Hollywood's Canada: The Americanization of Our National Image." In *Canadian Culture: An Introductory Reader*, edited by Elspeth Cameron, 37–56. Toronto: Canadian Scholar's Press, 1997.

Callaghan, Morley. *The Loved and The Lost: A Novel.* New York: Macmillan, 1951.

Canadian Encyclopedia. http://www.canadienencyclopedia.ca/en/article/expo-67. http://virtuolien.uqam.ca/tout/UQAM_BIB000180179 (G153.4R36.2003).

Caritey, Christophe. "Manuels scolaires et mémoire historique au Québec: Questions de méthodes." *Histoire de l'éducation* 58 (May 1993): 137–64.

Carpentier, Frances. *Canada and Her Northern Neighbors.* New York: American Book Company, 1946.

Cather, Willa. *Death Comes for the Archbishop.* New York: Alfred A. Knopf Inc., 1927.

– *Shadows on the Rock.* New York: Alfred A. Knopf Inc., 1931.

Cazelais, Normand, et al., eds. *L'espace touristique.* Ste-Foy: Les Presses de l'Université du Québec, 1999.

Chamberland, Line. "Remembering Lesbian Bars: Montreal, 1955–1975." *Journal of Homosexuality* 45, no. 3 (1993): 231–70.

Chambers, Erve. *Native Tours: The Anthropology of Travel and Tourism.* 2nd ed. Long Grove, IL: Waveland Press Inc., 2011.

Chhabra, Deepak, Robert Healy, and Erin Stills. "Staged Authenticity and Heritage Tourism." *Annals of Tourism Research* 30, no. 3 (July 2003): 702–19.

Choko, Marc, Danielle Léger, and Michèle Lefebvre. *Destination Québec: Une histoire illustrée du tourisme.* Montreal: Les Éditions de l'Homme, 2013.

Clarke, George Elliott. *George and Rue.* Toronto: Harpercollins Canada, 2005.

Clement, W.H.P. *The History of the Dominion of Canada.* Toronto: William Briggs, The Copp Clark Co. Ltd., 1898.

Coates, Colin, and Cecilia Morgan. *Heroines and History: Representations of Madeleine de Verchères and Laura Secord.* Toronto: University of Toronto Press, 2002.

Cocker, M. *Loneliness and Time: British Travel Writing in the 20th Century.* London: Secker and Warburg Ltd., 1992.

Cohen, Erik. "Authenticity and Commoditization in Tourism." *Annals of Tourism Research* 15, no. 3 (1988): 371–86.

– "'Primitive and Remote': Hill Tribe Trekking in Thailand." *Annals of Tourism Research* 16 (1989): 30–61.

Cook, Ramsay. "L'observateur empathique: L'art de dépeindre de Cornelius Krieghoff." In *Krieghoff: Images du Canada*, edited by Dennis Reid, 145–63. Toronto: Musée des Beaux-Arts de l'Ontario, 1999.

Craik, Jennifer. "The Culture of Tourism." In *Touring Cultures: Transformations of Travel and Theory*, edited by John Urry and Chris Rojek, 113–36. New York and London: Routledge, 1997.

Cronin, Michael. "Fellow Travellers: Contemporary Travel Writing and Ireland." In *Tourism in Ireland: A Critical Analysis*, edited by Barbara O'Connor and Michael Cronin, 51–67. Cork: Cork University Press, 1993.

Currien, Pauline. "L'identité nationale exposée: Représentations du Québec à l'Exposition universelle de Montréal 1967." PhD thesis, Political Science, Université Laval, 2003.

Curtis, Barry, and Claire Pajaczkowska. "'Getting There': Travel, Time and Narrative." *Travellers' Tales: Narratives of Home and Displacement*, edited by George Roberson et al., 198–214. New York: Routledge, 1994.

Dagenais, Michèle. "Fuir la ville: Villégiature et villégiateurs dans la région de Montréal, 1890–1940." *Revue d'histoire de l'Amérique française* 58, no. 3 (Winter 2005): 315–45.

Davies, Blodwen. *Gaspé: Land of History and Romance*. 2nd ed. Toronto: Ambassador Books Ltd, 1949.

– *Quebec: Portrait of a Province*. Toronto: William Heinemann Ltd., 1951.

– *Romantic Quebec*. Toronto: McClelland and Stewart, 1932.

Davis, Donald F. "Dependent Motorization: Canada and the Automobile to the 1930s." *Journal of Canadian Studies/Revue d'études canadiennes* 21, no. 3 (Fall 1986): 106–32.

Davis, Susan G. "Landscapes of Imagination: Tourism in Southern California." *Pacific Historical Review* 68, no. 2 (1999): 173–91.

Dawson, Michael. "A 'Civilizing' Industry: Leo Dolan, Canadian Tourism Promotion, and the Celebration of Mass Culture." *American Review of Canadian Studies* 41, no. 4 (December 2011): 438–47.

– "From 'Business as Usual' to 'Salesmanship in Reverse': Tourism Promotion in British Columbia during the Second World War." *Canadian Historical Review* 83, no. 2 (June 2002): 230–54.

– *Selling British Columbia: Tourism and Consumer Culture, 1890–1970*. Vancouver: UBC Press, 2004.

– "Taking the 'D' out of 'Depression': The Promise of Tourism in British Columbia, 1935–1939." *BC Studies* 132 (Winter 2001/2002): 31–56.

– "'Travel Strengthens America'? Tourism Promotion in the United States during the Second World War." *American Review of Canadian Studies* 41, no. 4 (2011): 438–47.

De Blois, Martin Charles. "Tourisme et patrimoine: Les rendez-vous manqués." *Continuité*, no. 76 (1998): 37–40.

– "Survol historique des pratiques touristiques au Québec." *Continuité*, no. 81 (Summer 1999): 28–31.

de Saint-Maurice, Faucher. *Promenades dans le golfe Saint-Laurent – une partie de la Côte Nord, Île aux Œufs, l'Anticostie, l'Île Saint-Paul, l'Archipel de la Madeleine*. Quebec: Typographie de C. Davreau, 1879.

Desmond, Jane. *Staging Tourism: Bodies on Display from Waikiki to Sea World*. Chicago: University of Chicago Press, 1999.

Des Roches, Jacques, and Brian Foss, eds. *1920s Modernism in Montreal: The Beaver Hall Group*. Montreal: Montreal Museum of Fine Arts, 2016.

Dickenson, John, and Brian Young. *A Short History of Quebec*. 3rd ed. Montreal and Kingston: McGill-Queen's University Press, 2003.

Donald, J.M. *Quebec Patchwork.* Toronto: Macmillan Company of Canada Ltd at St Martin's House, 1940.

Dorland, Arthur. *The Romance of Canada.* Toronto: Copp Clark Co. Ltd., 1949.

Drouin, François. "Promotion touristique, gestion du réseau et autonomie provinciale de la voirie du Québec de 1922 à 1954." *Cap-aux-Diamants: La revue d'histoire du Québec* 111 (Autumn 2012): 27–30.

Drouin, Martin. "Le tourisme dans le Vieux-Montréal: Une fonction au cœur de sa rennaissance et de sa réhabilitation." *Téoros: Revue de la recherché en tourisme* 28, no. 1 (2009): 93–6.

Druick, Zoë. "Documenting Government: Re-examining the 1950s Films about Citizenship." *Canadian Journal of Film Studies* 9, no. 1 (Spring 2000): 55–79.

– *Projecting Canada: Government Policy and Documentary Film at the National Film Board of Canada.* Montreal and Kingston: McGill-Queen's University Press, 2007.

Drummond, Henry. *The Habitant and Other French Canadian Poems.* New York and London: G.P. Putnam's Sons, 1897.

Dubé, Philippe. *Charlevoix: Two Centuries at Murray Bay.* Translated by Tony Martin Sperry. Montreal and Kingston: McGill-Queen's University Press, 1990.

– "La villégiature dans Charlevoix: Une tradition séculaire, un patrimoine encore vivant." *Téoros: Revue de la recherché en tourisme* 14, no. 2 (1995): 4–7.

Dubinsky, Karen. "'Everybody Likes Canadians': Canadians, Americans and the Post–World War II Travel Boom." In *Being Elsewhere: Tourism, Consumer Cultures and Identity in Modern Europe and North America*, edited by Shelley Baranowski and Ellen Furlough, 320–47. Ann Arbor: University of Michigan Press, 2001.

– *The Second Greatest Disappointment.* Toronto: Between the Lines, 1999.

Dulles, Foster Rhea. *Americans Abroad: Two Centuries of American Travel.* Ann Arbor: University of Michigan Press, 1964.

Dumont, Micheline. "Growing Up In … /Grandir en …" *Historical Studies in Education/ Revue d'histoire de l'éducation* 19, no. 1 (Spring 2007): 141–52.

Dupuy, Pierre. *Expo 67 ou la découverte de la fierté.* Montreal: Les Éditions la presse, 1972.

Durand, Irène. "Essai d'analyse de la pratique de l'artisanat au Québec." MA thesis, Sociology, Université du Québec à Montréal, 1981.

Durie, Alastair J. *Making Ireland Irish: Tourism and National Identity since the Irish Civil War.* Stirling, Scotland: University of Stirling, 2010.

– *Scotland for the Holidays: A History of Tourism in Scotland 1780–1939.* East Linton, Scotland: Tuckwell Press Ltd., 2003.

Endy, Christopher. *American Tourism in France: Cold War Holidays.* Chapel Hill: The University of North Carolina Press, 2004.

– "US Tourism in France: An International History, 1944–1971." PhD thesis, University of North Carolina, 2000.

Engerman, David. "Research Agenda for the History of Tourism: Towards an International Social History." *American Studies International* 32, no. 2 (October 1994): 3–31.

Esmen, Marjorie R. "Tourism as Ethnic Preservation: The Cajuns of Louisiana." *Annals of Tourism Research* 11, no. 3 (1984): 51–67.

Fabre, Gérard. "Présentation: Écrits de voyageurs européens sur le Québec." *Recherches sociographiques* 54, no. 2 (2013): 223–38.

Fawcett, Clare, and Patricia Cormak. "Guarding Authenticity at Literary Tourism Sites." *Annals of Tourism Research* 28, no. 3 (2001): 686–704.

Faugier, Étienne. "De la codépendance à l'indépendance: Automobilisme et tourisme dans la Province de Québec, 1906–1936." *Téoros: Revue de la recherche en tourisme* 32, no. 2 (2013).

Ferland, Jean-Baptiste. "Journal d'un voyage sur les côtes de la Gaspésie." *Littérature canadienne*, 1863.

Ferland, Philippe. *Paul Gouin*. Montreal: Guérin Éditeur, 1991.

Filteau, Gérard. *La civilisation catholique et française au Canada: Manuel d'histoire à l'usage des écoles secondaires*. Montreal: Trifluvi, 1960.

Francis, Daniel. *The Imaginary Indian: The Image of the Indian in Canadian Culture*. 2nd ed. Vancouver: Arsenal Pulp Press, 2013.

– *National Dreams: Myth, Memory and Canadian History*. Vancouver: Arsenal Pulp Press, 1997.

– *Selling Canada: Three Propaganda Campaigns That Shaped the Nation*. Vancouver: Stanton Atkins and Dosil Publishers, 2011.

Frow, John. "Tourism and the Semiotics of Nostalgia." *October* 57 (Summer 1991): 123–51.

Furlough, Ellen. "Making Mass Vacations: Tourism and Consumer Culture in France 1930s–1970s." *Comparative Studies in Society and History* 10, no. 3 (1998): 247–86.

Gagnon, France. "Du cheval au rail: l'évolution des circuits touristiques québécois au XIXe siècle." *Le Pays laurentien au XIXe siècle*, Cahier 1, 101–33, 1992.

Gagnon, François-Marc. "Un Regard sur l'Autre: l'iconographie canadienne-française et indienne de Krieghoff." In *Krieghoff: Images du Canada*, edited by Dennis Reid, 207–33. Toronto: Musée des Beaux-Arts de l'Ontario, 1999.

Gagnon, Serge. "Au fondement du potentiel touristique d'un territoire: Un processus de nature anthropologique et géopolitique." *Loisir et Société* 20, no 1 (Spring 2007): 23–42.

– *L'échiquier touristique québécois*. Ste-Foy: Les Presses de l'Université du Québec, 2003.

– "L'émergence de l'identité rurale et l'intervention du gouvernement québécois en tourisme (1920–1940)." *Téoros: Revue de la recherche en tourisme* 20, no. 3 (Autumn 2001): 24–38.

– "L'intervention de l'État québécois dans le tourisme entre 1920–1940." *Hérodote* 4, no. 127 (2007): 151–66.

Garceau, Henri-Paul. *Chronique de l'hospitalité hôtelière du Québec de 1880–1940: Les pionniers*. Montreal: Les Éditons du Méridien, 1990.

– *Chronique de l'hospitalité hôtelière du Québec de 1940 à 1980*. Montreal: XYZ Éditeur, 1995.

Gauthier, Serge. *Charlevoix ou la création d'une région folklorique: Étude du discours de folkloristes québécois, 1916–1980*. Québec: Les Presses de l'Université Laval, 2006.

Gauvreau, Michael. *The Catholic Origins of the Quiet Revolution, 1931–1970*. Montreal and Kingston: McGill-Queen's University Press, 2005.

Geller, Peter. "Visions of a Northern Nation: Richard Finnie's View of Natives and Development on Canada's Last Frontier." *Film History Cinema and Nation* 8, no. 1 (Spring 1996): 18–43.

Géromini, Martine. "L'émergence des lieux du tourisme et de la villégiature." In *L'Espace touristique*, edited by Norman Cazelais, Roger Nadeau, and Gérard Beaudet, 197–212. Quebec: Presses de l'Université du Québec, 1999.

– "Imaginaire français en Amérique du Nord: Genèse d'un tourisme de distinction à Québec et à la Nouvelle-Orléans: Notes de recherche." *Anthropologie et société* 25, no. 2 (2001): 151–66.

– "Permanence paysagère et consommation touristique: Le cas du Vieux Québec." *L'Espace touristique*, edited by Norman Cazelais, Roger Nadeau, and Gérard Beaudet, chapter 4. Quebec: Presses de l'Université du Québec, 1999.

– "Québec dans les discours des guides touristiques, 1830–1930." *Folklore Canadien/ Canadian Folklore, Transactions identitaires/Identity Transactions* 18, no. 2, special volume (1996): 69–90.

– *Québec et la Nouvelle-Orléans: Paysages imaginaires francais en Amérique du Nord.* Paris: Éditions Belin, 2003.

Gerson, Carole. *A Purer Taste: The Writing and Reading of Fiction in English in Nineteenth-Century Canada.* Toronto: University of Toronto Press, 1989.

Gilbert, David. "'London in All Its Glory – or How to Enjoy London': Guidebook Representations of Imperial London." *Journal of Historical Geography* 25, no. 3 (1999): 279–97.

Gillepsie, Greg. "'I Was Well Pleased with Our Sport Among the Buffalo': Big Game Hunters, Travel Writing, and Cultural Pluralism in the British North America West, 1847–1872." *Canadian Historical Review* 83, no. 4 (December 2002): 555–84.

Gilmore, John. *Swinging in Paradise: The Story of Jazz in Montreal.* Montreal: Véhicule Press, 1988.

Glassberg, David. "History and Memory: Public History and the Study of Memory." *The Public Historian* 18, no. 2 (Spring 1996): 7–23.

Gold, J.R. *Imagining Scotland: Tradition, Representation and Promotion in Scotland Tourism since 1750.* Seattle: University of Washington Press, 1994.

Gordon, Alan. "Entre l'invention et la réalité: Paysages et histoire vivante dans les villages musées de pionniers au Canada." *Histoire sociale/Social History* 49, no. 99 (June 2016): 347–67.

– *The Hero and the Historians: Historiography and the Uses of Jacques Cartier.* Vancouver: UBC Press, 2010.

– *Making Public Pasts: The Contested Terrain of Montréal's Public Memories.* Montreal and Kingston: McGill-Queen's University Press, 2001.

– *Time Travel: Tourism and the Rise of the Living History Museum in Mid-Twentieth-Century Canada.* Vancouver: UBC Press, 2016.

– "'Where Famous Heroes Fell': Tourism History and Liberation in Old Quebec." In *Remembering 1759: The Conquest of Canada in Canadian History*, edited by Philip Buckner and John Reid, 58–81. Toronto: University of Toronto Press, 2012.

– "What to See and How to See It: Tourists, Residents, and the Beginnings of the Walking Tour in Nineteenth-Century Quebec." *Journal of Tourism History* 6, no. 1 (2014): 74–90.

Gordon, Bertram M. "Warfare and Tourism: Paris in WWII." *Annals of Tourism Research* 25, no. 3 (1998): 616–38.

Gouin, Paul. "Au pays de Québec rien ne doit mourir et rien ne doit changer ..." *Culture, Revue trimestrielle/A Quartely Review* 12, no. 1 (March 1951).

– *Servir – 1. La cause nationale*. Montreal: Les Éditions du Zodiaque, 1938.

Gow, James Ian. *Histoire de l'administration publique québécoise, 1867–1970*. Montreal: Les Presses de l'Université de Montréal, 1986.

Graburn, Nelson, ed. *Ethnic and Tourist Arts: Cultural Expressions from the Fourth World*. Berkeley: University of California Press, 1976.

Graham, Gwenthalyn. *Earth and High Heaven*. Garden City, NY: Sun Dial Press, 1945.

Graham Bonner, Mary. *Canada and Her Story*. New York: Alfred A. Knopf, 1942.

Greg, Richard. "Politics of National Tourism Policy in Britain." *Leisure Studies* 14 (1995): 153–73.

Grenier, K.H. *Tourism and Identity in Scotland, 1770–1914*. Hants: Ashgate, 2005.

Gruffudd, Pyrs, David Herbert, and Angelina Piccini. "In Search of Wales: Travel Writing and Narratives of Difference, 1918–50." *Journal of Historical Geography* 26, no. 4 (2000): 589–604.

Guénette, Marie-Claude, and Pierre Hétu. "Le tour du bout du monde: Un siècle de tourisme en Gaspésie." *Téoros: Revue de la recherche en tourisme* 14, no. 2 (Summer 1995): 8–11.

Halbwachs, Maurice. *The Collective Memory de Maurice Halbwachs*. Translated by Francis J. Ditter Jr and Vida Yazdi Ditter. New York: Harper & Row, 1980.

Hall, C. Michael. "Packaging Canada/Packaging Places: Tourism, Culture, and Identity in the Twenty-First Century." In *The Canadian Distinctiveness in the XXIst Century/La distinction canadienne au tournant du XXIè siècle*, edited by Chad Gaffield and Karen L. Gould, 199–214. Ottawa: Les Presses de l'Université d'Ottawa, 2003.

Hamel, Natalie. *La collection Coverdale: La construction d'un patrimoine national*. Quebec: Les Presses de l'Université Laval, 2009.

– "Coordonner l'artisanat: L'artisanat et le tourisme, ou comment mettre en valeur le visage pittoresque du Québec, 1915–1960." *Histoire sociale/Social History* 34, no. 67 (May 2001): 97–114.

– *"Notre maître le passé, notre maître l'avenir": Paul Gouin et la conservation de l'héritage culturel du Québec*. Quebec: Les Éditions de l'IQRC, Les Presses de l'Université Laval, 2008.

Handler, Richard. "In Search of the Folk Society: Nationalism and Folklore Studies in Quebec." *Culture* 3, no. 1 (1983): 103–14.

– *Nationalism and the Politics of Culture in Quebec*. Madison: University of Wisconsin Press, 1988.

Handler, Richard, and Eric Gable. *The New Story in an Old Museum*. Durham and London: Duke University Press, 1997.

Handler, Richard, and Jocelyn Linnekin. "Tradition, Genuine or Spurious." *Journal of American Folklore* 97, no. 385 (July–September 1984): 273–90.

Harris, Liela Gott, and Kilroy Harris. *Canadian Ways*. Bloomington, IL: McKnight and McKnight, 1939.

Hart, E.J. *The Selling of Canada: The CPR and the Beginnings of Canadian Tourism.* Banff: Altitude Publishing Ltd., 1983.

Harvey, Jean-Charles. *Québec: La Douce Province.* Chemin de fer National du Canada, 1925.

Hawrysh, Michael. "Une ville bien arosée: Montréal durant l'ère de la prohibition, 1920–1933." MA thesis, History, Université de Montréal, 2014.

Hémon, Louis. *Maria Chapdelaine.* Translated by W.H. Blake. Toronto: Macmillan Co. of Canada Ltd., 1921.

– *Maria Chapdelaine.* Translated by W.H. Blake. Toronto: Macmillan Co. of Canada Ltd., 1948.

– *Maria Chapdelaine: A Tale of French Canada.* Translated by W.H. Blake with an introduction by Michael Gnarowski. Toronto: Dundurn Press, 2007.

Henderson, Stuart. "'While There Is Still Time . . .': J. Murray Gibbon and the Spectacle of Difference in Three CPR Folk Festivals, 1928–1931." *Journal of Canadian Studies/Revue d'études canadiennes* 39, no. 1 (Winter 2005): 139–74.

Heron, Craig. *Booze: A Distilled History.* Toronto: Between the Lines, 2003.

Highlights of Montreal: The Graphic Digest for Travellers. Montreal: Travel Publications Ltd., 1948.

Holland, Patrick, and Graham Huggan. *Tourists with Typewriters: Critical Reflections on Contemporary Travel Writing.* Ann Arbor: The University of Michigan Press, 1998.

Hollier, Robert. *Montréal: Ma grand'ville – A Grand City.* English text by Gordon Black. Montreal: Librairie Décom, 1963.

Houellebecq, Michel. *Plateforme.* Paris: Flammarion, Éditions J'ai lu, 2001.

Hulan, Renée. "The Past Is an Imagined Country: Reading Canadian Historical Fiction in English." In *Settling and Unsettling Pasts: Essays in Canadian Public History,* edited by Nicole Neatby and Peter Hodgins, 591–614. Toronto: University of Toronto Press, 2012.

Hulme, Peter, and Tim Young, eds. *Travel Writing.* Cambridge: Cambridge University Press, 2002.

Igartua, José. *Arvida au Saguenay: Naissance d'une ville industrielle.* Montreal and Kingston: McGill-Queen's University Press, 1996.

– "The Genealogy of Stereotypes: French Canadians in Two English-Language Canadian History Textbooks." *Journal of Canadian Studies/Revue d'études canadiennes* 42, no. 3 (Fall 2008): 106–32.

– *The OTHER Quiet Revolution: National Identities in English Canada, 1945–71.* Vancouver: UBC Press, 2006.

Jackle, John. *The Tourist: Travel in Twentieth-Century North America.* Lincoln: University of Nebraska Press, 1985.

Jasen, Patricia. "Native People and the Tourist Industry in Nineteenth-Century Ontario." *Journal of Canadian Studies/Revue d'études canadiennes* 28, no. 4 (Winter 1993): 5–27.

– *Wild Things: Nature, Culture, and Tourism in Ontario, 1790–1914.* Toronto: University of Toronto Press, 1995.

Jaumain, Serge. "'Une grande capitale moderne': Bruxelles dans les guides touristiques de la deuxième moitié du XXe siècle." In *Mondes urbains du tourisme*, edited
by Philippe Duhamel and Remy Knafou, 308–22. Paris: Belin, 2007.

– "L'image de Bruxelles dans les guides touristiques (XIXe–XXe siècles)." In *Bruxelles,
175 ans d'une capitale*, 155–66. Sprimont: Madaga, 2005.

Jessup, Lynda. "The Group of Seven and the Tourist Landscape in Western Canada,
or The More Things Change." *Journal of Canadian Studies/Revue d'études canadiennes* 37, no. 1 (Spring 2002): 144–79.

Jessup, Lynda, Andrew Nurse, and Gordon E. Smith, eds. *Around and About Marius
Barbeau: Modelling Twentieth Century Culture*. Ottawa: Canadian Museum of Civilization, 2008.

Johnson, Nuala. "Framing the Past: Time, Space and the Politics of Heritage Tourism." *Political Geography* 18 (1999): 187–207.

– "Where Geography and History Meet: Heritage Tourism and the Big House in Ireland." *Annals of the Association of American Geographers* 86, no. 3 (1996): 551–66.

Johnston, Russell. *Selling Themselves: The Emergence of Canadian Advertising*. Toronto:
University of Toronto Press, 2001.

Kirby, William. *The Golden Dog (Le Chien d'Or): A Legend of Quebec*. New York:
Lovell, Adam, Wesson & Co, 1877.

– *Le Chien d'or: Légende canadienne*. Translated by Pamphile Le May. Montreal: Imprimerie de L'Étendard, 1884.

Korte, Barbara. *English Travel Writing from Pilgrimages to Postcolonial Explorations*.
Translated by Catherine Matthias. New York: Saint Martin's Press Ltd., 2000.

Koshar, Rudy. "'What Ought to Be Seen': Tourists Guidebooks and National Identities in Modern Germany and Europe." *Journal of Contemporary History* 33, no. 3
(July 1998): 323–40.

Kröller, Eva-Marie. *Canadian Travellers in Europe, 1851–1900*. Vancouver: UBC Press,
1987.

– "Expo 67: Canada's Camelot?" *Canadian Literature/Littérature canadienne* 152/153
(Spring/Summer 1997): 36–51.

Kuffert, L.B. *A Great Duty: Canadian Responses to Modern Life and Culture, 1939–
1967*. Montreal and Kingston: McGill-Queen's University Press, 2003.

Kuplowsky, Adam. "A Captivating 'Open City': The Production of Montreal as a
'Wide-Open Town' and 'Ville ouverte' in the 1940s and 1950s." MA thesis, Department of History and Classics, McGill University, 2015.

Kyte, Shelley. "'V–8 or Make and Break' – An Investigation of the Development of
Tourism in Canada: A Case Study of Nova Scotia." MA thesis, Queen's University,
1997.

Lambert, Maude-Émmanuelle. "À travers le pare-brise: la création des territoires à
l'ère de l'automobile." PhD thesis, History Department, Université de Montréal,
2013.

– "Automobile Tourism in Quebec and Ontario: Development, Promotion and Representations, 1920–1945." In *Moving Natures: Mobility and the Environment in Canadian History*, edited by Ben Bradley, Jay Young, and Colin M. Coates, 299–322.
Calgary: University of Calgary Press, 2016.

- "'Québécoises et Ontariennes en voiture!' L'expérience culturelle et spatiale de l'automobile au féminin 1910–1945." *Revue d'histoire de l'Amérique française* 63, no. 2–3 (Autumn 2009–Winter 2010): 305–30.

Lamonde, Yvan. *Histoire sociale des idées au Québec, 1896–1929*, vol. 2. St-Laurent: Fides, 2004.

- "La modernité au Québec: Pour une histoire des brèches (1895–1950)." In *L'avènement de la modernité culturelle au Québec*, edited by Yvan Lamonde and Esther Trépanier, 299–311. Quebec: Institut québécois de recherches sur la culture, 1986.

Lamonde, Yvan, and Esther Trépanier, eds. *L'avènement de la modernité culturelle au Québec*. Quebec: Institut québécois de recherches sur la culture, 1986.

Lamontagne, Sophie-Laurence, and Fernand Harvey. "De l'économie familiale à l'artisanat: Les textiles domestiques." *Cap-Aux-Diamant: La revue d'histoire du Québec* 50 (Summer 1997): 20–4.

Lapierre, Richard. "Aspects géographiques du tourisme à Montréal." *Cahiers de géographie du Québec* 3, no. 6 (1959): 295–303.

Larose, Jean-François. "A l'aventure! Les débuts du tourisme routier." *Cap-aux-Diamants: La revue d'histoire du Québec* 45 (Spring 1996): 26–9.

Laviolette, Guy. *Histoire du Canada, 6e et 7e années: L'épopée canadienne*. La Prairie, QC: Frères de l'Instruction Chrétienne, 1954.

Leacock, Steven. *Leacock's Montreal*. 2nd ed. Toronto-Montreal: McClelland and Stewart, 1948, 1963.

- *Montreal: Seaport and City*. Toronto: McClelland and Stewart, 1948.

Lears, T.J. Jackson. *No Place of Grace: Antimodernism and the Transformation of American Culture, 1880–1920*. Chicago: The University of Chicago Press, 1983.

- "Packaging the Folk: Tradition and Amnesia in American Advertising, 1880–1940." In *Folk Roots, New Roots: Folklore in American Life*, edited by Jane S. Becker and Barbara Franco, 103–40. Lexington: Museum of Our National Heritage, 1988.

Lebel, Jean-Marie. "Quand *Le Terroir* faisait rêver les citadins." *Cap-aux-Diamants: La revue d'histoire du Québec* 65 (2001): 24–6.

Lebel, Jean-Marie, and Alain Roy. *Québec: 1900–2000: Le siècle d'une capitale*. Éditions Multimondes, Commission de la capitale nationale du Québec, 2000.

Lemelin, Roger. *The Plouffe Family*. Translated by Mary Finch. Toronto: McClelland and Stewart, 1950.

- *The Town Below*. Translated by Samuel Putman. Toronto: McClelland and Stewart, 1961.

Le Pan, Marie-Christine. "Les images d'Albert Tessier: Regard sur la culture, regard sur l'identité." In *Produire la culture, produire l'identité?* Ste-Foy: Presses de l'Université Laval, 2000.

Létourneau, Jocelyn, and Sabrina Moisan. "Young People's Assimilation of a Collective Historical Memory: A Case Study of Quebeckers of French-Canadian Heritage." In *Theorizing Historical Consciousness*, edited by Peter Sexias, 109–28. Toronto: University of Toronto Press, 2006.

Levenstein, Harvey. *Seductive Journey: American Tourists in France from Jefferson to the Jazz Age*. Chicago: Chicago University Press, 1998.

- *We'll Always Have Paris: American Tourists in France since 1930*. Chicago: University of Chicago Press, 2004.

Lévesque, Andrée. "Éteindre le Red Light: Les réformateurs et la prostitution à Montréal entre 1865–1925." *Urban History Review/Revue d'histoire urbaine* 17, no. 3 (February 1989): 191–201.

Levine, Marc. *The Reconquest of Montreal: Language Policy and Social Change in a Bilingual City.* Philadelphia: Temple University Press, 1990.

Lindsay, Claire. *Contemporary Travel Writing of Latin America.* New York: Routledge, 2010.

Linteau, Paul-André. *Histoire de Montréal depuis la Confédération.* Montreal: Boréal, 1992.

– *La rue Sainte-Catherine: Au coeur de la vie montréalaise.* Montreal: Les Éditions de l'Homme, 2010.

Linteau, Paul-André, et al. *Histoire du Québec contemporain: Le Québec depuis 1930.* 2nd ed. Montreal: Boréal, 1989.

Little, Jack. "In Search of the Plains of Abraham: British, American and Canadian Views of a Symbolic Landscape, 1793–1913." In *Remembering 1759: The Conquest of Canada in Canadian History*, edited by Philip Buckner and John Reid, 82–109. Toronto: University of Toronto Press, 2012.

– "'Like a Fragment of the Old World': The Historical Regression of Quebec City in Travel Narratives and Tourist Guidebooks, 1776–1913." *Urban History Review/ Revue d'histoire urbaine* 40, no. 2 (Spring 2012): 15–27.

– "Travels in a Cold and Rugged Land: C.H. Farnham's Quebec Essays in *Harper's Magazine*, 1883–89." *Journal of Canadian Studies/Revue d'études canadiennes* 47, no. 2 (Spring 2013): 215–45.

– "'A Fine, Hardy, Good-Looking Race of People': Travel Writers, Tourism Promoters, and the Highland Scots Identity on Cape Breton Island, 1829–1920."*Acadiensis* 44, no. 1 (Winter/Spring 2015): 1–13.

– "Natives Seeing Icebergs and Inuit as Elemental Nature: An American Transcendentalist on and off the Coast of Labrador, 1864." *Histoire sociale/Social History* 49, no. 99 (June 2016): 243–62.

Lollar, Sam A., and Carlton Van Doran. "US Tourist Destinations: A History of Desirability." *Annals of Tourism Research* 18, no. 4 (1991): 622–38.

Longstreth, T. Morris. *The Laurentians: The Hills of the Habitant.* Kessinger Publishing Co., 1922.

– *Quebec, Montreal and Ottawa.* New York: The Century Co., 1933.

Lortie, André, ed. *Les années 60 Montréal voit grand.* Montreal: Centre Canadien d'Architecture, 2004.

Lusignan, Marie-Janou. "Comment Montréal est devenu Paris pour les Américains!" *Téoros: Revue de la recherche en tourisme* 14, no. 2 (Summer 1995): 20–3.

MacCannell, Dean. "Reconstructed Ethnicity: Tourism and Cultural Identity in Third World Communities." *Annals of Tourism Research* 11 (1984): 375–91.

– "Remarks on the Commodification of Culture." In *Hosts and Guests: The Anthropology of Tourism*, edited by Valene Smith, 380–90. Philadelphia: University of Pennsylvania Press, 1977.

– "Staged Authenticity: Arrangements of Social Space in Tourist Settings." *American Journal of Sociology* 79, no. 3 (November 1973): 589–603.

– *The Tourist: A New Theory of the Leisure Class*. Rev. ed. Berkley: University of California Press, 2013.

MacDonald, Edward. "A Landscape … with Figures: Tourism and Environment on Prince Edward Island." *Acadiensis* 40, no. 1 (Winter/Spring 2011): 70–85.

MacDonald, Edward, and Alan MacEachern. "Rites of Passage: Tourism and the Crossing to Prince Edward Island." *Histoire sociale/Social History* 49, no. 99 (June 2016): 289–306.

MacDonald, Monica. "Railway Tourism in the 'Land of Evangeline,' 1882–1946." *Acadiensis* 25 (Fall 2005): 158–80.

MacEachern, Alan. "'No Island Is an Island': A History of Tourism on Prince Edward Island." MA thesis, History, Queen's University, 1991.

Mackenzie, John M. "Empires of Travel: British Guide Books and Cultural Imperialism in the 19th and 20th Centuries." In *Historical Tourism: Representation, Identity and Conflict*, edited by John Walton, 19–38. Clevedon: Channel View Publishers, 2005.

Mackenzie, John, and Marjorie Mackenzie. *Quebec in Your Car*. Toronto: Clarke, Irwin and Company Ltd., 1952.

Mackenzie, Scott. *Screening Quebec: Québécois Moving Images, National Identity and the Public Sphere*. Manchester: Manchester University Press, 2004.

MacLennan, Hugh. *Two Solitudes*. Toronto: Collins, 1945.

MacRae, Matthew. "The Romance of Canada: Tourism and Nationalism Meet in Charlottetown, 1939." *Acadiensis* 34, no 2 (Spring 2005): 26–45.

Malack, Dominick. "Le dévelopment du tourisme: L'exemple du Château Frontenac." In *Atlas historique du Québec: Québec, ville et capitale*, edited by Serge Courville and Robert Garon, 322–5. Ste-Foy: Les Presses de l'Université Laval, 2001.

Maoz, Darya. "The Mutual Gaze." *Annals of Tourism Research* 33, no. 1 (2006): 221–39.

Marchand, Roland. *Advertising the American Dream: Making Way for Modernity, 1920–1940*. Berkeley: University of California Press, 1985.

Martin, Paul-Louis. "La conservation du patrimoine culturel: Origines et évolution." In *Les chemins de la mémoire: Monuments et sites historiques du Québec*, vol. 1, edited by La Commission des biens du Québec, 1–17. Quebec: Les publications du Québec, 1990.

Mason Clarke, John. *The Heart of Gaspé: Sketches in the Gulf of St Lawrence*. New York: Macmillan, 1913.

– *Sketches of Gaspé*. Albany: J.B. Lyon, 1908.

Mattison, David. "The British Columbia Government Travel Bureau and Motion Picture Production, 1937–1947." In *"Flashback": People and Institutions in Canadian Film History*, edited by Gene Waltz, 79–104. Montreal: Mediatexte Publications, 1986.

– "Discovering an Island: Travel Writers and Tourism in PEI." *Island Magazine* 29 (1991): 8–16.

McCullough, David. *The Greater Journey: Americans in Paris*. New York: Simon and Schuster, 2011.

McInnis, Edgar. *The North American Nations*. Toronto: Dent, 1963.

McKay, Ian. "'Cashing In on Antiquity': Tourism and the Uses of the Past in Nova Scotia, 1890–1960." In *Settling and Unsettling Pasts: Essays in Canadian Public History*, edited by Nicole Neatby and Peter Hodgins, 454–90. Toronto: University of Toronto Press, 2012.

– "Handicrafts and the Logic of Commercial Antimodernism: The Nova Scotia Case." In *Antimodernism and Artistic Experience: Policing Boundaries of Modernity*, edited by Lynda Jessup, 117–29. Toronto: University of Toronto Press, 2001.

– *The Quest of the Folk: Antimodernism and Cultural Selection in Twentieth-Century Nova Scotia*. Montreal and Kingston: McGill-Queen's University Press, 1994.

– "The Rise of Tourism." In *Interpreting Canada's Past, Vol 2: Post-Confederation*, edited by J.M. Bumsted, 487–512. Toronto: University of Toronto Press, 1993.

– "Tartanism Triumphant: The Construction and Uses of Scottishness in Nova Scotia, 1934–1954." *Acadiensis* 21, no. 2 (1992): 5–47.

McKay, Ian, and Robin Bates. *In the Province of History: The Making of the Public Past in Twentieth Century Nova Scotia*. Montreal and Kingston: McGill-Queen's University Press, 2010.

McNaughton, Janet Elizabeth. "A Study of the CPR-Sponsored Quebec Folk and Handicraft Festivals, 1927–1930." MA thesis, Memorial University of Newfoundland, 1982.

Meunier, E., and Jean-Philippe Warren. *Sortir de la "Grande noirceure": L'horizon personnaliste de la Révolution tranquille*. Sillery: Septentrion, 2002.

Miedema, Gary. "'For Canada's Sake': The Centennial Celebrations of 1967, State Legitimation and the Restructuring of Canadian Public Life." *Journal of Canadian Studies/Revue d'études canadiennes* 34, no. 1 (Spring 1999): 139–60.

– *For Canada's Sake: Public Religion, Centennial Celebrations, and the Re-making of Canada in the 1960s*. Montreal and Kingston: McGill-Queen's University Press, 2005.

Money-Melvin, Patricia. "Historic Sites as Tourist Attractions: Harnessing the Romance of the Past: Preservation, Tourism, and History." *The Public Historian* 13, no. 2 (Spring 1991): 35–48.

Montgomery, Ken. "Banal Race-Thinking: Ties of Blood, Canadian History Textbooks and Ethnic Nationalism." *Paedagogica Historica* 41, no. 3 (June 2005): 313–36.

Montpetit, Édouard. "Prends la … route: Montre-moi le décor de ta vie et je te dirai qui tu es." Montreal: Éditorial du *Devoir*, 940 (reprinted in the *Revue trimestrielle Canadienne*, December 1939).

Moore, Brian. *Wreath for a Redhead*. Toronto: Harlequin Books, 1951.

Morgan, Cecilia. "A Choke of Emotion, a Great Heart-Leap: English Canadian Tourists in Britain, 1880s–1914." *Histoire sociale/Social History* 77 (May 2006): 11–43.

– *"A Happy Holiday": English Canadians and Transatlantic Tourism 1870–1930*. Toronto: University of Toronto Press, 2008.

Morisset, Lucie. "Voyage au pays de l'identité: De la définition d'un paysage touristique à la création de la spécificité culturelle canadienne-française." In *L'espace touristique*, edited by Normand Cazelais et al., 213–36. Ste-Foy: Presses de l'Université du Québec, 1999.

– "Un ailleurs pour l'Amérique: Notre patrimoine et l'invention du monument historique au Québec." *Revue Internationale d'études québécoises* 10, no. 1 (2007): 73–105.

Morisset, Lucie, Patrick Dieudonné, and Jean-François Simon, eds. *Réinventer pays et paysage*. Brest Centre de recherche bretonne et celtique, Institut de géo-architecture, Université de Bretagne occidentale 2003. Actes du colloque Québec Bretagne, Réinvention des pays et des paysages dans la seconde moitié du 20ᵉ siècle à l'Université de Bretagne occidentale 2001.

Morrison, James H. "American Tourism in Nova Scotia, 1871–1940." *Nova Scotia Historical Review* 2, no. 2 (1982): 40–51.

Murphy, Peter E. "Tourism: Canada's Other Resource Industry." In *Tourism in Canada: Selected Issues and Options*, edited by Peter Murphy, 3–23. Victoria: Department of Geography, University of Victoria, 1983.

Murton, James. "'La Normandie du Nouveau Monde': La société Canada Steamship Lines, l'antimodernisme et la promotion du Québec ancien." *Revue d'histoire de l'Amérique française* 55, no. 1 (Summer 2001): 3–44.

– "'The Normandy of the New World': Canada Steamship Lines, Antimodernism and the Selling of Quebec." In *Settling and Unsettling Pasts: Essays in Canadian Public History*, edited by Nicole Neatby and Peter Hodgins, 419–53. Toronto: University of Toronto Press, 2012.

Muzzey, David S. *An American History*. Rev. ed. Boston: Ginn and Company, 1925.

Nadeau, Brigitte. "Albert Tessier, agent de transmission d'une idée du Québec en France entre 1930 et 1950." *Mens: Revue d'histoire intellectuelle et culturelle* 12, no. 2 (2012): 61–101.

Neatby, Nicole. "Leaving the Past Behind: From Old Quebec to 'La Belle Province.'" In *Settling and Unsettling Pasts: Essays in Canadian Public History*, edited by Nicole Neatby and Peter Hodgins, 491–537. Toronto: University of Toronto Press, 2012.

– "Meeting of the Minds: North American Travel Writers and Government Tourist Publicity in Quebec, 1920–1955." *Histoire sociale/Social History* 36, no. 72 (November 2003): 465–95.

– "Notes bibliographiques." *Revue d'histoire de l'Amérique française* 55, no. 2 (Autumn 2001): 314–15.

– "Remembering the Conquest: Mission Impossible?" In *Remembering 1759: The Conquest of Canada in Historical Memory*, edited by Phillip Buckner and John G. Reid, 251–78. Toronto: University of Toronto Press, 2012.

Nelles, H.V. *The Art of Nation-Building: Pageantry and Spectacle at Quebec's Tercentenary*. Toronto: University of Toronto Press, 1999.

NFB. *Show Girls: Celebrating Montreal's Legendary Black Jazz Scene* (film). http://www.nfb-onf.gc.ca/eng/collection/film/?id=33572.

Nicks, Trudy. "Indian Villages and Entertainments: Setting the Stage for Tourist Souvenir Sales." In *Unpacking Culture: Arts and Commodity in Colonial and Postcolonial Worlds*, edited by Ruth Philips and Christopher Steiner, 301–15. Berkeley and Los Angeles: University of California Press, 1999.

Nixon, Larry. *See Canada Next*. 1st ed. Boston: Little, Brown and Company, 1940.

Noppen, Luc. "L'Île d'Orléans: Mythe à découvrir." *Cap-aux-Diamants: La revue d'histoire du Québec* 5, no. 1 (1989): 23–6.

Nord, Douglas. "American Images of Canada – Courtesy of the Canadian Tourism Industry." *North Dakota Quarterly* 52, no. 3 (1984): 257–78.

– "Canada Perceived." *Journal of American Culture* 1, no. 9 (1986): 23–30.

Norkunas, Martha. *The Politics of Public Memory: Tourism, History and Ethnicity in Monterey California.* Albany: SUNY Press, 1993.

North, Gary. "Textbooks as Ideological Weapons." http://www.lewrockwell.com/north/north461.html.

Nurse, Andrew. "'The Best Field for Tourist Sale of Books': Marius Barbeau, the Macmillan Company, and Folklore Publishing in the 1930s." *Papers of Bibliographical Society of Canada* 36, no. 1 (1998): 7–30.

– "'But Now Things Have Changed': Marius Barbeau and the Politics of Amerindian Identity." *Ethnohistory* 48, no. 3 (Summer 2001): 433–72.

– "Tradition and Modernity: The Cultural Work of Marius Barbeau." PhD thesis, History, Queen's University, 1997.

Oakley, Amy. *Kaleidoscopic Quebec.* Illustrated by Thornton Oakley. New York: D. Appleton-Century Company, 1947.

O'Barr, William M. *Culture and the Ad: Exploring Otherness in the World of Advertising.* Colorado: Westview Press, 1994.

O'Connor, Barbara. "Myths and Mirrors: Tourist Images and National Identity." In *Tourism in Ireland: A Critical Analysis*, edited by Barbara O'Connor and Michael Cronin, 68–85. Cork: Cork University Press, 1993.

O'Connor, Barbara, and Michael Cronin, eds. *Tourism in Ireland: A Critical Analysis.* Cork: Cork University Press, 1993.

Osborne, Brian S. "The Iconography of Nationhood in Canadian Art." In *The Iconography of Landscape: Essays on the Symbolic Representations, Design and Use of Past Environments*, edited by Denis Cosgrove and Stephen Daniels, 162–78. New York: Cambridge University Press, 1993.

Olins, Wally. "Branding the Nation – the Historical Context." *Journal of Brand Management* 9, no. 4/5 (April 2002): 241–8.

Ouellet, Pierre Olivier. "'Nos routes se couvrent de touristes à la recherche de nos reliques du passé': Les débuts de la Commission des monuments historiques (1922–1928)." *Revue d'histoire de l'Amérique française* 61, no. 2 (Autumn 2007): 235–51.

Ousby, Ian. *The Englishman's England: Taste, Travel and the Rise of Tourism.* Cambridge: Cambridge University Press, 1990.

Overton, James. *Making a World of Difference: Essays on Tourism, Culture and Development in Newfoundland.* St John's: ISER, 1996.

Owram, Doug. "'Quaint Quebec': British Views of French Canada." In *Imperial Dreams and Colonial Realities: British Views of Canada, 1880–1914*, edited by Doug Owram and R.G. Moyles, 87–113. Toronto: University of Toronto Press, 1988.

Palmer, Catherine. "An Ethnography of Englishness: Experiencing Identity through Tourism." *Annals of Tourism Research* 32, no. 1 (2005): 7–27.

Parfum de Livres. http://parfumdelivres.niceboard.com/t9524-gabrielle-roy.

Park, Hyung Yu. "Heritage Tourism: Emotional Journey into Nationhood." *Annals of Tourism Research* 37, no. 1 (2010): 116–35.

Parker, Gilbert. *The Lane That Had No Turning.* Toronto: Morang & Co., 1900.

– *The Seats of the Mighty: A Romance of Old Quebec.* New York: Appleton, 1896.

– *When Valmont Came to Pontiac.* Chicago: Stone and Kimball, 1895.

Pearce, Philip, and Gianno Moscardo. "The Concept of Authenticity in Tourist Experiences." *The Australian and New Zealand Journal of Sociology* 22, no. 1 (March 1986): 121–32.

Pelletier, P., C. Vallée-Tremblay, and R. Malo. "La fonction symbolique des ouvrages fortifiés du Vieux-Québec." *Cahiers du centre de recherches en aménagement et développement* 8, no. 4. Quebec: Université Laval, 1984.

Percival, W.P. *The Lure of Montreal.* Rev. ed. Toronto: Ryerson Press, 1947.

– *The Lure of Quebec.* Rev. ed. Toronto: Ryerson Press, 1946.

– *The Lure of Quebec.* Rev. ed. Toronto: Ryerson Press, 1965.

Phillips, Ruth. *Trading Identities: The Souvenir in Native North American Art from the Northeast, 1700–1900.* Montreal & Kingston: McGill-Queen's University Press, 1998.

Pocius, Ferald L. "Tourist, Health Seekers and Sportsmen: Luring Americans to Newfoundland in the Early Twentieth Century." In *Twentieth Century Newfoundland: Explorations,* edited by James Hiller and Peter Neary, 47–77. St John's: Breakwater, 1994.

Podmore, Julie. "Gone 'Underground'? Lesbian Visibility and the Consolidation of Queer Space in Montreal." *Social and Cultural Geography* 7, no. 4 (2006): 595–625.

Poirier, Christian. "The Clergy and the Origins of Quebec Cinema: Fathers Albert Tessier et Maurice Proulx." *Encyclopedia of French Cultural Heritage in North America.* http://ameriquefrancaise.org/en/article-367.

Popp, Richard K. *The Holiday Makers: Magazines, Advertising, and Mass Tourism in Postwar America.* Baton Rouge: Louisiana State University, 2012.

Potvin, Damasse. *The Saguenay Trip.* 3rd ed. Canada Steamship Lines, 1927.

Pratt, Mary-Louise. *Imperial Eyes: Travel Writing and Transculturation.* London: Routledge, 1992.

Prévost, Réjean. "1900–1929: Affirmation du Québec comme destination touristique." *Téoros: Revue de la recherche en tourisme* 14 (Summer 1995): 15–19.

Prévost, Robert. *Trois siècles de tourisme au Québec.* Sillery: Septentrion, 2000.

Prévost, Robert, Suzanne Gagné, and Michel Phaneuf. *L'histoire de l'alcool au Québec.* Montreal: Stanké, 1986.

Proulx, Daniel. *Le Red Light de Montréal.* Montreal: VLB éditeur, 1997.

Province de Québec: Paradis du touriste. 3rd ed. Montreal: Société Nouvelle de Publicité Incorporée, 1956.

Racine, Michelle. *La légende de Maria Chapdelaine.* Montreal: VLB éditeur, 2004.

Ramsay, Lucie. "L'image de Montréal dans les guides touristiques." MA thesis, Urban Studies, Université du Québec à Montréal, 2003.

Redfoot, Donald L. "Tourist Authenticity, Tourist Angst, and Modern Reality." *Qualitative Sociology* 7, no. 4 (Winter 1984): 291–309.

Reid, Denis. "Cornelius Krieghoff: 1845–1865." In *Canadian Culture: An Introductory Reader*, edited by Elspeth Cameron, 31–6. Toronto: Canadian Scholar's Press, 1997.

Renauld, Robin. "Un charmant paradis d'été de l'aristocratie sherbrookoise: Le Petit Lac Magog de 1892–1917." *Revue d'études des Cantons de l'Est* 25 (Autumn 2004): 79–105.

Richler, Mordecai. *The Apprenticeship of Duddy Kravitz*. Don Mills, ON: Deutsch, 1959.

Riley, Roger, Dwayne Baker, and Carleton S. Van Doren. "Movie Induced Tourism." *Annals of Tourism Research* 25, no. 4 (1998): 919–35.

Ringer, Greg. *Destinations: Cultural Landscapes of Tourism*. London: Routledge, 1998.

Rivard, Adjutor. *Chez Nous*. Quebec: L'Action sociale catholique, 1914.

– *Chez Nous (Our Old Quebec Home)*. Toronto: McClelland and Stewart Publishers, 1924.

Roby, Yves. *Les Franco-Américains de la Nouvelle-Angleterre: Rêves et réalités*. Sillery: Septentrion, 2000.

Rochelea-Roukeau, Corine. *Laurentian Heritage*. Edited by W.F. Langford. Toronto: Green and Co., 1949.

Rojek, Chris. "Indexing, Dragging and the Social Construction of the Tourist Sight." In *Touring Cultures: Transformations of Travel and Theory*, edited by John Urry and Chris Rojek, 52–74. London: Routledge, 1997.

Rombout, Melissa. "Imaginary Canada: Photography and the Construction of National Identity." *VIEWS: The Journal of Photography in New England* 12, no. 2 (Spring 1999): 4–9.

Rose, Jonathan. *Making Pictures in Our Heads: Government Advertising in Canada*. Westport: Praeger Publishers, 2000.

Rothman, Hal K. *Devil's Bargain: Tourism in the Twentieth-Century American West*. Lawrence: University Press of Kansas, 1998.

– "Selling the Meaning of Place: Entrepreneurship, Tourism and Community Transformation in the Twentieth Century American West." *Pacific Historical Review* 65, no. 4 (1996): 525–57.

Rouillard, Jacques. "La Révolution tranquille: Rupture ou tournant?" *Journal of Canadian Studies/Revue d'études canadiennes* 32, no. 4 (1998): 23–51.

Rouleau, Célyne. "La fille du gouvernement. L'École des arts domestiques: La transmission du savoir dans les arts textiles et l'artisanat." *Histoire Québec* 14, no. 2 (2008): 23–7.

Roy, Alain. "Le Vieux Québec, 1945–1963: Construction et fonctions sociales d'un lieu de mémoire nationale." MA thesis, History, Université Laval, 1995.

Roy, Fernande. *Histoire des idéologies au Québec au XIXe et XXe siècles*. Montreal: Boréal, 1993.

Roy, Gabrielle. *The Tin Flute*. Translated by Hannah Josephson. New York, 1947.

Rudin, Ronald. "Revisionism and the Search for a Normal Society: A Critique of Recent History Writing." *Canadian Historical Review* 73, no. 1 (March 1992): 30–61.

Rutche, Joseph Père, and Athanase Forget. *Précis d'histoire du Canada pour les élèves des classes supérieurs de l'enseignement secondaire*. Montreal: Librairie Beauchemin, 1932.

Savard, Pierre. "Les 'caractères' nationaux dans un manuel de géographie des années 1930." *Recherches sociographiques* 23, nos. 1–2 (1982): 205–15.

Schmeller, Erik S. *Perceptions of Race and Nation in English and American Travel Writers, 1833–1914.* New York: Peter Lang, 2004.

Scott, Duncan Campbell. *In the Village of Viger.* Boston: Coupland and Day, 1896.

Sears, John F. *Sacred Places: American Tourist Attractions in the Nineteenth Century.* Amherst: University of Massachusetts Press, 1989.

Selwyn, Tom, ed. *Image: Myths and Mythmaking in Tourism.* West Sussex: John Wiley and Sons, 1996.

Shackley, Myra. "The Legend of Robin Hood: Myth, Inauthenticity, and Tourism Development in Nottingham, England." In *Hosts and Guests: the Anthropology of Tourism,* edited by Valene Smith, 315–22. Philadelphia: University of Pennsylvania Press, 1977.

Shaffer, Marguerite. *See America First: Tourism and National Identity, 1880–1940.* Washington, DC: Smithsonian Institute Press, 2001.

– "Seeing America First: The Search for Identity in the Tourist Landscape." In *Seeing and Being Seen: Tourism in the American West,* edited by David Wrobel and Patrick T. Long, 165–93. Lawrence: University Press of Kansas, 2001.

Sheehy, Colleen. "American Angling: The Rise of Urbanism and the Romance of the Rod and Reel." In *Hard at Play,* edited by Kathryn Grover, 77–92. Rochester: University of Massachusetts Press, 1992.

Sicotte, Hélène, and Michèle Grandbois. *Clarence Gagnon, 1881–1942: Rêver le paysage.* Quebec: Musée national des beaux- arts du Québec, Les Éditions de l'Homme, 2006.

Simard, Sylvain. *Mythe et reflet de la France: L'image du Canada en France, 1850–1914.* Cahiers du CRCCF no. 25. Ottawa: Les Presses de l'Université d'Ottawa, 1987.

Simon, Sherry. "William Hume Blake or, the Translator as Amateur Ethnologist." In *Writing Between the Lines: Portraits of Anglophone Translators,* edited by Agnes Whitfield, 19–36. Waterloo: Wilfrid Laurier University Press, 2006.

Smith, Allan. "Seeing Things: Race, Image and National Identity in Canadian and American Movies and Television." *American Review of Canadian Studies* 26, no. 3 (Autumn 1996): 367–90.

Smith, Valene, ed. *Hosts and Guests: The Anthropology of Tourism.* Philadelphia: University of Pennsylvania Press, 1977.

– "War and Tourism: An American Ethnography." *Annals of Tourism Research* 25, no. 1 (1998): 202–27.

Sobieszek, Robert. *The Art of Persuasion: A History of Advertizing Photography.* New York: H.N. Abrams, 1988.

Squire, Shelagh J. "Ways of Seeing, Ways of Being: Literature, Place and Tourism in L.M. Montgomery's Prince Edward Island." In *A Few Acres of Snow: Literature and Artistic Images of Canada,* edited by Paul Simpson-Housley and Glen Norcliffe, 137–47. Toronto: Dundurn Press, 1992.

Stanonis, Anthony. *Creating the Big Easy: New Orleans and the Emergence of Modern Tourism, 1918–1945.* Athens: The University of Georgia Press, 2006.

Steele, Byron. *Let's Visit Canada, a Practical Guide for Tourist, Sportsman and Vacationist.* New York: Robert M. McBride and Co., 1948.

Stokes, Charles W. *Here and There in Montreal and the Island of Montreal*. Toronto: The Musson Book Company, 1924.

Sukin, S. *Landscapes of Power: From Detroit to Disney World*. Los Angeles and Berkeley: University of California Press, 1991.

Swartz, Joan. "The Geography Lesson: Photographs and the Construction of Imaginative Geographies." *Journal of Historical Geography* 22, no. 1 (1996): 16–45.

– "Lofty Images: Government Photography and the Canadian Rockies." *The Archivist* 14, no. 2 (March–April 1987): 6–7.

Tessier, Albert. *Rapport sur le tourisme*. Ministère des Affaires municipales, de l'industrie et du commerce, Province de Québec, 1939.

– *Les valeurs nationales et économiques du tourisme*. Quebec: Comité permanent de la survivance française en Amérique, *Pour Survivre*, volume 5, 1943.

Thompson, Carl. *Travel Writing*. London and New York: Routledge, 2011.

Towner, John, and Geoffrey Wall. "History and Tourism." *Annals of Tourism Research* 18, no. 1 (1991): 71–84.

Trépanier, Esther. *Peinture et modernité au Québec 1919–1939*. Quebec: Éditions Nota bene, 1998.

Trudel, Marcel, and Geneviève Jain. *Canadian History Textbooks*. Ottawa: Queen's Printer for Canada, 1970.

Urry, John. *The Tourist Gaze: Leisure and Travel in Contemporary Societies*. London: Sage Publications, 1990.

Urry, John, and Jonas Larsen. *The Tourist Gaze 3.0*. Los Angeles: Sage, 2011.

van den Berghe, Pierre L. *The Quest of the Other: Ethnic Tourism in San Cristobal, Mexico*. Seattle: University of Washington Press, 1994.

– "Tourism as Ethnic Relations: A Case Study of Cuzco, Peru." *Ethnic and Racial Studies* 3, no. 6, 375–92.

van den Berghe, Pierre, and Charles Keyes. "Introduction: Tourism and Re-created Ethnicity." *Annals of Tourism Research* 11, no. 3 (1984): 343–51.

Vanlaethem, France. "Modernité et régionalisme dans l'architecture au Québec: Du nationalisme canadien de Percy E. Nobbs au nationalisme canadien-français des années 1940." In *Architecture, forme urbaine et identité collective*, edited by Luc Noppen, 157–77. Sillery: Septentrion, 1995.

Villeneuve, Lynda. *Paysage, mythe et territorialité: Charlevoix au XIX siècle, Pour une nouvelle approche du paysage*. Ste-Foy: Les Presses de l'Université Laval, 1999.

Walters, Evelyn. *The Beaver Group and Its Legacy*. Toronto: Dundurn, 2017.

Wang, Ning. "Rethinking Authenticity in Tourism Experience." *Annals of Tourism Research* 26, no. 2 (1999): 349–70.

Warren, Jean-Philippe. "L'Opération McGill français: Une page méconnue de l'histoire de la gauche nationaliste." *Bulletin d'histoire politique* 16, no. 2 (Winter 2008): 97–115.

Wertsch, James. *Voices of Collective Remembering*. Cambridge: Cambridge University Press, 2002.

West, Nancy Martha. *Kodak and the Lens of Nostalgia*. Charlottesville: University Press of Virginia, 2000.

White, Richard. "The Retreat from Adventure: Popular Travel Writing in the 1950s." *Australian Historical Studies* 28, no. 109 (October 1997): 90–105.

Wientraub, William. *City Unique: Montreal Days and Nights in the 1940s and '50s.* Toronto: McClelland and Stewart, 1996.

William, M. O'Barr. *Culture and the Ad: Exploring Otherness in the World of Advertising.* Boulder: Westview Press, 1994.

Williams, Raymond. "Advertising: The Magic System." In *The Canadian Studies Reader*, edited by Simon During, 320–36. London: Routledge, 1993.

Williams, Stephen. *Tourism Geography.* London: Routledge, 1998.

Williams, William H.A. *Creating Irish Tourism: The First Century.* London and New York: Anthem Press, 2010.

Williamson, Judith. *Decoding Advertisements: Ideology and Meaning in Advertising.* London and New York: Marion Boyars, 2002.

Wood, Robert E. "Ethnic Tourism, the State and Cultural Change in Southeast Asia." *Annals of Tourism Research* 11, no. 3 (1984): 353–74.

Wright, Donald. "W.D. Lighthall and David Ross McCord: Antimodernism and English Canadian Imperialism, 1800s–1918." *Journal of Canadian Studies/Revue d'études canadiennes* 32, no. 2 (Summer 1997): 134–54.

Wrobel, David, and Patrick T. Long, eds. *Seeing and Being Seen: Tourism in the American West.* Lawrence: University Press of Kansas, 2001.

Wrong, G.M. *The Canadians: The Story of a People.* Toronto: The Macmillan Company of Canada Ltd at St Martin's House, 1938.

Wylie, Herb. *Speaking in the Past Tense: Canadian Novelists on Writing Historical Fiction.* Waterloo: Wilfrid Laurier Press, 2007.

Zeppel, Heather, and C. Michael Hall. "Selling Art and History: Cultural Heritage Tourism." *Journal of Tourism Studies* 2, no. 1 (1991): 29–45.

Zuelow, Eric G.E. *Making Ireland Irish: Tourism and National Identity since the Irish Civil War.* Syracuse: Syracuse University Press, 2009.

Zukin, Sharon. *Landscapes of Power: From Detroit to Disney World.* Los Angeles and Berkeley: University of California Press, 1991.

INDEX